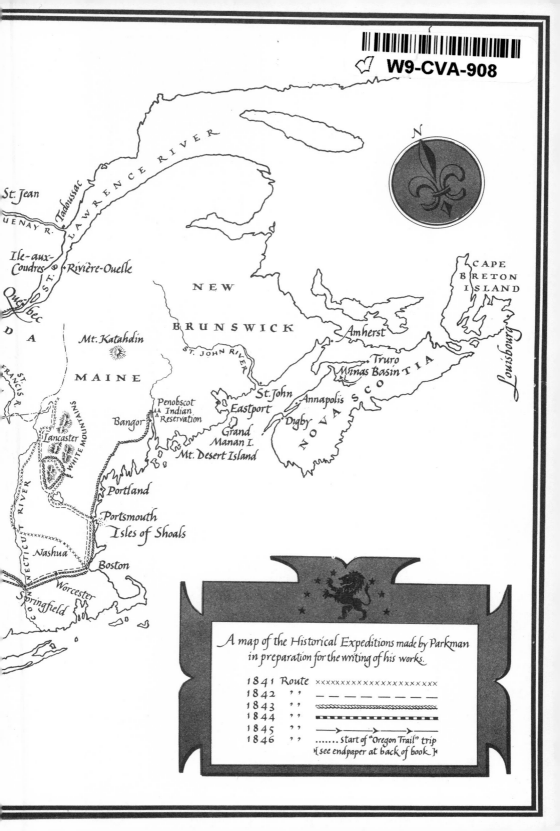

N

St. Jean

SAGUENAY R.

Tadoussac

St. LAWRENCE RIVER

Ile-aux-Coudres

Rivière-Ouelle

Québec

CANADA

ST. FRANCIS R.

Mt. Katahdin

MAINE

ST. JOHN RIVER

NEW

BRUNSWICK

CAPE BRETON ISLAND

Amherst

Truro

Minas Basin

NOVA SCOTIA

Louisbourg

Penobscot Indian Reservation

Bangor

St. John

Eastport

Annapolis

Digby

WHITE MOUNTAINS

Lancaster

Grand Manan I.

Mt. Desert Island

CONNECTICUT RIVER

Portland

Portsmouth

Isles of Shoals

Nashua

Boston

Worcester

Springfield

A map of the Historical Expeditions made by Parkman in preparation for the writing of his works.

1841 Route ×××××××××××××××××××××××
1842 ,, – – – – – – – – – – –
1843 ,, ∽∽∽∽∽∽∽∽∽∽∽∽∽∽
1844 ,, ▬▬▬▬▬▬▬▬▬▬
1845 ,, ⟶⟶⟶⟶⟶⟶
1846 ,, ... Start of "Oregon Trail" trip
}[see endpaper at back of book]{

Francis Parkman

Francis Parkman

HEROIC HISTORIAN

BY

MASON WADE

ARCHON BOOKS

1972

Library of Congress Cataloging in Publication Data

Wade, Mason, 1913–
    Francis Parkman; heroic historian

    Bibliography: p.
    1. Parkman, Francis, 1823–1893.
E175.5.P28 1972   970'.077'2024   [B]   72-6564
ISBN 0-208-01213-3

Preface

THE necessity of writing the history of a historian is not at
once self-evident, and perhaps demands an apologia. Yet the
biography of a historian may be as revealing in the insights it affords as that of any statesman, soldier, or other public figure, and
a life lived largely in the study may be as adventurous and colorful
as a life of action, and in the end far more important in the history
of mankind. The captains and the kings depart, once they have
fulfilled their roles, and the memory of their deeds soon grows dim;
but the scholars and the writers leave monuments of words, often
more enduring than the lifeless brass and stone.

Yet books, like all human things, fall prey to time to a greater or
lesser degree, and therefore each successive generation tends to
revise its estimate of the intellectual heritage of mankind. In no
field of human endeavor is the need for such revaluation so acute
as in the case of literature, and consequently in no other field is
the tendency more pronounced for each age to write its own esti-
mates of the great figures of the past. Few careers in the history
of American literature may be reconsidered to greater advantage
today than that of Francis Parkman, who devoted his life to chronicling the struggle between France and England for domination of
the North American continent.

Parkman has a triple claim upon our attention. He is perhaps the
greatest American historian; certainly the greatest writer among
that goodly nineteenth-century company of Sparks, Palfrey, Bancroft, Ticknor, Prescott, Motley, Adams, Channing, Fiske, Winsor.
Both at home and abroad his great achievement was underesti-
mated in his own time, for there was then little interest in the
origins of the American nation. Prescott's *Conquest of Mexico* and
Motley's *Rise of the Dutch Republic* received far more attention
from Parkman's contemporaries than his epic of *France and England in North America*. Today Prescott and Motley seem stiff and
wooden, and are read only as romance and rhetoric; but much

research and investigation has shaken only details and not the broad conclusions of Parkman's work in the field which he cleared as a pioneer, and his pages still live, as do those of no other nineteenth-century historian, for the modern reader.

As Van Wyck Brooks has pointed out, Parkman was not only the "climax and the crown" of the great Boston historical school, he was a Brahmin of the Brahmins—and the last great figure of that caste. He came of a long line of New England divines, and while he rejected their creed he retained their pride of learning and pride of power. Though he cordially disliked Puritanism, he could not help being a Puritan: he was unalterably stamped with the characteristics of the caste which combined the roles of priest and soldier. He was harsh by nature and a lover of hard truths; a rigorous ascetic who spared neither himself nor others. Perhaps more than any other of his contemporaries he represents the old New England order, for the circumstances of his life insulated him from the influence of the new ideas and interests. More than half his life was passed in the isolation demanded by the precarious condition of his health; and the means which he inherited from his grandfather, who had been the wealthiest merchant of the Boston of his day, made that isolation more complete. Abolitionism, the Civil War, universal suffrage, the woman's-rights movement, universal education—all the great ideas and causes of his era hardly touched him. He remained true to the ideals of the old order, and devoted a lifetime to a self-imposed task for which he received only a slight return—and that in reputation rather than in money. He believed firmly in his class and its superiority to all others, and made few friends outside it; he was an aristocrat by temper and conviction, who distrusted the new notion of democracy and despised the morality of commerce. Even before he entered college he had become preoccupied with the past and had lost interest in the present; and this preoccupation became more dominant as ill health deprived him of action and left him only the resources of his own mind, which was peopled with a colorful company of savages, soldiers, explorers, adventurers, and priests. And his greatness lies in his ability to make these creatures of his mind come alive on the pages which he laboriously compiled, so that the reader is translated into an enthralling new world, whose history is a great drama played out by a heroic company.

For Parkman was a romantic, despite his Puritanism, and a lover of heroes. His ideal of manhood was by his own admission "a little medieval," and one of his claims to greatness is the degree to which he wrought his own life in the heroic mold. His life was an unceasing struggle against great odds, and in the successful conduct of that struggle he displayed the heroic virtues: courage, self-reliance, perseverance, austerity, modesty. His life has been called the most heroic in the annals of literature, and with much justice. The blessings of position, means, and a good heritage which were bestowed upon him at the outset were soon counterbalanced by ill health of both body and brain and the early loss of his wife and his only son. A lover of action and the strenuous life, he was condemned to semi-invalidism while still a young man. First his heart gave trouble, then his eyes, then he was half crippled, and then beset by indigestion and insomnia. Thus barred from the active life that he loved, he was threatened also with loss of the life of the intellect by the failure of his eyesight and an obscure nervous disorder. For many years he often was able to work only five minutes at a time and for but two hours a day at best, and twice he was unable to do any intellectual work for periods of some years. Yet he never resigned himself to invalidism and went ahead as best he could with the historical epic whose outlines he had mapped out in his youth. He lived to fill out the design and revise the earlier parts, and there are few evidences in the whole great canvas of the agony and effort that were involved in its making.

The importance of Parkman as the main figure of our historical literature, as a representative of a vanished class which left an indelible mark on American life, and as a great personality, has never been properly estimated. There are, of course, good reasons for the inadequate recognition he has received. He was the last of a great company of scholarly writers, and their established reputations overshadowed his as it was made and gradually grew. Then, when his fame was at its peak, the world underwent a revolution, and emerged from it in no mood to accept the standards of a past with which it was less concerned than with the present and the future. Not until recent years did his subject become again of general interest to Americans. He is more highly regarded in Canada today than he is in his own country, for Canadians still care more and know more about the early history of their continent and ours than we Americans do. His importance as one of the greatest of the Brahmin caste could not be properly estimated until that class had become virtually extinct, and while its blood was beginning to run thin by the time of Parkman's death, its eclipse was not then foreseen. Though his greatness as a personality was appreciated in his last years and after his death, its full measure was not revealed, both because of his own reticence and that of those members of his class who knew him best. His earlier biographers, Charles Haight Farnham and Henry Dwight Sedgwick, were handicapped by inadequate materials—Farnham astigmatically characterized them as "extraordinarily scanty"—and by being too close to their subject in time, mentality, and environment. One cannot write the true biography of Francis Parkman solely in terms of Boston and the Boston state of mind. Through his work and its demands upon him Parkman escaped from the mold which nevertheless stamped him with its image. In their preoccupation with that mold—which they understood because they, too, were formed by it—Farnham and Sedgwick neglected to assess at their proper value the other influences which were brought to bear upon their subject.

The passage of the years has increased considerably the store of materials for a life of Francis Parkman. Certain sources of information which the earlier biographers neglected or were barred from have been made accessible to the present writer. Time provides a better perspective and permits the use of techniques which were not available forty years ago. And finally it is the writer's hope that his own heritage of New England blood and the Catholic faith has enabled him to do fuller justice to a great New Englander who described with remarkable impartiality the struggle between "feudal, militant, and Catholic" France and "democratic, industrial, and Protestant" England for domination of the New World.

A few words might well be said about the method of this book. Disagreeing with the view of Farnham that Parkman's active life was unimportant, I have tried to meet the need for a comprehensive chronological narrative, thus adopting Parkman's own literary method. What a man writes is determined very largely by what he is, and Parkman could not have written as he did unless he had lived as he did. He left a much fuller written record of his life than previous biographers have indicated, and since so much of his life was hidden from the world, this record remains the best authority. Hence my greatest debt in writing this book is to Francis Parkman himself, for, not presuming to rewrite a great writer, I have used his own words to a considerable extent, particularly in dealing with those active early years which were so vital a preparation for the later life of the study. To an extraordinary extent, Parkman's youth determined the course of his manhood. This fact, together with the circumstance that because of illness Parkman left little record of his later years, determined the proportions of this book.

I owe the suggestion of my subject to Van Wyck Brooks; his view of Parkman and Parrington's helped me to frame my own. Bernard DeVoto guided and criticized my treatment of Parkman's Oregon Trail trip; I owe much to his knowledge of the West and its literature. Miss Elizabeth Cordner immeasurably aided my work by putting Parkman's diaries and a mass of his correspondence at my temporary disposal. For permission to quote from this material, as well as from the Parkman papers already in their possession, I am greatly indebted to the Massachusetts Historical Society, now the owners of the manuscripts. I am under obligation to the following libraries and their staffs for furthering my researches and granting permission to quote from manuscript material in their possession: the Harvard College Library, the Boston Athenaeum, the Library of Congress, the Parliamentary Library of Canada, the Public Archives of Canada, the Bibliothèque de la Ville Montreal, the Redpath Library of McGill University, the Archives of the Séminaire de Québec, the Quebec Literary and Historical Society, and the Archives of the Province of Quebec. I am particularly indebted to the Dartmouth College Library for extending to me extraordinary facilities for research.

I have incurred too many personal obligations to list all the individuals in the United States and Canada who have aided my work. My gratitude is not less because their names do not appear here. I must particularly thank Mr. Daniel Sargent, my sister Mrs. Raymond C. Labarge, Mr. and Mrs. John B. Frosst, Mr. A. J. H. Richardson, the late Aegidius Fauteux and l'Abbé Arthur Maheux, Colonel William Wood, M. Pierre-Georges Roy, Mgr. Camille Roy, Dr. Roger Gaudry, Dr. Wayne Stevens, and Mr. Alexander Laing.

MASON WADE

Cornish, N. H.
August 17, 1942

Contents

Illustrations

Part One

THE MAKING OF A HISTORIAN

1823–1845

1: The Making of a Boston Brahmin

Had he been born in Jerusalem under the shadow of the Temple and circumcised in the Synagogue by his uncle the high priest, under the name of Israel Cohen, he would scarcely have been more distinctly branded, and not much more heavily handicapped in the races of the coming century, in running for such stakes as the century was to offer. . . .
—THE EDUCATION OF HENRY ADAMS

FRANCIS PARKMAN, JR., was born on September 16, 1823—the year of the Monroe Doctrine—in his father's house in Somerset Place (now Allston Street) on the northern slope of Beacon Hill in Boston. The Hill was to be his lifelong dwelling place, and he was to be among the most notable of the goodly company that made of it a Brahmin citadel. The great golden dome of the State House crowns the Hill and is the epicenter of the Hub, but the dwellers in the Bulfinch houses lining the narrow streets and alleys which aimlessly crisscross the slopes have done more to make Massachusetts great than any temporary tenant of the capitol. Their fortress has now become a shrine and the slums creep up on the sacred precincts, but the Hill remains the most charming as well as perhaps the most historic quarter of any American city.

Parkman was born to the purple and with a golden spoon in his mouth. He was the oldest son of the Reverend Dr. Francis Parkman and Caroline Hall Parkman, who were descended from the oldest Massachusetts families. His ancestors were men of note in the colonies of Massachusetts Bay and Plymouth in the earliest days, and the strain showed no signs of thinning out after two hundred years. His father was minister of the New North Church in Boston for thirty-six years and was regarded as a worthy disciple of Dr. William Ellery Channing and a leading Unitarian divine of the day. The church over which he presided for so many years was

3

founded in 1712 by a group which included his great-grandfather William, and his father Samuel was long a deacon and pillar of it. This Samuel Parkman, the grandfather of the historian, was a remarkable man. He had come to Boston from the village of Westboro as a poor boy, the twelfth son of a clergyman, to make his fortune, and make it he did. He began as an errand boy in a tavern, the Bunch of Grapes, and ended as the richest merchant of the Boston of his day. His worldly success did not make him forget the God of his fathers: he was deacon of the New North for twenty-three years and gave that society much money as well as much time. In 1814 he conveyed a twenty-three-thousand-acre township in Maine to Harvard College, this princely gift being intended for the support of a professor of theology.

Samuel Parkman died just a year after his grandson was born, but eleven children and his great mansion on Bowdoin Square long kept his memory green. He was typical of the great merchant princes of the Federalist era: a man of fine presence and courtly manners, always faultlessly dressed. He usually appeared in public in a blue coat with brass buttons and a ruffled shirt, in the front of which he wore a magnificent diamond. His four daughters married Blakes, Shaws, and Tuckermans—members of the ruling caste. After the death of Samuel Parkman in 1835, Dr. Parkman's family occupied the great house at No. 5 Bowdoin Square. It was a large square brick mansion of three stories, whose front was sheathed with wood designed to imitate beveled courses of stone. There was a great entrance hall and a staircase with spiral balusters, which the historian valued so greatly that he had them carefully removed when the mansion was demolished and placed on the stairs of his own Jamaica Plain house. In front there was a green, shaded by chestnut trees and enclosed by an iron fence with tall square pillars at the corners. In the rear there was a large paved court, and beyond, where the ground sloped away sharply to the north, was a terraced garden devoted to fruit rather than flowers. The great merchant was interested in combining beauty with profit even in his hobby. The same fortune which had smiled upon him in trade favored him as a fruit-grower, and the lusciousness of his bergamot pears became legendary. The barn, on the Chardon

Street side of the property, was later remodeled into a chapel, and in 1840 was the scene of the famous convention of "madmen, mad-women, men with beards, Dunkers, Muggletonians, Come-Outers, Groaners, Agrarians, Seventh-Day Baptists, Quakers, Abolitionists, Calvinists, Unitarians, and Philosophers," as Emerson character-ized the gathering. Dr. Parkman, who had no love for reformers, always referred to the Chardon Street Chapel as "my mother's barn."

But this Samuel Parkman's father, the Reverend Ebenezer Park-man, is the paternal ancestor whose traits were best represented in his great-grandson, the historian. Ebenezer was born in Boston in 1703 and graduated from Harvard when seventeen. At twenty-one he was ordained minister of the church at Westboro, some few miles west of Boston on the Worcester road, and he held this posi-tion for fifty-eight years until his death in 1782. Like the minister of Rowley, Ebenezer Parkman, when asked by a stranger to West-boro: "Are you, sir, the person who serves here?" might have replied: "I am, sir, the person who rules here." He was a benevolent despot of a theocratic era, and not only wrote the history of his town, but made it. He was the most prominent and influential man in that part of the state in religion and in public affairs, and was regarded as a literary ornament of Massachusetts, though he pub-lished only a few sermons and a historical sketch of the town.

Ebenezer Parkman kept a private diary during the whole period of his pastorate, and this journal of frontier life was a source of de-light and information to his great-grandson. Ebenezer lacked the simplicity of the earlier Puritans—on his tombstone he is styled "the first Bishop of the Church in Westborough"—and it did not offend his scruples to keep a slave purchased in Boston of his father, William Parkman. This slave, whose name was Maro, died a year after he had trudged out to Westboro behind Ebenezer's horse, and his master noted in the diary: "Dark as it has been with us, it became much darker about the sun-setting, the sun of Maro's life Sat." The minister married twice and had sixteen children, eight boys and eight girls. The boys inherited their father's vigor and his willingness to shed blood like a good Christian—Ebenezer was a notable Indian fighter—for one carried a musket at Ticonderoga in 1758 and another was a minuteman in 1775. With these followers of the arts of war their great-nephew felt more affinity than he did with their brother Samuel, who cultivated those of peace and, as Josiah Quincy put it, "through assiduity and talent . . . rose to eminence and opulence among the merchants of Boston."

For the rest, Francis Parkman seems to have derived little from his paternal ancestors, though some of his characteristics are those of the Devon stock from which his earliest American ancestor, Elias Parkman of Dorchester, sprang. The line on his mother's side is more notable, and perhaps more important, since the one who knew him best judged that "Whatever characteristics Frank inherited from his parents came from her." John Cotton of Boston, the renowned divine and grandfather of the still more renowned Cotton Mather, was the first of that line. His son John removed to Plymouth, where he was pastor of the church for many years. He was expert in the language of the Indians and preached to them in their own tongue during two years as the missionary Mayhew's assistant at Martha's Vineyard. He also revised and corrected the last edition of the Apostle Eliot's Indian Bible. According to his son he "was a man of universal acquaintance and correspondence, so that he had and wrote (perhaps) twice as many letters as any man in the country." This son, Rowland Cotton, like his father, was a graduate of Harvard, and was for more than seventy years the pastor of the church at Sandwich on Cape Cod. He was a famous preacher, though he never allowed his sermons to be printed, a great letter writer, and also well versed in the Indian language, preaching to the savages once a month. His wife Elizabeth was the only daughter of Nathaniel Saltonstall and a great-grand-daughter of Sir Richard Saltonstall. Their daughter married a minister of Haverhill, and the daughter of this union married the Reverend Edward Brooks of Medford, who was called to a church at North Yarmouth, Maine, a few years after he graduated from Harvard in 1757. After five years he was dismissed "on account of his too liberal views"— the only record of liberalism among Parkman's highly conservative ancestors—and returned to Medford. The Reverend Edward Brooks had some of the same martial spirit as the Reverend Ebenezer Parkman, for, as his son relates, "On the 18th of April 1775, he went over to Lexington, on horseback, with his gun on his shoulder and in his full-bottomed wig." As befitted his cloth, however, his most notable deed of the great day was saving the life of a wounded British officer. In 1777 he was made chaplain of the frigate *Hancock* and soon after was captured and sent as a prisoner to Halifax by the British. He took the small-pox there, and, when released, returned to Medford in shattered health and died at forty-eight. His daughter married Nathaniel Hall of Medford, whose daughter was Parkman's mother. It is probable that Parkman derived some of his dislike of clergymen from the constant hymning of the glories of this overwhelmingly clerical ancestry; and it is barely possible that his distrust of the mingling of the civil and religious functions was a heritage from the Pilgrims of Plymouth, who differed in this matter from their neighbors of Boston and, unlike them, were plain and simple peo-ple, according to Governor Bradford, "not aquainted with trads nor traffique . . . but . . . used to a plaine countrie life, and ye innocente trade of husbandrey."

At all events it is certain that Francis Parkman was a scion of the ruling class, and a Brahmin of the Brahmins by inheritance. His ancestry gave him a personal interest in the early history of America and particularly in that Old French War—the American part of the Seven Years' War—which early captured his fancy and led him into devoting his life to writing history. His share of his grandfather's wealth freed him from the necessity of making a living. He came upon the New England scene just as the old the-ocracy, the Standing Order, was finally breaking up, and, like the majority of his contemporaries, he rebelled against the clerical tradition and struck out for himself. And it happened that an un-healthy and unhappy childhood gave him a passion for the wilder-ness.

There is only one anecdote preserved of Francis Parkman's early childhood. When he was about six or seven, the family moved from Somerset Place to No. 1 Green Street, a large house, formerly the residence of Samuel Gore, which stood next to Samuel Park-man's mansion. Young Francis showed his energy and independ-

ence by insisting upon moving his own effects from the old residence to the new upon his sled, though the month was April and
there was no snow upon the ground. Fortunately the route was all
downhill. Despite this demonstration of hardiness, he was a sickly
youngster and when he was eight his family decided to send him
to his grandfather Hall's farm in Medford. Here he remained for
some four or five years, attending the school kept by Mr. John
Angier in the town and roaming the wild and rough woodland now
known as the Middlesex Fells but then as the Five Mile Woods.
Of his life at this time Parkman wrote fifty years later: "I walked
twice a day to a school of high but undeserved reputation, about a
mile distant, in the town of Medford. Here I learned very little,
and spent the intervals of schooling more profitably in collecting
eggs, insects, and reptiles, trapping squirrels and woodchucks, and
making persistent though rarely fortunate attempts to kill birds
with arrows." Nathaniel Hall's land bordered on the Fells, a four-
thousand-acre tract of rocky wilderness which abounded in hills,
ponds, and pools. The early settlers' attempt to make farmland of
it had long been abandoned, and it was left untouched except for
occasional woodcutting. Four years of roaming this boy's paradise
gave Parkman an enduring taste for the forest and the things that
live or grow there, and an incentive to explore still more untouched
wilderness, where Indians and large wild beasts might yet be
found. Here, too, he began the collection of minerals which some
years later brought him his first academic honor, a vote of thanks
from the Harvard Natural History Society, when he donated part
of it to that body.

His father, who drove out to Medford every Saturday and
brought the boy back to Boston in his chaise for Sunday with the
family, must have decided that his son was growing too wild, and
perhaps was alarmed by Francis's habit of deliberately adopting
upon these occasions the dazed and bewildered air proper to a
country boy on his first visit to the city. At any rate the boy was
brought back to town permanently, much to his regret. Deprived
of his opportunity of observing nature in the wilderness, he developed a passion for experiments in chemistry, "involving," as he
himself described it, "a lonely, confined, unwholesome sort of life,

baneful to body and mind." Parkman was inclined to blame some of his later ill health on this youthful pursuit, and the three or four years that he devoted to this hobby "served little other purpose than injuring him by confinement, poisoning him with noxious gases, and occasionally scorching him with some ill-starred explosion." To his mind this taste for chemistry was an indication of bodily inferiority rather than of mental superiority.

Possibly Parkman attached too much importance to this scientific interlude as he looked back upon it in later life. It does not seem so "baneful to body and mind" today when many boys are given to such harmless pursuits, and it does not seem to have cut him off from his fellows. The following announcement, printed by a contemporary, has been preserved:

GRAND EXHIBITION!

Mr. F. Parkman, grateful for receiving, and always desirous of returning the favours of his friends and of the public in general, begs leave to announce most respectfully, that at the request of a large proportion of the citizens of this "great metropolis," he has consented (at a great expense and labour), to exhibit his truly astonishing, not to say wonderful and amazing exhibition of

PHISYORAMIC PYROTECNICON!!
or—PYRRIC FIRES!

Mr. P., having studied many years under Malzael, that original inventor, can assure the public that they are fully equal to his. The performances will comprise,

The pyramids and globes
The full sun (This piece cost $200.)
Magic wheel
Transparency of Lord Nelson, &c.
The whole to conclude with his powerful MAGIC LANTERN, containing 18 glasses, comprising elegant and beautiful forms.

This scientific entertainment seems to have been given in the Star Theater, which was launched in the fall of 1835 by Parkman, several of his cousins, and some other boys. An unused barn in the rear of the Green Street house served as headquarters for this enterprise. The boys wrote or adapted the plays they put on, painted their own scenery, and made their own costumes or borrowed more elaborate ones from the good-natured Pelby, manager of the National Theater. Even the playbills were printed by F. Minot, one of the company. Performances were generally given on Saturday afternoons, though occasionally on Wednesdays. The Star Theater flourished for two seasons, and attracted not only contemporaries of the company, but also their elders. Now and then a dame brought her school to witness a performance, for the names of the company and the site of the theater—on the eminent Dr. Parkman's property—sufficed to give a highly respectable air to the enterprise in a day when the theater was generally regarded as "low."

Parkman was a leading spirit in the Star Theater. He was stage hand, lighting expert, designer, and actor. He frequently took feminine roles, for which his good looks and high voice suited him. His Distaffina in *Bombastes Furioso* is said to have been charming, and he played Katharina in *The Taming of the Shrew*. He also distinguished himself by acting the title role of *The Dumb Boy of Genoa* entirely in pantomime. In addition to playing Fag in "the celebrated play of *My Fellow Clerk*" he concluded the performance with "some interesting experiments in Chemistry, by Mr. Parkman, being his first appearance as a chemist." One year he appeared as Harry Hammer in *The Golden Farmer, or Vell, Vot of It!* and the next (by which time the subtitle had become *The Last Crime*) as Elizabeth, the leading lady. The company included his cousins George Francis Parkman, Quincy Adams Shaw, and J. Coolidge Shaw; F. Minot, William A. Marston, P. and C. Dexter, C. F. Shimmin, S. Eliot, G. Haskell, C. Williams, F. Lee, and W. Johnson. Minot and Marston frequently lowered the curtain with comic songs, and Lee translated a farce, *The Chicken,* from the French "expressly for the Star Theater."

There is no evidence as to what brought about the setting of the Star. Probably the boys lost interest in it and turned to other recreations. About this time Parkman was placed in Mr. Gideon Thayer's school, where he remained until he went to Harvard. Thayer's institution, later known as the Chauncy Hall School, was conducted in Chauncy Place. One of his teachers there, Mr. Thomas

Cushing, then fresh from Harvard and later the principal for many years, recalls him as "a quiet, gentle, and docile boy, who seemed to appreciate the fact that school meant an opportunity for improvement, and always gave an open and willing mind to instruction." This does not agree with the accounts of Parkman as a student, either before or after this period, and may be suspect, since it was written shortly after the distinguished pupil's death, when he was being eulogized on all sides. Another of Mr. Cushing's recollections seems more trustworthy: that while Parkman was a fair enough Latin and Greek scholar, he excelled "in the rhetorical department":

His compositions were especially good, and he used sometimes, as a voluntary exercise, to versify descriptions of heroic achievements that occurred in his reading. I remember that he put into verse the whole description of the Tournament in Scott's *Ivanhoe,* and then used it afterward in declamation, and it was so much liked that other boys used it for the same purpose. I think he might have excelled in narrative and descriptive poetry (the poetry of action) had he not early imbibed the historical idea.

Toward the end of his life Parkman contributed an account of his early training in writing to an English volume called *The Art Of Authorship, personally contributed by leading authors of the day.*

When fourteen or fifteen years old I had the good luck to be under the direction of Mr. William Russel, a teacher of excellent literary tastes and acquirements. It was his constant care to teach the boys of his class to write good and easy English. One of his methods was to give us lists of words to which we were required to furnish as many synonyms as possible, distinguishing their various shades of meaning. He also encouraged us to write translations, in prose and verse, from Virgil and Homer, insisting on idiomatic English, and criticizing in his gentle way anything flowery or bombastic. At this time I read a good deal of poetry, and much of it remains verbatim in my memory. As it included Milton and other classics, I am confident that it has been of service to me in the matter of style. Later on, when in college and after leaving it, I read English classics for the express purpose of improving myself in the language. These I take to be the chief sources of such success as I have had in this particular.

One composition of this early period, written in August 1839, has been preserved. It is entitled "Studies of Nature" and starts off in the best prosy essay style: "Of all pursuits the cultivation of natural science tends most to improve the mind and improve the understanding." It goes on to justify the study of nature in the field and in the laboratory—Parkman's favorite pursuits—against the objections of the utilitarian: "I answer that whatever tends to increase our knowledge of the globe we inhabit is of use, and that objects which appear to be too trifling to be noticed may, at some future day, be found of great benefit to mankind." Certainly Parkman's minute study of the wilderness later stood him in good stead in those matchless descriptions which make the forest of the Indian and the pioneer appear before our eyes. This early essay is a rhetorical exercise, showing competence, a strong moralistic tendency, and little else, but it is interesting evidence of Parkman's intellectual self-consciousness at the age of sixteen.

There was only one college for a Boston boy of Parkman's background. Dr. Parkman was an overseer of Harvard from 1819 to 1849; and in 1840, the year of his son's entrance into college, he made a donation of $5000 to supplement his father's gift for the theological professorship, which had realized only a fourth of the sum intended because of the decline in Maine land values. Young Parkman was admitted to Harvard on August 28, 1840, less than a month before his seventeenth birthday. The records indicate that he was conditioned in "compound interest and simple equations" and that he was placed in the second of the three divisions into which the entering class was divided by scholarship. Subsequently he was promoted to the third division, which was the highest in rank. Dr. Parkman, doubtless concerned about the temptations of college life to a home-bred boy, arranged with his friend Benjamin Apthorp Gould, master of the Latin School, that their sons should "chum," or room together, during their freshman year.

This arrangement, like many evolved by well-meaning parents, was not a complete success, and No. 9 Holworthy Hall was the scene of some dissension. Parkman, late in life, described this "chumship" as in its beginnings "a little breezy, I might say squally, but the foundation and beginning of a lifelong friendship." He also mentioned the fact that "the average scholarship of Holworthy 9 was exceedingly creditable," for Gould, who became a famous astronomer, more than made up for Parkman's mathematical deficiencies.

Harvard in the early 1840's hardly deserved the name of a university. Francis Parkman's class had sixty-two members in its first year, and the whole student body, including graduate students, numbered only four hundred and forty. Josiah Quincy was President, and the faculty notables included Joseph Story, Dane Professor of Law; Dr. Jacob Bigelow, Professor of Materia Medica; Edward Tyrrel Channing, Boylston Professor of Rhetoric and Oratory; Dr. John W. Webster, Professor of Chemistry and Mineralogy; Daniel Treadwell, Rumford Professor of Science; James Walker, Alford Professor of Philosophy; Jared Sparks, McClean Professor of History; Henry Wadsworth Longfellow, Smith Professor of French and Spanish Languages and Literature and Professor of Belles-Lettres; Cornelius Felton, Professor of Greek; Charles Beck, Professor of Latin; and Charles Stearns Wheeler, Tutor in Greek and Instructor in History. The graduate students were mostly studying law or medicine, for the secular professions had risen to dominance in the institution which had been founded in dread of "leaving an illiterate ministry to the churches when our present ministers shall lie in the dust."

The undergraduate course was severely classical—the admission requirements included Virgil, Caesar, Cicero, Latin prosody and composition, and Felton's *Greek Reader,* the Four Gospels of the Greek Testament, and Greek prosody and composition—and was just beginning to show the effect of the new educational trends. Longfellow was the first professor of modern languages in an American college, and it was scarcely recognized as yet that there were literatures other than English, Latin, and Greek. Jared Sparks was the first historian to concern himself with the American past from an academic post, and Daniel Treadwell was a pioneer in the teaching of physics. In the freshman year there was no option as to courses, and but little thereafter. The academic year was divided into two terms, August to January and February to July, with Commencement on the fourth Wednesday of August. The final examinations came on the Monday and Tuesday of Commencement Week, beginning, as an ominous note in the catalogue put it, "precisely at 6 o'clock a.m." The course was so severe that the class reports of the period reveal an appalling number of breakdowns in health, mental and physical, and of complete or partial blindness at the outset of life. Part of this high mortality may have been due to the old New England custom of trying to make a scholar of the family weakling who was unsuited to practical pursuits. Parkman had a particular detestation of this type, evidenced in his later essay, "The Tale of the Ripe Scholar," and in his own undergraduate career.

In the first term of his freshman year he was obliged to read Xenophon's *Memorabilia* and Herodotus, study Greek grammar and "antiquities," and write Greek; read Livy and study Latin grammar and "antiquities," and write Latin; master Peirce's *Geometry and Algebra;* study French; and attend lectures "on the means of preserving health." The second term's work included Thucydides and more Xenophon, Cicero's *Brutus* and more Livy, plane and spherical trigonometry and more algebra, and Keightley's *History of Greece and Rome.* Since a cousin and classmate, George F. Parkman, has given evidence that "Whatever he liked, he would take hold of with the utmost energy; what he did not like he would not touch," it is not surprising that Francis Parkman failed in freshman mathematics. His account of this failure is revealing:

I remember the last examination when Professor Peirce in the presence of a committee examined us, and I was required, according to the cruel custom of the times, to work out a problem on the blackboard. I had not opened my algebra for six months, having devoted to rifle-shooting the time which I was expected to devote to mathematics. A problem was proposed. I said "Don't know it, sir." Professor Peirce with great kindness then proposed another, to which I replied, "I cannot do it, sir." He then tried a third. "I don't know anything about it, sir." "Mr. Parkman, you may go."

Since none of his courses at this time particularly interested him, Parkman grew fonder of roaming the Cambridge marshes with his rifle than of perusing his books. Still his scholarship was good enough to win him a "Detur" (an award given to deserving students under the will of Governor Edward Hopkins, *"pro insigni in studiis diligentia"*) in the first term of his sophomore year.

This second year brought him under the instruction of Professor Edward Tyrrel Channing, who taught Emerson, Holmes, Dana, and Motley, and was thus hymned by Holmes:

> Channing, with his bland, superior look,
> Cold as a moonbeam on a frozen brook,
> While the pale student, shivering in his shoes,
> Sees from his theme the turgid rhetoric ooze.

But thanks to William Russel's training, Parkman's themes were not turgid with rhetoric and he got excellent marks for them. His high rank in this subject helped him to win a place among the first eight of his class for the second term, and the right to a "part" at the first Exhibition of his class on July 13, 1842. His choice was an English version of the "Speech of an Insurgent Plebeian" from Machiavelli's *History of Florence*. The other subjects of the sophomore year may also have been more to his taste. In the classics he read the *Iliad* and Cicero's *De claris oratoribus;* in English he wrote themes, translations, and gave declamations, as well as studying Lowth's *Grammar*, Campbell's *Rhetoric*, and Porter's *Analogies*. In history he read Sismondi's *Fall of the Roman Empire*, with Guizot's *History of Civilization* as an elective. Mathematics may have proved more palatable when it included "astronomy, the use of globes, and surveying instruments," as well as plane and spherical trigonometry. There was an elective course in natural history, in which Marcel's *Vegetable Physiology* was studied, and a choice of French, Spanish, German, Italian, or Portuguese among the modern languages. In the second term the *Electra, Antigone, Prometheus Bound,* and *The Clouds* were read in Greek, Juvenal in

Latin; there was a course in chemistry given by that Professor Webster who some years later murdered Parkman's uncle in the Medical School laboratory; Hallam's *Constitutional History of England* and Ray's *Animal Economy* were read.

Parkman's chumship with Gould was dissolved at the end of the freshman year, and for the rest of his college course he roomed alone—during the sophomore year at Mrs. Ayer's on the corner of Garden Street and the Appian Way, and later in Massachusetts Hall. During this year he took advantage of his solitude to begin his own course of study, designed to fit him to write history. In an autobiographical letter written to his friend Martin Brimmer in 1886, he thus described his early historical ambition:

> Before the end of my sophomore year my various schemes had crystallized into a plan of writing a story of what was then known as the "Old French War"—that is, the War that ended in the conquest of Canada—for here, as it seemed to me, the forest drama was more stirring and the forest stage more thronged with appropriate actors than in any other passage of our history. It was not till some years later that I enlarged the plan to include the whole course of the American conflict between France and England, or, in other words, the history of the American forest; for this is the light in which I regarded it. My theme fascinated me, and I was haunted with wilderness images day and night.

He had long intended to be a literary man, but now he put aside poetry, his first love, and decided to "confine his homage to the Muse of History, as being less apt than her wayward sisters to requite his devotion with a mortifying rebuff." His plan was made, but he was beset with doubts about his ability to realize it. Therefore he entered upon a self-imposed training "tolerably well fitted to serve his purpose, slighted all college studies which could not promote it, and pursued with avidity such as had a bearing upon it, however indirect."

One of his classmates noted that Parkman "even then showed symptoms of 'Injuns on the brain.' His tales of border life, his wampum, scalps, and birch-bark were unsurpassed by anything in

Cooper." This is not surprising, for Parkman's great literary en-
thusiasms were Cooper, Scott, and Byron. Cooper was the only
American writer who had recognized the importance of the Indian
and the forest in the development of the nation, and Scott's tales
of border frays found their parallels in the less vivid factual accounts over which Parkman pored in his secret lucubrations, for
he kept his plans and purposes to himself. One of his classmates,
Daniel Denison Slade, shared his enthusiasm for the woods and
the Indians—thus winning the college nickname of "The Chief-
tain"—and so came to share his walks and hunting expeditions
through the wilder sections of the countryside within range of
Cambridge. Slade could not understand Parkman's habit of always
carrying a gun on these tramps, and the proffered explanation, that
"a man should always carry a gun," did not throw much light on
this practice. Slade seems to have been an unimaginative soul, who
did not understand that Parkman's vivid fancy metamorphosed an
expedition to Fresh Pond or the Middlesex Fells into a wilderness
journey, and the small birds and squirrels which they shot into
larger game. This was not play, but training for the real wilderness
expeditions which Parkman hoped to make, and did make, before
his health forsook him. He walked at so rapid a pace that it was
hard to keep up with him, but fortunately Slade possessed "a length
of limb which admirably fitted him for pedestrianism." Their walks
took them down Long Wharf and about Fort Hill, to Roxbury and
Dorchester, to the marshes about Fresh Pond, and over Prospect
Hill to Medford and Parkman's beloved Five Mile Woods. In the
vacations longer and more strenuous expeditions into the real wilderness were made, but these are so important in Parkman's life
that they will have several chapters to themselves.

Parkman was not such a self-dedicated student and ascetic as
these preoccupations might seem to indicate. During most of his
college career he boarded at Mrs. Schutte's, whose excellent table
at a moderate price attracted a numerous and lively company. Most
of Mrs. Schutte's boarders soon acquired a nickname by which they
were known to their table companions. Parkman's was "The Lo-
quacious," which was a shaft aimed at his habit of doing more
listening than talking when in general company. Among close

friends this reticence left him, and he was a chosen companion of the wildly exuberant William Morris Hunt, whose buoyance led first to "rustication" in Concord and then to a severed connection with the college, and George Blankern Cary, who was regarded as the wit and rake of the class. Parkman could also be moved to articulate action by what he regarded as injustice. In his sophomore year Professor Beck adopted the arbitrary habit of calling the roll in his Latin class precisely on the hour, instead of some minutes after, as the immemorial Harvard custom decrees, and of marking as absent all those who were late. Parkman drew up a memorial against this iniquitous novelty, got it signed by the principal members of the class, and sent it to the faculty. The rebellion was successful, though President Quincy, between the two fires of an irate son of an overseer and a formidable member of the faculty, tactfully induced Dr. Beck to abandon his practice by a private remonstrance rather than by faculty action.

Both by family right and by personal character many social honors came to Parkman from his college mates. At the end of his freshman year he became a member of the Institute of 1770, then a literary and debating society. He gave a lecture on the Puritans, demonstrating "in a very original and humorous style the front, flank, and rear of their offending." He was also appointed to maintain the affirmative of the question, "Does attendance on theatrical exhibitions have a bad effect on the mind and morals?" which he did in opening the debate, but then changed sides—perhaps swayed by recollections of the Star Theater and by his enduring taste for the drama—and supported the contrary opinion. He was also a member of the Hasty Pudding Club, of which he was first vice-president and then president; and of the Harvard Natural History Society, of which he was Corresponding and Recording Secretary and Curator of Mineralogy. He was also a pillar of the mysterious I.O.H., in which he was known as "The Dominie"— which must have irritated him—and of another society known as the C.C. to its members but to the rest of the college as the Lemonade Club. Its members were his closest college friends: George Blankern Cary, James Gordon Clarke, George S. Hale, Horatio J. Perry, Charles B. Snow, James Parker Treadwell, and Edmund

Dwight. The mystic letters stood for Chit-Chat, and the meetings "usually took place once a fortnight, when the members read such compositions of their own as they had felt the inclination to prepare, and the evening's entertainment concluded with a supper, which at first was anything but sumptuous, though in this respect a considerable change afterward took place." The gatherings were not quite so highminded as this account, written by Parkman for the mother of his classmate Cary after the latter's sudden death in 1846, might indicate. A number of letters to and from Parkman and his college friends show a rather surprising familiarity on the part of Dr. Parkman's son with the taverns and playhouses of Cambridge and Boston, and a strong interest in the less simple forms of food and drink.

Indeed, the two strains in Parkman, the Puritan and the patrician, both made themselves evident during his college years, and perhaps the nervous tension of which he was conscious derived partly from their conflict. The Puritan drove him to his books, to a self-imposed schooling in history in addition to his college course, and to a rigorous program of physical training, designed to harden him and fit him for wilderness life. He rowed on Fresh Pond, as well as hunted on its borders. He learned to ride circus style from an acrobatic rider who gave lessons in Cambridge. In his junior year Harvard acquired its first gymnasium. It was a small wooden building, provided with parallel bars, lifting machines, and such other apparatus as was then common, presided over by one Mr. T. Belcher Kay, "a pugilist and popular teacher of the art of self-defense." Parkman, of course, made the most of the opportunities thus afforded. He took boxing lessons from Belcher Kay, and applied himself to the devices designed for muscular development with such eagerness that he is thought to have thus strained his heart. Overexertion in the college gymnasium is the reason commonly assigned for his leaving college in the fall of his senior year for a long trip abroad, though it seems probable that this excursion was intended more to afford relief from nervous strain than from heart trouble, for he did some arduous traveling in rough country and climbed cathedral towers and mountains like the most indefatigable tourist. His own account of his preparation for his chosen lifework, as given in the first autobiographical letter, written to his friend George Ellis, is a remarkable psychological document:

The task, as he then reckoned, would require about twenty years. The time allowed was ample, but here he fell into a fatal error, entering on this long pilgrimage with all the vehemence of one starting a mile heat. His reliance, however, was less on books than on such personal experiences as should in some sense identify him with his theme. His natural inclinations urged him in the same direction, for his thoughts were always in the forests, whose features, not unmixed with softer images, possessed his waking and sleeping dreams, filling him with vague cravings impossible to satisfy. As fond of hardships as he was vain of enduring them, cherishing a sovereign scorn for every physical weakness or defect, deceived, moreover, by a rapid development of frame and sinews, which flattered him with the belief that discipline sufficiently unsparing would harden him into an athlete, he slighted the precautions of a more reasonable woodcraft, tired old foresters with long marches, stopped neither for heat nor rain, and slept on the earth without a blanket. Another cause added not a little to the growing evil. It was impossible that conditions of the nervous system abnormal as his had been since infancy should be without their effect on the mind, and some of these were of a nature highly to exasperate him. Unconscious of their character and origin, and ignorant that with time and confirmed health they would have disappeared, he had no other thought than that of crushing them by force, and accordingly applied himself to the work. Hence resulted a state of nervous tension, habitual for several years, and abundantly mischievous in its effects. With a mind overstrained and a body overtasked, he was burning the candle at both ends.

But if a systematic and steady course of physical activity can show no better result, have not the advantages of such a course been overrated? In behalf of manhood and common sense, he would protest against such a conclusion; and if any pale student, glued to his desk, here seeks an apology for a way of life whose natural fruit is that pallid and emasculate scholarship of which

FRANCIS PARKMAN AT TWENTY

From a daguerreotype taken shortly before his departure on the Grand Tour.

From C. H. Farnham's *Francis Parkman*, by permission of the publishers, Little, Brown & Co.

New England has had too many examples, it will be far better that this sketch had not been written. For the student there is, in its season, no better place than the saddle, and no better companion than the rifle or the oar. A highly irritable organism spurred the writer to excess in a course which, with one of different temperament, would have produced a free and hardy development of such faculties and forces as he possessed. Nor, even in the case in question, was the evil unmixed, since from the same source whence it issued came also the habit of mind and muscular vigor which saved him from a ruin absolute and irremediable.

In his own behalf, he is tempted to add to this digression another. Though the seat of derangement may be the nervous system, it does not follow that the subject is that which, in the common sense, is called "nervous." The writer was now and then felicitated on "having no nerves" by those who thought themselves maltreated by that mysterious portion of human organism. This subterranean character of the mischief, early declaring itself at the surface, doubtless increased its intensity, while it saved it from being a nuisance to those around.

There is perhaps no better self-portrait of a Puritan than this remarkable document, which Parkman destined for a friend's eye after he himself was dead. Driven by a passionate devotion to his chosen task, tormented by the sexual stirrings of adolescence, fired by romantic ideals and a vivid fancy, crucifying the flesh both out of principle and with a purpose, the simultaneous victim of restraint and excess, it is not surprising that Parkman's health collapsed and that it was necessary for him to leave college and go abroad.

So much for the Puritan. The patrician is less fully recorded, but is no less important because of that fact. The young patrician usually scorns the work of the world—as Parkman did much of his college work—and delights in the more aristocratic pleasures: hunting, riding, the society of his peers, eating, and drinking. Parkman, the solitary student, the bookish worshiper of the woodsman and the pioneer and of the simple life of the forest, was also Frank

Parkman, one of a convivial company of well-to-do young men who neglected their studies to go bird-shooting or deer-hunting, who found learning equestrian feats under the direction of a former circus rider more instructive than mastering trigonometry and alegbra, who were perhaps more familiar with the resources of Murdoch's Tavern than those of the Harvard Library. His chosen companions were like himself the offspring of prominent and wealthy parents. When Parkman went abroad he was annoyed to have it assumed on all sides that Harvard was a rich man's institution, but it was beginning to be so, even if the tuition was $75 and rent $15 a year ("Students find their own board and furniture"), board $90 for forty weeks, and washing $3 to $5 per quarter. Harvard had become a stronghold of Federalism, and the influence of men of substance had replaced that of men who were rich in faith alone. The Reverend Dr. Parkman did not stint his son, but even so he was alarmed by the rate at which the money went. Doubtless much of it went for historical books and maps, but it is clear that some also went for ale, porter, and flip, for dinners at Murdoch's, for wine parties in Massachusetts Hall, and into the tills of the Boston playhouses. Parkman's crowd went to the Boston balls, and paid long visits to the abodes of their young ladies. This extracurricular life made Parkman considerable of a snob, and gave him an unfortunate inability to get along with the general run of his fellow-men—a handicap that prevented him from making the most of his Oregon Trail opportunities. If a man interested him sufficiently or could help his purpose, Parkman could forget the prejudices of environment and class, but his early diaries and later letters provide ample evidence that Harvard stamped him with some unfortunate habits of thought and points of view. Though in later life he largely escaped in his work from the provinciality of Boston, he never lost the Brahmin attitude and he was more than physically blind. His wilderness journeys and his travels abroad were liberalizing influences, though he was not free from the Boston habit of transferring his own culture momentarily upon every place he visited, of seeing the world outside of Boston through a local haze, "composed of a desire to escape plus an admiration for our tradition," as George Apley put it.

2: The Making of a Woodsman—I

His thoughts were always in the for-
ests, whose features possessed his
waking and sleeping dreams, filling
him with vague cravings impossible
to satisfy.
F.P., LETTER TO ELLIS, 1864

PARKMAN never could have written so vividly of the forest and of the men, savage and civilized, who peopled it, without knowing wilderness life as well as they did. Indeed, the history of the great French and English struggle for North America may well have been neglected until his day for the very reason that no armchair scholar dared to tread such unfamiliar ground. Even as a youth Parkman saw that the most important part of his preparation for his lifework lay not in books but in personal experience, and he set about acquiring this experience with characteristic vigor and impetuosity. In his eagerness to examine the scenes of the conflict that obsessed him before they were ruined by cultivation and exploitation, and to come to know the Indian and the pioneer before they perished at the hands of a rapidly developing industrial civilization, he nearly ruined his health beyond remedy and thus almost frustrated his purpose at the outset. But there is no record, not so much as a hint, that he ever regretted the price he paid for his intimate personal knowledge of the scenes and the men he was to perpetuate on the printed page.

Parkman's wilderness education began unconsciously in his eighth year as he roamed the Middlesex Fells in response to an obscure impulse that drove him to the woods rather than to his books. Five years spent largely in this tract of woods gave him an enduring taste for outdoor life and the beginnings of wilderness wisdom. He not only played the imaginative games that any boy would play, given such a playground, but acquired some practical knowledge of the natural sciences. He collected birds' eggs, insects, and reptiles, as well as minerals; trapped squirrels and woodchucks;

and tried his hand at fishing and hunting. His career as a fisherman began even earlier than this, for there is a story of his catching horned pouts in the Frog Pond on Boston Common, with no more elaborate tackle than a pin-hook, in the company of his cousin. The fish were seasoned with cinnamon and broiled over a fire in Dr. Parkman's garden. Such a natural talent for sporting pursuits blossomed when given larger scope by the Fells, and Parkman became an impassioned collector of zoological specimens, his clothing habitually bulging with fearsome objects. He once frightened the life out of a little girl at school when a snake stuck its head out of his coat pocket. Another time, when in Boston for a Sunday with his family, he amused bystanders considerably by bringing up the rear of the august family train, led by Dr. Parkman in his gown, on its way back from church, with a dead rat held by the tail at arm's length. Dr. Parkman regarded this performance as an injury to the dignity of his cloth, and Frank's protestation that he wished to take this valuable specimen home to stuff was met with a sharp order to relinquish the rat and walk decorously as befitted a Christian on the Sabbath. When brought back to Boston from Medford, and thus deprived of the company of wild beasts, he formed a lifelong fondness for cats—as an old man he had no less than forty-two pictures of them in his study. He also grew silkworms in the family garden, and never lost his fondness for fishing, although he doubtless scorned the Frog Pond on the Common after having had the freedom of Spot Pond in Medford, which covers many acres.

There is a mention in one of his diaries of a visit to Lake Winnipesaukee and the White Mountains in 1838. This may have been a vacation journey in the company of his father, but there are no other records of it. The first wilderness journey of which a full account is preserved is that to the White Mountains in 1841, in the summer vacation of his freshman year. His companion was his classmate Daniel Denison Slade. Another classmate, Tower, was to have been of the company, but fell sick on the day of departure, July 19, "having imprudently gorged himself with pie yesterday." Slade's enthusiasm for the expedition was not so great as Parkman's—it became negligible during the course of it—and he regarded Tower's defection as an inauspicious omen. From his point of view he was

doubtless justified. On these expeditions Parkman drove himself
and his companions so hard that they invariably wearied and grew
despondent, while he was sustained by the inner flame of his passion for feats of endurance and hardiness.

Parkman and Slade took the train at seven o'clock in the morning from Charlestown, reaching Portsmouth at ten and Dover at
half-past eleven. After a lunch which left them *cibo et poto graves,*
as the learned young diarist records it, they took the stage for Alton.
The carryall was designed for four and was made to hold seven,
plus an inordinate amount of luggage. Parkman and Slade were
obliged to share the front seat with the driver, "a portly man," and
also to sit bolt-upright, for two women occupied the seat behind,
with their backs to the young men, and "an attempt on our part
to lean would have pitched the nymphs, head first, into the laps of
their neighbors opposite." Twenty miles of this "disagreeable pro-
pinquity" was enough, and they got out and walked the remaining
twelve miles to Alton. "The way was long and the burden heavy,"
but the colossus Slade was the first to call a halt, though little Parkman carried, besides a knapsack, a heavy gun, a ponderous double
shot-pouch, and a powder-flask. Slade constantly shifted his knapsack, which was galling his shoulders, and tried carrying it first in
one hand and then in the other. Finally his flagging spirits were
raised by the assurance of a farmer at his haying that Alton Bay
was only "two miles strong" away. And at last they saw Lake Winnipesaukee, and found a good supper and lodging by its shore, though
the tavern was most "unpromising-looking."

The next morning they discovered that the "Winnipissiogee
steamboat" had foundered the preceding year and the only sailboat
was out of commission, so perforce they set off on foot for Center
Harbor. But the day proved hot, and there was little shelter from
the broiling July sun. Parkman records bitter observations on "the
folly which had deprived us of shelter and comfort by ridiculously
burning the forests, in the zeal for making clearings, though the
land lies utterly waste and the sole effect of the operation is to ruin
the scene and lay the road open to the baking sun." His zeal was
flagging like Slade's, for "the road had become most disgustingly
hilly and dreary." With frequent stops to bathe in some stream, for

bread and milk at some hospitable farmhouse, or merely to rest in a patch of shady woods, they finally reached Meredith Bridge, where they collapsed in the tavern parlor. From an easy chair Slade said: "Last time you catch me walking this time of day," and Parkman replied: "Amen. We will set out before sunrise tomorrow"— which must have completed Slade's collapse. The expedition was thoroughly out of sorts, for the only good thing that Parkman could find to say of Meredith—"a disgusting little manufacturing village, with no single point of attraction"—was that there was an apocryphal story of a ten-pound trout having been taken there some days before.

Despite their early start, they found no respite from the scorching heat the following morning and, after a nine-mile walk to Meredith Village before breakfast, they hired a wagon to take them on to Center Harbor. Slade fell snoring on his bed upon arrival, and Parkman sat reading Irving's *Alhambra* on the balcony of their room, for it was too hot to stir outdoors. That evening they went out on the lake in a leaky boat and then bathed, "to the indescribable horror and inexpressible consternation of a party of ladies, who had been out in a leakier boat and who were advancing into the darkness directly into the midst of us until we signified the peculiar delicacy of our situation by splashings in the water and unequivocal callings to one another." The outraged ladies sheered off with a chorus of "Oh's!" "Ah's!" and "Did you ever's!"

The next morning they started before sunrise for Red Hill, which rises two thousand feet above the head of the lake and usually affords a superb panoramic view. Leaving their horse and wagon at the foot, they toiled up, with Parkman muttering maledictions on the "Yankee spirit of improvement" which was clearing the slopes and destroying the chief ornament of the country. The smoke of the fires and dull clouds obscured the view they had hoped to find and which Parkman had seen in its perfection on his previous journey to this region. Slade cared little, being too exhausted, and, sitting himself down on the stone, snorted: "First-rate prospect! I tell you what, Frank, I guess my shoes won't stand this much longer!" Parkman had had enough of this faint-heartedness, and on the way down proposed that he go on alone to the White Mountains, while Slade could wait at Center Harbor for Tower and re-join him at Crawford's tavern in the Notch. But Slade would neither be left behind nor go on cheerfully, and Parkman regretted the imprudent pie which had deprived the party of its third mem-ber—for if Tower had come, the more eager pedestrian could have pressed on alone and been freed of his grumbling companion.

At two that afternoon they took the stage for Conway, the heat remaining Tartarean. This mode of conveyance proved less wear-ing to the party's nerves, and Parkman found the country "ex-tremely wild and beautiful." They went past Ossipee Pond, "not choked up, like Winnipissiogi, by a too great number of islands" and "Chicoriuye *alias* Chorcorua Mountain, the highest peak of a noble range." But the wide patches of burnt wood and half-culti-vated land, continually increasing, made Parkman feel like emulat-ing the Indian chief who gave the mountain his name by plunging from its summit in despair at the encroachments of the white man. They arrived at Conway at eight, and Parkman occupied himself during the evening in writing a letter home, like a dutiful son.

The following morning they set out from Conway by stage at six, breakfasted at Bartlett at eight, and went on to the mountains. It was a misty day, with occasional showers, but to Parkman the view of this wild and mountainous country was sometimes the more interesting on this account. Soon after they reached Abel Craw-ford's, eight miles from the Notch, it began to pour, and the out-side passengers on the stage, who included two ladies as well as Parkman and Slade, were soon drenched:

At first we put up umbrellas, but the rain came down like a thundershower, and I, who sat on the driver's seat, and whose umbrella, consequently, conducted a small torrent of dirty water directly into the laps of the ladies behind, judged it expedient to lower my miserable shelter and receive the bounty of heaven in full. This, indeed, subjected me to no additional drenching, for, in the situation in which I was, the umbrella was like a dam of bulrushes against the Nile. We made sport of the matter, al-though the driver averred he had not gotten such a ducking for four years—the ladies especially exhibited much philosophy, though of the kind denominated "laughing philosophy," and, altogether, the ducking was an extremely agreeable affair.

It is clear from this and some other entries in the diary that these heroic young ladies were to Parkman's exacting taste, and one of them was long the object of his attentions. Though all were soaked to the skin, they reached the Notch House in fine fettle, and a little brandy and water and a change of clothing revived them, though the gallant Parkman noted that in view of the company "a reviving process was almost needless." The ladies and the occasional glimpses they had caught coming through the Notch of "craggy and savage hills, scored with avalanche tracks and white with torrents," had lent fuel to the momentarily flickering flame that burned within Parkman.

The account of the next day's activities is too well done to be recorded in any other words than his:

> This morning I went fishing, following downwards the stream of the waterfall which comes down through the Flume. I basketed about thirty trout. The weather was dull and cloudy; the clouds hid the peaks of the mountains and rolled in huge masses along their sides. Early in the morning the mist was rolling, in a constant stream, from the narrow opening of the Notch, like a furnace disgorging its smoke.

> This afternoon I achieved the most serious adventure it was ever my lot to encounter. I walked down the Notch to the Willey House and, out of curiosity, began to ascend in the pathway of the avalanche on the mountain directly behind. This pathway is a deep ravine, channelled in the side of the mountain which in this place is extremely steep. In the bottom of this gulf a little stream comes down from a spring above and renders the precipitous rock as slippery as clay. The sides of the ravine, which runs straight up and down the mountain, are of decaying granite, while the bottom is formed by a trap-dike. I ascended at first easily, but the way began to be steeper and the walls on each side more precipitous. Still I kept on until I came to a precipice about forty feet high and not far from perpendicular. I could see that this was followed by a similar one above. Professor Silliman,

a year or two ago, ascended in this place, until, as he says, "further progress was prevented by inaccessible precipices of trap-rock." The exploit of the professor occurred to me as I stood below, and I determined that "inaccessible precipices" which had cooled his scientific ardor should prove no barrier to me. I began to climb and with considerable difficulty and danger, and with the loss of my stick which went rattling and bounding down the ravine many rods before it found a resting place, I surmounted both precipices. I climbed on, but finding that I was becoming drenched by the scanty stream, and seeing, moreover, a huge cloud, not far up, setting slowly towards me, I bethought me of retracing my steps. I knew that it would be impossible to descend by the way I had come, and, accordingly, I tried to get out of the ravine to the side of the mountain, which was covered with woods which I could grasp hold of to assist me. But I was enclosed between two walls fifty feet high and so steep and composed of such material that an attempt to climb would only bring down the rotting granite upon my head. So I began to descend the ravine, nothing doubting that I should find some means of getting out before reaching the critical point. But it was impossible; and I found myself at the top of the precipice with no alternative but to slide down, or clamber the perpendicular and decaying walls to the surface of the mountain. The former was certain destruction, as I proved by suffering a rotten log to slide down. It glanced by the first descent like an arrow, struck at the bottom, bounded six feet into the air, and leaped down the mountain, splintering into twenty pieces as it went. The other method was scarcely less dangerous, but it was my only chance, and I braced my nerves and began to climb. Down went stone and pebbles clattering hundreds of feet below and giving me a grateful indication of my inevitable fate in case my head should swim or my courage fail. I had got half-way up and was clinging to the face of the precipice, when two stones, which supported my feet, loosened and leaped down the ravine. My finger ends, among the rotten gravel, were all which sustained me, and they, of course, would have failed, had I not thought, on the instant, of lowering my body gradually, and so diminishing its weight, until my feet found new supports. I sank the length of my arms and then hung for the time, in tolerable safety, with one foot resting on a projecting stone. Loosening the hold of one hand, I took my large jack-knife from my pocket, opened it with the assistance of my teeth, and dug with it a hollow among the decayed stones large enough to receive and support one foot. Then thrusting the knife as far as possible into the wall to assist my hold, I grasped it and the stones with the unoccupied hand and raised my foot to the hollow prepared for it. Thus, foot by foot, I made my way and in ten minutes, as time seemed to me, I seized a projecting root at the top and drew myself up. During the whole time of climbing I felt perfectly cool, but when fairly up, I confess I shuddered as I looked down at the gulf I had escaped. A large stone, weighing, perhaps, a hundred pounds, lay on the edge. I thrust it off with my foot and down it went, struck the bottom of the ravine with a tremendous crash, and thundered down, leaping from side to side until it lodged, at last, far below against a projecting rock. I descended the **mountain** by means of the trees and bushes, cut a fishing pole at the bottom, and, having amused myself with an hour's fishing went to the tavern, and astonished the company with a recital of my adventure. Crawford expressed considerable astonishment at my escape, and the young lady in whose company I got my ducking on the stage transferred an account to her journal, but refused to let me see it, promising to send me a copy the moment her book was out of the press.

This account gives a good notion of Parkman's quality as a writer and a man at the age of seventeen. He had the solitary courage which is rarer and finer than the more public kind, and he took the opportunity of a lonely hour to master his jangled nerves before seeking the company of his fellows and thrilling them with a tale which doubtless was casual to a degree, though not free of a restrained touch of vainglory. The terse and vivid narrative is put down in the diary with but five or six slips of the pen and one interlineation. His natural way of writing was to compose the narrative in his head before he set a word on paper, and this practice stood him in good stead in the years to come.

On the next day, July 25, Parkman was one of a party of ten men and women, who set out on horse and foot for Mount Washington by the newly enlarged Crawford Path at ten in the morning. For two hours they climbed Mount Clinton through the forest, though at the summit the forest was "of the gigantic height of two feet— a complete miniature of the larger woods we had passed." Then they went on to Mount Pleasant, where they were blessed with a most glorious view of the valleys on each side, with the clouds rising and falling about the summits of the surrounding mountains. Then, with one of those almost momentary revolutions of the weather common here, the clouds closed down on the party and they descended Mount Pleasant and began the ascent of Monroe in darkness. But suddenly the sun broke through again, "the mists gathered themselves and rolled down the mountainsides, quivered an instant, then boiled up through the ravines and gorges, scattered, and were borne along glistening in the sun, among the thousand mountains that lay beneath and around us. At the same moment a peal of thunder sounded below and a rainbow arched, for a minute, the peak before us." Parkman could not savor such beauty to the full in company, and reined in his horse on a ridge while the rest zigzagged up the steep path.

As he watched his companions moving slowly in a long line, bending and winding in twenty directions, he thought that no scene among the Andes could be more wild or picturesque, for the fluttering shawls of the ladies and the outlandish garb of the men lent color to the picture. Then he rejoined his companions on the summit of Monroe, and marveled at the view: "The mountains were like a sea of lashing waves; the valley of the Connecticut was visible for fifty miles, with the river winding through it like a thread, while in the valley below, the forests seemed, from the tremendous height we stood upon, like fields of mown grass intersected by the channels of streams, whose waters, at intervals, flashed in the sun." Then they went on toward the cloud-capped summit of Washington, along the ledge above the precipice of Mount Franklin, overlooking Oakes Gulf, and on past the Lakes of the Clouds and the snowpatches in the hollows of Washington's summit slopes. A cold wind and mist mixed with sleet drove along the mountain top and they were glad to take shelter at the summit in a pyramid of huge rocks, whence the first arrivals bellowed "Old Hundred" to the winds. Crawford had brought food and brandy, and the latter was particularly welcome as a hard storm of sleet and rain soon came on. Balked of the best view in the mountains, they began the return trip after a three-quarters of an hour rest, soon reaching warmth and sunlight. Two of the party fell from their horses and all the ladies were faint-hearted or tired, with the exception of Parkman's new object of adoration, Miss Prentiss of Keene, "whose strength and spirit and good humor would have invigorated at least a dozen feeble damsels." They got back to the tavern at seven in the evening. Parkman, with his usual insistence on making things hard for himself, walked all but a mile of the six to the summit and all but twice that in returning.

The next day was dull and promised rain. But it held up in the morning and Parkman climbed the "High Rock in the Notch"— probably Mount Willard—finding the ascent passable but the descent abominable. There was a path which he chose to ignore, making his way "through a tangled wood, rocky, bushy, and strewn in all directions with rotten trunks, many of which, when stepped upon, straightway burst to pieces, and, unless I was extremely careful, seated me among their rot." When he got back to the tavern he was dismayed to find dinner over and "all the pleasant company gone to Franconia, whither I shall go tomorrow." The entry closes with a reference to his bad temper and a malediction upon the Notch House, "a place which, though one of the pleasantest in the world at other times, is the perfection of dullness in bad weather." He liked neither the enforced inaction of this afternoon and evening nor the sudden departure of Miss Prentiss. He dismissed some other members of the company still at Crawford's as "the most consummate fools I ever saw." Savagely he saw them set off for Washington the next morning, among them a lady who "uttered the most piercing shrieks her limited power of lungs could compass the instant she was in the saddle. A fit person she is, truly, to climb a mountain of seven thousand feet!"

He and Slade set out on foot for Franconia, both the morning and the road being the finest they had yet had. At Fabyan's they found that Tower, their intended companion, had arrived there, but had gone to climb Washington with George Cary, Henry Parker, and Edward Wheelwright. They went on, however, and lunched on the banks of the Ammonoosuc off a partridge and a wild pigeon, which Parkman had shot, and some crackers. After walking another eight miles they reached Franconia Village, having walked twenty-two miles during the day. The next day they went to the Notch, and inspected the Old Man of the Mountain, rowed about Echo Lake, and then walked down through the Notch to Lincoln, planning to examine the Flume in the morning. The sole tavern and only house there bore a discouraging aspect, but they had no choice, and in the company of "a most comical-looking Yankee pedlar" they dined on raw cucumbers, "backed by an anonymous pie with a crust like lignum vitae." The host was drunk and they had trouble in obtaining clean sheets. A pump was the sole provision afforded by the tavern for travelers with a passion for cleanliness. Before breakfast they set out for the Flume, but missed the path and followed the banks of the Pemigewasset. They took the wrong branch, and after a difficult struggle through the almost impenetrable forest, which brought a "Hang your dirty Flume!" from Slade, they came out at the Pool. They got out of their difficulties here by scaling the steep, smooth cliffs which rise directly from the water and finally came out on the road, two miles from the tavern. Thence they returned, to breakfast off a large partridge and several wild pigeons which Parkman had shot the preceding afternoon.

Having procured a guide, they then set out for the Flume again. They were comforted to learn that visitors seldom attempted to find the place without help and frequently got badly lost. From Parkman's long account of the place, it is clear that he thought the sight well worth the trouble it had cost him. Then they walked back through the Notch until they came to a tavern kept by a man

named Fifield, who went fishing with them in the afternoon. Parkman followed a steam in an opposite direction from the others and was almost benighted in the woods, but made his way first by the sun and then by a familiar peak, and reached the road before darkness overtook him.

The next day, July 30, Parkman and Slade went north to Lancaster, for the former had been inflamed at Crawford's by an account of Dixville Notch, "said to be the equal or superior in grandeur to the Notch of the White Mountains." Parkman had never before heard of this pass, and the assurance that moose and other big game were still common in this wilderness, which was traversed only by a new and impassable road, determined him to see it. At Lancaster he hoped to find an Indian guide named Anantz, a Dartmouth graduate who lived by hunting and guiding parties through the wilderness on the borders of New Hampshire and Canada. When Parkman reached Lancaster he found that the celebrated hunter was absent in Vermont, but he fell in with the State Survey party. Dr. Charles T. Jackson, its head, and his assistants gave him an account of the country and of what he would need for an expedition there. One of the assistants, M. B. Williams, had hunted with Anantz last season and, as Parkman noted excitedly, "between them they shot two moose!" Williams provided a map and mentioned places where temporary guides might be obtained, and the proper price to pay for such services. Jackson made a catalogue of the requisites, "as if we were bound on an exploring expedition to Hudson's Bay," which dismayed Slade, who fell to muttering about "not engaging to come so far." Parkman was obliged to accuse him of a tendency to "funk out," being now unwilling to dispense with company for the canny reasons that he did not want to travel alone through the wilderness and that the cost to him would be only half as great if Slade came. Parkman was cheerfully setting off into the unknown, for whither their route led after traversing the Notch and reaching Umbagog Lake and the Megalloway River, "the Lord knows where." Slade was only dragged into the excursion by an overpowering barrage of arguments, and Tower, whom they had finally met at Littleton, had gone home sick and discouraged. So much for the value of enthusiasm in coping with physical hardship.

Parkman and his unwilling companion engaged a private wagon to convey them to Colebrook, the jumping-off place, there being no public conveyance to that settlement. It took them seven hours to make the journey north along the banks of the Connecticut, but the little town of a few hundred souls, then the largest north of Lancaster, seemed pleasant enough and there was a "neat little tavern." The next day was Sunday, August 1, and Parkman's record of it opens: "Sunday in the country is a day of most unmitigated and abominable dullness." Aflame as he was for the wilderness, he managed to endure a civilized Sabbath by going through some old copies of a Baltimore magazine which he found in the house. He went to church in the morning, but "the minister being unfortunately an Unitarian, the dullness of his discourse and the squall of his choir were not varied and relieved by any novel fanaticism or methodistical blunders."

He soon found life more to his taste. After passing a few farmhouses scattered along the roadside outside Colebrook, they saw no more of villages, cultivated fields, or civilization. The way now ran through a forest "so thickset and tangled that we could scarce see two rods in any direction, except before and behind." The road might be called such, "but the term was grievously misapplied" in Parkman's opinion. It was surfaced with stones, stumps, and roots, and boughs arched overhead. Only ruts gave indication that it was occasionally traveled by wheeled traffic. They met but one traveler on the way, an armed horseman from Brag's settlement on the other side of the mountains. At first there seemed to be no opening in the green wall which blocked their passage, but as they emerged upon an unwooded plain,

. . . a gap in the range appeared, with bare and pointed rocks starting upward from the forests that covered the mountains and looking down upon us as we entered the passage. These rocks were many hundred feet high and the pass between extremely narrow. Looking upward on either side, the mountains were almost perpendicular. Fire had stripped them of their verdure and left them covered with blackened trunks and rocks rolled from the sharp peaks above. In picturesque effect the scene was superior to the Notch of the White Mountains, but in grandeur it fell far below it. Instead of the vast rounded summits of the Notch, these mountains were surmounted by peaks and needles of rock, which from below looked like ruined towers standing out in relief against the sky.

Nevertheless Parkman did not hurry on. They lunched in the Notch off some fresh-caught trout and newly shot pigeons, cooked "after a style wholly original." While Slade let his dinner settle, Parkman climbed one of the mountains and got a fine view of the pass and the surrounding country. Then they pushed on eastward, passing only a few log cabins until they reached Captain Brag's settlement on the "Amariscoggin" [Androscoggin] at sunset. Here they slept to the roar of the rapids that ran close to the house, and Parkman was cheered to find a fresh bearskin nailed on the barn to dry. At last, when only seventeen, he had reached the real wilderness he had often dreamed of in his childhood. He gave himself so wholeheartedly to wilderness life that he neglected his diary for a week, but made entries covering the whole period upon his return to Colebrook. It is clear from his account that Brag's settlement on the Androscoggin, "not far from Lake Umbagog and a few miles west of the Margalloway," was the modern village of Errol. He speaks of rapids extending more than a mile upstream here, and of two-mile rapids on the Megalloway, some miles above where it joins the lake's outlet and forms the Androscoggin, "passable only by means of a ragged and difficult portage."

Parkman was unable to obtain a guide and a boat at Brag's as he had hoped, but was assured by the captain that both could be procured on the Megalloway. This frontier worthy accompanied the two youths a mile or so on the path that led through the woods to these settlements. His directions as he left them must be given word for word as Parkman recorded them:

"The first house," he said, "is five or six miles further on. When you get about a mile you will have to cross a brook. On the other side there are logging paths, and one thing another branching out like, right and left. All you have got to do is to pick out the one you see has been most travelled by the cattle, because all the others run a little ways, and then come to nothing. Then go on a little further and you will come to a guzzle that they say is pretty bad this season thought I ha'nt seen it myself. However, it a'nt more than two rods wide, so I guess you can get across. Just keep, all along, where the cattle have been most, and you can't miss the way."

With these admirable directions and added injunctions to avoid quagmires and mistaking rabbit tracks or cattle paths for the road, Parkman and Slade went on alone. The path was about four inches wide, choked with undergrowth and blocked by fallen logs. They found five miles along such a track equivalent to twenty along any other. They crossed the brook and found the right cattle track, progressing at the rate of a mile an hour; got their first view of the Megalloway and came upon the "guzzle," whose nature had been a mystery to them until they saw it:

A kind of muddy creek, very deep and dirty, extended from the river directly across the path. It was, as the captain said, about two rods wide, with muddy and slippery banks and no earthly means of crossing but two slender poles, laid one from each bank and resting on a floating log in the middle. On the opposite bank, however, lay a heap of logs with their ends in the water, and bearing to the careless eye an appearance of tolerable solidity. With a commendable spirit of prudence, I induced Dan to make the first attempt. He cut him a long pole to steady himself, and, adding two or three additional supports to the frail bridge, essayed to cross. He planted his pole firmly in the mud and leaned hard against it, but he was not a foot from shore before the bridge began to sink, inch by inch. Daniel's ponderous frame was too much for it, and, wherever he stepped, down sank logs, poles, and branches, and resting place for his foot he had none. Dan got flurried. He splashed here and there, lost his balance, gave a leap in desperation at the treacherous pier of logs on the other side, they tilted up, and in plunged Dan, floundering among the fragments of the demolished bridge and sputtering the dirty water from his mouth. He gained the bank and shook himself like a dog. "Ha! Ha! Ha!" laughed I from one side. "Haw!

Haw! Haw!" responded he from the other. "Now let's see you cross," said Dan. I accordingly rearranged the bridge with his assistance and succeeded in getting over, though wet to the knees.

At length they came to the clearing of one Bennet, "a man strong and hardy and handsome, though I never saw an Indian darker than exposure had made his features." Bennet was a famous hunter and would have liked to join the party, but he was in the midst of haying. He suggested that Joshua Lumber [Lombard], who lived near by and had a boat and oxen to drag it round the falls, was just the man for them. Bennet's son ferried them across the river, which the path crossed here, and they went on five miles to Lumber's abode at the foot of the falls. This house was the last but one on the river, "Captain Wilson holding a 'clearing' a mile further up—all above as far as the Canada settlements is one vast forest varied, as yet, with not the slightest trace of man's hand, unless it be the remains of the hunter's encampment." This was Parkman's dish, and he insisted on spending the night in the forest, though Lumber offered the accommodation of his rude log cabin, already well filled with a wife and a number of stout boys.

Parkman's description of the place is worth noting, for it is at this point that he became confused in his geography: "His place is situated just within the borders of Maine. A high and picturesque mountain rises on the west, with summits some rounded, some steep and broken. The river flows at its base through fertile plains which Lumber's industry has cleared of timber and covered with a growth of grain and grass. *Asesquoss* is the name of the mountain." Now if Parkman was below Wilson's clearing (the modern Wilsons Mills), Aziscoos Mountain was to the east, while the peak to the west to which he gave a phonetic version of that name is Black Mountain. From here on it is impossible to follow Parkman's course on a modern map, for the damming of the Megalloway above Wilsons Mills has covered his path with the waters of Aziscoos Lake.

Lumber and his sons, and a stranger whom Parkman soon discovered to be an Indian, paid them a visit that night as they sat about the fire in their camp. The Indian proved to be the nephew of the learned Anantz and an excellent hunter, and since he was going up the river in a few days, Parkman appointed a meeting place thirty miles upstream, where they might engage him to guide them on to Canada in case they decided to return that way. The next morning a light skiff, "built after the fashion of a birch canoe and weighing scarce more," was drawn on a sledge by oxen over the three-mile portage, which frequently had to be cleared of logs and fallen trees by the ax as they went along it. Lumber aptly summed up the arduous journey with "Considerable of an enterprise, sir," when they stood at last upon the banks of the river above the rapids. Some hasty repairs were made on the boat, which had suffered from the rough passage, and then they pushed off.

Without Lumber's guidance, the party might well have come to grief. They had only six pounds of bread, some salt, and some butter; no blankets and no nets for protection against the flies. They hoped to catch all the fish they needed and perhaps meet larger game. Soon they passed the mouth of a "cold stream" where they got some trout, though "the flies bit infinitely more than the fish." That night they camped on the river bank, with only a bed of spruce boughs and a roaring fire as protection. The next day brought a change in the character of the river. It grew shallow and the current more swift, so that it took all their force to move upstream. It also followed a winding course, so that they made little progress. They ran aground on shallows or among rocks, and frequently had to get out into the water and push their craft along. The flies became so intolerable that they lit a smudge in the frying pan, which they placed in the bow of the boat. They found no trout and had to dine off chubs. They passed at last the meadows, where the river wound in great bends through a flat and marshy tract of low bushes, and then re-entered the forest:

. . . A most wild and beautiful appearance did the river shores present. From the high banks huge old pines stooped forward over the water, the moss hanging from their aged branches, and behind rose a wall of foliage, green and thick, with no space or opening which the eye could penetrate.

The river was no longer still and deep here, but swift and broken by cascades, "a change which, how much soever it might improve the effect of the scene, was of no advantage to the navigation." Finally they reached the appointed meeting place, where the river divided into two branches, one of which led to the New Hampshire line, the other to Parmachenee Lake and thence to the Boundary Mountains.

Here they awaited the Indian, who was expected at sunrise the next day. Lumber built a lean-to of boughs, and his companions caught a mess of "most magnificent trout, some of them being not less than a foot in length, though this is an unfavorable season for them." Their camp was on the tongue of land between the two streams, and though the tumbling waters did not bother Parkman, mosquitoes and the black flies did. His treatise on these pests is admirable:

> As usual our chief annoyance was from flies and mosquitoes, of which the latter swarmed in numbers unprecedented, but their attacks were as nothing in comparison with that of clouds of black flies—animals not much larger than the head of a pin, but inflicting a wound twice as large as themselves and assaulting with such eagerness that nothing but being in the midst of a thick smoke will keep them off. They seemed to take a particular liking to me, and I was bitten to such a degree that I am now— nearly four days after—covered with their wounds as if I had the smallpox. There is another cursed race, denominated from their microscopic dimensions "no-see-ems." Their bite is like the prick of a needle, but not half so endurable, and they insinuate themselves through pantaloons, stockings, and everything else.

But in spite of these unwelcome visitations, the exhausted party slept and was only aroused at daybreak by a shout from the river as Jerome the Indian guided his canoe to the shore. He had shot a moose downriver and hoped to find her in the morning, but as he had been paddling since nine the morning before in order to keep his bargain, he promptly wrapped himself, head and all, in his blanket and went to sleep.

Later that morning the party held a council of war. Their bread was almost gone, and in the absence of that and blankets, it seemed foolhardy, even to Parkman, to attempt to push on to Canada. Yet he was clearly regretful:

My chief object in coming so far was merely to have a taste of the half-savage kind of life necessary to be led, and to see the wilderness while it was as yet uninvaded by the hand of man. I had had some hope of shooting a moose but that hope seemed doomed to be disappointed, although, had we kept on, there was a very considerable chance of finding them. Slade, however, became utterly discouraged and refused to proceed, and this alone would have prevented me even if there had been no other obstacles.

So they turned back the way they had come after breakfast, the Indian in his bark canoe having vanished down the swift stream like a bubble. The descent was nothing like the upstream journey, since they were borne without effort past the scenes of their previous difficulties, and the landscape proved twice as inviting under these circumstances. They had gone some miles when they saw a young moose far in front splash across the river. Parkman dropped his paddle and stood in the prow with cocked rifle, but by the time they reached the spot there was no sign of the beast but its tracks on the bank. A bend in the river blocked their view, but they heard another plunge and the snap of a gun missing fire, and as they came around the bend they saw a large moose climbing the bank while Jerome, on the opposite shore, hastily picked the lock of his gun. Parkman took quick aim at the back, fired, and the moose tumbled down the steep bank into the river with a severed spine:

The poor beast lay an instant in the water and then, with a convulsive effort, staggered to her feet and stood in the river where it was about a foot deep. Jerome aimed at her head, fired, and missed altogether. I reloaded and, aiming at the eye, struck the head just below the root of the ear. Jerome took a long aim and fired again. He hit her fair and full just between the eyes. For an instant she did not move; then her body declined slowly to one side and she fell, gave a short plunge, and lay dead on the bottom.

This was the same moose that Jerome had wounded on his way up, and thus the prey was his by forest law. But he gave Parkman's party as much of the meat as they wanted, for the young man's rifle practice from a tossing boat had been good enough to win his admiration.

Jerome stayed behind to load his canoe—the beast was larger than a horse—and the others dined off moose meat at their first night's camp, and then went on to the starting place at the head of the rapids, which they reached an hour before sunset. They topped off their thirty miles of paddling with the walk to Lumber's, where they "preferred the fresh hay of his barn to the chance of what we might encounter in the shape of log-cabin sheets." Since their vacation time was growing short, they determined to make Colebrook in a day's journey, though the distance was forty miles. Leaving Lumber's an hour before the sun rose, they reached Bennet's half an hour after it was up, where they hired a skiff and paddled down to Brag's. They reached the settlement at half-past ten, and ate a monstrous breakfast which cost them ninepence. The pie, cake, bread, and quarts of fresh milk which they consumed at this first civilized meal in a week did not ride well, and Slade was sick. A bath in a freezing-cold stream revived them and they passed back through Dixville Notch in the early afternoon. Here Parkman again got his directions twisted, in noting the appearance of the pass:

> . . . The scene appeared to much greater advantage on entering from the west [east] than when seen from the opposite side. The road, which has been constructed within a few weeks, adds greatly to its effect. It is a causeway strongly built of stone against the side of steep precipices which on the one hand rise abruptly from it, while on the other a shallow ravine, the bed of a winter torrent, is interposed between the road end and the crags which overlook it. These, steep as they are, afford in the crevices root-hold for large trees and a thick growth of saplings which, over-shadowing the road, make with the rocks above a beautiful per-

spective to one entering the pass. Further on, the rocks rose higher and fire has stripped them of their woods, so that in the heart of the defile nothing meets the eye but the tall pinnacles shooting upward abruptly and with black and fire-scorched rocks scattered about their bases.

They reached Colebrook long after nightfall, having traveled thirty miles on foot and paddled ten. Neither Parkman nor Slade seems to have had any objection to a most Calvinistic Sabbath on the following day. Parkman described his chief occupations as sleeping and writing up his journal for the previous week. But by Monday he was restored and restless again, and tarried in Colebrook only under "the imperative necessity of my clothes undergoing a cleansing operation."

On Tuesday they started south on foot, reaching Lancaster that night, where Parkman wrote these prophetic words in his diary:

> For myself I am loath to abandon so soon the excitements and the enjoyments of the last few weeks, though many of them have been purchased with "toil and sweat." My pilgrimage, however, must come to an end, and next Saturday will find me at home. I regard this journey but "as the beginning of greater things" and as merely prefatory to longer wanderings.

At the tavern in the Connecticut Valley where they stopped for lunch this day, they again encountered Dr. Jackson's survey party, now bound for Colebrook. They spent an hour and a half, "most satisfactorily to me," discussing backwoods matters. The obliging Williams offered Parkman the use of his notebook of his journeys with Anantz, who was well versed in the traditions of his tribe. Parkman, eager student of the Indians that he was, noted: "I shall certainly avail myself of his offer." Having thus lost time in talk, and perhaps being willing to rest upon their laurels as pedestrians, they took a wagon to Lancaster. Parkman made some notes on the country through which they passed, as was his lifelong custom: "As through the greater part of the valley of the Connecticut, the level and beautiful meadows through which the river flows are shut in by parallel ranges of hills, some high and craggy—all wild and beautiful in their appearance. Distant mountains of considerable elevation overlook Lancaster on the east." The following afternoon he proceeded to Littleton, whence he departed at four the following morning for Windsor, by way of "Hallowell" [Haverhill] and Hanover. Arriving in Windsor he only had opportunity—or inclination, after the exhausting stage ride—to note that "Ascutney Mountain overhangs the village" and "I deem it expedient to retire immediately to bed, since I must be off at two in the morning." Starting at that hour by coach, he reached Nashua in time to catch the late afternoon train for Boston, where he arrived in another two hours. Vacation was over, and a second year of college lay ahead before he could return to the forest life he loved so well.

The journal of this first wilderness adventure ends with these words, "And a joyous month it has been, though one somewhat toilsome—may I soon pass another as pleasantly," and with the initials "F.P." and two great flourishes of the pen. The flame still burnt with undiminished intensity after surviving a trial which had only lent it fuel. Parkman's passion for the wilderness was an enduring thing.

3: The Making of a Woodsman—II

I spent all my summer vacations in the woods or Canada, at the same time reading such books as I thought suited in a general way to help me towards my object. I pursued these lucubrations with a pernicious intensity, keeping my plans and purposes to myself, while passing among my companions as an outspoken fellow.
F.P., LETTER TO BRIMMER, 1886

IN 1842, during the summer vacation of his sophomore year, Parkman made another and more ambitious wilderness tour. His companion on this expedition was Henry Orne White, who was in the class above him at Harvard and shared his passion for the woods. Slade, his former companion, may not have wanted to involve himself in so extensive a trip as this was to be, though he had shared Parkman's shorter expeditions to points near Cambridge during the past college year. The plan was to start north from Albany, visit the battlefields of the French and Indian Wars in the region of Lake George and Lake Champlain, and then cut across the northern boundaries of Vermont and New Hampshire into Canada, returning by way of Mount Katahdin in Maine. This was an ambitious and adventurous month's undertaking for an eighteen-year-old youth at this period, when the region was still largely wilderness.

Parkman and White started off from Boston at half-past six on the morning of July 15, 1842, and reached Albany that night. Parkman noted that it was the longest day's journey he had ever made, but that he "would rather have come thirty miles by stage than the whole distance by railroad, for of all methods of progressing, that by steam is incomparably the most disgusting." The train made a meal stop at Springfield at noon, and Parkman was initiated, much to his disgust, into this old American custom: "White ran off to see his sister and I stayed and took 'refreshment' in a little room

at the end of the car-house, where about thirty people were standing around a table in the shape of a horseshoe, eating and drinking
in lugubrious silence." Then the train started off again and crossed
the Connecticut. Parkman was vastly annoyed by the parapet on
the bridge, which both cut off the view and drove all the sparks
from the engine into his eyes. Later on, as the train began to dodge
around the high cliffs in the foothills of the Berkshires, he found
this method of transportation doubly irritating, because the speed
permitted him to see only enough of the country to make him wish
to see more, while a shower of red hot sparks poured in the window like a hailstorm and half blinded him. Glimpses of this lovely
countryside tantalized him and he resolved to see it to better advantage another time. But the train relentlessly carried him on
through Becket, Hinsdale, Pittsfield, and over the New York border
to Chatham, Kinderhook, and Schodack. At half-past six that evening he saw the Hudson, "moping dismally between its banks
under a cloudy sky, with a steamboat solemnly digging its way
through the leaden waters," and in a few minutes more the dirty
spires of Albany came in sight. They crossed the river by a ferry
and put up at the Eagle Hotel. They were both eager to leave cities
behind them, particularly since Albany "impressed us at once with
its antiquity by the most ancient and fish-like smell, which invaded
our shrinking nostrils."

The next day they went on to Caldwell (the modern Lake
George) largely by train, for it was impossible to proceed up the
Hudson to Fort Edward by boat as Parkman had hoped to do. The
long train ride the previous day had clearly disagreed with him,
for the diary opens with a devout hope that he may never see
Albany again and goes on with the note: "Railroad the worst I
was ever on; the country flat and dull, the weather dismal." He
had been prepared to find Schenectady "something filthy" but not
"quite so disgusting as the reality." Since the Mohawk Valley in
this era has come to be thought romantic, perhaps his picture of it
is worth recording:

Canal docks, full of stinking water, superannuated rotting canal
boats, and dirty children and pigs paddling about formed the

forefront of the delicious scene, while in the rear was a mass of tumbling houses and sheds, bursting open in all directions, green with antiquity, dampness, and lack of paint. Each house had its peculiar dunghill, with the group of reposing hogs. In short, London itself could exhibit nothing much nastier.

Here he got a train for Saratoga, which traveled at the "astonishing rate of seven miles an hour." At the Springs he was glad enough to abandon the cars for the Caldwell stage, but took time to walk through one or two of the famous hotels of the spa; though "after perambulating the entries filled with sleek waiters and sneaking fops, dashing through the columned porticoes and enclosures, drinking some of the water and spitting it out again in high disgust, I sprang onto the stage, cursing Saratoga and all New York." At Glens Falls his smoldering bad temper flared up again at the sight of a clumsy bridge thrown over the noble cataract and of some twenty mills around the dam above the bridge; though the Yorkers had not succeeded in spoiling the place entirely for him, and he got satisfaction from the fact that "still the water comes down over the marble ledges in foam and fury, and the roar completely drowns the clatter of machinery." He inspected the rock caverns at the foot of the falls, guided by two little boys who fell to quarreling over the identification of the caves in terms of Cooper's *Leather-stocking Tales*. Parkman ended the literary controversy with two cents.

Dinner at the tavern here and a subsequent conversation with the stage-driver changed Parkman's mood for the better. Then the sight of French Mountain and the far-off Green Mountains, scarcely visible through the haze, completely cured him of what he called the "blue-devils." He was moving now in a land whose every mark had meaning for him, thanks to his study of the Old French War in books. In 1755 French Mountain was the scene of one of the most desperate and memorable battles in that conflict; two piles of stone by the roadside marked the grave of Colonel Ephraim Williams, "that accomplished warrior and gentleman"; and a little farther on was the lookout rock on which the colonel received his mortal wound. Then came the scene where McGinnis cut up the

French as they retreated from their defeat at the lake; and then Bloody Pond, "a little slimy dark sheet of stagnant water, covered with weeds and pond-lilies, and shadowed by the gloomy forest around it . . . the place where hundreds of dead bodies were flung after the battle, and where the bones still lie." A few miles more, and Lake George lay before them, the mountains and water confused and indistinct in the mist. Mist or no, this was Parkman's El Dorado and his Promised Land.

The tavern was full of fashionable New Yorkers—"all of a piece" —who looked upon White and Parkman, who looked like the Old Nick, in a manner corresponding. So Parkman went off to spend a Sunday morning inspecting the fortifications and the battlefields. Fort William Henry proved a disappointment: "The enterprising genius of the inhabitants has made a road directly through the ruins, and turned bastion, moat, and glacis into flourishing corn-fields, so that the spot so celebrated in our colonial history is now scarcely to be distinguished." But he was able to trace Montcalm's lines and the burying ground of the French who fell in the siege, though these were now in the midst of a gloomy pine wood. Fort George, a little to the east, was in a much better state of preservation, being under the special protection of Mr. Caldwell, the feudal proprietor of the village. But its ruins lacked sufficient historical associations to capture Parkman's interest, and he soon betook himself to the near-by Prospect, a two-thousand-foot pathless mountain which he climbed in the heat of the day. Though he was almost "suffocated with heat and thirst," the view down the lake toward Ticonderoga rewarded him sufficiently for his efforts. Upon his return to Caldwell, he went to church in a half-filled little edifice, whose congregation consisted of "countrymen; cute, sly, sunburnt slaves of Mammon; maidens of sixty and of sixteen; the former desperately ugly, with black bonnets, frilled caps, peaked noses and chins, and an aspect diabolically prim and saturnine; the latter for the most part remarkably pretty and delicate." The minister, who long kept this gathering waiting for him, was the image of a Yankee plowboy, but he read the Episcopal service in a manner satisfying even to the highly critical Parkman. The text was "The Lord is a man of war" and every figure of the sermon was taken from warfare, which seemed singularly appropriate to the place and to Parkman, who was a militant and not a milk-and-water Christian. After the service he fell into conversation with the tavern-keeper and heard legends of the remains of a great Indian feast near by; of spikes and timbers, of Abercrombie's sunken vessels, which might be seen lying on the bottom of the lake when the water was still and the sunlight strong; and of the remains of the old batteries on French Mountain. That evening he visited the French graves, but recorded no mention of his thoughts.

The next day, which was sultry and oppressive, Parkman and White set out upon the still lake in a hired boat. Fishing and bathing, sleeping in the sun and reading Goldsmith, they passed a lazy day, camping for the night on uninhabited Diamond Island. The next morning they coasted along the eastern shore, having followed the western on the preceding day. For the first time the scenery seemed to match the extravagant ideas Parkman had formed of it in his fancy. Perhaps the appearance of a strong south wind, which whipped the lake into waves and dissipated some of the mist and sultriness, helped to make the place more pleasing. They drove along with the wind at their back, and, since the storm was becoming furious, landed on the extremity of Tongue Mountain, at the entrance of the Narrows. That night they camped on an island, and the next morning entered the Narrows. They spent the day rowing up and down this strait, and toward evening they drove down to Sabbath Day Point, "the famous landing place of many a huge army," before a fierce wind. At the Point two savage mountains rose abruptly from the water, with precipices resembling castle walls, and near the beach was a rickety old house where they sought shelter.

The owner of this "dingy shingle palace" turned out to be Captain Patchin, a Revolutionary pensioner, and his tales of campaigning, of rattlesnakes, deadly beasts, and deadly diseases delighted Parkman. They tarried here two days, fishing and hunting deer and rattlesnakes with members of the captain's household. While looking for rattlers on Catamount Mountain, Parkman came upon the top of a precipice overlooking the lake. Putting one arm around a gnarled tree, he leaned over and discharged his rifle, "Satan," into the gulf, at whose bottom some crows, looking like beetles from the height above, flew cawing over the treetops. From another height he got a good view of two-thirds of the lake, which seemed like a swift clear stream in the bottom of a deep glen. Parkman felt that: "There would be no finer place for gentlemen's countryseats than this, but now, for the most part, it is occupied by a race of boors about as uncouth, mean, and stupid as the pigs they seem chiefly to delight in." He exempted Captain Patchin's household from this indictment, but he refers to other natives he encountered on the shores of the lake as "deformed abortions," "Brobdingnagian sons of the plow," and so on. He was no democrat, though capable of exempting someone who interested him from his general contempt for the masses. The tables were nicely turned on him a little later when he was mistaken for a deckhand by a scorned "paddy tailor."

On Friday the twenty-second, Parkman and White left old Patchin's, the captain having unsuccessfully offered his abode to Parkman for $5000, as the whole household "calculated" to emigrate to Illinois in the fall. Since they had broken an oar and wished to mail a letter, they put in at a little hamlet on the western shore, near the foot of the lake. Here the combination tavern and post-office was kept by one "Judge" Garfield, who guided them to a carpenter. Parkman took advantage of the delay to follow a brook into the hills. Then he returned to Garfield's, where he found White in trouble with the carpenter. White had offered a Naumkeag Bank bill in payment, but this worthy had replied: "Don't know nothing about that money: wait till Garfield comes and he'll tell whether it's genuine or not." Parkman took a hand in the discussion:

"There's the paper," said I. "Look and see." He looked—all was right. "Well, are you satisfied?" "How do I know but what that 'ere bill is counterfeit? It has a sort of counterfeit look about it to my eyes. Deacon, what do you say to it?" The deacon put on his spectacles, held the bill to the light, turned it this way and that, tasted of it, and finally pronounced that, according to his calculation, it was good. But the carpenter was not contented. "Bijah, you're a judge of bills; what do you think?" Bijah, after a long examination, gave as his opinion that it was counterfeit. All parties were beginning to wax wroth when the judge entered and decided that the bill was good.

Thus acquitted of the suspicion of passing counterfeit bills, Parkman and White took to the lake again and soon reached a narrow strip of dark water between two grim mountains which "had witnessed, in their day, the passage of twenty vast armies in the strait between; and there was not an echo on either side which had not answered to the crack of rifles and screams of dying men."

They ran their boat ashore at the foot of Anthony's Nose, opposite Rogers' Slide, and sought a camping place, for Parkman could not bear to hurry past this historic strait. To their surprise, they found a little roofless log enclosure, which they piled with hemlock boughs for beds. But the camp, at the foot of a steep rock and surrounded by cedars and hemlocks, was alive with mosquitoes, "no-see-ems," and innumerable swarms of other bugs. Despite nets, which Parkman had had the foresight to take along this time, they suffered as if under a shower of molten iron, and White cursed the woods and his companion for bringing him there. Parkman tried to laugh it off, but the best even he could manage after a while was to suffer in silence. Eventually they fell into a doze, from which Parkman was awakened late in the night by the sound of loud voices and a shout of "Now then, G-d damn it, pull for your life—every stroke helps!" Fearing that their boat was being stolen, Parkman dashed down to the shore, only to find a man who had become exhausted rowing against a strong head wind and had put ashore through the breakers, thus encouraged by a hardier friend who kept on. The wind drove the bugs away along the shore, so Parkman, White, and their new acquaintance built a fire and prepared to sleep there. "As the light fell on his matted hair, his grisly unshorn countenance, haggard with drinking, and his tattered and patched clothes, and then again flared up on the cliffs and savage trees, and streamed across the water, I thought

that even that shore had seldom seen a more outlandish group—
we in our blankets, he in his rags." The stranger was talkative, and
so they got but little sleep.

The next morning they started back up the lake to pick up some
washing at Patchin's, and had a bad time of it, for it was twelve
toilsome miles against a severe head wind, with the waves running
high and tempers running short.

"Well," said White, "you call this fun, do you? To be eaten by
bugs all night and work against head winds all day isn't according to my taste, whatever you may think of it."

"Are you going to back out?" said I.

"Back out, yes, when I get into a bad scrape, I back out of it as
quick as I can"—and so he went on with marvelous volubility
to recount his grievances. Lake George he called a "scrubby-
looking place"—said there was no fishing in it—he hated camping and would have no more of it—he wouldn't live so for another week to save his life, etc., etc.

Verily, what is one man's meat is another man's poison. What
troubles me more than his treachery to our plans is his want of
cash, which will make it absolutely necessary to abandon our
plan of descending through Maine. His scruples I trust to overcome in time.

It is worth noting that on every one of Parkman's wilderness expeditions his companions grew weary and discouraged and wanted
to turn back while he was still enthusiastic and eager to press on.
The fault could not have been entirely theirs; it is clear that Parkman in his zeal for hardening himself and approximating the living
conditions of his historical heroes, tried the flesh beyond normal
endurance. His passion for the wilderness and his secret purpose
in these expeditions gave him a sort of manic intensity that made
him a poor fellow-traveler. Eventually he paid dearly for his ex-
cesses, and his sorely tried companions were avenged by nature.

It seems clear that Parkman was more interested in hearing
Captain Patchin's tales again than in obtaining fresh linen. His

portrait of the captain is a good bit of characterization, as revealing of its author as of its subject:

> We reached Patchin's at last, and were welcomed by the noble old veteran as cordially as if we were his children. We dined, and sat in his portico, listening to his stories. He is eighty-six. Three years ago he danced with great applause at a county party, and still his activity and muscular strength are fully equal to those of most men in the prime of life. He must once have been extremely handsome; even now his features are full and regular, and when he tells his stories he always sets his hat on one side of his head, and looks the very picture of an old warrior. He was several times prisoner. Once, when in Quebec, an English officer asked him, as he tells the story, "What's your name?" "Patchin." " 'What, Hell-Hound Patchin!' says he." At another time an officer struck him without any provocation but that of his being a rebel. Patchin sprang on him and choked him until he fainted, in the streets of Quebec. He served in the Indian campaigns of Butler and Brant about Ft. Stanwix—at the recovery of Ft. Ann after it was taken by Burgoyne—was present when Sir John Johnson fled from the Mohawk with his property, and tells how narrowly that Tory made his escape from the pursuing party on Champlain. He wants us to come back and hear more of his stories.

And no doubt Parkman wanted to do so, but White found fishing more to his taste and he had to be humored if their excursion was to be accomplished in its entirety.

Back down the lake they went, "White still continuing comtumacious," and so being left at Garfield's, while Parkman camped by himself on an island some miles off. He left his pantaloons to be washed by the action of the waves, and wrapping himself in a blanket, read a book as long as he could see. The next day being Sunday, Parkman lingered at Garfield's, having been kindly and hospitably received by the "judge." After a taste of a different life, Parkman was already losing some of his Bostonian near-sightedness about human beings, for he wrote a democratically flavored note

about the Garfields, whom he had previously regarded only as
amusing country bumpkins. On Monday Parkman went hunting
and fishing with White and a fellow-guest named Gibbs, whose
wife was a "vocalist." That afternoon they witnessed a spectacle
which brought out another unexpected burst of democratic feeling in the young Boston patrician:

> . . . The arrival of the great Nabob, Mr. Caldwell, the founder
> and owner of the village of that name, who comes here on a long
> promised visit in a little barge of his own, with flags at prow and
> stern, and a huge box of wines for his private refreshment. Ask
> anybody here what kind of man Mr. Caldwell is, and he will
> answer with a shrug of the shoulders, or if he is unusually deli-
> cate or cautious, it will be, "Oh, he is a very good sort of man,"
> or else, in the emphatic tone of one defending an accused person,
> "He is a very clever man, sir, a very clever man." But the truth
> is that he is a consummate tyrant and fool. He refused to pa-
> tronize the steamboat unless it was called after his name and
> fired a salute on approaching the village whenever he was pres-
> ent, which is accordingly done. It is impossible to get any favor
> from him without the humblest deference. He treats the towns-
> men, his vassals, with favor or the contrary according as they
> yield him due reverence. Tonight the report of a piece from his
> boat gave the signal of his approach. Patrick, the Irishman, stood
> on the beach with the Judge's best gun and answered with a
> salute, for so it must be, or the great man would be displeased.
> Somehow or other, the Judge himself, though I believe him as
> sensible a man as I ever met, regards his humble roof as honored
> by the mighty presence. Caldwell is of course reported vastly
> rich, as perhaps he is, but he got all his property from his father,
> an Irish immigrant who built himself a fortune by trading at
> Albany.

Possibly the young Boston patrician was patronized by the Irish
landlord and resented it. The sensation of not being a central
figure in the picture was new to Parkman, and none too agreeable.
And in addition he had a genuine grievance: the great man's ret-
inue crowded every corner of the little tavern, and two of his

satellites were crowded into the same room with Parkman and White, and kept them awake all night "with snorings so diversified and so powerful that I wished myself at camp in spite of the storm."

Declining a proffered swap of rifles with Garfield after a trial lasting half the morning, Parkman started off for Ticonderoga on Tuesday afternoon. There they found the steamboat tied up to her wharf at the outlet of the lake, and went on board to renew their acquaintance with an old deckhand, whom they had met at Caldwell. His most treasured possession was a box of rattlesnakes, which had once been stolen by some rascal, who took the rattling for the sound of some valuable piece of machinery but abandoned his loot in a hurry when he examined it. Parkman arranged to have their skiff returned to Caldwell by the steamer captain, and then took the stage for Ty, "a despicable manufacturing place." The inhabitants were as bad as the place in Parkman's view: the "paddy tailor" of whom he ordered a new pair of breeches annoyed him not a little by asking if he did not work on the steamboat, and another fellow of whom he asked the way to the fort replied: "Well, I've heered of such a place, seems to me, but I've never seen it, and couldn't tell ye where it be." He dismissed this villager as an idiot, but others proved as ignorant. It was Parkman's first contact with the profound apathy of the America of his day in regard to its origins. At last he got the direction, and after a two-mile walk came upon a ditched parapet running through the woods, which he took to be the French strongpoint against Abercrombie's assault. Next came an abundance of breastworks, then two or three square redoubts, and finally the old stronghold itself:

At length, mounting a little hill, a cluster of gray ruined walls, like an old château, with mounds of earth and heaps of stone about them, appeared crowning an eminence in front. When I reached them, I was astonished at the extent of the ruins. Thousands of men might have encamped in the area. All around were ditches of such depth that it would be death to jump down, with walls of masonry sixty feet high. Ty stands on a promontory, with Champlain on one side and the outlet of Lake George on the other; his cannon command the passage completely. At the very extremity is the oldest fort of the fortress—a huge mass of masonry with walls sinking sheer down to the two lakes. All kinds of weeds and vines are clambering over them. The senseless blockheads in the neighborhood have stolen ton upon ton of the stone to build their walls and houses of—may they meet their reward.

Parkman was to devote his life to chronicling the struggle in which a major role was played by this mighty fortress in the wilderness, but there is no further account of it in this early journal, except a note that he went over the ruins again the next morning, before taking the Champlain steamer for Burlington.

The first words penned by Parkman upon his return to New England from the land of the Yorkers were: "In Yankeeland again, thank heaven." Back home, he regained his sense of superiority, for upon his arrival at Burlington on the evening of July 27 he visited the college there, remarking upon the ugly buildings and the students lounging about or making "abortive attempts at revelry in their rooms." The two young Harvard men soon decided that these Vermont collegians were "all green"—a favorite term of patronizing contempt—and so sought their beds, making invidious comparisons between Harvard and the University of Vermont as they went. The next morning they started off on their walking tour of the northern frontier. At first they followed the Onion River, now mercifully restored to its original Indian name of the Winooski, Parkman observing that its falls, one of the sights of Vermont, had been ruined by dams; then they continued on by way of Essex and Jericho. Mount Mansfield loomed up directly in front of them, in the midst of a long line of wild mountains which bounded the horizon, and far off to their right Parkman noticed Camel's Hump—the singularly shaped peak which had been a landmark to the French in their border forays, under the name of Lion Couchant. Beyond Underhill they rested in a rocky glen near the road, having put sixteen miles behind them. Late that afternoon they pushed on nine more miles to Cambridge, "White making by the way several abortive attempts to shoot birds and squirrels." Parkman was taking notes of the region, which has the finest scenery in northern Vermont:

> The country was rather hilly, tolerably cultivated near the road, but covered with woods elsewhere. On a hill before us stretched a line of forest, remarkably dense and lofty, and over the tree-tops and among the boughs dozens of crows were wheeling about, croaking in hoarse concert. Ascending this hill, we found ourselves going down into a deep valley on the other side, flanked by barren rocky hills, with flocks of sheep perambulating among the rocks and stunted trees. In front of us was a noble spectacle of mountains, with an intervening country of low hills, forests, and cultivated fields. We turned an angle, and descended into another valley. Mansfield Mt. appeared through an opening on the right, and on the left was a succession of high rolling hills, one behind the other, all covered with forests, with the sinking sun blazing among the trees on the summit of the most distant, and flinging streams of light and shadow over the whole.

At supper in Cambridge Parkman and White encountered an inquisitive old Yankee who wanted to know who they were, where they came from, and where they were going. This inquisition irritated Parkman unreasonably, but White answered the queries after a fashion, and the old fellow gave them a sharp glance and observed, "whoever we were, we had some kind of prospects to look forward to." Not getting any help from his victims on this line, he astounded Parkman by asking him if he were not an Indian:

> I assured him that I was not, on which he coolly shook his head and said he made it a principle never to contradict any man. He did not consider it any disgrace, for his part, to be an Indian: "he had knowed Indians well edicated, afore now. He was very far from meaning to offend." He proved, after all, a fine old fellow; his sins being all of ignorance. Far from being offended, I favored his belief, for the joke's sake, and he firmly believes us both to contain a large share of Indian blood. He invited us to his house, if we passed "his way." We have been taken, on this

journey, for people of almost every nation on earth, but this is a consummation we hardly expected.

Once over his irritation at the social inquisition of Yankeeland, Parkman was secretly delighted to be taken for one of the savages in whose exploits he had long reveled. In his old and worn clothes, and deeply tanned by the exposure of the last ten days, he may well have reminded the old farmer of Anantz, the cultivated Indian guide, who often hunted in this region.

The following day Parkman and White walked on to Johnson, being taken on the way for members of the British Army, which was then very much on the minds of people in the frontier region because of the tension between the two countries. Their route led along the banks of the Lamoille River, which were infested by hawks whose shrieks and cries startled the travelers as they passed through deep woods. At Johnson they took the stage for Stanstead, just over the line in Canada. Except for greater speed, this arrangement had little advantage to offer over walking. The stage was a broken-down carryall, stuffed with passengers—one tubercular—and luggage, and it was drawn by two sickly horses "over a road of diabolical roughness." As they lumbered along by mountain lake and stream, Parkman was charmed by the consumptive's sister, who was pretty, never down-hearted, lively, and talkative, though she had been up all the preceding night nursing her brother. As they rattled on northward through Eden and Lowell, Parkman was struck by the wildness of the mountainous country. High cliffs hung over the road, and now and then there would be a new clearing among the wooded hills, which "lay in all the dismal deformity of charred trunks and stumps." They spent the night at Troy, near Lake Memphremagog, where eighteen-year-old Parkman was much taken with a girl, a year or two younger than himself, who sat with them at supper: "a pretty, innocent little thing, too timid to speak above a whisper. She kept her great black eyes always turned downwards."

The next day they went on to Stanstead in Canada by way of Newport, in the same stage. There was a furious intermittent rain, and mist veiled the trees and hills and the mountains were hidden in the clouds. The prospect from the stage was not a cheery one: "tracts of half-burned forests, steaming and smoking, some blasted trunks standing upright, others prostrate among charred trunks and tangled underwood, all looking supernaturally dismal through mist and rain." The only dwellings they passed were miserable log cabins, and the road now consisted of corduroy, rocks, and water. After one of the horses had fallen on a hill, and all the company had had to get out in the rain, they came at last to Lake Memphremagog: "A direful composition of great sheets of leaden water, scarce distinguishable from the fog that enveloped it, and a border of melancholy trees which stood apparently lamenting and pouring forth copious tears above it. All nature was in a fit of the bluedevils"—and so apparently was Parkman. A few miles on was Stanstead, which seemed like a Yankee town until they dismounted at the tavern, where a party of thirteen British soldiers under a cornet was quartered. These defenders of the frontier, all provincials, were gathered around a fire in the barroom, "smoking or telling stories, or indulging in a little blackguardism and knocking one another about the room." Parkman liked them well enough and accepted their invitation to join them in a pot of mead, the house being a temperance establishment. The military were planning to acquire a barrel of cider to offset this unfortunate circumstance.

Even on a diet of mead the soldiers managed to keep Parkman and White awake well into night, as they regaled themselves with the din of bugle and drum, which served as accompaniment to their singing and dancing. The next morning being still rainy and dismal, all the company gathered about the stove in the barroom. Thus given a further opportunity to observe the soldiers of the Queen, Parkman noted that "Their conversation was about as decent and their jokes as good as those of a convocation of Harvard students." The corporal proposed a conspiracy to make the young cornet, who detested tobacco, a slave of his pipe and ingenious ways of doing this were discussed. Parkman attended the military roll-call, and then church; dined, wrote letters, ate supper, and, the weather clearing, went out for a walk in the company of the stage-driver, who entertained him with smuggling stories. That evening Chase, the temperate landlord, invited Parkman and White and the cornet to attend the private devotions of his family in the inn kitchen:

> We went and found Mrs. C., her daughter, son, and another youth with a mouth like a gaping oyster seated along a table with their psalm books before them, humming, coughing, and *do-ra-me*-ing preparatory to the commencement. The cornet, who painfully professed himself fond of music, with a few of his soldiers, was in the room. The family stood up behind the singers, except Chase himself who established himself in front to dictate and pronounce judgment. They sang well, especially the son. With every pause, the old man—a downright puritan—would criticize the performance; and the unfortunate cornet declared that it was very good music indeed. They finished—having previously been reinforced by a long-faced individual, apparently a deacon—with the tune of "America," singing, in order to satisfy all the auditors, the stanzas of the republican song, and adding to each one "God save the Queen." The cornet succeeded in retiring before the end, but his men seemed to like it and crowded into the room.

Thus Parkman got evidence of the New England character of the Eastern Townships of Quebec, which remain to this day largely Yankee in aspect and blood, and more closely related to New Hampshire and Vermont than to the French Quebec of which they are a prosperous part.

The next day, August 1, they started off in Chase's wagon for Barnston, Quebec, where Parkman and White planned to jump off for the Indian Stream country and the Megalloway, since they were unable to return home by way of Mount Katahdin as originally planned. Parkman could console himself with the reflection that he was retracing the path of some of Rogers's Rangers on their return from their expedition against the St. Francis Indians. Their route led across Stanstead Plain, a fertile tract. Parting from Chase at Barnston, where they found another handful of soldiers quartered in the town, they started off on foot for Canaan, Vermont. They soon left the good road behind them and had to follow a path

through the woods. Shortly after they crossed the Coaticook on a
log bridge they were overtaken by rain. They found shelter in a
log cabin, where the "old man" received them hospitably and the
"old lady"—"a damsel of twenty-two, who sat combing her hair
in the corner"—discussed with them the doctrines of Millerism,
then a ferment at work all along the frontier, and was distressed by
their abuse of the holy prophet of the sect. The rain ceasing, they
pushed on amid a striking scene:

> High rolling hills bounded the horizon, all covered with an ocean
> of forest. The clouds hung heavy upon them, but would break
> every instant and admit a stream of sunshine, which would pass
> across the great carpet of woods, illuminate it in spots for an
> instant, and then give place to the black shadows of the clouds
> . . . Now and then there would be a clearing with its charred
> stumps, its boundary of frowning woods, and its log cabin, but,
> for the most part, the forest was in its original state. The average
> depth of the mud in the path was one foot. Scarce a ray of sun-
> light ever reached there through the thick boughs overhead.
> The streams that ran through the wood had no bridges, and most
> of them seemed to have preferred the artificial channel afforded
> by our path to the one they had worked for themselves among
> the mossy stones and decaying trunks of the forest. So we had
> to wade in deep water about two-thirds of the way. Of course,
> we were soon covered with mud to the eyes.

At last they came upon a better path, practicable for a stout
wagon, and stopped at a cabin where they got a decent dinner,
though subject to the giggling attention of the girls spinning by
the fire and the stiff contemplation of the boys who sat upright in
their homemade chairs to observe these strange figures from out
of the forest world. It was eight long miles to the next clearing,
through a dismal swampy tract, with the mud up to their knees.
But the path was wild and impressive, cut as it was through a
wilderness:

> Huge trees flanked and arched it—maples, pine, cedar, cypress,
> and a thousand others; bending over it, and intertwined with one

another, two high walls of foliage and wooden columns. Below, a frieze of high bushes along the path hid the bases of the trunks, but, looking through, the ground was hid with matted masses of green mossy logs, and heaps of rot, with a tangled undergrowth, all wet with the moisture that never leaves a forest like this.

Alternately wet and dry, as showers gave way to sun, they plodded on and reached a clearing, where they met two men about to set off on horseback. Going through the now familiar—though still distasteful—ritual of shaking hands and answering questions, they continued through two more miles of forest and came to another clearing, "of an aspect so wild and picturesque that a painter might have won the credit of being an astonishing genius by only copying things as they were." Here there was a swift, cold stream, into which they walked to wash off the mud which covered them. A little farther on they came to the "microscopic" village of Canaan, which then numbered some three hundred inhabitants, where they found a good tavern. Though they were quartered in the hall, they found no fault with their lodging after their arduous walk through the wilderness. The village lay beside the Connecticut, rapid here and full of rocks and foam. They were to follow its banks to the lakes which are the river's source, and then turn homeward, following the mountainous spine of the state of which the Connecticut is the majestic western border.

The next morning, Tuesday, August 2, they set out after breakfast for the First Connecticut Lake, some twenty miles distant. The day was cold and blustery, and they did not welcome the shade of the road along the west bank of the roaring river, which was "about as good as a cart-track through the woods about Boston." Two miles on their way, White discovered that he had left his powder-flask behind and had to go back for it. After losing an hour or more thus, they pressed on, being hailed at every house or cabin, for travelers were the "walking newspapers of this wilderness region." At one house where they stopped for a drink, Parkman suffered an unfortunate accident:

. . . I rested my rifle against a hogshead standing by a pump trough. A sudden jar knocked it down. It fell so that the muzzle struck with great force upon the trough. I picked it up and walked on without imagining that it had been much hurt, till some way further, when I found the stock split, the breech-pin broken short off, and other damage done which made the gun almost useless. This was worse than anything that could have happened, short of the loss of our cash, but we determined to keep on to the Margalloway still and make shift as we could.

"Satan" was their only rifle and it was hazardous to travel through the wilderness without one, particularly when they carried little in the way of supplies, lacked money to acquire more, and had planned to live off the country for the most part. But Parkman had succeeded so well in rousing White with tales of the giant Megalloway trout that the latter had quite lost his apathy and was willing to continue the expedition despite this accident.

The Connecticut Valley, already familiar to Parkman, did not surprise him by its richness and fertility, but here, unlike the scene farther south, the encompassing hills and mountains were one broad unbroken expanse of forest. That afternoon they got their first view of the source of the great river of New England:

. . . We reached a hilltop and a vast panorama of mountains and forests lay before us. A glistening spot of water, some miles to the north, girt with mountains which sloped down to it from all sides with a smooth and gradual descent, was Lake Connecticut. As far as we could see one mountain of peculiar form rose above the rest which we afterwards learned was the Camel's Hump.*

Crossing a rapid river [Indian Stream] as they went, they came at the end of the day to the First Lake, on whose banks stood two houses, Barnes's and Abbot's, and by the rapids at the lake's outlet, a mill. At Abbot's they got supper and lodging, and when they inquired about a guide to the Megalloway, Abbot himself, "a stout, round-shouldered, frank-looking man," volunteered to go, though he had never been that way before and did not know the

* Rump Mountain in Maine.

country. Parkman observed: "This was nothing to the purpose. A compass was guide enough. I hired him for a dollar a day."

Their supper was rough but clean, as was everything about the place, except the swarm of children. Since the youngest of the "eight or ten imps of both sexes" rejoiced in the name of Henry Harrison, Parkman deduced that their father was a fellow-Whig, for all that he seemed "a rough-hewn piece of timber" and his wife "a perfect barbarian." Both were frank and hospitable, however, and Parkman had long since reconciled himself to the well-worn principle of doing in Rome as the Romans do. He got on better thus with the Abbots than did White, who "tried the polite," and he painted a good picture of frontier home life:

> We spent that evening about their enormous cavern of a fire-place, whence a blazing fire gleamed on rows of suspended stock-ings, the spinning wheel, the churn, the bed, and walls covered with an array of piled-up cheeses, plates, milk pails, and clothes, all clean and all in order; while the older children were dodging about the furniture of the crowded room and the younger ones venting precocious snorings from a box under the bed. Abbot soon began to rail against Tyler, etc., then diverged to stories, which we kept going among us, the little schoolmistress taking her part, till a pretty late hour, when we were shown to a good bed in the opposite room.

Their host soon found Parkman's great interest, and regaled him with tales of a relative named Kenfield who had fought at William Henry, and at the massacre, "seeing an Indian about to strip a fallen officer, caught him, raised him in his arms, and dashed him to the ground with such violence as to make him senseless." James Abbot prided himself on the strength which had long distinguished his family and Parkman admiringly observed: "He himself no way dishonors his race in that respect."

They spent the following day loafing about the old settlement, which had stagnated for many years, going out on the lake in a dugout canoe and finding no fish at first, but later hooking some large trout at the foot of the rapids and also a lunge, a fish which Parkman had never seen before. There were moose, bear, and

wolves among the surrounding mountains, and a beaver dwelt on
Perry Stream, which Parkman mistook for Indian Stream, farther
to the west, which gave its name to the short-lived republic set up
in this region a few years before, when the territory was in dispute
between Canada and the United States. The backwoods style of
life was not unpleasant to Parkman: sugarless tea for dinner, a
common drinking mug for the company, and Mrs. Abbot's announcement of meals by a "Here, supper's ready. Where's that other
man gone to?" Abbot cobbled his shoes against the expedition and
amazed Parkman by announcing that he was not a disciple of St.
Crispin, but only an occasional follower. Again at supper he came
out with a comparison of the Jacksonian Democrats to Procrustes,
who wished to reduce all men to the same dimensions. This from
a rude figure "squatting on his homemade chair, one leg cocked
into the air, shirt-sleeves rolled up to his elbows, bushy hair straggling over his eyes, and eating meanwhile as if his life depended on
his efforts!" Parkman, who shared this pioneer philosopher's contempt for the Democrat "levelers," discovered that his host had
read a vast amount of history and a good deal else, "all fact, however, for fiction, he says, he cannot bear." As a young man—Abbot
was now thirty-six—he had defended himself in court and won his
case and his legal opponent's admiration for his knowledge and
memory.

On Thursday, August 4, they started for the Megalloway. At
first they headed north along a path which soon failed them, and
so made it necessary for them to force their way through the
tangled woods. In a few hours they reached the west bank of the
Second Connecticut Lake, where they had to make a raft in order
to cross. On the other side, ridge after ridge rose between them
and their goal, "covered with an unbroken and pathless forest,
never trod except by hunters." Striking southeast by compass, they
plunged into the woods, pack on back. Parkman gives a vivid account of their difficulties:

Ten thousand decayed logs scattered here and there, piled one
on the other, a thick growth of strong and tangled underwood,
rocks, fallen trees, gullies, made the forest almost impassable.

It was a constant straining of muscle and sinew. Boughs slapped us in the face, swarms of flies stung us, we trod on spots apparently solid and sank to the thighs in masses of rotten timber.

It did not take much of this to discourage White, who already had had a tumble in the lake to cool his ardor and had hurt his ankle the day before. He lagged behind, and the others had to wait for him, while they were tortured by flies. Soon they struggled up a mountain, but could see nothing from the top because of the thick growth. At an opening near the summit they came upon a buck, which sprang up and leaped down the mountain before Parkman could level his damaged rifle. Descending the mountain, they came upon a little stream, where White insisted that they encamp, although Abbot and Parkman wished to go on. By this stream, in a thick growth of firs, spruces, and birches, they built their fire and cooked their supper. Their provisions for this wilderness journey consisted only of seven pounds of bread, six and a half of rice, some butter, an ounce of tea, and salt. Eating with their knives, they soon put away a mess of rice served on a birch-bark platter; then they lay down upon their spruce-bough beds, cooled by a light rain and cheered by their blazing fire.

The next morning they breakfasted on rice, bread, and plain tea, and set off again. The powerful Abbot led the way, forcing a path through the forest by sheer strength. They were still following a southeasterly course, up another mountain. White grumbled and lagged behind, until Abbot cursed him and said "he never knew a fellow of so little pluck." At last they reached the summit, but could see only about a rod around, for the forest remained dense. By climbing to the top of a tall maple, however, Parkman got a noble view and their bearings:

Far off rose the Margalloway Mountain, with a sea of smaller hills about it, all pale and indistinct in mist. Lake Connecticut glistened among them like a surface of polished silver. Right beneath us was the valley of Diamond Stream. A line of steep and lofty bluffs marked its course, for the river itself was buried too deep among mountains to be visible. In front, close to us, heaved up a long ridge of mountains, sloping away to the left down to the Margalloway.

In all probability, Parkman stood on Bosebuck Mountain at this moment.

After fighting their way down the rough and precipitous side of the mountain, still bearing to the southeast, they heard the sound of plunging water and emerged from the forest onto the banks of a wild stream, which came rushing down in a succession of rapids and falls over broad shelves of granite. This they took to be the western branch of the Megalloway. As if to celebrate the attainment of their goal, the "sun came out from the clouds and lit up the long avenue of trees that followed the course of the stream, and made the water sparkle and glisten in welcome contrast to the somber shades we had just left." Even White was cheered, and, mysteriously recovering from his lameness, rushed up and down the river's rocky bed, finding a fish in every pool. They had a good dinner of trout and then followed the stream downward. At first they walked in the channel, which was no more than knee-deep, but soon the river became so swollen from tributary brooks that they had to take to the woods. A few miles farther on they came to a place where the waters plunged over a four-foot ledge of granite into a deep basin, and, finding traces of an old encampment, they decided to establish themselves here, though they had hoped to reach Parkman's former camp at the forks of the Megalloway before nightfall. At the foot of the fall they caught in ten minutes a dozen trout, averaging a foot in length, and so they dined luxuriously off broiled fish, rice, and tea. Spruce-bough beds and the plunging falls soon lulled them to sleep.

The next morning, Saturday, August 6, they held a grand council of war as to how to descend the river—at least Abbot and Parkman did, for White was still snoring on the spruce boughs. They had three choices: "Abbot could make a raft, thought he could make a spruce canoe, and was certain that he could make a log one." They settled on the last, and Abbot picked and felled a suitable pine, while Parkman set off on an exploring expedition. White, who had been aroused for breakfast, had fallen asleep again. Parkman waded downstream, sometimes up to his waist in water, a considerable distance, then took to the woods and after a half-mile of forcing his way through them in a southerly direction came upon the familiar basin where the branches of the Megalloway met:

> The old place, though in the midst of a howling wilderness, looked to me quite like home. It was the spot which had listened to Slade's lugubrious lamentations, the extreme point of my last year's pilgrimage; the place where Jerome had joined our party, and, to crown all, it was scarce five miles distant from the scene of that astounding exploit of knocking over the wounded moose. There lay the great black basin of dull waters, girt with its fringe of forests, but the appearance of things was altered since I had seen it before. The basin was fuller, the water blacker and deeper. Some hunter—Jerome, we found afterwards—had visited it since Slade and I had been there and made a good camping place of split boards. Two or three vessels of birch-bark, a setting pole, and a fishing pole were scattered around. There was a fragrance of rotting fish in the atmosphere which told that the visit had not been many months back.

Parkman picked up the pole and in an hour caught enough trout for several meals for his whole party, while lunching on a biscuit and a cup of water from the basin. On his way back to camp he stumbled over a half-finished spruce canoe, which Abbot had begun to make, for the felled pine had proved rotten. Parkman was not pleased at this change of plans, but gave what help he could, since the thing was begun, and by nightfall they had finished "something which had the semblance of a canoe, but, owing chiefly to haste and want of tools, had such a precarious and doubtful aspect that White christened it the Forlorn Hope." Upon trial it leaked, so they stuffed the seams with pounded spruce bark, chewed spruce gum, and bits of cloth. It still leaked, but they hoped that with diligent bailing it would serve to carry them to the settlements. Then they rolled themselves in their blankets and went to sleep before the fire.

Adopting the sailor's maxim of "No Sunday off soundings," for their slender store of provisions was failing, they set off downstream after a breakfast of trout, rice, and tea, "one item, at least, of which would have been considered an extreme luxury at the breakfast table of the richest man in Boston." Parkman sat in the bow, Abbot in the stern, and White in the middle to bail. They glided downstream swiftly, but soon they passed through a stretch of rapids, which made the frail craft quiver and shake and grate on the bottom, but she survived this first trial and carried them on through the smooth deep waters below. Another rapid came:

> She entered it, grated heavily over the stones, and struck hard against a large one before her. The water spouted in like a stream from a pump. It would not do. The experiment was an utter failure. We left Abbot with the canoe to conduct that and the baggage as he could down to the basin and waded to shore ourselves to walk there through the woods. We had not gone a quarter of a mile when, "Hallo, there," came from the river. "What's the matter, now?" shouted we in return. "The canoe's burst all to pieces!" Sure enough, we found it so. Abbot stood in the middle of a rapid, up to the knees, holding our baggage aloft to keep it dry, while the miserable remnant of the demolished canoe was leisurely taking its way down the current.

As they pushed through the woods to the basin, they determined to build a raft, which would take only an hour or two to make, and run their chances with its insecurity in the rips and its lack of speed. Demolishing Jerome's camp for materials, they stood in waist-deep water, pelted by a furious rain, while Abbot bound together with withes the timbers they held. After about two hours of this, the raft was finished. It drew more water than they had hoped, but they pushed off, in no mood to make another.

Like the canoe, the raft passed the first rapid safely, though here, of course, the rapids were much deeper than above. But when they came upon a second rapid,

> . . . the machine seemed to quiver in direful expectancy of its approaching destruction. Presently it grunted loud and dolefully. We set our poles and pushed it into the deepest part. For a while it bumped and blundered downward; at length there was

a heavy shock, a crash, a boiling and rushing of many waters.
The river spouted up between the logs. We were fixed irrecov-
erably aground. The water coursed savagely by us, and broke
over the end of the raft, but it could not be moved. The result
of this second experiment was more dismal than of the first. We
were in the middle of the river; the trees on both sides loomed
gloomily through rain and mist, and a volume of boiling and
roaring waves rolled between.

They got to the bank safely and Parkman, having had enough of
experiments, ordered Abbot to make a log canoe. Before night he
had nearly finished it, while Parkman and White kept a fire going
and cooked and plied him with tea to keep his spirits up. That
night it rained hard, and they made a rude tent of White's blanket,
with Parkman's as ground sheet, before a roaring fire. To Parkman,
"the continual dropping and plashing of rain through the forest
had a sound singularly melancholy and impressive"; and since
neither he nor Abbot felt sleepy, they talked until after midnight.
In spite of his prejudices and his pride of class, Parkman was impressed:

> Our guide is a remarkably intelligent fellow, has astonishing
> information for one of his condition, is resolute and as independ-
> ent as the wind. Unluckily, he is rather too conscious of his
> superiority in these respects, and likes too well to talk of his own
> achievements. He is coarse and matter-of-fact to a hopeless ex-
> tremity, self-willed and self-confident as the devil; if anyone
> would get respect or attention from him, he must meet him on
> his own ground in this matter. He is very talkative. I learned
> more, from his conversation, about the manners and customs
> of the semi-barbarians he lives among than I could have done
> from a month's living among them.

And despite his patronizing tone, he had the grace to add: "That
night in the rain, leagues from the dwellings of man, was a very
pleasant one."

After a few hours of sleep, they rose before it was fairly light,
Abbot to finish the canoe and the others to make breakfast. Soon

after, they launched their new craft and pushed off downstream under a leaden sky and a heavy rain. They had determined to reach the settlements that night, and paddled hard all day, stopping only to lunch off their last biscuit. White paddled faintheartedly, "showing much of that kind of resignation which consists in abandoning oneself to fate instead of fighting with it." When Abbot and Parkman upbraided him, he threw down his paddle and sulked, bundled up in his blanket in the bottom of the canoe. As night came on they saw a loggers' camp on the bank and went ashore to inspect it, not relishing the notion of remaining out of doors in such weather. It proved to be dry, with a slanted roof which had been well thatched, leaving only a hole to let out smoke. A cart-track led away from it, and this they thought might be a short cut to the settlements, so, leaving "the certain to pursue the uncertain," they raced along the wretched path for a mile, before it fanned out in countless directions and lost itself in the wilderness. They had followed a logging trail leading only to the heart of dismal swamps, where the best timber was found. One path seemed older and better marked than the rest, and down this they ran amid the roaring of the wind, the beating of the rain, and the creaking of boughs. Without warning they suddenly plunged up to their necks in mud. As they struggled out, they thought longingly "of warm taverns, hot suppers, soft beds, and brandy and water." But the best they could do for themselves that night was to return to the abandoned camp, which at least offered shelter. Since Parkman fortunately had secured his matches in a tin case, they were able to build a fire with the aid of some dry birch-bark they found in the hut. So successful was the blaze that it burned down one side of the hut, and might have burned the rest if the logs had not been rain-soaked, but this did not bother them, exhausted as they were. They hung up their outer clothing to dry before the blaze and lay down in the clean straw which covered the floor.

Much to their surprise they fared as well in the hut as they had in their fancy. The beds of straw were so comfortable that they did not rise until late, and then they found their clothes dry and their muscles limber from the steam which filled the hut. They had had practically nothing to eat since the morning before, and now they made their last mess of rice, boiled all their tea, and seasoned their breakfast with the last of their butter. After this very "fair and satisfactory meal," they started off and found "the forest about us glittering.in the morning sun with the raindrops of last night; mists floated above the river and among the trees; the clouds that half covered the sky were light and thin and promised to scatter soon." And best of all, in the morning stillness, they could hear the distant rumbling of the rapids which marked their goal. Three miles downstream they came upon the line of white foam stretched across the river and, turning to the bank, found the true path to the settlements. An hour's walk brought them to Lombard's cabin—Parkman finally got the name right—and on their way they met Jerome the Indian cleaning a moosehide in a field. He gave Parkman a fervent welcome, but White "after muttering a salutation which Jerome did not hear, and half extending a hand which Jerome did not see—or pretended not to—stood fixed in awe and abhorrence at the sinister look of the fellow's face, the diabolical size of his mouth, the snaky glittering of his deep-set eyes, the hollowness of his cheeks, and the black marks dissipation has made on his countenance." Parkman summed up his savage acquaintance as a rascal and an outcast from his tribe for various misdeeds, "too many and too gross to particularize," but concluded: "Jerome is an admirable hunter. He killed more than twenty moose this spring."

At Lombard's cabin, his wife welcomed them and gave them a lunch of bread, milk, and cheese, which the woodsmen demolished in miraculous quantity. They found Lombard himself, "dirty, big, rough, ogre-like, and hearty as ever," at work on the road near by; and he presented Parkman with the smoked ears of the moose the latter had shot the summer before. The settler had meant to send them on to Boston by the first opportunity, but "such opportunities are not of very frequent occurrence on the Margalloway." With these valuable relics tucked in a pocket, Parkman took the road for Brag's settlement. A storm broke over the peaks like a gray curtain, but Parkman's hope of preserving a dry skin that day was not yet doomed, for it soon cleared.

At Bennet's clearing, where it was necessary to cross the river, they hallooed to no purpose for a passage across. The boat was gone. White collapsed in helpless resignation on the river bank; Parkman ran back a mile to another clearing to obtain a boat, but in vain; and Abbot began to make a raft, but the wood proved too heavy to float well. Parkman and Abbot goaded White to swim the river and get a boat at some houses farther down, and at last he did so, pushing his clothes across on a little raft which Abbot made. Parkman and Abbot made another raft to hold their baggage, and were just stripping to swim across with it when Bennet called to them that there might be a boat hidden in a muddy creek near by. Here they found a broken log canoe, in which they managed to get across by constant bailing. White finally appeared with a lanky, lantern-jawed farmer named Hibbard, who had a boat but was afraid that these strangers might not pay for it. At last they persuaded him to row them the ten miles downstream to Captain Brag's for a dollar, since the rains had made the path through the woods impracticable. Abbot persuaded this reluctant ferryman, who was confessedly a delicate man who always took cold when he got wet, that the black lowering clouds and muttering thunder did not forebode a storm, and so they set off, with the gunwales only an inch above water. All paddled or rowed except White, who rested on his laurels, but despite their efforts they did not outrun the storm, which burst upon them furiously:

. . . Down came a deluge of rain on us that seemed as if it would beat our skiff and us to the bottom. Even the sound of the thunder peals seemed stifled in the dismal hissing and roaring of this portable cataract. It fell with such violence that the whole surface of the river was white. Our view was confined to a few rods round us. The wall of trees on each side could only be seen dimly and indistinctly as if in the night. Feeling somewhat uncomfortable, we ran the boat ashore and waited in the woods until the first fury had past, and then drove down the river in double quick time towards our destination. There was a long line of dead pines, rising up high above the other trees, and flinging their knotted and twisted arms in such fantastic style through the mist and rain that they looked like so many tall imps of the devil, stationed there on purpose to plague and torment us. In about two hours, straining our eyes through the vapors, we saw a line of white objects in front of us, rising, sinking, approaching, falling back, and apparently performing a sort of ghostly dance across the river. These were the waves dashing against the rocks, at the head of the rapids of the Androscoggin, and spouting into the air as they struck.

Here they ran ashore and plunged and crawled through mud, water, and slime, until they dashed into Brag's kitchen. Mrs. Brag took pity on them, and soon had them steaming before a huge fire, filled with hot supper, and sent to comfortable beds, from which they heard with pleasure the "impotent malice of the rain as it beat upon the windows." The delicate Hibbard chose a buffalo robe before the fire as his couch.

The next day they walked to Colebrook, burdened with wet blankets and their other gear. About six miles along the path they came up with a wagon, in which White got a jolting ride the rest of the way and in which they deposited all their baggage, except Parkman's knapsack, "which I chose to keep with me." Again Parkman remarked on the superiority of the eastern approach to Dixville Notch, and shortly after passing through, he took leave of Abbot, who turned off on a side road for the north and his home. The next day Parkman and White were forced to remain at Colebrook, "for want of means to get off." Every day seemed like Sunday in "the villainous little hole of a tavern," and Parkman found no pleasure in the place's scrupulous neatness and the "starched and precise, and, of course, grossly stupid" landlady, though she supplied their only amusement of the day, some old magazines. The stage came in next morning from Canaan, and Parkman was glad enough to see it, though it was only a milkcart. At Lancaster White stopped, "being reduced to his last quarter of a dollar, to see his uncle and borrow the needful of him." Parkman kept on to Littleton, and the next day started for home by way of Franconia Notch and Plymouth:

Riding down through the Franconia Notch, the mountains, rolled up heads and all in their blankets of mists, the lake, the martial countenance of the Old Man, and all the other familiar objects of that noble pass seemed to press me to stay in a manner that nothing but necessity enabled me to resist.

Parkman found all but the scenery changed, however, as he picked up gossip from the tavern-keepers he had known and from their successors. After backwoods life, he enjoyed talking to "accommodating driver and a pleasant party of ladies and gentlemen—one of the former exceedingly handsome, romantic, and spirited," and the time passed well enough until they reached Plymouth late at night. One fellow-passenger particularly amused him:

There was a general on board, a man of exalted character and vast political influence which he exerted on the righteous side of radical democracy, fiercely maintaining that ninepence was better than a million dollars, insomuch that the possessor of the first is invariably a good man and contented with his lot, while the owner of the last is always a grasping avaricious child of the devil. When the general alighted at his own tavern, he saluted the first loafer who met him at the door as "major"; the next but one was "colonel," while our driver answered to the title of "captain."

Thus restored to his Brahmin sense of superiority to all and sundry, Parkman passed Sunday in Plymouth; the morning at church, "where a toothless old scarecrow, who had been a preacher twenty-five years ago, mumbled a sermon which nobody could hear"; and, the afternoon in a walk to Livermore's Falls. Then he returned to Boston, to home and his third year at Harvard, none the worse for another expedition into the wilderness and wiser in the ways of man and nature.

4: The Making
of a Citizen of the World–I

*For the student there is, in its season,
no better place than the saddle, and
no better companion than the rifle or
the oar.*
F.P., LETTER TO ELLIS, 1864

PARKMAN'S passion for the North Country was unsatisfied by
the two long trips he had already made through it. He spent the
winter vacation of his junior year in Keene, visiting his classmates
Hale and Perry and renewing his attentions to the Miss Prentiss
who had won his heart by her "laughing philosophy" in Crawford
Notch and on Mount Washington. That summer he made another
excursion, still more extensive but not so arduous as the preceding
vacation trips. This journey was designed to satisfy the historical
student rather than the woodsman, although Parkman did not fail
to allow himself some days of the life he loved to lead. The itinerary
included Schenectady, Lake George, Lake Champlain, St. Jean,
Chambly, Montreal, Quebec, and the return to Boston by way of
the White Mountains. Hardly had he finished this extensive journey before he set out for Maine, where he went as far as Bangor
in order to study the Penobscot Indians. And during the fall, winter, and early spring he made the grand tour of Europe. These experiences did much to cure him of his provinciality and to make
him a citizen of the world.

When viewed by a student rather than by a vacationist hungry
for the wilderness, Schenectady offered more than the stinking
canals, tumbledown dwellings, and streets filled with hogs and
dunghills which Parkman had observed there on his first visit. In
the midst of these drawbacks he now met the "best of American
antiquarians," Giles F. Yates, who possessed an extensive knowledge of the colonial history of New York. From a clergyman of the
place, the Reverend Mr. Williams, he heard of another minister,

Mr. Kerney of Clermont, Columbia County, who was a grand-nephew of Sir William Johnson; and he learned that the Germans of the Mohawk Valley were steeped in the lore of this frontier prince who played such a vital role in the French and Indian Wars.

One fellow-antiquarian in Schenectady delighted him by his "most extensive and minute information." The house of this man's ancestor, with one other dwelling, had alone escaped the burning of the settlement, for this reason:

His ancestor, an old Dutchman, saved a Jesuit priest whom the Mohawks were about to burn at their "burning place" near Schenectady. The priest was secretly packed in a hogshead, boated down to Albany, and thence sent home to Canada. The old man accounted to the Mohawks for his escape by the priest's omnipotent art—magic. This priest accompanied the war party, and protected the house.

The grandfather-in-law of the antiquarian was saved when at the stake by Joseph Brant, the great Indian leader, because he made a Masonic sign. Brant was a Mason and interfered. As if these stories were not enough to intrigue Parkman, his new acquaintance told him of excavations made at the Mohawks' "burning place," which had brought to light the fragments of a skull and some bones. When Parkman went on to Lake George, he was determined to do some digging himself, and carried out his intention with interesting results. On a little hill near Fort George, he found a flat rough stone with the inscription: "1776. Here lies Stephen Hodges . . ." The rest was unreadable, but there seemed to be other graves near by. The boy with Parkman at the time found a buckshot and an old coin about the size of a fifty-cent piece in a newly plowed field, and Parkman himself picked up a musket ball and a copper coin.

Fresh from these discoveries, Parkman pressed on up Lakes George and Champlain and into Canada along the Richelieu River, the great waterway warpath of the French and Indian Wars. Then he went on to Montreal, to form his first impressions of the French who so long had fought the English and the settlers in the regions to the south which were now familiar to him. More to his taste than the cathedral and the Hôtel-Dieu was the sight of the 71st Highlanders and the 89th Regiment, then stationed in the town, while a part of the 43rd was on the island a short way off. At St. Jean he had noticed a small fort and barracks, and at Ile-aux-Noix "a strong and admirable establishment." But at Quebec he found the sort of thing that really aroused his enthusiasm: the Hope Gate, whose defenses he sketched with careful notes and which he found precisely resembled "the description of the place where Montgomery was killed," though "it does not resemble the reality." Below this rocky fortress with its bastions rising sharply from the St. Lawrence and St. Charles, the little expedition of New Englanders had struggled in 1775 to maintain a siege until their gallant leader was killed in a New Year's Eve assault of the well-nigh impregnable walled city. The Wolfe and Montcalm monument also stirred him, though he recorded in his notebook only the fine inscription: *"Mortem virtus communem—famam historia—monumentum posteritas— dedit."* He also sketched the Wolfe memorial, with its eloquent "Here died Wolfe, victorious."

The notebook of this 1843 excursion is tantalizing in its crypticness, for a full record of the first impact of these scenes on their future historian would have much more than a sentimental interest. But there is no further record of his Canadian tour except two notes about books: *"Emily Montague*—a novel to be read forthwith" and "Butler—*Jesuits."* The next entry deals with a ride up the Notch of the White Mountains at sunset from Old Crawford's: "The whole scenery at that hour, especially about the entrance of the Notch, wild and exciting to the highest degree." From his host Abel Crawford, the patriarch of the region, he gathered local history. That father of eight strong sons, all more than six feet tall, prided himself on being "the first of the Crawfords," having settled some fifty-five years before at Fabyan, on a grant from the state. His most famous son, Ethan Allen Crawford, the Paul Bunyan of the White Mountains, had just returned from Guildhall, Vermont, and taken up the tavern belonging to one Dennison, near Fabyan, while Tom kept the Notch House, built by his father and brother in 1828. At Abel's the company consisted of: "a little, thin, cadaverous youth called Joshua Waterhouse and his bride, a pretty, lively, tall damsel—both from Portland, and both stamped Yankee." Park-

QUEBEC AT THE TIME OF THE ENGLISH CONQUEST

This was the image of the city that Parkman held in his mind as he wrote Montcalm and Wolfe.

From the engraving of A. H. Ritchie.

man went fishing with the honeymooners and found the volunteered company of the lady agreeable. She amused him by referring to a mother and daughter who had been at Tom Crawford's recently as "Miss Thornton and her daughter Sarah."

Parkman explored two rock caverns in the Notch. Of one there is no record save a withered flower which resembles a white violet, pressed between two pages of his notebook on which is written: "This delicate little flower, whatever it be, I place here in memory of the grimmest, dismallest den on earth, where it grew among moist precipices and rotting logs." The next entry was written in the second cavern:

> I write at the bottom of a den more savage than the first. Turn to the left as you approach Crawford's, enter a gateway of rock, and you will reach two dens that look like the very bottom of Hell. Nothing but great piles of damp mossy rocks, rotten timber, huge black cliffs fencing you in, with trees stretching across from their edges. A stream is plunging somewhere underground, and breaking out into a black pool among the moss. Behind is a great heap of rocks where you descended. In front a steep descent, choked with fallen timber, and such a tangled mass of vegetation that a bear could scarce get through. These ferns shall be a memento.

But seemingly these dismal dens were more to Parkman's taste than the company he found at Tom Crawford's tavern. The place was crowded with botanists and mineralogists, to whom Parkman devoted some biting paragraphs. The botanists particularly annoyed him: "They actually reached the top of one of the Notch Mts. today, though one of them nearly killed himself in the attempt, and, as he elegantly remarked, 'got sick as a horse and puked.'" This unfortunate scientist annoyed Parkman by spreading his weary length on the parlor sofa, alternately grunting with fatigue and assisting with a "here—that ain't the way to press" a sentimental lady who was journalizing and arranging flowers. The mineralogists, "tough broad-shouldered men, apparently schoolmasters," were more to Parkman's taste than the ungainly botanists. The company also included two pedestrians from Maine, one of whom had served as a lieutenant in the recent Aroostook border fray with Canada. On Monday, his fourth day in the mountains, Parkman rode up along the Crawford Path to Washington, starting at six in the morning and getting back too late for the stage, so that Crawford had to take him north in a wagon to overtake it. Evidently the ascent was highly satisfactory, despite the lack of company:

> Was about six hours gone. Lay down, thrusting my face into the Lake of the Clouds, and drank a copious supplement to a gill of brandy wherewith I had previously regaled myself. My horse fell twice. Had a glorious time of it.

Parkman got a ride from Bethlehem, on his way to Franconia Notch, from a wagoner named Russell who edified him by a serious discussion of religion. Their progress was interrupted for theological and economic debate when they encountered a minister on the road who owed Russell a debt. Russell admired this clergyman, and pronounced him a "loud one." At Franconia, Parkman passed two days very agreeably at Knapp's tavern, hunting, spearing fish, and otherwise amusing himself. Going down to Plymouth in the stage, he was startled to find the driver an admirer of the scenery of his route, which made him "a perfect phenomenon in his way," for it was usually left for the visitors from the city to discourse on the marvelous views. But the driver confessed to having always "felt a kind of comfort as he rode through the Notch."

At Center Harbor Parkman inspected a collection of Indian relics gathered by the local lawyer, which included gorges, pestles, and arrowheads. There were some Indian graves about four miles off, and Parkman concluded that "The mineral spring on Ossipee hills was evidently a place of resort." Meanwhile he was learning of books that might be useful to his purpose and listing them: *Wars of Canada,* Charles Fenno Hoffman's wilderness books, Barstow's *New Hampshire,* Dunlap's *New York.* From Center Harbor he retraced his steps to Conway and then visited Fryeburg, just over the line in Maine. Here he inspected Lovewell Pond—the scene of an Indian fight in 1725—and saw Chief Paugus's gun, "so called," as he said with historical caution. Then he returned to Conway and the Notch, putting up again at Abel Crawford's. Here he encountered a strange pedestrian named Wells:

> I heard downstairs a tremendous noise of tongues and found this
> gent. reading aloud from the *Northern Traveller* and catechizing
> old Crawford, reserving all the talk to himself, and making noise
> enough for a dozen. This done he read us a piece in the news-
> paper. He had been something of a traveller, loved to talk of his
> experiences, and assumed the chief command. "Now, Mr. Craw-
> ford, we are all rather tired with our hard day's work, and, if you
> please, we will retire to our rooms. What do you say, gentlemen,
> shall we protract our sitting?"

Despite this pompous fellow-lodger, Parkman stayed a day or two
at Abel's before pushing on to Ethan's, where he found Lucy Crawford at work on her account of her husband's adventures.

He was soon shown the manuscript, which she published three
years later. Parkman was interested in her narratives of Nash and
Sawyer's discovery of the Notch and of the Willey catastrophe,
which last he found excellent. For all its roughness and simplicity
her account of the early settlers struck him as very well done and
he was stirred by the story of Eleazer Rosebrook, Ethan's grandfather, who settled near Colebrook in 1775, though the place was
eighty miles from the northernmost settlements at the time. He
also was so much impressed by Ethan Crawford's tale of the great
slide that he took full notes on it. Since this disaster was used by
Hawthorne as the basis of his tale of "The Ambitious Guest," it is
interesting to see what Parkman made of it when barely twenty:

> Ethan's original seat was by the "Giant's Grave," where his house
> was burnt.
>
> On the night of the slide, their situation was tremendous. In
> the morning, their fields were flooded, all the bridges for a score,
> and more, of miles swept away, great part of their roads torn up
> —and a bright unclouded sun showed the extent of the desola-
> tion. In the still morning they heard the waters pouring from
> the mountains. Ethan carried an impatient traveller across the
> swollen Ammonoosuc and left him to find his way to the Notch.

He struggled on to the Willey House—found it empty. The children's beds had been slept in—the others had not. The house had started from its foundation and fallen in. The horses were dead—the oxen still alive, and he found an axe and released them. This done, he crept into one of the beds and slept till morning, hoping the family had escaped to old Crawford's. A dog of Willey's, which at first refused him admission, was his only companion. Next day he found they were not at the old man's, and he passed on carrying the news to Bartlett and Conway. The neighbors and the relatives of the Willeys assembled—a dog pointed out the first body—the flies moving about the drift timber the rest. The night after the traveller had left, when several people had assembled, Ethan C., who was there and anxious to get back to his own house, probably on account of his own loss, groped his way up the Notch in the darkness, though the road was ruined.

Either from Mrs. Crawford or another at the tavern, Parkman heard of a book called *The Captivity of Mrs. Johnson,* published in Windsor, Vermont, in 1807, which he recorded as "A book worth getting—Frontier life in '54, etc." Whoever his informant, the information was correct. Mrs. Johnson, a native of Old No. 4, or Charlestown, New Hampshire, was captured there by Indians and carried overland to Champlain and thence to Montreal and Quebec, finally returning home by way of London. Her story is an epic of the French and Indian Wars and proved of great value to Parkman's purpose.

On his way down to Conway in the stage, Parkman met Stephen Meserve, who gave him a detailed account of his own experience on the night of the Willey disaster and of his discovery of the bodies,—from which every shred of clothing had been torn by the avalanche—thanks to his dogs, who refused to leave the mound of debris which contained the corpses. And on the stage from Conway to Dover, Parkman met old Mr. Willey, the father of the victim and a veteran of the Revolution. He and his daughter gave Parkman the true story of Nancy's Brook, where the betrayed servant girl of Colonel Whipple had perished while pursuing her faithless lover and her equally faithless employer. He was also regaled with the story of how the close-fisted colonel, who carried a bag of half-cents to make exact change, was pilfered of his corn by a group of poorer neighbors to whom he had refused a supply when they were starving. They dressed as Indians and scared him away, then bored a hole in the floor of his granary and filled their bags with corn, while the colonel took to the woods. During the Revolution the doughty colonel had made a plucky escape from English, Tories, and Indians, who seized him in his house, by squeezing through a small window in a back room where he had been allowed to go and dress.

These stage rides seemed to have been singularly pleasant and informative to Parkman. By now he had developed a technique of pumping his fellow-travelers for historical information. The stage-driver showed him a brook in Ossipee where Lovewell had am-bushed a band of Indians, and told of "the pond in Wakefield which goes by his name from a fight of his there." Parkman later celebrated Lovewell's last fight in a resounding ballad, one of his first publications. The diary breaks off abruptly here, with the statement: "Robert Southey had in his possession the whole of Wolfe's correspondence." Parkman had become hungry for the materials of the history he wanted to write, now that he had made himself familiar with its scenes and legends.

Soon after his return to Boston, he set off for Maine to gather material from the only Indians now left in the East, those Penob-scots who now made their headquarters at Old Town near Bangor. Leaving his sister Carrie to pay a visit in Gardiner, he proceeded alone to his goal. He found the hazards of travel in more or less civilized regions as rigorous as in the wilderness, for the wagon which accommodated him and another overflow passenger from the stage broke an axle and deposited him by the roadside. His companion, "a stupid young downeaster," went off at snail's pace to get help, despite Parkman's exhortations to hurry, and Parkman rescued himself and went on in the stage to Bangor, with "a mis-erable old wretch of a speculator" and a former shipmaster as com-panions.

He went over to see the Indians soon after his arrival, and learned that there were some four hundred in the tribe, though many were away at the time. He met one named François, who seems to have been his chief informant, and found the squaws "extremely good-looking with their clubbed hair and red leggins." Two of the Indians paddled him a short distance up the Penobscot, and thus he got a taste of the early explorers' life. For the first time he saw wampum in use, and encountered a squaw proudly parading a necklace of it said to be worth six dollars. Red-shirted loggers filled the tavern bar, and with amusement Parkman recorded their comment on an exhibition called "The Lord's Supper":

> One expressed his disapprobation of the character of the exhibition as follows: "G-d d-m it, I should like to take that fellow by the nape of the neck and pitch him into the road. He's no right to serve that 'ere up for a show in that way."

Parkman acquired some wampum from François's squaw, which supposedly had been bought from the Caughnawagas near Montreal twenty-five years before. With true New England caution, Parkman observed: "It is, however, sometimes made by the whites in Canada." When he mentioned the Mohawks he drew an outburst from François's brother:

> "You no 'fraid Mohawks? We 'fraid. They bad Indians—look too cross." Whereupon François began the following story, which he told with some excitement, mixing up the name of Castine with it in a way I did not understand. Several hundred Mohogs (as he called it) came upon the Penob. and took prisoners and killed a large number. Many of the old prisoners were burnt—the young thrust upon sticks which were stuck in the ground. Soon after the Mohogs were famine-stricken. Fifteen P. prisoners were left who volunteered to go out and hunt. The M.'s consented. The P.'s brought in plenty of game, feasted their enemies till they were overpowered with repletion, then fell upon them and killed all but one, whose ears and hand they cut off and sent him home.

The tribe, however, had fallen on evil days, and cunning had replaced its legendary bravery. In one hut Parkman met a young Indian named Mitchell who "seemed to be a perfect adept in all the vices of cities." He had advertisements, printed like bankbills, which he planned to pass off as money on some unwily fellow-savage. He was fond of Boston and "talked learnedly about the mysteries of Ann St., appealing to me if his reasonings were not correct." Parkman found him much easier to talk to than the others, and observed that "it would have been hard to cheat him with his quick observation and cunning." From this shady character the student learned that wampum was made from the sea-clam ("called quahog"), and that the French Canadians, as well as the Indians, made it. And he got an explanation of the change in Indian manners:

> "What use fight—take scalp—no do any good. Spose me kill snake—no get nothing at all. Spose um kill men, they no get anything."
> François says he is glad Indians have left off fighting. "Ought to be peaceable," he says. Even hunting, he added, is getting out of date, on account of the loggers, and the Indians are now farmers.

Such tame creatures as these, altered beyond recognition from their forebears and reconciled to civilization, were disappointments to Parkman, who had fed his fancy on Cooper and still believed in the "noble savage." But it was clear to him now, after meeting Jerome and the Penobscots, that he would have to go farther afield to encounter Indians who bore some resemblance to those who had devastated the early settlements, and played one white race against the other in the long three-cornered struggle for the continent.

Parkman strained his constitution during his junior year at Harvard, though in just what respect it is now impossible to determine among the welter of explanations that he had fallen from a trapeze in the college gymnasium, hurt his heart by too much violent exercise, and was suffering from nervous exhaustion. The last is the most probable, when it is considered how he drove himself, both mentally and physically, in his ascetic zeal, though he was not naturally robust; and when the evidence of his behavior during his trip to Europe "for rest and recreation" is weighed. Evidently the trouble, whatever it was, first made itself felt early enough in 1843 so that his vacation travels of that year to Canada, the White Mountains, and Maine were tame affairs in comparison to those of the preceding years. Seemingly the journeys were made entirely by train, stage, and horseback; and Parkman's disgust at this effete way of traveling, and perhaps his nervous condition, is mirrored in the briefness of his journal for that period, in contrast to the expansiveness of the earlier diaries. But the holiday did not suffice to restore his health and it was necessary for him to leave college in the midst of the first term of his senior year. He was sick enough for this rather drastic step and also sick enough to be sent abroad for an eight-month grand tour, which even the well-to-do Dr. Parkman must have thought twice about; but he was well enough to travel alone and to travel rather arduously. In the first part of his journal of this trip there is a confusion about days and dates which may be taken as a symptom of the nervous exhaustion which other indications support as his real malady at this time.

He sailed for the Mediterranean in the barque *Nautilus* from Central Wharf on Sunday morning, November 12, 1843. His family, who came down to see him off, did not contribute to the gaiety of the occasion. His youngest sister Eliza, who later became his amanuensis, recalls that their mother, who was usually very calm, was "very much overcome at parting" with her oldest child, for whom she had a particular tenderness. But Parkman seems to have been too excited by what lay ahead to allow such painful farewells to dampen his spirits. While his sister recalls the day as gloomy, Parkman described it as "fine weather, and a noble west wind." Soon after dropping the pilot, they saw the frigate *Cumberland*, which was also bound for Gibraltar but chose to follow a more southerly course and soon was out of sight. But Parkman had little opportunity to enjoy his first sight of the sea from a ship, for the *Nautilus* soon started pitching in a vicious swell:

The barque tossed about like a cork, snorted, spouted the spray all over her deck, and went rushing along like mad in a great caldron of foam she raised about her. At the same time it grew cloudy, and the wind became stronger. The sea rose and fell in great masses, green as grass—the wind driving the spray in clouds from their white tops. As I came from the cabin, I beheld, to my great admiration, a huge wall of water piled up in front, into which the vessel was apparently driving her bows; a moment more and the case was reversed—her bowsprit and half her length rose straight from the water, and stood relieved against the sky. In consequence of which state of things, I, like a true greenhorn, grew seasick by the time we were fairly out of sight of land. Accordingly I got into my berth as soon as it was dark, and stayed there twelve hours.

When I came on deck in the morning the weather had changed, nowise for the better. The same short seas were running—the vessel flung herself about in the same villainous style—a great black cavern on one side, and a huge mountain on the other, and a great pile of water rolling after stern—but the wind had become contrary, and the whole sky was black with clouds. Two or three land birds fluttered about the ship, driven by the wind from shore, which the unfortunates were destined never to see again. I wrapped myself in my cloak, and sprawling on the poop-deck read *The Bible in Spain*. A schooner, with only topsails set, went scouring past us, before the wind, homeward bound—also, in the afternoon, a brig, tossing so that her keel was almost visible. A troop of porpoises went tumbling about us, and I ransacked the vessel for a musket in vain to get a shot at them.

Though Parkman soon passed through the first stages of complete collapse from seasickness and was able to get about and even to meditate revenging himself upon porpoises, he proved a fair-weather sailor, much to his disgust.

The third day out was the worst yet. As he came on deck he was drenched by two hogsheads of water which came over the gunwale at that moment. It was cold, dark, and wretched, and the ship was lashed by a mixture of snow, sleet, and rain, blown on a savage head wind. Foam and spray shot over the bows and spouted far up among the sails, and the decks were swept every other moment. Parkman found an india-rubber cloak belonging to a former captain, and wrapping himself in it to the chin, braced himself in a corner to watch the surging ocean, to listen to the wind, and to observe the oilskin-enveloped crew struggling to perform their tasks like drowning rats. With a fluttering report, the jib blew itself to pieces; and at this Parkman went below, to spend the morning in his berth, "reasonably miserable with seasickness—cogitating, meanwhile, on things human and divine, past, present, and to come." He answered the captain's invitation to dinner, but a sudden lurch cleared the table just as they were about to begin. "With an execration, the captain grasped the beef and potatoes, and elevated them above his head—while he himself slid down the transom, and joined the medley on the floor." The steward shoveled up the ruins and they dined off the captain's salvage. Supper was not a cheery meal either, the captain and mate both being thoroughly out of humor at this sample of North Atlantic winter weather. The mate swore the *Nautilus* was the wettest craft he had ever sailed in, and vowed never to embark in her again, not even for the princely consideration of a five-dollar raise. Parkman spent a bad night, flung about in his berth listening to "the groaning and creaking of the timbers, the shouts of the men, the sullen thumps with which the seas struck the ship, making her shiver through her whole length, and, immediately after, the shock of the water descending in a torrent on her deck." The wind howled wildly without, and within a fiery stove made the stateroom as hot as Tartarus. Such were the pleasant conditions under which Parkman began his rest cure.

In a day or two the storm blew itself out, and the weather became warm and pleasant, although they were plagued by head winds, as indeed they were for much of the voyage. This did not make for cheeriness in the cabin, for it was the captain's first voyage in command and he desired a quick passage. But soon they had some days of prosperous wind and weather, which the captain celebrated by shaving for the first time since leaving port. They passed a school of sperm whales and then drove through the fogs of the Grand Banks, amid thousands of gulls, noddies, and baglets which skimmed the water. Parkman regretted that "the wind is too good to suffer us to lie to and fish," but within a day he was complaining about a head wind, which caused them to progress not a league, though they tacked back and forth all morning. In the calm he found time to describe the ship's company: three officers, himself as the only passenger, the steward, the six men of the crew—a Yankee, a Portuguese, a Dane, an Englishman, a Prussian, and an old Dutchman, "the best sailor in the ship." His portraits of the officers show a sharp eye for character, and are also self-revealing:

Of the officers, the Captain is a sensible gentlemanly man; the mate has rather more individuality, being, as to his outer man, excessively tall, narrow-shouldered, spindle-shanked, and lantern-jawed—with a complexion like dirty parchment. Mr. Jonathan Snow is from Cape Cod, a man of the sea from his youth up. When I first came on board he was evidently inclined to regard me with some dislike, as being *rich* (!). He constantly sighs forth a wish that he had five thousand dollars, "then ketch me going to sea again, that's all." He is rather given to polemic controversies, of which I have held several with him, on the tenets of Baptists, Unitarians, Universalists, Christians, etc. etc.!! Of course, he imagines that men of his rank in life labor under all sorts of oppressions and injustice at the hands of the rich. Harvard College he regards with particular jealousy, as a nurse of aristocracy. "Ah! riches carry the day there, I guess. It's a hard thing to see merit crushed down, just for want of a thousand dollars."

Mr. Hansen, second mate, is the stoutest man on board, and has seen most service, but being, as Mr. Snow remarks, a man of no education, he has not risen very high in the service. He accompanied Wyeth's trapping party to the Rocky Mts., where he was more than once nearly starved and within a hair's breadth of being shot. He speaks with great contempt of Indians, but not with quite so much violence as I have known from some others of his stamp. He plumes himself on having killed two or three. "Oh, damn it, I'd shoot an Indian quicker than I'd shoot a dog." He is now seated at supper, amusing me and himself with some such discourse as follows:

"I've lost all my appetite—and got a horse's! Here, steward, you nigger, where be yer—fetch along that beefsteak. What do you call this here? Well, never mind what it be; it goes down damned well, anyhow." Here he sat stuffing a minute or two in silence, with his grisly whiskers close to the table, rolling his eyes, and puffing out his ruddy cheeks. At last pausing, and laying down his knife a moment, "I've knowed the time when I could have ate a Blackfoot Indian, bone and all, and couldn't get a mouthful, noway you could fix it." Then resuming his labors—"I tell you what, this here agrees with me. It's better than doctor stuff. Some folks are always running after the doctors, and getting sick. *Eat!* that's the way I do. Well! doctoring is a good thing, just like religion—to them that likes it; but damn the doctors for all me; I shan't die."

Parkman soon got on very good terms with Mr. Hansen by treating him with brandy and water, and then drew him out on his Oregon experiences, which doubtless were as inflaming to Parkman as the brandy was to Hansen. Hansen made much of the merit of the frontier ideas of retributive justice and a society based upon a man's worth rather than his wealth, and Parkman longed for the presence of "a consumptive minister, with his notions of peace, philanthropy, Christian forgiveness, and so forth," on whom he could set Hansen loose for sport.

After a spell of remarkably fine weather and smooth seas, the *Nautilus* was suddenly caught in a severe storm, which came up in a furious squall one night. Parkman was awakened by Snow calling the captain, and then the shouts and trampling on deck and the crack of canvas whipped by the wind kept him awake. Soon the furniture and baggage were bounding about the stateroom, and he was tossed about in his berth in "execrable style." At daybreak he went on deck, and found the ship scouring along under two or three sails, lying over with her lee gunwale in the water, and clouds of spray flying as high as the mainyard. He stayed on deck some time, with the spray pricking his cheeks like needles; then, "being thoroughly salted," went below, changed, and read *Don Quixote* until called by Mr. Snow with "You're the man that wants to see a gale of wind, are ye?":

The wind was yelling and howling in the rigging in a fashion that reminded me of a storm in a Canada forest. The ship was hove-to. One small rag of a topsail set to keep her steady—all the rest was bare poles and black wet cordage. I got hold of a rope by the mizzenmast, and looked about on a scene that it would be perfect folly to attempt to describe—though nothing more, I suppose, than an ordinary gale of wind. The sailors clung, half drowned, to whatever they could lay hold of, for the vessel was at times half inverted, and tons of water washed from side to side of her deck. The sea, like the sky, was of a dull gray color. The violence of the wind seemed to beat down the waves, but the sea rose in huge misshapen masses, marked with long diverging trains of foam as the wind flew over their surface. As for the usual horizon, it had disappeared—we seemed imbedded among moving mountains. Now and then a towering ridge of waters would heave up to windward and bear down upon the ship, with a line of tumbling foam crowning it as it rolled on. All held their breath and clung fast as it approached. It would strike the ship with a crash, and deluge her with water from stem to stern. The wind has not yet abated. It is with much ado that I can brace myself in my seat to write.

For all the "perfect folly" of attempting to describe the scene, he did so with remarkable success, and evidently to his satisfaction, for he used much of this passage verbatim in his autobiographical novel, *Vassall Morton,* which he wrote thirteen years later. For a landlubber and a mountain man by choice, Parkman did full justice to the sea with his pen, though he was still an apprentice to his trade at this time and just twenty years old.

The gale was followed by a false calm, which soon gave way before another violent wind and sea, and the *Nautilus* had to heave to for some hours in the redoubled fury of the storm. Cuffie, the steward, who had his troubles getting some victuals into the gullets of the cabin mess before the food was dashed to ruins upon the deck, opined that "he never saw the like," despite his seven voyages to Canton. The storm followed them until they were in the neighborhood of the Azores, but despite their trials they lost not a sail nor a spar. Then for ten days they had "a series of accursed head winds," which kept them tacking back and forth

vainly, within thirty-six hours' sail of Gibraltar. The captain was
driven half mad by this bad luck, and walked about swearing
quietly to himself. Snow's philosophy vanished, and as for Parkman, he remarked: "I never had any." Hansen alone remained calm
and indifferent, and amused himself by whittling. Parkman decided to follow his lead, producing an "indescribable trinket"
which excited vainly the curiosity of Mr. Snow, who confessed
to having been told by a Brewster phrenologist that he had a
remarkable bump of this characteristic. Parkman was in no mood
to answer inquisitive questions, and in the dead calm, amid the
stupid flapping of sails and creaking of masts, he quoted:

> "Day after day, day after day,
>   We stuck, nor breath nor motion;
>   As idle as a painted ship
>   Upon a painted ocean."

The captain, who was less articulate and had no well-stored memory to draw comfort from, could only repeat: "By George! This
is *too* bad! I never see the beat of this!"

Day after day the calm or adverse winds continued, until Parkman felt himself going mad with boredom. Mr. Hansen was his
sole resource, and Parkman valued to the full his acquaintance's
humor, volubility, and "much good feeling." With his way of occasionally overcoming the handicaps of his environment and his
class consciousness, he found that Hansen had "too much coarse
rough manhood in his nature to be often offensive in his speech.
Moreover, one man may say a thing, with very good grace, that
would be insufferable from the mouth of another." And so it was
with Hansen and Snow. Finally they succeeded in beating up
against the wind to a position within view of the Spanish coast,
but then were driven back by a violent offshore wind. Parkman
imagined that a shovel-nosed shark which followed in their wake
was an incarnation of the evil spirit that had been persecuting
them, and concluded an entry in his journal thus: *"Thirty days
from Boston.* Old Worthington promised that I should see Gibraltar
in eighteen, but he is a deacon." The wind they wanted came, but
always from the wrong quarter, and they alternately backed and
filled within maddening nearness to their goal. But bit by bit they

gained, and after several days succeeded in passing Tarifa and entering Gibraltar Bay, while Parkman "looked up with infinite satisfaction at the warlike rock which rose right above us—with a gray and savage aspect—indented all over with portholes and scored with zigzag lines of battlements and military roads." But they had still further difficulty in making the anchorage amid the forest of masts at the foot of the great rock. After beating up the bay in the face of squalls, they let out six fathoms of cable, the captain being unable to "stand this longer, nohow," but the anchor dragged and they began to drift rapidly ashore. Two of the six seamen were sick, and thus shorthanded they could not raise the anchor. Meanwhile they drifted ever nearer to the Algeciras shore. Up went the flag at half-mast, in token of distress, and a boatload of rescuers came from the American frigate *Congress,* which lay under the Rock, and in a few hours had them safely moored beside the frigate.

Parkman had had enough of the *Nautilus* and could not wait to get ashore, though there was scarce time to do so before the gates were closed for the night. He persuaded three rascally Spaniards in a bumboat to race the signal gun, but they failed to thread the labyrinth of strange-looking vessels in time, and perforce he returned to the *Nautilus,* after an argument with the boatmen, who tried to collect an inordinate fee from this eager newcomer. The next day, December 21, 1843, he came ashore in the ship's boat, got his papers put in order at the consulate, and established himself at the King's Arms. On the mole he was beset by fifty porters, who besought him in as many languages for the privilege of carrying his luggage. He selected the "most decent-looking, who was a slender-built fellow, with a sickly countenance." Much to Parkman's astonishment this apparent weakling swung the heavy trunks on his back and trotted off up the steep streets at a pace which Parkman could barely match. He dined with the consul and explored "this singular city—the world in epitome."

One evening he went to watch the Sunday promenade of the inhabitants upon the large parade ground just without the walls. The spectacle was very colorful, and still more vivid to one who knew only the drab broadcloth of Boston and the sober Puritan;

I established myself at the foot of a bronze statue of the defender of Gibraltar—I forget his name (General Eliot)—but there he stands, towering above the trees and aloes at the summit of a hill above the parade, with the emblematic key in his hand, and with a huge cannon and a mortar on each side of him. Here I had a specimen of every nation on earth, it seemed, around me. A dozen Moors with white turbans and slippered feet lolled on one side; Jews by couples in their gabardines; the Spanish gentleman in his black cloak and sombrero—the Spanish laborer with his red cap hanging on one side of his head—the Spanish blackguard in bespangled tights and embroidered jacket. On benches among the trees officers and soldiers carried on successful lovesuits; on the parade below, English captains were showing forth good horsemanship to the best advantage. The red coats of soldiers appeared everywhere among the trees and in the crowd below. There were women in cloaks of red and black—ladies with the mantilla and followed by the duenna —no needless precaution—and ten thousand more, soldier and civilian, bond and free, man and woman and child. Not the least singular of the group were the little black slaves belonging to the Moors, who were arrayed in a very splendid and outlandish attire; following after their masters like dogs. Bands were stationed on the parade and around a summerhouse among the trees. The evening gun dissolved the pageant—"God Save the Queen" rose on the air: then the crowd poured through the gates into the town.

No wonder that Parkman, with his love of the colorful and the dramatic, was moved to write: "I have seen more noble-looking men in this place than ever it was my lot to see before." He particularly admired the physique and the facial beauty of the Moors, so well set off by their dress. The *hamalos*, the Arabian Jews who acted as porters, amazed him by their extraordinary appearance and strength: smaller than the average woman, leathery of face and sandy of beard, wearing little black skullcaps, broad blue pantaloons of Turkish cut, and carrying a bundle of cords to sling their burdens on their backs; with the calves of their legs swollen

to thrice the natural size from clambering up and down the steep
streets under heavy burdens.

With some difficulty Parkman obtained permission to visit the
excavations in the Rock, which he found well worth his trouble.
The galleries and great vaulted halls, hewn out from the solid
stone to shelter countless cannon which pointed to every quarter
of the sea and land a thousand feet below, moved him strangely,
and peering from a porthole he saw the whole region spread out
like a map before him, with black specks of soldiers shooting on
the plain below, the white smoke being visible some time before
the report reached his ears. He dropped a stone, which fell to the
sands without once striking the Rock in its descent, so sheer and
bold was that face of the mountain. At a lookout he found an
"armchair carved, of massive dimensions, out of the rock, facing
towards Africa—where, perhaps, the holder of this tremendous
fortress might sit and overlook the passage which he commands."
Descending on a road hewn through precipices, as in the Alps, he
found another lonely lookout occupied only by a howitzer and a
cannon, where the white breakers could be seen, but not heard,
breaking on the rocks below. That evening Parkman summed up
his impressions of the great key to the Mediterranean:

> Look upon this Rock as a phenomenon of nature alone; or
> only for the miracles of military art which it contains; or for the
> motley population which inhabit it; or, finally, as the scene of
> that bloody attack and repulse during our Revolution—in either
> mode of regarding it, the "Pillar of Hercules" deserves to be
> considered one of the wonders of the world.

And having been warned by a sentry while lounging among the
rocks not to pass in a certain direction, because they were blasting
there, he marveled that hundreds of men should be kept at work
adding "new strength to a place that now might defy the whole
earth."

Though Captain Newton of the *Missouri* stirred him with an
account of Granada, Parkman determined to postpone his proposed tour of Spain until spring, a better season for seeing that
country, and, having wearied of Gibraltar, determined to sail on

a government steamer for Malta. His last picture of Gibraltar was
an admiring one of the *hamalos* who carried his luggage to the
boat, a distance of about half a mile:

> The little wretch shouldered it all—looking like an Atlas sup-
> porting the world—and trotted at a round pace through the
> streets and onward to the mole, the muscles of his bare legs
> gathering into solid knots with every step. He was a mass of
> bone and sinew.

Though Parkman was no hewer of wood and drawer of water, he
was capable of admiring those who toiled with the sweat of their
brow, though not, perhaps, of understanding them. But he was
learning how to meet men who were not Brahmins and Bostonians
on their own terms, which is one of the most useful tricks of
travel. Prepared for the *"hauteur,* approaching to insolence, of a
certain class of English naval officer," he was surprised by the
cordial reception he received from Lieutenant Sparks, who commanded the little vessel on which he was the only passenger. The
two spent half the first night at sea in talk, and Sparks offered
Parkman the run of his library and produced "an endless variety
of wines." The first day out being Sunday, the captain mustered
his sailors and marines in the cabin and read Divine Service, "not
forgetting a special prayer for the British Navy and the success
of British arms." Sparks had known Sir John Moore, Sir Peter
Parker, and other heroes of yore; had shaken hands with Blücher;
and had fought the French by sea and land. And this *rara avis*
of a British naval man was a great reader, "not only of English
works, but of all the eminent American authors."

Parkman was impressed by his first taste of Europe and particularly by the Britons with whom he had been thrown. This new
but ancient world was far more to his taste than the one he had
left behind him:

> Here in this old world, I seem, thank heaven, to be carried
> about half a century backwards in time. As far as religion is
> concerned, there are the ceremonies of the Catholic Church;
> and the English litany, with rough soldiers and sailors making

the responses. A becoming horror of dissenters, especially Unitarians, prevails everywhere. No one cants here of the temperance reform, or of systems of diet—eat, drink, and be merry is the motto everywhere, and a stronger and hardier race of men than those round me now never laughed at the doctors. Above all there is no canting of peace. A wholesome system of coercion is manifest in all directions—thirty-two-pounders looking over the bows—piles of balls on deck—muskets and cutlasses hung up below—the red jackets of the marines—and the honest prayer that success should crown all these warlike preparations, yesterday responded to by fifty voices. There was none of the newfangled suspicion that such belligerent petitions might be averse to the spirit of a religion that inculcates peace as its foundation.—And I firmly believe that there was as much hearty faith and worship in many of those men as in any feeble consumptive wretch at home, who when smitten on one cheek literally turns the other likewise—instead of manfully kicking the offender into the gutter.

Strange thoughts on Christmas Eve for the young student, son of an eminent Unitarian divine and disciple of Dr. Channing! Yet not so strange, for the Toryism known as Federalism in New England is here, with a large strain of the sentiments of those hard-drinking, hard-riding Cavaliers who rode down or died before the Puritan Ironsides; though the underlying framework of thought is that of Calvinism, a religion of force and strict control of the masses, with a certain indulgence permitted to the elect; a warlike faith which won converts by the sword—not the religion of decorous behavior and social service which was replacing the old rock-ribbed Standing Order. The Puritanism of his day was not puritanical enough for young Frank Parkman, who nevertheless loved good food and drink and the sight of a pretty girl, as befitted a young man of the patrician class. But still more he loved the past, which was at once more rigid and more colorful than the present in his eyes; and soon he came to live entirely in it, heedless of the great changes which remade his country in his lifetime.

5: The Making
of a Citizen of the World—II

*Here in this old world, I seem, thank
heaven, to be carried about half a century backwards in time.*
F.P., DIARY, 1843

AFTER a Christmas celebration—during which every man jack
of the crew became "more or less elevated" as they drank
a double ration of grog and danced in an astonishing style to the
music of a fiddle, drum, and triangle, and the wardroom enjoyed
an "admirable" Christmas dinner—Parkman landed at Malta, five
days from Gibraltar. The harbor of Valletta was filled with ship-
ping, and as Parkman went ashore the great British men of war
lying in the roads seemed black and sullen by contrast with the
pervading yellow of Malta, which was broken only by the guns
on the batteries and the red coats of the soldiers. Upon landing
he found that he had the choice of waiting ten days for the next
steamer for Messina or leaving that night, and, though he was reluctant to rush away, he determined upon the latter course. But
he saw as much of Valletta as was possible in the short time: particularly the ancient palace of the Knights of Malta, where the portraits of the Grand Masters still hung in long and splendid galleries
and the armory still boasted the "complete panoply and weapons
of all the most distinguished of these defenders of Christendom."
Parkman was impressed by the gigantic armor of La Valette, "a
man of tremendous frame, differing in this respect from many of
the less renowned brethren of the order, who seem to have been
of rather small stature." He was annoyed that the English, who
used the palace as the governor general's residence, should have
placed some thirty thousand muskets and other modern arms here,
"in villainous contrast to the ancient weapons of the Knights of
St. John." There were also some Turkish weapons, including a

98

rope cannon, preserved here in memory of the defeat their owners had suffered before these walls.

That night Parkman visited the church of St. John. It was closed, but after much pounding of oaken doors, a survey of the neighboring coffee houses, and vociferous aid in bastard Arabic from some Maltese loungers, the sexton was finally roused and induced to guide them through the church. In the half-light of the tapers they held in their hands, Parkman saw splendidly decorated chapels and tombs, and the subterranean chamber which contained the resting places of the Grand Masters. Opposite that of La Valette, which was surmounted by an effigy with sword and helmet, was another of a Grand Master who had been a cardinal "and lay there in his pontifical robes, with his sword girt to his side and his hands crossed on his breast. He looked like a gallant soldier, who had done good service to Christianity by dealing death to its enemies." In the church itself, lit only by candles before the numerous altars, Parkman was struck by their faint glimmering in the distance, by the reverberating voices of his companions, and by the paving stones, every one of which "bore the name and the arms of a knight who lay below." He was reluctant to leave "the church where so many brave men had kneeled to God for His blessing on their matchless enterprises," for this was a kind of Christianity that appealed to him far more than the bloodless Boston brand, but he had to rush off to his boat.

The next morning he found himself unable to converse with anyone on board the *Francesco Primo* except by sign language, until a sleek-looking fellow came up and accosted him in fair English. His new acquaintance proved to be Giuseppe Jackson, a Sicilian with some English blood, who had been a cook at the Albion and at Murdoch's Tavern—Parkman's favorite haunts at home— knew some of the Cambridge students, and even was a frequenter of Fresh Pond. Parkman, a little homesick in his solitary travels, noted: "I was right glad to see him, cook though he was," and found him useful as an interpreter. At breakfast Parkman had exchanged many bows and other attentions short of conversation with an old man "of severe countenance and tremendous mustache," whom he now discovered to be no less than "il Principe

Statelli, a general of the Sicilian army—but Sicilian 'Principes' are apt to be humbugs."

Having caught his first glimpse of smoking Mount Etna, Parkman landed at Syracuse, where he was at once repelled by the sight of some Neapolitan officers "with grizzled mustaches and a peculiarly swinish expression." On the dock he was ensnared by an English-speaking guide, one Jack Robinson, who had served in both the English and American navies, though in no more martial capacity than that of laundryman. Under his guidance Parkman inspected Dionysius's Ear, a tremendous prison-yard cut from solid rock and boasting a famous whispering gallery which Jack Robinson and "Signor Francesco" tested; the ancient amphitheaters hewn out of rock; the temple of Minerva which had now become a Franciscan church and in whose catacombs Parkman wandered, picking a bone or two from the tombs and musing over the story of a schoolmaster and his pupils who lost themselves in the maze and were not found for years. Upon returning to the city, Parkman dined with his guide in a wine cellar and then inspected Robinson's home, before going off to the steamer. The little square-built English-looking fellow, whom Parkman summed up as "an honest man, an exceedingly *rara avis* in these quarters," was so satisfied with the dollar and a half that he received for his day's labor that he said farewell in Sicilian style, kissing Parkman on each cheek.

The next morning Parkman arrived at Messina, where his culinary friend Giuseppe Jackson, late of Murdoch's Tavern, proved of the greatest service in showing him how to bribe a customs officer and how to treat a Sicilian landlord if one desired excellent accommodations at a reasonable price. Parkman had already found his ignorance of the language a considerable handicap, and soon learned to speak Italian after a fashion. He was oppressed by the filth and age and ruinous condition of everything he saw, and dismissed the people of Messina as "the scum of humanity." Only the sight of distant mountains, "almost as wild and beautiful as our mountains of New England," cheered him, though he half wished himself at home among well-remembered peaks. Repelling as it was to him, nevertheless the spectacle before his eyes was colorful and interesting enough to make him soon forget his homesickness. In the company of a chance acquaintance, of whom he had asked the way to the theater, he went to the Cathedral to watch the New Year's festival, finding a spectacle "indeed worth seeing":

> The cathedral was a blaze of light from many hundred candles, while all below was a black sea of heads. The priests were chanting, and the incense smoking. Every few moments there would be a blast of trumpets and a burst of solemn music, at which every one of the thousands there knelt on the pavement, and then rose again with a deep rushing noise, produced by the simultaneous motion of such a multitude.

Meanwhile his new friend lectured on the beauties of the church and translated the *Te Deum,* until Parkman explained that he understood Latin. The service ended with a thunderous explosion of fireworks in the galleries, "which filled the church with an insufferable smell of gunpowder." Perhaps disturbed by this reminder that he was flirting with brimstone by assisting at the hellish practices of papistry, Parkman left the church hurriedly in the company of his guide, who in great fear of pickpockets had urged him to "hasten to go out, previously to the crowd of people."

On the second day of the new year Parkman set out for an expedition through the Sicilian countryside, in the company of Don Mateo Lopez, a Spanish gentleman who spoke good English. They had a fine day for the start and Parkman found the scenery "noble beyond expression . . . I never imagined that so much pleasure could be conveyed through the eye." He disliked the dirty villages and their people, whom he dismissed as "a gang of ragamuffins," but the country impressed him vastly:

> These disgusting holes of villages only added zest to the pleasure of the scenery; a pleasure not inferior, and not unlike, that of looking upon the face of a beautiful woman. In many respects our own scenery is far beyond it; but I cannot say that I have ever looked with more delight on any of our New England mountains and streams than upon these of Sicily. The novelty of the sight, and the ruined fortresses on the highest crags, add much to the effect.

At noon on the second day they reached Catania, a city so old
that the Cyclopes are thought to have founded it. It had been held
in turn by Greeks, Romans, Saracens, and Christians, and each had
left an enduring mark upon it. But its real master is Mount Etna,
which "knocks it to pieces or floods it with lava" every few centuries. The city is paved, built, and partly buried in lava. Parkman
was particularly impressed by the fountain which Prince Boscari
had restored after it had been buried sixty feet deep in lava in
1669, and by the Benedictine monastery and church, to whose very
walls the lava had come and then turned aside. And in Prince
Boscari's museum, amid antiquities and precious fragments of the
art of earlier cultures, he found a Chippewa birch canoe: "I welcomed it as a countryman and an old friend."

That evening Parkman was surprised to find Don Mateo, whom
he had judged to be the staidest and soberest of men, prowling
about the town "on his own errands" as soon as it was dark.
Amused at the old reprobate, Parkman went off to the opera,
where he met a young Spanish friend of the Don, who joined the
party in its return to Messina. The newcomer diverted Parkman
greatly by his youthful eccentricities as he rattled away and imi-
tated every beast they met upon their way. The three traveled in
a sort of calèche, which boasted, in addition to the driver, a crew
of assistants:

> . . . A small boy ran along by our side, or clung behind, ready
> to do what offices might be required of him. A still smaller one
> was stowed away in a net, slung between the wheels, where he
> kept a constant eye on the baggage. The larger one employed
> himself in tying knots in the horses' tails as he ran along or he
> would dart along the road before us, clamber on a wall, and sit
> till we came by, when he would spring down with a shout, and
> run on again.

It is not surprising that with this equipage they attracted a swarm
of beggars at every stop, to the detriment of Parkman's purse. He
could not resist the wiles of one little rascal who stood about a
foot and a half tall and mocked Don Mateo's solemnities so clev-
erly that Parkman burst out laughing. Thus encouraged, the mani-

kin danced a hornpipe which won him a *grano* (a third of a cent). This "unparalleled generosity" brought out a crowd of beggars from whom Parkman barely escaped in the carriage. But he got a vivid impression of the poverty of Sicily when he and the young Spaniard threw a few coppers to a mute girl, who burst into a perfect frenzy of delight:

> She danced about among the crowd; flinging both hands into the air—then kissing the coins, and pressing them against her breast; tossing them on the ground before her, and gathering them up again; till her ugly face seemed absolutely good-looking with the excess of her pleasure.

That night they put up at a flea-ridden tavern, where the *padrone* proudly showed them in the register the comments of his guests on their entertainment. Since the *padrone* could not read English, he was unaware that these included warnings that the beds were full of fleas and the food unfit to eat. The next morning was rainy and Parkman feared that he had had his last sight of Etna. In the company of the young Spaniard he set out on muleback to visit Taormina, where a well-preserved amphitheater and a Saracen castle capping a steep cliff impressed him once more with the romantic and classic associations of this ancient country. By nightfall they had reached Messina, and Parkman had a chance to think over the sights he had seen. His reflections conclude with this notable observation:

> The church of the Benedictines is the noblest edifice I have seen. This and others not unlike it have impressed me with new ideas of the Catholic religion. Not exactly; for I reverenced it before as the religion of generations of brave and great men— but now I honor it for itself. They are mistaken who sneer at its ceremonies as a mere mechanical farce: they have a powerful and salutary effect on the mind. Those who have witnessed the services in this Benedictine church, and deny what I say, must either be singularly stupid and insensible by nature or rendered so by prejudice.

But though his attitude toward the Church had changed radically, he still was no lover of clergymen. In Messina he observed that the priests stood out as fat and good-looking men among the "dregs of humanity" from whom "they draw life and sustenance —just as tall pigweed flourishes on a dunghill." Time after time in his European travels Parkman makes this distinction between the Church, which he respected, and its ministers, whom he congenitally disliked. He was not so much anti-religious as anti-clerical.

In Messina Parkman also revised another opinion of his—as to the beauty of Sicilian women. On his journey from Catania he had summed them up flatly as "not handsome." But the sight of some ladies of high rank, on their way to and from the devotions of Epiphany, moved him to speak of "the black eye, the warm rich cheek, and the bright glance that belong to southern climates; and are beautiful beyond all else." Parkman attended the ceremonies in the cathedral, where, in addition to finding reason to make the observation just mentioned, he saw five or six noblemen established on a throne of crimson silk:

> They wore rich black dresses, massive gold chains on their breasts, and the enormous ruffs of several centuries ago: making them look as if their heads were screwed down between their shoulders, without the intervention of a neck. A motley concourse of soldiers and women, princes and beggars, filled the church.

On the following day, a Sunday, he took leave of the hospitable American Consul, Mr. Payson, and sailed away in the steamer for Palermo. Evening sailings were great social events in Sicily, and Parkman marveled at the farewell kissings amid the boatmen's curses, heard his name bellowed out as "Signor Park-a-man" as the passenger list was read by way of roll-call, and soon found himself passing between Scylla and Charybdis. Etna loomed up in the darkness like a thundercloud; the ship left a long train of phosphorescence in its wake; and the moon cast a long path of light across the sea. Parkman thought it a place well worth being cast away in, but this unwonted classical humor was rudely broken off when he went below and found a cabin full of seasick wretches.

The next morning they entered the mountain-bordered harbor of Palermo, with the city midway between the horns of the crescent-shaped bay. As soon as they anchored, the sea around the ship was paved with boats and Parkman had to have his baggage transported over six boats into a seventh, which bore him and it ashore. He hired Giuseppe Jackson as guide and Italian teacher, and with him saw the numerous sights of Palermo. Parkman liked the city: "It is a place as gay as any in Europe—the people moreover have the faculty of being gay on the smallest means." One day he rode up Monte Pelligrino, the dwelling place of Palermo's patroness, St. Rosalia, who had saved the city from a pestilence several centuries after her death. Every year half the city made a pilgrimage to her shrine on the mountain top, while the valley below blazed with illuminations in her honor. Parkman's account of his visit to the shrine is notable, in its contrast to his later observations on such "papistical mummery":

The priests guided me through the church, into the grotto behind—a huge black den hung with broken stalactites, whence water icy cold was dripping onto the floor. The snow had found its way through a large cleft above: altogether, the habitation of the young saint wore a most somber and cheerless aspect. The lamps were burning in a remote part of the cavern before her shrine. The priest kneeled before a grating beneath the altar, and motioned me to look in between the bars. Two or three lamps were burning there, but for some time I could discern nothing else. At length I could distinguish a beautiful female figure, sculptured in marble and clothed in a robe of gold, lying with a crucifix in her hand and a skull beside her. The white transparency of the marble showed beautifully in the light of the lamps, and suited well the mild enthusiastic expression on her face. I scarce wondered at the devotion of the Palermitans. Drinking some of the water that trickled from the roof into a stone basin by the side of the altar, I left the grotto, which was as cold and chilling as a New England winter.

With a last look at the ancient, moss-grown church amid the black cliffs, he turned downward through the snow, getting a noble view of the Palermo valley, "green and bright as an emerald" set between the circling snow-capped mountains and the sea. It was the Neapolitan king's birthday, and a pall of smoke from saluting cannons hung over the city.

After a visit to the Capuchin monastery, where thousands of mummies were preserved in underground vaults, Parkman arranged to have a Mass said among the sepulchers at four o'clock the next morning. Giuseppe roused him and they set off through the streets on which many were already abroad, although it lacked two hours of daybreak. Fires burnt outside the cafés, and around them clustered ragamuffins and *filles de joie* to warm themselves in the chill of dawn. At the convent five or six monks awaited him and conducted him down to the tombs by lamplight:

> The mummies, each from his niche in the wall, grinned at us diabolically as we passed along. Several large cats, kept there for the benefit of the rats, stared at us with their green eyes, and then tramped off. When we got to the little chapel, the prior put off his coarse Capuchin dress, and arrayed himself in white robes—the curtain was drawn aside from the image of the Virgin behind the altar—the lamps lighted—and the Mass performed. When all was over, one of the fathers lighted a torch to show the catacombs by its light. Coffins piled up below— men, shrunk into a mere nothing, but clothed as they used to be above ground, all ranged along the wall on either hand—a row of skulls under the cornices—this made up the spectacle, which was rather disgusting. There were one or two children, just dead, and a few men, flung down in corners, waiting for the drying process. Women are placed here, as well as men. The virgins all wear crowns of silver paper, from beneath which they grin and gape in a most alluring fashion.
>
> I soon cried enough, and returned to the upper air. The morning Mass in the church was just begun. One of the monks conducted me to an ancient apartment behind the altar: here the whole convent was kneeling, telling their beads—the faint light,

their dark cowls, their beards, and their deep murmurings at their devotions made quite an impressive scene. The little church itself was half full of people, though it was not yet daylight. I looked awhile at the old pictures about the rooms and passages, then bade adieu to the fathers, who thought me mad, and departed.

The good Dr. Parkman would have probably concurred in the Capuchins' verdict if he had known of his son's doings. Not content with his ecclesiastical sightseeing in Palermo itself, Parkman visited the noble church of the Benedictines at near-by Monreale. Parkman admired the mosaics which covered its walls with representations of Bible stories, but he did not admire the rapacity of the inhabitants, one of whom tried to sell him bits of mosaic stolen from the church while it was undergoing repairs. Such conduct did not befit, in his opinion, the lowly neighbors of the noble monks, for this monastery, like that of Catania, drew its members from the nobility of the island.

The fountains of Palermo—"water gods, horses, serpents, fishes, and every other imaginable variety of figure, pouring forth the pure water of the mountains into basins full of goldfish or over rocks of marble covered with a growth of water plants"—deeply impressed Parkman with their beauty. With Giuseppe as guide he made pilgrimages on donkeyback to a ruined church at the foot of the mountains, and to the convent of Santa María de Gesù on the summit of a rock overlooking the valley of Palermo. One day in the city he saw a review of several thousand Neapolitan conscripts, whom King Ferdinand had sent to Sicily while he kept his Sicilian troops in Naples. To Parkman these were slight and feeble-looking men, many of them mere boys, and they lacked the precision and unity of the English troops he had seen at Gibraltar and Malta. He recalled that "the Neapolitans were the only nation of whom Napoleon could not make soldiers."

Wearying of Palermo at last, Parkman engaged a *vetturino* named Luigi Rannesi to conduct him to Girgenti at the southern extremity of the island, at the inclusive cost of four dollars a day. He knew that traveling in Sicily at this season was hazardous, and by thus engaging a courier he avoided all chance of being imposed upon or robbed along the way. Though Luigi enjoyed good repute, Parkman extracted a written agreement from him, having "laid it down as an inviolable rule to look on everybody here as a rascal of the first water, till he has shown himself by undeniable evidence to be an honest man." Giuseppe, who regarded it as beneath his dignity to receive wages but did not take offense at a present of half a dollar a day, had proved a good servant, his only fault being that he continually stopped to kiss his acquaintances on the street. " 'It is 'trange Mist'r Park-a-man,' he modestly remarked the other day, 'that I cannot go nowhere but what all the people seem to like-a me, and be good friends with me.' " Parkman found him vain, ostentatious (noting that he "dresses infinitely better than I ever did"), and a great coward, but prompt and ready for all kinds of service and understanding perfectly how to cheat everybody —including his large acquaintance. But he had served admirably to initiate Parkman into Italian ways, while his recollections of Boston and Cambridge no doubt comforted the solitary traveler, who had had his momentary moods of homesickness in this new and strange land.

From the very first Luigi proved himself a jewel. Parkman had told him to be ready on Thursday, January 18, at two: he came at noon, said all was prepared and the carriage at the door. He displayed every item of the provisions he had laid in for the journey, "extolling the qualities of each—and they deserved all his praise—and always ended by pounding himself on the breast, rolling up his eyes, and exclaiming: 'Do you think Luigi loves money? No! Luigi loves honor!' " Parkman soon became very fond of this diminutive Sicilian, with his thin brown face, his alert air, and his constant attention to his employer's wants; and considered him as a particular friend. It was well that he had chosen so good a guide, for the trip through rugged country was by no means an easy one at this season, and Parkman would have passed many cheerless nights in comfortless *albergos* if Luigi had not anticipated his wants so well. Indeed, the only criticism Parkman had to make was that he fared too sumptuously—and far above his expectations, for he had contracted only to be kept alive on the road.

They passed the first night at the village of Marineo, where they abandoned the carriage and took to mules. Luigi provided dinner and conversation, kissed his patron's hand in farewell, then reappeared with a decanter of wine and a book on the antiquities of the island, as good-night gifts. Early the next morning they set off for Girgenti on the opposite side of the island. In the village *albergo* where they passed that night, "nothing but fleas was to be had." The next morning there was a cold raw wind sweeping over the mountains, which reminded Parkman of a New England November. Their road had been washed out, so they made a long detour through the fields, forded many streams, and followed a rough pathway along a mountainside, so ancient that the stones of the way were worn through. Some of these mountain brooks again reminded Parkman of his chosen haunts at home, but the bare and cultivated hills, the olives in the valleys below, and the aloes and Indian figs upon the banks soon dispelled the illusion. As they were beaten by a violent wind sweeping through a narrow gorge, they got a glimpse of Castel Termini in a hollow of the mountains, and there they eventually fought their way against the buffets of the wind. Luigi was a great antiquarian—the best pass- port in Sicily—and his hobby introduced him and his employer everywhere. That night a fellow-antiquarian, a judge, took Park- man to a *conversazione,* where the *signore Americano* became the lion of the evening, much to his embarrassment and irritation. An officer of gendarmes, from one of the Greek villages of the islands, tried to converse with the guest in this language, "but made an absolute failure." Parkman nevertheless found him admirable, "a broad-shouldered and athletic fellow, remarkably intelligent and well informed"—this last, seemingly, because he asked whether Boston were not near Charlestown.

After a night in a cheerless inn he was glad to be among the mountains again, early the next morning. The path here was paved with alabaster, with which the country abounds. Even the mule troughs were hewed from it. In a valley where they forded a stream Parkman first noted the change in physical type among the inhabitants, for the two men who helped travelers across the ford were "noble specimens of flesh and blood." And in a mountainside village, whose steep street and walls were gray with gypsum, "the women were sitting in the hot sun, on heaps of stone outside their doors, arranging their hair, or nursing their children; some lay stretched at full length asleep. Many were pretty—all wore the appearance of full health and vigor. They seemed like the women of earlier times—the partners of the primeval inhabitants of Sicily of whom the pastoral poets speak." The lines of Theocritus came alive in Parkman's mind as he surveyed these scenes.

Here he visited a sulphur mine, descending a shaft solid with it, without any trace of foreign ingredients. Then they rode on, the mule track giving way to a good carriage road on which they were passed by some English travelers from Cantanizetta. At last they saw the battlements and church spires of Girgenti on a high hill before them, and Luigi was struck with a fit of enthusiasm:

> He began to lash his mule and drive him along over mud and rocks at such a rate that I thought him mad till he told me that it was necessary—*per besogno*—to get to Girgenti before the Englishmen. "*Coraggio*, my brave mule! *Coraggio, signore*," he shouted, "we shall be the victors!" At that, he drove full speed up the steep hill toward the gate. Nothing would stop him. He leaped over ditches—scrambled through mud and stones, shouting "*Coraggio!*" at the top of his lungs. At last an insuperable gully brought him up short. He clapped his hand to his forehead, exclaiming "*Santissima María!*" in a tone of wrath and despair—then recovered his spirits and dashed off in another direction. We succeeded. When we got to the top the carriage was a quarter of a mile off, and Luigi shouted "*Vittoria!*" as he rode into the gate, as much elated as if he had accomplished some great achievement.

As if in honor of this great victory, all Girgenti was in festive garb, with square white caps above the ruddy dark brown faces. Parkman admired the hardiness of these people, and envied them their short strong necks and broad and prominent chests. He could not reconcile himself to the differences in race and type and manners which seemed to occur between one village and the next: dedicated student of history that he was, he did not recognize that he saw the living memorials of the various races who had ruled the island. But from the battlements of Girgenti he got a stronger reminder of history, for between the town and the sea could be seen the remains of ancient Agrigentum. He inspected the five or six temples which still stood in ruins on the abrupt ridge which marked one boundary of the ancient city, but he left a further description to "the more classically disposed, having little inclination to it myself."

But Luigi made up for his employer's lack of antiquarian enthusiasm. Triumphantly he brought in pocketfuls of old coins and was injured by Parkman's indifference to them. He dove into houses and shops, and stopped *contadini* at work in the fields, in his quest for *antica moneta*. His all embracing enthusiasm amused the reticent Parkman: whether it expressed itself in this collecting passion or in accounts of his many loves, culminating in his elopement with his wife; in the singing of love songs or, in more martial vein, shouts of *"Coraggio!"* and defiances to wind, rain, and torrents. Parkman had but to mention a plan for him to fall in enthusiastically with it. Every night he brought his employer rare coins, and the dresses and utensils of the people for examination. At every stop he put the inn into a turmoil, ransacked the town for the best of everything, and served each dish with a eulogy, repeating always: "Ah, signore, do you think Luigi loves money? No, Luigi loves honor!" And to make good his motto, he had something to give to every beggar he met.

Parkman accompanied him to the house of a certain Signor Politi, who was as "rampant with antiquarian zeal" as Luigi, and an amateur of the fine arts. Luigi presented this local connoisseur with an ancient cameo as *un piccolo complimento*, and Parkman marveled at Politi's cavalier acceptance of the gift until he understood that it was made Indian fashion, and saw Luigi retire with a return gift of a handkerchiefful of antiquities. The cunning Luigi was never without something *per fare un complimento* to his wide acquaintanceship, which ranged from princes to beggars. Parkman was later introduced through his cicerone to a Marchese Giacomo, who possessed a "most admirable picture gallery—among the rest was an original of Guido," and to a *barone*, whose wife received

Parkman in her bedroom, the only other ground-floor room besides the kitchen in the baron's simple house. Parkman marveled
over this occurrence: "I was inclined to suspect a little humbug
about the baron and his establishment, till I got to Palermo, and
I found by inquiry that noblemen of his description were very
common in Sicily." Not every solitary traveler has his way cheered
by the present of a melon and some nuts, brought and served by
a baron!

At Girgenti, too, he met a blind traveler, a Mr. Holeman, at the
English consul's. Holeman had traversed Siberia, New Holland,
and other remote regions, and written seven volumes about his
solitary travels. He confessed to an itching foot and a passion for
travel, which would not allow him to stay at home. Parkman admired his indomitable energy, which would not yield to his handicap, and the picture he made as he set off the following morning
in the company of a guide: "His strong frame, his manly English
face, his gray beard, and mustaches, and his sightless eyeballs gave
him a noble appearance in the crowd of wondering Sicilians about
him." Parkman little thought that he might be forced to emulate
this Englishman before many years had passed, and to surpass him
in the struggle against physical handicaps. When that dark time
came, the memory of this wandering blindman doubtless served
to strengthen a will which brooked no check and a temperament
that lived on action.

From Girgenti Parkman and Luigi went westward over the
mountains on a wretched mule track. Among the hills he met a
herdsman, with tangled hair, unshorn beard, shaggy goatskin
breeches, and a dog as savage as himself, and Parkman reflected
that the American frontier could show no wilder group than this
encountered in a land over which many civilizations had passed.
That night they passed at Mont' Allegro, among alabaster mountains, and paved and built of the same stone. Parkman noted here
the permanence of village life, which remained much the same as
it had been centuries before. But these musings were interrupted
by the effervescent Luigi, who came to hold a *discorso* with his
employer over the wine:

He takes a glass of wine in his hand. "*Viva l'onore, signorino mio!*" rolling up his eyes and flourishing his hands, "*viva Bacco; viva Dio; viva il console Americano!*" and so on, the finale being a seizure and kissing of my hand; after which he inquires if I shall want him, looks about to see that all is right, kisses my hand again, and goes off.

The next morning Parkman visited the convent of St. Calogero, with its vapor baths which Diodorus speaks of, and which are said to have been arranged by Daedalus. Parkman stripped and sweated in the steam until he was forced to cry enough and flee to the dressing room. Afterwards the monk in charge of the baths showed him a similar issue of steam from a hole in the mountain-side, and a view of Sciacca with its white battlements, its church domes, and the ruined castle of Count Perolla, the grandson of Ruggiero, who drove the Saracens from Sicily. Then next day their journey took them over a great plain, which Parkman found uninteresting, for only mountain scenery stirred him. But he did admire the *contadini*, guiding their clumsy wooden plows through the fertile fields under the scorching fire of the January sun: "The men were noble fellows, with gigantic busts, and massive limbs, and a wild untaught look." That afternoon they passed the ruins of Selinus, which the Carthaginians had besieged and leveled. Only one column of the temple of Jupiter still stood. Parkman puzzled over the great sculptured blocks of stone which lay about, for since time immemorial the method of transporting building stone here had been on donkeyback. After a "needlessly luxurious dinner of cold sole, oranges, almonds, wine, etc.," among the ruins, they pressed on to Castrovetrano, enlivened on the way by the antics and songs of their muleteer Michele.

The next morning they set off in a cold storm, and soon reached the quarries of Campo Bello, whence had come the stone for Selinus:

It is a most extraordinary place. About the base of a little hill, near an old plantation of olive trees, are lying fragments of columns cut from the rock thousands of years ago. Further on are others completely carved, but not yet severed from the mother rock. The process of cutting them out was this: A circle, of the same diameter with the column wanted, was marked out on the flat rock. The workmen then hewed down into the rock, around this circle, until the column was long enough, when it was cut off and drawn out, leaving an orifice like a well. There were some where the circle had just been traced—others where the column was standing ready to be drawn out of the hole— others where the hole was empty, and the column was rolled down to the foot of the hill.

At Mazzara, some distance on, he saw the effigy of Count Ruggiero, riding down the prostrate Saracens. They rode to Marsala that night through a hard rain, Parkman deriving a gloomy satisfaction from traveling in bad weather, but feeling like a starved wolf when they reached their goal at last, having ridden from sunrise to sunset without food.

A certain local type of capote, "ten times coarser and thicker than a Mackinaw blanket, and accommodating itself to the person about as well as a garment of sheet iron," seems to have impressed Parkman more than the famous wine of the place, particularly when worn by the broad-shouldered fishermen, who took on gigantic status in this rig. Beyond Marsala they had a brush with the legendary bandits of the island, but nothing worse befell than the bad scare which Luigi suffered, so that "the natural ruddy brown of his face was changed to a most cadaverous yellow." In their confusion they lost their path and got thoroughly soaked before they reached Trapani with its tremendous fortifications. From the rocks by the sea, outside the city gate, Parkman saw the reef where Aeneas placed the green bough when he held games in this place in honor of his father. And also in sight was the rock of Malo Consiglio, where the Sicilian Vespers were planned. Behind the city rose Mount Eryx, the second highest mountain in Sicily, and Parkman climbed it to visit the shrine of Venus "founded by Eryx —enriched by Aeneas—resorted to by the old Sicanians, and in later times by the Romans." The walled city on the summit was almost deserted, and was swept by a wind "as cold and sharp as a January day at home." Nevertheless Parkman found the view "charming beyond measure" and mused over the legends of the place: the sickle-shaped harbor of Trapani, where Saturn dropped his sickle or Ceres lost hers as she went to look for Proserpine; the mountain itself where Hercules slew Eryx and Anchises was entombed; and the shrine of Rome's favorite goddess, where "a *thousand* fair and kind priestesses" waited to welcome the pious pilgrims. Parkman felt himself less fortunate: only a few crest-fallen robbers, then confined there, showed him about the ruined castle which was tumbling to decay on top of the ruins of the temple.

Pushing on from Trapani, they rode through solitary and pathless hills to the ruins of Segesta, "a city as old as the Trojan War, and afterwards noted for its riches and misfortunes." The tyrant Agathocles had leveled it, save for one temple and an amphitheater too massive to be destroyed, after massacring its men and women and selling its children into slavery. Parkman was beginning to fall into the antiquarian mood amid such sights, and wrote: "I have seen nothing in art so striking and majestic as this solitary temple. . . . Standing as it does a monument of the fate that overtook its builders, and in the midst of a scene so sublime by nature." It was with regret and reluctance that at sunset he turned from the last glimpse of the melancholy temple, after descending the mountains which surrounded it, and rode into the dark and dirty city. The next night they stayed in a wretched village, grateful enough for the dismal shelter it offered against the continual rain. Parkman had an eerie experience when his lamp ran out of oil, and he wandered through the dark passages and chambers of the *albergo*, which reminded him of a deserted castle. His explorations and cries brought no answer save a dead silence, until he stumbled upon a party of gendarmes, drinking wine about a brazier of charcoal, who directed him to the people of the house, who dwelt in an outbuilding across the muddy yard. A thunderstorm during the night added to the eeriness of the place, and the next morning Parkman was astounded to see every mountain white with snow. During the day, on their way through a mountain pass, they were beset by a driving snowstorm, and as they waded through the drifts they heard heavy dull peals of thunder, "a novel circumstance to me." They met no one for miles, and the brigand-fearful Luigi agonized as they passed a solitary stone house, which he thought to be a lurking place of the *briganti.* But soon the valley of Palermo lay before them, "green among the white mountains around it," and Parkman's tour of Sicily was nearly done. They made a detour, though, to inspect the Benedictine monastery of San Martino, another noble house whose resources startled and shocked the young Puritan ascetic:

> Everything is on a scale of magnificence and luxury—pictures, fountains, the church, the chapels, the library, the interminable galleries of the enormous building. There are no tawdry ornaments; everything is in good taste—but for ascetic privations, and mortification of the flesh, look elsewhere than at San Martino. The fathers were at table. I was served with a dinner of lampreys and other delicacies which a prince might have envied. There is a preserve of wild game, a formidable establishment of cooks and scullions, a beautiful *conversazione,* and billiard rooms, for the diversion of the pious devotees. In a palace-like hall, below the surface of the ground, sustained by columns and arches of the richest marbles of Sicily, and lighted from above, is a noble statue of San Martino. He is a young soldier on horseback, with as little savor of the saint about him as any of his votaries in this luxurious monastery.

The Puritan had become more Roman than the Romans, after two months' exposure to Catholicism.

Soon after his return to Palermo, Parkman took the steamer for Naples. Luigi presented him with some valuable ancient coins, and could scarcely be restrained from giving him a hundred more in his sorrow at leavetaking. There were farewells to be said, too, to his American friends, the Marstons and the Gardiners, who had helped to make his Sicilian tour successful by their advice. And then Parkman followed the three *facchini* who carried his luggage on board the *Palermo.* Evidently he was moved at leaving this wild and romantic island, for he almost succumbed to an "unwonted feeling of benevolence to a Sicilian beggar." An old Franciscan monk was begging for his patron's benefit, promising a pleasant voyage and perfect safety to all donors, and Parkman found his humble and miserable figure so moving among the inattentive nobles and exquisites crowding the deck that he tried to catch his eye to give him something. But just then all visitors were warned off, and the old monk tumbled over the side into the boat of a charitable *facchino*.

Parkman's first glimpse of the Bay of Naples was wretched and miserable enough, since it was lashed by an easterly storm and Vesuvius was barely visible. He put up at the Hotel de Roma, and passed the first day at the Royal Museum, debating the merits of the Farnese Hercules and the Venus of Praxiteles. The following day he drove out to Pozzuoli through the grotto of Posilipo, a wide road tunneled through a mountain of rock. Parkman found this wonder "as dark as Tartarus, and excessively damp and cold." The lamps provided only a "mockery of light," and the shouts of drivers and the rumble of wheels made a tremendous uproar which was echoed by the rock walls. Upon arrival at his destination he chose a guide from among the fifty who fell upon him, and rode down to Lake Avernus and the grotto of the Cumaean Sibyl. "A particularly modest piece of sculpture" above one door of one of the Sibyl's apartments was the only feature that caught his attention, aside from the darkness and sootiness of the cavern, which the guides' torches did nothing to relieve. These guardians raised such an outcry of disappointment at the smallness of his *bonamano* that he was forced to use stern measures to disperse them and also some peddlers of mosaics and bronze amulets, remarking loftily that "These fellows fear a cane as much as a thieving dog does."

He followed the beaten tourist track around Baiae and Cumae, where he tasted some Falernian wine made from grapes growing on the same spot as Horace's; grew weary of temples and was disappointed by the extinct volcano of Solfatara. His zeal for classical sightseeing was dampened by constant grumbling demands for *bonamano*, requests to buy antiquities ("manufactured in great profusion at Naples"), and the persistent intercessions of a swarm of beggars. Nero's vapor baths interested him, however, though he found them not unlike those of Sciacca. The next day he visited

Lake d'Agnano and tested the powers of the Grotto del Cane, whose cicerone kept mongrels on whom to demonstrate the strength of the natural gas, which overcame them in a few minutes. But he had his most colorful experience in attempting to wrest a memento from the tomb of Virgil, on Mount Posilipo:

. . . Seeing a bush which from its position had escaped the violating hands of former travelers, I determined to get a branch of it. The tomb stands at the edge of a rock about two hundred feet high above the street; this bush was on the side of the cliff just outside an opening in the back part of the tomb. There was a stout iron bar to hold on by—no man of ordinary nerve and muscular strength would have the slightest cause of apprehension. So I told the cicerone to hold my cloak, grasped the bar, leaned from the opening, and got hold of the plant, which I was about to secure when I heard a simultaneous shout from both guides, who sprang upon me and seized me fast. I looked round at them. Both were pale as ghosts, with their mouths wide open, and eyes staring out of their heads. I asked them what the devil was the matter—they replied by seizing me by the arms and shoulders and pulling me away from the hole. I got free of them by a sudden effort, but they sprang at me again, and began to roar for help. "Oh, come this way, signore! Come this way: you must not go there." I was a good deal vexed, but could not help laughing at being mistaken for a madman. I thought I would try a little intimidation, so aimed a blow with my fist at the nearest fellow's face. They dodged off for a moment, but returned to the charge with faces doubly earnest and anxious, and pinioned me from behind. "Oh, signore!" they said. "We don't want money; only come up with us to the gate." I saw the folly of contending with the idea that had got possession of them, so told them that I would go. Thus I went out from Virgil's tomb a prisoner. I thought my quiet compliance would have allayed their fears a little—no such thing; nothing would do but I must mount with them to the garden gate above. Half-way up appeared a gang of men rushing in hot haste to secure the madman. They were soon about me, when confiding in their numbers they loosened my arms. I was resolved not to lose my relic of Virgil, so dispatched a boy to pluck a leaf from the door of the tomb, since the men would on no account suffer me to go myself. I got this memento of my adventure, and departed. I had some little suspicion that all this terror of my guides was counterfeited in order to give them a chance to pick my pockets; but all my money was safe.

Strangely enough, this dearly won prize is not preserved among the leaves of Parkman's notebook of this journey, as are many flowers from less celebrated and more accessible places. But doubtless he needed no reminder of his frustrated attempt at "suicide" at Virgil's tomb.

At the house of Mr. Rogers in Naples, Parkman encountered Dr. Theodore Parker, the eminent Boston divine and man of letters, and a Mr. Farnum from Philadelphia. Upon the following day they went up Vesuvius together. The volcano was unusually active at the time, and Parker exclaimed: "What stock in trade for an orthodox minister!" As they stood on the rim of the great crater, showers of lava shot hundreds of yards into the air from the huge central cone, out of which smoke and fire streamed. These minor eruptions were accompanied by a dismal bellowing and shocks like the discharge of a cannon within the mountain. The wind drove the smoke and fumes of sulphur about the crater, more than a thousand feet deep and floored with a crust of lava, through which the liquid fire beneath was visible here and there. Parkman agreed with his friend: it was indeed "a lively picture of Hell." They were fascinated by the sight and determined to have a closer view of the subterranean monster. Scrambling down into the crater, where the lava scorched their shoes, they passed over fissures and holes which poured out fumes of brimstone and set their canes on fire. They went as near to the cone as they dared, occasionally driven back by clouds of smoke blown down upon them, or forced to hold their heads in crevices to avoid being suffocated. Their guides were more daring, approaching the base of the cone and nimbly dodging the falling masses of lava which showered down from the periodic explosions. Some lumps weighed as much as a ton, and spread out over a large surface as they fell. The guides dashed at them, detached a small portion with a pole, and, carrying it to a safe place, stamped it with a copper coin. Parker and his young friend did the same and thus secured several trophies. Their enterprise was not a tame one, for the very floor of the crater on which they stood had been a sea of molten lava only three days before.

At a house half-way down the mountain, they paused to refresh themselves with some of the famous Lachryma Christi wine; then returned to Naples, whose outskirts they found deserted in mid-afternoon. It was Sunday, and the great day of the Carnival, which King Ferdinand had opposed and reduced to a mere nothing in recent years:

This year, in consideration of the distress of tradesmen, he has consented, much against his inclination, to make a fool of himself. This was the day appointed for a grand masked procession, in which the king and his ministers were to pelt his subjects with sugar-plums, and be pelted in turn. There was a great crowd, as we entered a square upon the Toledo—the main street of Naples. While we were slowly driving through it, the head of the procession appeared. First came a dragon about fifty feet long, with his back just visible above the throng of heads, as if he was swimming in the water. He was drawn by a long train of horses. Five or six masked noblemen were on his back, pelting the crowd and the people in the galleries of the house on each side. Then came a sort of car, full of bears, cats, and monkeys, all flinging sugar-plums. The horses of this vehicle were appropriately ridden by jackasses. Then came a long train of carriages, which we joined. The crowd was enormous. The Toledo was one wide river of heads, the procession slowly moving down on one side and returning on the other. Along the middle, a line of dragoons set motionless, with drawn swords. Mrs. P. was hit on the nose by a formidable sugar-plum, flung by a vigorous hand from one of the balconies. She was in great trouble, but there was no such thing as retreat. We got our full share. Mr. Farnum's dignity was disturbed—Mr. Parker had a glass of his spectacles broken—I alone escaped uninjured. At length the royal carriage appeared. Ferdi-

nand—a gigantic man, taller and heavier than any of his subjects
—was flinging sugar-plums with hearty goodwill, like all the rest.
As they passed our carriage, the royal family greeted us with a
broadside, which completed Mrs. Parker's discomfiture. They
threw genuine sugar-plums—the others were quite uneatable.
The king wore a black silk dress which covered him from head
to foot. His face was protected by a wire mask. He carried a
brass machine in his hand to fling sugar-plums with. His uncle,
his mother, his wife, and all his chief noblemen soon appeared,
all protected by masks.

The procession passed several times up and down the Toledo,
with occasional stoppages. One of these happened when the
king's carriage was not far before us, while directly over against
it, on the other side of the street, was a triumphal car full of
noblemen. Instantly there began a battle. Ferdinand and the
princes sent volley after volley against their opponents, who returned it with interest. The crowd set up a roar, and made a rush
for the spoils. There was a genuine battle for the sugar-plums
that fell between the two carriages—rushing, scrambling, shouting, yelling, "confusion worse confounded"; till the dignified
combatants thought proper to separate.

No doubt Mrs. Parker reflected that evening that no good ever
came of such brazen Sabbath-breaking as exploring a volcano and
mingling in a carnival.

One peculiar feature of Naples life seems to have made a great
impression on Parkman. He covered pages of his journal with accounts of the countless dramas in which the clown Pulcinella
figured. He liked the little boxes on the quay where these dramas
were performed several times a day, whenever a handful of
loungers, sailors, and children could be enticed within, far better
than the theater of San Carlo, "one of the largest and finest in
Europe." Possibly these performances reminded him of those of
the Star Theater in his father's barn in Boston: at any rate it is clear
that he was much taken with this puckish Tyll Eulenspiegel of a
Neapolitan, who ridiculed the most serious moments of a tragedy,
indulged in "most particularly indecent" evolutions, and did not

hesitate to knock over the Devil himself or kick a sultan in the face, amid the roars of his devoted following. The Punch and Judy shows also fascinated Parkman; but Pulcinella had first hold upon his heart, and he could not see enough of these performances to satisfy him.

As he wandered about the city, he saw many sights strange to him. There was a funeral procession, led by a soldier and a group of men "in white robes, with white broad-brimmed hats, and white cloth covering their faces." The coffin, covered with gilding, came next, borne on a machine gay with gold and tinsel. Then came a group of men all in black, carrying little death's-head banners. He found out that the men in white were members of a company of penitents, while those in black came from the king's poorhouse. Then he witnessed a great review of the military in the square before the royal palace, "with the sunlight shimmering on the bayo-nets and the helmets of the cavalry," the king's guard selected for their great stature and fine appearance, and a body of Swiss mer-cenaries uniformed all in white. The Toledo, always teeming with life, enthralled him:

> The Toledo is a noble street. Every hour of the day it is thronged with a dense crowd of men and women of every kind and degree. Carriages and carts drive along at full speed with a noise that would split the head of a nervous man. The shops are small but elegant, and open on the street. Priests and monks, in every variety of dress—troops of military scholars, in cocked hats—straggling soldiers, mustachioed to the eyes—women in very neat and beautiful costumes—criers of various commodities—and a host of well-dressed men of all nations, together make up the crowd that swarms night and day in this street. The houses are very high and elegant. There are no sidewalks; woe to the absent man—he will be knocked down and run over twenty times a day, and have his pocket picked a hundred. A gayer and livelier place could scarcely be imagined.

But the remoter and more obscure streets intrigued him quite as much. The endless variety of costume was captivating, and he found the women particularly attractive, though "not handsome, properly speaking." He roamed all over the city, marveling at the infinite variety of humanity and dress and manners which greeted him, but always returned to the little play boxes on the quay, to witness Pulcinella's exploits or to see canaries trained to fire cannon, play dead, drag each other in carriages, and perform other such feats. With the present so absorbing, he got little pleasure from a visit to Pompeii, whose palatialness and elegance surprised him, and he dismissed Herculaneum as "scarce worth seeing after Pompeii."

6: A Puritan in Rome

*This will I say of Rome—that a place
on every account more interesting—
and which has a more vivifying and
quickening influence on the faculties—
could not be found on the face of the
earth—or, at least, I should not wish to
go to it if it could.*

F.P., JOURNAL, 1844

ON SATURDAY, February 17, 1844, Parkman set off by diligence for Rome, traveling with Mr. and Mrs. Parker. They
had a bad start, for on a hill just outside Naples, "the six consumptive horses attached to the ponderous machine were utterly unable
to drag it up, though the postilions sputtered and swore *carzo,* and
kicked their gigantic boots against the gaunt ribs of the miserable
beasts, and lashed until they split their livery jackets." A crowd of
ragamuffins was enlisted to tug at the wheels, but nothing availed
until the horses were taken out and oxen substituted. Then the
diligence lumbered forward, but there was a crack and a jounce,
greeted by a scream from the much tried Mrs. Parker, and the diligence came to a halt with a broken spring. The whole party returned to Naples for refitting and started off again after a three-
hour delay. Soon after midnight they paused at the customs for a
last tribute to the minions of King Ferdinand and a first to those of
the Pope. Three or four customs officials had to be bribed, porters
rewarded, and postilions tipped, before peace was restored. Parkman noted bitterly:

This road is notorious above most others for custom-house exactions. An American, jealous of his rights as a traveler, refused a
few days since to satisfy their illegal demands. His trunk was
broken open in a moment, and searched to the very bottom, especial care being taken to tear and soil everything as much as
possible.

At dawn Parkman woke to find the diligence passing the Pontine Marshes, the wide meadows being white with dew and the distant mountain ranges half veiled in mists and clouds, which dissipated as the sun rose on a clear cool morning. At once he noted a contrast between the villagers here and the Neapolitans. They lacked the gaiety and vivacity of their southern neighbors, and he soon wearied of their solemn stares. Then he caught a glimpse of St. Peter's, and as they passed ruined temples, aqueducts, and tombs, Theodore Parker became inspired and spouted Cicero and Virgil, to the accompaniment of three young Roman beggars, who ran beside the carriage for a mile, hat in hand, wailing: *"Eccellenza, Eccellenza! Povero miserabile, molto di fame!"* Mrs. Parker, "a pretty, timid, gentle little woman," looked up everything dutifully in the guidebook, while her husband meditated on the ruins of Rome. Soon after they passed the city gate, Mrs. Parker exclaimed: "Oh, only look here; *do* tell me what this is!" Accordingly Theodore looked, "burst out with rather an untheological interjection, and caught me by the shoulder, 'The Colosseum!' " But they caught only a glimpse of a mountain of arches piled one upon another, before the narrow streets shut off their view of the towering pile. They had difficulty in finding rooms; the hotels were so full that some English travelers were forced to walk the streets all night.

They had arrived just in time for one of the great days of the Roman Carnival. Undaunted by their experiences in Naples, the Parkers and their young friend braved the crowded streets to see the show. There were maskers on foot and in carriages, who packed the streets until a blast of trumpets cleared the Corso for a parade of the Papal soldiers, sappers, infantry, and cavalry, whose appearance was designed to preserve order. After they had passed by, the Carnival spirit prevailed:

It was not the solemn sugar-plum foolery of Naples, but foolery entered into with right heartiness and goodwill. There were devils of every description, from the imp of two feet high to a six-foot monster with horns, hoofs, and tail, and a female friend on each arm. There were harlequins with wooden swords, or with bladders tied to poles, which they beat over the heads of all they met—Pulcinellas, and an endless variety of nondescripts. Some of the carriages were triumphal cars gaily ornamented— full of maskers; men and girls, in spangled dresses. Instead of sugar-plums they flung flowers at one another. Some of the women wore wire masks or little vizards, which left the lower part of the face bare; many, however, had no covering at all to their faces. Few had any regular beauty of features, but there was an expression of heart and spirit, and a loftiness, besides, which did not shame their birth. They flung their flowers at you with the freest and most graceful action imaginable. To battle with flowers against a laughing and conscious face—showering your ammunition thick as the carriage slowly passes the balcony —then straining your eyes to catch the last glance of the black-eyed witch and the last wave of her hand as the crowd closes around her—all this is no contemptible amusement.

Parkman seems to have enjoyed himself thoroughly this day in Rome. He found even "the inferior class of woman," walking the streets rather than riding in a carriage or watching from a balcony, attractively dressed, and approved of those who were disguised as boys and wore "fierce mustaches, which set off well enough their spirited faces." That evening he went to the theater, and found Pulcinella in great form. He was pleased to learn that this favorite was not, as he had been told, peculiar to Naples.

The next day was the last of the Carnival—"a concentration of all its frolics." Again the Corso and the surrounding squares and streets were jammed with merrymakers, on foot and in carriages. The usually staid and stately Corso wore an altered air: windows and balconies were thronged with people and draped with rich hangings, while a shouting, laughing, dancing crowd of maskers filled the street. At a cannon signal the carriages withdrew and troops cleared a passage down the center of the street, their lines holding back the crowd:

The horses were to start from the upper end of the Corso, where it expands into a square, surrounded by fine palaces and churches. The people sat on raised benches on each side of this square; a strong rope was stretched across the upper end, to restrain the horses till the signal should be given. Near this, under a canopy, sat the officers of the state.

At length a body of dragoons rode in, circling around the space, while their officer made his obeisance before the seats of the senate. They then passed out. There was a yell from the crowd without, and the horses were brought in, each by two grooms, snorting and plunging with terror. They had leaden balls set round with needles, hung against their sides, to spur them as they ran, which they do without riders. There were large sheets of thin metal and gilded paper tied to their manes and backs. For a moment there was an active struggle between the grooms and the frightened horses—then, at a signal, down went the rope, and the horses sprang away at full speed down the Corso. The yells of the people passed down the street along with them, growing more and more faint, till they were lost entirely.

It was now almost dark. When I went back to the Corso, the street seemed on fire through its whole length, to the very roofs of the houses. The carriages had returned; the crowd was as active as a swarm of bees; thousands of wax torches were tossed about, extinguished, and lighted again. This is the game with which the Carnival concludes. Everybody carries a torch which he tries to keep burning, while he extinguishes his neighbor's. Flappings of handkerchiefs, flinging of flowers, blowing, and twenty other means were used to put out the lights. At every successful attempt, the man shouted: *"Senza moccolo!"* These sounds mingled into one roar which filled the street. The light of the torches glaring on the gaily dressed figures in the carriages and balconies, and then suddenly extinguished—the glittering forms of the maskers leaping into the air to preserve their own light or put out that of another—the shrill cries of the girls, who fought like little Amazons, and had strong arms, as I can testify —made altogether an appropriate finale to the Carnival.

Compared to these vivid street scenes, Parkman found nothing to notice at a masked ball that evening, nor at the American colony's

Washington's Birthday dinner the following day, which seemed "like a visit home." Though he thought some of the many American artists then in Rome "fine fellows," he was annoyed that his countrymen should seem so slight, pale, and thin, unlike the ruddy, beefy Englishmen who also abounded in the city then; so very quiet and apparently timid, "speaking low to the waiters, instead of roaring in the imperative tone of John Bull"; so lacking in "that boisterous and haughty confidence of manner that you see among Englishmen." In fact he felt obliged to dismiss his compatriots as "a little green." He consoled himself with the thought that these Yankees, for all their thin faces, narrow shoulders, and awkward attitudes, were a full match for the blustering Englishmen in "genius, enterprise, and courage—nay, in bodily strength." But still he had to conclude: "Would that they bore themselves more boldly and confidently. But a time will come when they may meet Europeans on an equal footing." He considered the speeches of General Dix, Mr. G. W. Greene, the consul, and Dr. Howe to be fine specimens of American eloquence, though he deplored Mr. Conrade of Virginia's would-be stirring toast: "Washington and Cincinnatus! Patrick Henry and Cicero!"

After a week of "lionizing," as he called seeing the sights of the Eternal City, he recorded this observation in his journal: "I would not give a damn for all the churches and ruins in Rome—at least such are my sentiments at present." He found the Colosseum by moonlight unboundedly sublime, St. Peter's a miracle in its way, "but I would give them all for one ride on horseback among the Apennines." To the restless, energetic Parkman, going through the sightseer's mill of driving from church to church and ruin to ruin, from morning to night for a fortnight, was worse than seeing nothing. He recalled an acquaintance at Palermo, who was something of a self-satisfied philosopher, denying the faculty of imagination, and having only contempt for the childish amusement of looking at "old stones." This Mr. Smith was "an upstart speculator from New York, about five feet high and three inches broad—gulled and befooled at all hands, but fortunately about to depart this earth, for he was in consumption." Mr. Smith was articulately opposed to sightseeing, as practiced in Sicily:

"Don't tell me about your Tarpeian Rock. I've seen it, and what's more, the feller wanted I should give him half a dollar for taking me there. 'Now look here!' says I. 'Do you suppose I'm going to pay you for showing me this old pile of stones? I can see better rocks than this any day, for nothing; so clear out!' I'll tell you the way I do," continued Mr. Smith. "I don't go and *look* and *stare*, as some people do, when I get inside of a church, but I pace off the length and breadth, and then set it down on paper. Then, you see, I've got something that will keep!"

When he heard this in the Marstons's parlor at Palermo, Parkman had not anticipated that he would ever feel any sympathy with Smith, but a week of "lionizing" had given that materialist a fervent disciple. Only the prospect of a trip among the mountains in the near future kept Parkman dutifully at his sightseeing.

One of the sights that impressed him most was the Cloaca Maxima, the three-thousand-year-old common sewer of the city and the only Roman monument that retained unaltered its original character. The fish still came up to feed on offal at its outlet into the Tiber, as the pike did in Juvenal's day, and were caught in great flat nets for the market. Other fishermen, too, Parkman saw on Father Tiber's shores, grappling for driftwood against great odds, "for the current runs as it used to when Horatius Cocles and Clelia swam it." On the river bank alone did he feel that the past still lived: elsewhere the temples had been turned to cattle sheds or burnt into lime, and the Forum was used as a cow-yard. In the Colosseum, where the early Christians had been thrown to the beasts, he saw a procession of penitents, garbed in brown robes, parading from one to another of fourteen "chapels" placed around the arena, chanting prayers at each.

If the Empire was dead and its living traces few, the Church was much in evidence. Parkman, already well disposed toward it, despite his Puritanism, by what he had seen in weeks of travel in Catholic lands, now began to experience the force which draws many to Rome. After his account of the ceremony in the Colosseum, he wrote:

A Virginian named St. Ives, lately converted to Catholicism, has been trying to convert me, along with some of the Jesuits here. He has abandoned the attempt in disgust, telling me that I have not logic enough in me to be convinced of anything, to which I replied by cursing logic and logicians.

Parkman met St. Ives in Theodore Parker's rooms in the Via Babuino, and was at once reminded by the stranger's appearance of the English Puritans' title of "crop-eared knaves." Parker introduced them with a warning expression to Parkman: "This is a friend of your cousin Shaw." The visitor regarded Parkman with interest, saying: "I hope you will follow in your good cousin's path." Coolidge Shaw, who was the cousin in question and a playmate of Parkman in the Star Theater days, had been converted to Catholicism not long before, chiefly through St. Ives's agency; and later joined the Jesuits, though he died before being ordained as a priest. Parkman was fond of his cousin, who was five years older than himself, but he was at once repelled and filled with distrust by this friend's appearance: "a high forehead, a pale face, thin lips, and bright black eyes that gleamed with a keen but sinister light." Their subsequent acquaintance did nothing to relieve this unfavorable first impression. St. Ives boasted of his former recklessly dissolute life, which he claimed to have shorn off like his hair (which he now wore close-clipped) by the power of the true faith. Parkman often speculated as to what had brought St. Ives into the Church:

He hated democracy, and was fiercely arbitrary and domineering when he could be so unchecked, but was humble to those in high places. He had a keen intellect and a remarkably vivid imagination, to which he gave full rein. His vanity was great, and till he saw my incredulity, he entertained me with frequent stories of his adventures and exploits in his days of sin, always calling on me to observe the transformation wrought in him by his conversion. He was one of those to whom the imposing spectacle of organized power in the Roman Church appeals with fascination. Parker and I often speculated as to his position in regard to the Jesuits and other ecclesiastics with whom he was intimate, but we could come to no more definite conclusion than that, without trusting him, they made use of him to bring sheep into their fold.

Whether or not this conclusion was valid, and it may be suspect since Theodore Parker was in the habit of looking under his bed at night for papistical emissaries, St. Ives attempted Parkman's conversion, finding seemingly fallow ground, for Parkman noted:

> I had some slight suspicion that the exclusive claims of Rome might not be without foundation after all, and, though I disliked my preceptor, he appeared to be a new and interesting type of humanity. So I willingly listened to him, thus gaining what I particularly wanted, an acquaintance with certain English Jesuits to whom he made me known. I read their books and listened to their logic, but the conversion made no progress, and I remained where I was before, till, a year after, my cousin Shaw advised me to read a book which he pronounced sovereign against heresy. It was called, if I rightly remember, *Mill's End of Controversy*. I studied it from title-page to finis, thought to myself: "Is that all you have got to say?" and have remained ever since in solid disbelief as to the doctrines of Rome.

So wrote Parkman nearly half a century later, when he published in *Harper's* an account of his stay in a Roman monastery. Better evidence, perhaps, as to his feelings about the Church when he was twenty is supplied by his journal and his correspondence with Coolidge Shaw. Set apart in the journal by eight stars is this entry:

> I have now been three or four weeks in Rome—have been presented to His Holiness the Pope—have visited churches, convents, cemeteries, catacombs, common sewers, including the Cloaca Maxima, and ten thousand works of art. This will I say of Rome—that a place on every account more interesting—and which has a more vivifying and quickening influence on the faculties—could not be found on the face of the earth—or, at least, I should not wish to go to it if it could.
>
> It is as startling to a "son of Harvard" to see the astounding learning of these Jesuit fathers, and the appalling readiness and rapidity with which they pour forth their interminable streams

of argument, as it would be to a Yankee parson to witness his whole congregation, with church pulpit and all, shut up within one of the great columns which support the dome of St. Peter's —a thing which might assuredly be done.

The Catholics here boast that their church never stood at so high and happy a point as now—converts are pouring in—wisdom and sanctity abound.

It is clear from this passage that the pomp and circumstance of Catholic life in Rome, "the imposing spectacle of organized power in the Roman Church," which Parkman deemed influential in St. Ives's conversion, was not without considerable influence on himself, which is not surprising in view of his interest in history. In his *Harper's* article, Parkman speaks of his inclination for the monastic life, though it was not quite of the sort that the zealous St. Ives suspected:

The phenomena of religious enthusiasm, whether in its active or fossilized state, had an attraction for me. I had, moreover, a fancy for medievalism, and wished to get for a while out of the nineteenth century. I should have much preferred a feudal castle to a convent, but the castles had become the heritage of owls, while some convents were still living remnants of the thirteenth century. But by far the strongest and, indeed, the controlling motive lay in the fact that I had formed plans of a literary undertaking, since in some degree accomplished, which required clear impressions of monastic life, and of Roman Catholic ecclesiasticism in general. On a late muleback tour through Sicily I had visited all the monasteries on the way; but a more intimate acquaintance with them and their inmates was needful for my purpose. I was led into a convent by the same motives that two years later led me to become domesticated in the lodges of the Sioux Indians at the Rocky Mountains, with the difference that I much preferred the company of the savages to that of the monks.

Again the journal suggests that no little rationalization and some alteration of the facts went into this account written forty-six years later. Parkman was clearly drawn to the Church at this stage of his life, as well he might have been, since he found the Unitarianism of his father unsatisfactory and the Puritanism of his forebears uncongenial to a temperament that fed on romantic and colorful ideas rather than on drab God-fearing notions, that preferred the life of soldier and saint to that of godly merchant, that was fonder of the pomps and shows of history than of ideological hair-splitting. It is also clear from the journals of his stay in the Roman convent and of his months among the Indians that the last clause of the quotation is unconscious falsification, caused by subsequent bias, for his romantic notions of the Indians were thoroughly shattered by living among them, while he respected the monks all the more for a few days of living with them the life they had chosen. Those few days gave him considerable understanding of the clerical character—against which he had a basic prejudice—a respect for it which never yielded entirely to his anti-Catholic bias in later life, and an interest in Catholicism that remained strong enough a year later, when he was once more ensconced in the Puritan stronghold of Boston, to carry on a remarkably serious and sympathetic correspondence on the subject with his cousin, the young Jesuit student.

At this stage of Parkman's Roman stay, he fell in with a Harvard classmate, William Morris Hunt, and his brother John Hunt, who had been traveling in Europe with their family for some months. Parkman had last seen his classmate at Mrs. Schutte's table in Cambridge, and had no idea of his present whereabouts until the porter at the Hotel d'Allemagne informed him one day as he returned that his "brother" was inquiring for him. The two Hunts came downstairs six steps at a time to greet their friend, and carried him off to their lodgings, where the sight of *Peirce on Sound* and Whately's *Logic* carried Parkman back to Cambridge. John Hunt was now a Harvard freshman and William a suspended junior, but the family decided soon after this to remain in Europe, where William Hunt studied painting for ten years. Hunt was rather a particular friend of Parkman: his wild exuberance somehow struck an answering chord in his reticent classmate. Then through his ancestry Hunt was linked to the times and the places that Parkman loved, for his father, the Honorable Jonathan Hunt of Brattleboro,

Vermont, was a lawyer and a member of Congress, and his grand-father had been a distinguished soldier in the Revolution and as lieutenant governor did much to bring about the foundation of the state government and its union with the other states. And Hunt, with George Blankern Cary, was one of Parkman's boon compan-ions in college expeditions to the playhouses and Murdoch's Tav-ern. Unfortunately Hunt indulged himself in too many such excur-sions and neglected his studies, with which he had no difficulty but which did not attract him. Nature, music, and drawing were his chosen interests: he had inherited an artistic temperament from his mother and had early received training from a refugee Italian artist, one Gambadella. The college authorities were not willing to receive Hunt's constant sketching as an evidence of serious pur-pose, and he was first rusticated in Concord and then suspended. As his health was delicate, his mother determined to take him and the rest of her children, among whom was Richard Hunt, later a celebrated architect, abroad for travel and study. After some months they had settled down in Rome, where William drew in the studio of Henry Kirk Brown, the American sculptor.

Parkman could have asked no better luck than this chance en-counter. Here was a perfect companion for his projected trip among the Apennines, and an old friend who would not bombard him with theological arguments, of which Parkman was beginning to be weary. Confused and uncertain as he was about first principles at this time, it doubtless was a great relief to lapse into the old carefree existence of students on vacation. So one day soon after their meeting, Parkman and Hunt drove out to Tivoli with Mr. and Mrs. Parker, where they inspected the villas of Adrian, Cas-sius, and the modern dukes of Ferrara. Cascades, temples, and grot-toes were visited before a halt was called for dinner, after which the Parkers returned to Rome, while the two young men remained behind to begin their expedition through the mountains on the mor-row. If Parkman had had no difficulty in winning Hunt to his pur-pose, it is clear that Hunt had a certain influence on Parkman, for the journal for that day closes with a long discourse on the artistic beauties of Tivoli at sunset, with the Anio cascading under the arches of Maecenas's villa at the foot of the heights on which the town stood, the Campagna "a dimly seen ocean in front," and the whole forming a landscape "to which Claude Lorrain has not done justice."

The next morning they looked out on a piazza wet and wretched, with the mountains white with snow and the sky the color of lead. Parkman thought he was going to encounter Sicilian conditions again, but hardly had they set off on donkeyback when the clouds parted and scattered, while the sun poured down on the rain-freshened countryside. They met laughing black-haired girls upon the road, and were amused to see how the temporal got the better of the spiritual when a priest came jogging past on a donkey and greeted the girls. They followed the narrowing valley of the Anio until they reached a village perched on a rock at the top of the bank, where the guide showed them "Cyclopean" remains, although the stones were square and not polygonal. Farther on they came to the yard of the convent of San Cosinato, on the edge of a precipice which fell away hundreds of feet to the river. One of the monks led them down the cliff by a difficult and dangerous path. The face of the precipice was honeycombed with cells and chapels, the whole monastery of Benedictines having burrowed into the rock for a dwelling place. Parkman thought they showed admirable courage and enthusiasm. This was a monastery to his taste, clinging to the face of a savage cliff, above a roaring stream, facing a wild mountain, and with a wonderful view of the expanding valley, so he carried away a flower "as a memento of the gallant monks." Then they stopped at a dirty *osteria* to bait their asses, while he and Hunt ate off an upturned tub in the courtyard and regaled themselves with very good wine at three cents a quart:

This *osteria* was a fair specimen of its kind. In a long dirty stone room, some muleteers and others sat drinking at venerable wooden tables—while some monks were refreshing themselves hard by. I waded along through the mud and straw of the floor to the upper end, where some olive-sticks were burning under a huge tower-like chimney. In the recess of this chimney, all round the fire, low stone seats were built, from which you could look up into the black gulf above, and see volumes of smoke lighted by the rays of sunlight that came through the lateral holes where the smoke was to have escaped. A woman discharging the maternal function, two dirty girls, two cats, and several children were grouped around this singular fireplace, all staring at the stranger in silent admiration. An old sportsman, who was drinking a flask of wine, with his dogs at his knee, in one corner, told me that the wolves had lately made an irruption and carried off eighty sheep. Wild boars also abound here. I have seen them brought into Rome in numbers.

Leaving this rude inn, they rode on to Subiaco "in a perfect amphitheater of mountains." The air was clear and still; on their right the mountains were shadowed in dusk, for the sun was setting behind them; on the left the great bare rocks glared in the light, while the snow on their summits dazzled the eye. Along the mountainsides and even on the peaks gray villages perched, with light smoke hanging over them. The distant hills were sky-blue and peculiarly shadowed by the oblique light. Men and women—the latter full and graceful of form, and well set off by their tight bodices of red or green—were pruning the vineyards on the hillsides. Then the travelers came suddenly upon Subiaco, standing on a detached rocky spur. Since it was near sunset, the pathways leading down to the town from the surrounding mountains were filled with "goats, cattle, trains of mules and asses, women with jars of water on their heads, old woodsmen with the heavy crooked chopping knife in their girdles, and a bundle of fagots on their shoulders."

The town was already in shadow, save for the castle at the top, which was still touched by the sun's last rays. Within the gate the scene was not so charming. The streets, lined by high and crumbling stone houses, were so steep that a horse could not climb them, and served as common sewer for all the filth of the town. They were so narrow that only a strip of red sky could be seen between the rotting roofs. Women gathered to fill their water jars at the town fountain, or spun in corners of the square, or knelt singing vespers in the church, while the men lounged about in their red breeches, smoking and staring. This was Subiaco, but it might have been any of the other Italian country towns that Parkman saw.

The next morning they passed through a street lined by the shops of blacksmiths, "each of whom, covered with dirt and hair, was hammering and filing in a species of narrow den under the houses." Then they went up into the mountains, crossing the Anio on a bridge thrown across a deep and narrow ravine where the stream boiled savagely far below, half obscured by the olives and laurels that clung to the cliffs. A mile more, and they came to a Benedictine monastery, nestled under an overhanging rock at the summit, while the Anio twisted like a white thread among the rocks below. The porter was under the hands of the barber, and nearly concealed by the big brass basin held under his chin, so Parkman was shown around by the sacristan. The monastery was built over the cave where St. Benedict, who "must have had a peculiar taste for wild and lovely situations," had dwelt from his fifteenth year. Parkman was shown the very thicket of thorns into which the saint threw himself when the devil appeared to him in the form of an enticing woman. Though Parkman viewed this legend with some suspicion, he was charmed by the place:

I was under a strong temptation to beg the fathers to let me stay in their monastery a few days—it is as strange in its interior as in its situation. Full of relics of the Middle Ages—and contains halls and vaults built partly by art and partly formed by the natural rock. It seems doomed to speedy destruction. There is a deep crack in the cliff above, which leans forward, as if every moment to fall. I asked the fathers why they took no measures to secure it in its place. "Oh," they piously replied, "St. Benedict will see to that!"

But Hunt was less susceptible to the charms of monasteries, and they pressed on to Rocca di San Stefano, where St. Stephen is supposed to have been stoned to death. The *padrone* of the *osteria* and a vender of salt and tobacco were the only men left in the place, for the rest were at work in the Campagna on the lands of the Roman nobles. Parkman and Hunt amazed the pair by eating with an old dagger, the only good knife they had been able to find at Tivoli, and by the beef tongue which formed part of their provisions. This

strange food excited so much interest that samples were distributed:

> He looked at it—smelt of it—laughed a sort of gurgling laugh
> from the depths of his vitals; then mustered his resolution and
> ate it. The other man hesitated. He turned his piece over and
> over, as if it might be poison, which, though it suited us, would
> not agree with a Christian constitution. He ate half at last, and
> kept the rest, as he said, to show his friends.

The dagger, the strange new food, and the revelation that the visitors were neither *Inglesi* nor *Francesi* led to a certain evident suspicion that they must be devils. Then the pair went on through a
vast chestnut forest which covered the mountains, until they saw
a little village perched on one of the highest peaks. They clambered
up the steep pathway, gaining a great panorama of mountains, sea,
and the villages of the remote interior as they went. From the ruined
battlements, crumbling houses, and dirty people they anticipated
a bad night's lodging, but the old *padrone,* who was the great man
of the village, ushered them with lifted cap and many bows into
suites of rooms, tapestried and furnished with ancient beds and
chairs, and blackened pictures of knights in armor, priests, monks,
and cardinals. In this village of Civitella every stranger was known
as a *pittore,* because its attractions drew so many painters to the
spot. Parkman spent the early evening sitting in a square Pelasgian
fort, "older than the Bible," watching the scenery change with the
ebbing light while Hunt sketched furiously. The inn's fireplace reminded Parkman of a Yankee one, and he sat long before it that
night, trying to enlighten the old man on the subject of the Indians,
in which he was acutely interested and about whom he possessed
a little information. Some priests dropped in to see their friend
the *padrone,* "then came the full storm and rattle of Italian conversation, with the true gesticulations, shrugs, exclamations, and
offerings of the snuff-box."

The next day they went on to Palestrina, where they examined
Pelasgian walls and the ruined Temple of Fortune, with its extraordinary mosaic. The *albergo* here was remarkable in that it was kept
by two sisters of about twenty, "both handsome as the sun." The

ladies were not displeased by their guests' admiration, and the company spent a pleasant evening before the fire, though Hunt, who knew no Italian, had to keep up his share of the conversation by sign talk. Parkman remarked: "My Italian was not much better; but the girls were as intelligent as they were handsome, and, I think, as virtuous."

Roused at six in the morning by their guide's call from outside the window—the poor fellow had no means of telling the time and took up his station in that position like a faithful dog, until his lords and masters should deign to rise—they said farewell to their handsome hostesses, and went on to Cara, where they found only a dirty hole of an *albergo*, "but no match for the inns of Sicily." Since it was a *trattoria* or restaurant, its public room was filled with a strange assortment of people in the evening: old crones, like living skeletons in the corner; unshaven countrymen, fat loungers from the town, shabby dandies in cloaks, and children and dogs playing together on the hearth. Two or three savage-looking *contadini* stood erect and motionless in the firelight, and now and then the very pretty girl who waited on the customers would stoop over the fire, "so as to show to the best advantage her classic features and the enormous silver pin in her hair." And to complete the strangeness of the picture, Hunt and Parkman sat before the fire until it was reduced to embers, telling college stories and recalling their common memories. The following day they went on to Velletri, where they abandoned their asses and their faithful guide Giuseppe, and hired a carriage in which to return to Rome.

On his first Sunday back in Rome Parkman went to St. Peter's in the afternoon for what he described as High Mass but undoubtedly was Benediction. He was impressed by the hundreds of candles which made the altar one blaze of light, and by the line of Swiss halberdiers drawn up before the shrine, "with their black hats and the bright blades of their weapons rising above the kneeling crowd. The responses sounded through the gigantic church like a moaning of wind." The next Tuesday he went back over the last leg of his trip to Albano, to consult the Passionists of Rocca di Papa about sojourning in their monastery. He had learned that the Passionists were "the strictest of the orders of monks—wear haircloth next the skin—lash their backs with 'disciplines' made of little iron chains, and mortify the flesh in various other similar ways. I had some desire to see the mode of life of these holy men. . . ." But his request was refused as impossible without the permission of the superior of the order at Rome, and Parkman remounted the jackass which had borne him up from the village, planning to return to Rome and obtain the needed permission immediately. But the diligence had already left Albano, and he was left stranded. Undismayed, he walked out to see the Lake of Nemi, in the midst of a glorious morning and the beauties of the early Italian spring. Returning to Albano, he dined at an inn called the Locanda del Americano. No one knew the reason for the name, so that Parkman was left to debate "whether some enterprising Yankee had once actually set up a *locanda* in Albano, or whether the name was given out of pure love for the Americans." He had observed that the Americans were almost universally liked in Italy, "probably as contrasting favorably with the surly and haughty English." In conversation with a priest, some time before, Parkman's revelation of his nationality had been greeted with a low bow and a *bravo Americano!*

Upon his return to Rome the next day, Parkman sought permission to stay at the Capuchins' convent, but this was refused. At the Passionists' monastery near the Colosseum, he was told to return in the evening for a final decision. This turned out to be in his favor, for St. Ives had interceded with the director of a retreat for laymen then being held there. Theodore Parker shook his head over the scheme, reminding Parkman that the Inquisition still had its prison in Rome and suggesting darkly that it might be much harder to get out of the monastery than to get in. Parkman found this solemn warning added spice to the adventure he had conceived and, falling in with Parker's mood, requested that, if he did not reappear by Palm Sunday, representations be made to the consul, Mr. Greene, who could "invoke the Bird of Freedom in my behalf."

When Parkman returned to the monastery and asked for St. Ives's friend, Padre Lucca, he was promptly admitted and conducted to the narrow whitewashed chamber which was to be his abode for the next few days.

The monk told me that when the bell rang, I must leave my hat, come out and join the others—and then, displaying some lives of the saints and other holy works on the table, he left me to my meditations. The room has a hideous bleeding image of Christ, a vessel of holy water, and a number of holy pictures—a bed—a chair—and a table. Also, hung against the wall was a "Notice to persons withdrawn from the world for spiritual exercises, to the end that they may derive all possible profit from their holy seclusion!" The "notice" prohibited going out of the chamber without necessity—prohibited also speaking at any time—or making any noise whatever—writing, also—and looking out of the window. It enjoined the saying of three Ave Marias, *at least,* at night —also to make your bed, etc.

The devil! thought I, here is an adventure!

Parkman promptly exercised his Calvinistic right of private judgment by writing the foregoing account in his notebook; then taking up a copy of Cooper's *Pioneers,* which he had prudently brought with him "as a reminder of fresh air," he drew the chair to the window and sat looking out on the Colosseum, the Forum, and the more distant towers of the city, while he reflected on his situation:

The secret of my getting in so easily was explained. There were about thirty Italians retired from the world, preparing for the General Confession—and even while I was coming to this conclusion, the bell clanged along the passage, and I went out to join the rest. After climbing several dark stairs, and descending others—pulling off their skullcaps to the great images of Christ on the landing places, they got into a little chapel, and, after kneeling to the altar, seated themselves. The shutters were closed, and the curtains drawn immediately after—there was a prayer with the responses—and then a sermon of an hour and a half long, in which the monk kept felicitating himself and his hearers that they were of the genuine church—little thinking that there was a black sheep among his flock. The sermon over, we filed off to our rooms. In five minutes the bell rang again for supper—then we marched off to a *conversazione* in another part of the building—where the injunction of silence was taken off. I told the directing priest that I was a Protestant—he seemed a little startled at first—then insinuated a hope that I might be reclaimed from my damnable heresy, and said that an American had been there before, who had been converted—meaning my acquaintance St. Ives. He then opened a little battery of arguments upon me—after which he left me, saying that a lay brother would make the rounds to wake us before sunrise.

Parkman soon wearied of gazing at Rome from the window of his cell, though the sun, which had just set, tinged the fountains, gardens, ruined arches, walls, columns, and the distant dome of St. Peter's with ruddy light. The books—a *Life of Blessed Paul of the Cross,* the founder of the Passionists, and a devotional work called *Sainte Industrie*—had no appeal for him. Somewhat disgruntled at his simple supper of tea, bread, and butter, he went to bed on the narrow unpainted cot, "with sheets clean though coarse."

About midnight he was awakened by strange, chanting voices mixed with his dreams. Noticing a light shining through a hole above his door, he looked into the corridor, which was "full of cowled monks, like so many black specters, carrying flickering candles, and stalking in solemn procession to a midnight service in the chapel." Parkman had congratulated himself that he was quartered among the monks, while the other laymen were lodged apart on an upper floor, but after being thus awakened he regarded himself as less fortunate than he had supposed. At daybreak the lay brother appeared and told him that in fifteen minutes he was to join the others at Mass. This was followed by prayers and a long sermon, and then the retreatants were summoned to coffee. Parkman took only a glass of water, on account of his neuralgia, and judged that he was getting credit for mortifying the flesh, since he was stared at by some of his companions. Actually a report of his heresy had got abroad, and made him the center of curious attention. Several young Italians expressed sympathy for his unhappy condition, and one of them said that he would pray for his conversion. Parkman realized that he spoke in genuine kindness, and thanked him.

There was an hour's repose allowed—after which came another sermon in the chapel. This over, a bell rang for dinner—which was at eleven in the morning. The hall was on the lower floor—very long, high, and dark—with panels of oak—and ugly pictures on the walls—narrow oaken tables set all round the sides of the place. The monks were all there, in their black robes, with the emblem of their order on the breast. They had thin, scowling faces, as well they might, for their discipline is tremendously strict. Before each was placed an earthen bottle of wine, and a piece of bread, on the bare board. Each drew a cup, a knife, fork, and wooden spoon from a drawer under the table—the attendant lay brothers placed a bowl of singular-looking soup before each, and they ate in lugubrious silence. The superior of the order sat at the upper end of the hall—a large and powerful man, who looked sterner, if possible, than his inferiors. We who sat at another table were differently served—with rice, eggs, fish, and fruit. No one spoke, but, from a pulpit above, a monk read at the top of his lungs from a book of religious precepts, in that peculiar drawling tone which the Catholics employ in their exercises. There was, apparently, little fructification in the minds of his hearers. The monks ate and scowled—the laymen ate and smiled at each other, exchanging looks of meaning, though not a word passed between them. There were among them men of every age and of various conditions—from the field laborer to the gentleman of good birth. The meal concluded with a prayer, and the growling responses of the Passionists—who then filed off through the galleries to their dens, looking like the living originals of the black pictures that hung along the whitewashed walls.

Parkman had hardly got back to his chamber and begun to refresh himself with the *Pioneers,* when he was besieged by one of his hosts:

A monk has just been here, trying to convert me, but was not so good a hand at argument, or sophistry, as the Jesuits. I told him that he could do nothing with me, but he persisted, clapping his hand on my knee and exclaiming: "Ah! *figlio,* you will be a good Catholic, no doubt." There was a queer sort of joviality about him. He kept offering me his snuff-box, and when he thought he had made a good hit in argument, he would wink at me with a most comical expression, as if to say: "You see, you can't come round me with your heresy." He gave over at the ringing of a bell which summoned us to new readings and lecturings in the chapel, after which we were turned out into the garden of the convent, where we lounged along walks shaded with olives and oleanders. Padre Lucca, the directing priest, talked over matters of faith with me. He was an exception to the rest of the establishment—plump and well fed with a double chin like a bullfrog, and a most contented and good-humored countenance. As we passed the groups of Italians they took their hats off and kissed his hand reverently, and then immediately began to joke and laugh with him as if he were a familiar friend—as I suppose he was, as I have observed that many of the priests are to their parishioners.

One night in a monastery had given Parkman less of a passion for strict asceticism and more sympathy for the more human type of ecclesiastic, despite his earlier railings at the Benedictine convents he had seen in Sicily. And he was struck by the difference between the Catholic and the Puritan religious spirit:

There is nothing gloomy or morose in the religion of these Italians here, no camp-meeting long faces. They talk and laugh gaily in the intervals allowed them for conversation, but when the occasion calls it forth they speak of religion with an earnestness, as well as a cheerfulness, that shows that it has a hold on their hearts.

The next morning the devotion of the Way of the Cross was performed, and Parkman recognized it as the ceremony which he had witnessed in the Colosseum without knowing what it was. This exercise seemed to him idolatrous or in some other way objectionable, for he sat in his place in the chapel and declined to take part in it, thus incurring a mild rebuke from Padre Lucca. On his way back to his room, he was asked by one of the monks to come into his cell. Parkman gives an account of this visit in the *Harper's* article:

My host, the hollow-eyed monk, and his den needed nothing but a skull on the table to be artistically perfect. He was in grim and ghastly earnest, with no sign of the jocoseness shown by my lively visitor of the day before. The depth of my heresy seemed to fill him with horror, and when I told him that in the city of my birth there were many who did not even believe in the Holy Trinity, he rolled up his eyes in their discolored sockets, and stretched his long skinny neck out of his cowl, "like a turtle," says my diary, "basking on a stone in June." "Such a city as that," he observed, "must give the greatest pleasure to the devil." He had no skill in making proselytes, and his incoherent talk was very different from the heavy batteries of learning and logic which the English Jesuit Father Glover had before turned on me. My imperfect knowledge of Italian greatly tried him, till at length a happy thought came to his relief. He rose, opened a drawer, in his table, and after fumbling among the contents for some time, produced a small brass medal, equal in intrinsic value to about half a cent. On further search in the same receptacle he found a red string, which he passed through a hole in the medal, and, after knotting it securely, gave it to me. The medal was stamped with an image of the Virgin.

This medal he begged me to wear round my neck, and to repeat two or three Ave Marias now and then. It was by this means, he said, that Ratisbon the Jew was converted not long since; who, though he wore the medal and repeated the Aves merely to get rid of the importunities of a Catholic friend, yet nevertheless was favored with a miraculous vision of the Virgin; whereupon he fell on his knees, and was joined to the number of the faithful. I told the monk that I would wear the medal if he wished me to, but should not repeat the Aves. So I have it now round my neck, greatly to his satisfaction. Miracles, say all the Catholics here, happen frequently nowadays. The other day a man was raised to life, who had just died in consumption—and now is walking the streets in complete health!

Parkman missed the atmosphere of theological controversy, so typical of Puritan Boston, in the exercises of this retreat, in which he participated along with the Italians who were preparing to fulfill their Easter Duty and cultivating their religious sentiments undistracted by contact with the world. The retreat seemed to him too much a matter of rote and form:

> Their "exercises" are characteristic of the Church. The forms of prayer are all written down—they read—repeat—and sing; very little time is allowed them for private examinations and meditations, and even in these they are directed by a printed card hung in each of the rooms and containing a list of the subjects on which they ought to examine themselves—together with a form of contrition to be repeated by them. The sermons and readings are full of pictures of Christ's sufferings, exhortations to virtue, etc., but contain not a syllable of doctrine. One of the first in the printed list of questions which the self-examiner is to ask himself is— "Have I ever dared to inquire into the mysteries of the Faith?"

Aside from the fact that Parkman clearly did not understand the special meaning of the word "mystery" in this usage, it is clear that the sticking point in Catholicism, as far as he was concerned, was its insistence on corporate rather than individual religious practice, on authority arising from the corporate body of the Church rather than on the private judgment of the individual, no matter how enlightened. And his vast reticence, a Puritan heritage along with his intellectual pride, was opposed to public worship, to "making a fool of himself" by bowing and scraping and crossing himself.

That evening, his last in the monastery, he sat alone in his chamber, studying one of the books which had been left there for his instruction.

> It was the *Life of Blessed Paul of the Cross* whose tomb was somewhere in the building. After turning page after page of monotonous austerities and miracles, I came upon a chapter which recounted at great length the abhorrence borne by the venerable founder of the Passionists against all the daughters of Eve, as being the most killing bait with which Satan angles for the souls of men. I read how Blessed Paul was often heard to say: "I would rather my eyes were torn from their sockets than

fixed upon a woman"; how, when discoursing with one of the dangerous sex on matters pertaining to her soul, he would always, even were she old and ugly, insist that the door should stand wide open; and how, even meeting in the street a siren of enticing eye, he bent his looks on the ground, crossed himself, and passed over to the other side. As I perused these inspiring histories I felt a hand laid lightly on my shoulder, and heard in my ear the words, "*Bravo, mio figlio, bravissimo!*" It was Padre Lucca, who, the door being ajar, had stepped silently in to see what I was about, and seemed much pleased at the edifying nature of my employment.

The next day was Palm Sunday, the day which Parkman had set for his departure from the monastery. Though he had worn the medal for a day and a night, he had had "no vision of the Virgin— at least of Santissima María." His restlessness could brook the monastic life no longer and he was eager to get into the world once more, particularly since the impressive ceremonies of Holy Week were to be seen. So he took leave of Padre Lucca, who "was unfeignedly sorry to have me go with unimpaired prospects of damnation. He said he still had hopes of me, and, taking the kindest leave of me, gave me a book of Catholic devotions, which I shall certainly keep in remembrance of a very excellent man." Parkman made a little speech, which he had prepared beforehand, aware of his linguistic imperfection: "*Mio padre,* if I am in error, it is my fault only. It is not in my power to make any return to you or your brethren for the kindness you have shown me, but I hope I may be permitted to offer a trifling acknowledgment to the patron saint of this house." So with the gift of a few silver scudi, Parkman bade farewell to the Passionists and stepped out into the world once more, "rather glad to be free of the gloomy galleries and cells— which nevertheless contain so much to be admired." He went to Mass at St. Peter's, "where thousands of soldiers stood forming a hollow square, where a procession of bishops, cardinals, and all the high dignitaries of the Church, were moving round in procession with palm branches in their hands. The Pope was in the midst, seated on a species of canopied throne, borne on the shoulders of men, with his Swiss Guard about him, one of whom carried a sword whose blade—six feet long—represented flames of fire." Then he returned to the Via Babuino to report to Theodore Parker, who showed no curiosity whatever about his friend's experience and merely remarked: "Lucky you are an American heretic and not an Italian one, or you might not have come off so easily." And Parkman himself, in the excitement of the *Santissima Settima,* with its gorgeous ceremonials and motley crowds, forgot for the time being his experience of the monastic life.

On Wednesday he heard the *Tenebrae* sung in the Capella del Coro at St. Peter's; on Thursday he attended High Mass in the Sistine Chapel, and then the procession of the Host to the Altar of Repose in the Pauline Chapel.

> The cursing of the Jews, heretics, etc., and the blessing of the people was the next ceremony. The Pope was borne as before on the shoulders of men to the window of the Loggia in front of the church—a cardinal came forward and damned us all in a loud voice, the people taking off their hats, and most of the heretics imitating them, in ignorance of the compliment they were receiving. There were several regiments of the Pope's army drawn up in a hollow square, in the middle of the Piazza, which was thronged with an endless multitude. Some of them had brought bags of seeds and other things, which they held over their heads to receive the benefit of the Pope's blessing. His Holiness stretched his arms toward them, and immediately the bells of the city rang by a signal, cannon fired, and then the crowd rushed at full speed up the steps, and pushed fighting, scrambling, and laughing through the doors to see the Pope wash the feet of thirteen pilgrims, in imitation of the humbleness of Christ.

Parkman had a long wait for this ceremony before the door of the Loggia, in the midst of a turbulent crowd of screaming and fainting women and cursing men, who swayed to and fro, unable to stir an inch at their own will. Then a swelling roar was heard from the crowd in the courts and staircase below, and the Swiss guards struck the butt of their halberds on the floor to impose silence:

At length the pilgrims (they were no pilgrims, but priests, intended to represent the apostles), dressed in white, filed in and took their stand before the table. Some looked embarrassed, some tried to keep from laughing, and others coolly surveyed the crowd. The Pope came in surrounded by cardinals and prelates, to make an exhibition of his humbleness. He held a gold basin to each of the pilgrims, who pretended to wash his hands in it. They then took their seats. A cardinal kneeled and presented a dish to the Pope, who passed it to a pilgrim, who rose and received it, bowing with the profoundest reverence. When all were served, they began to eat, but apparently with no great relish. The Pope walked to and fro, with folded hands, looking as meek as a drowned kitten. He afterwards poured out a glass of wine apiece for the pilgrims, and then left them. The Italians seemed to regard the affair as an amusement; indeed one who stood by me said: "They expect us to feel reverence—it is impossible."

The soldiers marched to their quarters with reversed arms, in token of mourning for the death of Christ—to my thinking, one of the richest ceremonies of the day.

For all Parkman's lack of enthusiasm for this ceremony, he was sufficiently impressed by it to become thoroughly annoyed at an Englishman who exclaimed: "How long does this damned Pope expect us to stand here waiting for him?":

A priest who spoke English reminded him that since he had come to Rome, it was hoped that he would conform to the usages, or at least refrain from insulting the feelings of those around. The Englishman answered by an insolent stare; then, turning his back, he said: "The English *own* Rome!"

And this was nearly true, for of the forty thousand strangers then supposed to be in Rome, the English were the most numerous, "esteemed and beloved as usual" as Parkman ironically noted.

To him the famous Holy Week ceremonies would not have been worth seeing, were it not for the great crowds they drew together.

But he was impressed despite himself, and his last notes on Rome dealt with the celebrations on Easter and Easter Monday:

> On Easter Sunday the Pope blessed a huge army assembled in front of the church: for the second time. That night St. Peter's was illuminated by myriads of candles, disposed over its whole front, to the very top of the cross. It was a kind of phosphorescent light—faint and beautiful. At eight o'clock all changed in a moment. Bright fires kindled in a moment over all the church and the colonnade around the Piazza. St. Peter's was all at once a glare of light, and cast strong shadows among the dense crowd in front. It was a sight well worth all the rest of Holy Week.
>
> On Monday there was an exhibition of fireworks at the castle of St. Angelo, which in grandeur and magnificence more resembled an eruption of Mt. Etna than any artificial illumination I ever saw. This was the end of Holy Week.

And this, too, was the end of Parkman's stay in Rome, for on the following day he took the diligence for Florence. He left the Eternal City "with much regret and a hope to return." That hope was never fulfilled.

This firsthand acquaintance with Catholic life, coming as it did after several months of travel in Catholic countries and at a period when Parkman was rebelling against the Puritan tradition in which he had been bred, was invaluable preparation for the work he planned to do. Catholicism was one of the main forces behind the French colonial effort, and it would have been quite impossible to write the history of the French in North America without some understanding of their religion. Parkman could have fulfilled his task more adequately if he had been able to escape from his innate dislike for organized religion and ecclesiastics; but these youthful experiences did much to relieve him of the intense anti-Catholic prejudice which was part of his heritage as a Boston Puritan. Unfortunately the same chance that gave him a Catholic cousin brought him Dr. Theodore Parker as a companion in Rome; one influence largely canceled out the other, and Parkman did not attain as great an understanding of Catholicism under these circumstances as he might otherwise have done.

7: A Romantic on the Grand Tour

*Give me Lake George and the smell of
the pine and fir!*
F.P., JOURNAL, 1844

AFTER two days and nights in the diligence, traveling with a
young American named Marquand, Parkman reached Florence on April 10, 1844. During the course of the journey he had
become friendly with "a manly and soldier-like young Irish gentleman," Mr. William English of Castlerock, Dublin, and his sister.
Then there was an old Frenchman and his lady, who were convoy-
ing two young women, one of whom was "an English girl, very
spirited and intelligent, and a Catholic—but a few years too old to
make converts." The journey seems to have been pleasant enough
in such good company.

The first thing about Florence that struck Parkman was the
Gothic air which characterized the Duomo and the dark palaces
of the Piazza del Granduca. The very stones seemed to speak to
him of the Middle Ages and of the Medici. He found the collections
of the Pitti Palace and of the Galleria Reale far superior to those
of Rome as far as pictures went, but could admire only the equestrian statue of Cosimo I and the Venus de Medici among the sculpture of the city. He summed up his impressions briefly:

> A quiet and beautiful place—full of ancient palaces and churches
> —the Arno dividing it in the middle, with four noble stone
> bridges thrown across, and a perspective of mountains and woods
> beyond the lines of fine buildings, both up and down the stream.
> No beggars in the streets—the people civil and good-natured.

On Sunday night there was a public lottery in the Piazza, in celebration of the marriage of the grand duke's daughter to Leopold
of Bavaria, which Parkman went to see in the Duomo on the following day, in the company of his friend Mr. Payson, the American
consul at Messina, who had just arrived in Florence:

The church was illuminated and crowded with the scum of
Florence—we got wedged in the dirtiest part of it. Mr. P., who
is six feet and a quarter high, saw the top of the bride's headdress.
I saw nothing but a fat hog of a priest, who stood in his regi-
mentals just within the line of soldiers before me. Before it was
over I got out. The square in front was full. I had scarce got into
a breathing place when there was the rush of a signal rocket from
the dome of the church; then a tremendous cannonading in the
distance; then a stunning crash of musketry from two regiments
drawn up close by, followed by a general start and squall from
the women. I saw afterwards the bride and bridegroom, as they
left the church in their splendid carriage, covered with gilding
and liveried servants, and drawn by six noble horses.

Another day he visited the studio of the sculptor Powers, "a noble-
looking fellow and a wonderful artist." He had a glance at everything to be seen in Florence, and found himself falling under the
city's spell and wishing that he might remain there for months. He
liked the Florentines, too, finding them "as attentive and obliging
as the rest of the Italians—and the town is not infested with cice-
rones and other beggars." He was piqued by a handsome flower
girl, "with a most inimitable expression of arch impudence," who
fastened a large bunch of flowers in his buttonhole before he knew
what was up, laughed, and then ran off to do the same for someone else. "Her plan is to give flowers to all the strangers she can
find, and trust to their generosity for her pay at some future day.
She is sure to get twice the value of her flowers—at least if others
treat her as well as I did." That Wednesday he had to leave Florence, though reluctantly. He said farewell to Mr. and Mrs. Payson,
"of whose usual kindness to strangers I have certainly had my
share," and, after fighting his way through the funeral of the Tuscan
prime minister, got to the diligence office, where he took a place
for Bologna.

By now Parkman had made up his mind to press on to Paris and
to renounce his proposed tour of Granada, "thanks to the cursed
injury that brought me to Europe; for as I find no improvement, I
judge it best to see what a French doctor can do for me instead of

running about Spain." Though he does not mention it here, it is clear that he was also suffering from another kind of heart trouble: when he got among the Alps he was constantly reminded of well-known and beloved mountains at home in New England, and he was evidently lonely. His uncle lived in Paris, and the prospect of familiar company was no doubt another reason for hurrying through northern Italy and Switzerland. And then his time was running short, for he had to return in June in order to get his degree at Harvard in August, and much sightseeing still lay ahead of him if he was to accomplish the grand tour with due regard for tradition.

After a day and a night in the diligence, he reached Bologna, "a strange-looking place." He missed the rush, noise, gaiety, and endless variety of costume which had appealed to him at Naples and Rome; these northern Italians were grave, sober folk, who moved solemnly about their business through streets that seemed almost deserted after the teeming gutters of the southern cities. He liked the architecture, particularly the colonnaded porticoes above the sidewalks and the church of St. Petronica, with its lofty, slender columns and its splendid stained glass. Again he was conscious of the Gothic air which clung to the place and made him think of feudal times.

The next day he went on through Modena, meeting the duke in his carriage on the road and discovering an Italian translation of *The Last of the Mohicans* in the city itself. He was not surprised by this discovery, for he had come across translations of Cooper's works everywhere in Italy and Sicily. Europe, still under the influence of romanticism, was fascinated by the "noble savage." From Modena he went on to Parma, where he found the ducal gardens "filled with the song of birds, and cooled and shaded by fountains and high trees,—a most agreeable contrast to the dirt and hubbub of the city." They stopped here only for dinner, and at ten that night the diligence lumbered off for Piacenza, where they halted for breakfast. Here Parkman was struck again by the difference between the north and south: "the people looked as grave and solemn as the brick fronts of the palaces and churches." The market was just beginning to hum, and he noticed piles of live hens, "tied neck and heels as you see them in Canada." The farmers, in their breeks and broad hats, "with staffs in their hands and dickeys standing up erect, like diminutive Englishmen," stood about waiting for customers:

> High above this motley swarm of helpless humanity rose the statue of some great lord of the Farnese family, seated on horseback, holding his truncheon of command, as if at the head of an army; and looking as if one act of his single will or one movement of his armed hand would be enough to annihilate the whole swarm of poor devils below him.

Then crossing the Po on a bridge of boats, he entered Lombardy and the realm of the black double-headed Austrian eagle, whose minions detained them for an hour and a half, "to be searched, and to pay the fellows for doing it." Then the diligence went on through beautiful and fertile country, by way of Napoleon's battleground of Lodi, until it entered Milan at night, with its passengers well covered with dust.

The next day was Sunday, and Parkman found a quiet city, with a crowd of black-veiled women, like a flight of swallows, issuing from the cathedral, which he liked quite as well as St. Peter's and deemed worthy of Rome; gentlemen sauntering about listlessly or taking their coffee at sidewalk cafés; and porters and *contadini* sitting idle at the edge of the sidewalk. This city seemed well enough to him, but he still missed the southern liveliness, and he made a note that the girls of Milan were round and rich of face and figure, but "of the fiery black eye of Rome I have seen nothing; their eyes are blue and soft, and have rather a drowsy meek expression, and they *look* excessively modest." The Milan gentleman's way of life appealed to him as very agreeable:

> There is no place where you can be more independent than in one of these cities—when you are hungry there is always a restaurant and a dinner at a moment's notice—when you are thirsty there is always a café at hand. If you are sleepy, your room awaits you—a dozen sneaking waiters are ready at your bidding, and glide about like shadows to do what you may require, in hope of your shilling when you go away. But give me Ethan Crawford,

or even Tom, in place of the whole race of waiters and *garçons*. I would ask their pardon for putting them in the same sentence, if they were here.

He saw Leonardo's *Last Supper*, but found it "miserably injured, or rather destroyed by the dampness of three centuries and a half," and took more pleasure in the concierge's tales of Lodi and Marengo, where he had served as a sergeant. Napoleon had left his mark on the city, in the form of an amphitheater and a triumphal arch:

> I went to the top of the arch, and looking to the north saw what seemed light streaks of cloud, high in the air. As I looked at them, the idea crossed me, possibly they may be the Alps themselves! Yet I thought it very unlikely they could be seen on a sultry and hazy day like this, at such a distance. I watched them for a long time—they did not change position or figure, yet to my eye— not unpracticed in observing mountains—they looked more and more like thin clouds. I inquired of a man what they were—they were in fact the Alps! He pointed out the different peaks, and the situation of the various passes. The Splügen, the highest and wildest of all, and which I mean to pass, lay hidden in black piles of clouds that rose between it and the inferior mountains around the Lake of Como.
>
> This Triumphal Arch was designed by Napoleon as the termination of his road of the Simplon—curse him and his roads: he should have left the Alps alone. I will steer clear of him.

A funeral in the cathedral, with a procession of priests, laymen, women, and children with enormous wax candles in hand, and the noble chapel of the left transept hung with black for the occasion, somehow set off in Parkman an explosion of his congenital anticlericalism. The passage, coming as it does out of a clear sky, is almost inexplicable: it may have been the result of a reaction against his Roman mood, induced by the sight of mountains which brought back his old state of mind:

> The priests seemed not fairly awake—one fat bullfrog of a fellow would growl out of his throat his portion of the holy psalmody,

interrupting himself in some interesting conversation with his neighbor, and resuming it again as soon as the religious office was performed. Another would gape and yawn in the midst of his musical performances—another would walk about looking at the people, or the coffin, or the kneeling women, singing meanwhile with the most complete indifference and content on his fat countenance. I could imagine the subject of their conversation, as they walked out in a double file, leaving the coffin to the care of the proper officials, after they had grunted a concluding anthem over it. "Well! We've fixed this fellow's soul for him. It was a nasty job; but it's over now. Come! Won't you take something to drink?"

I used to like priests, and take my hat off and make a low bow, half in sport and half in earnest, whenever I met them—but I have got to despise the fellows. Yet I have met admirable men among them; and have always been treated by them with the utmost civility and attention.

It is only just to add, as Parkman did, that civility is almost universal among the Italians, and also, though Parkman did not consciously observe it, that the Latin attitude toward death is greatly different from the Puritan. In those lands death is festive, almost gay, and greeted with public pomp and circumstance; for it sets the soul free from the perils of a sorrowful world; in New England, where a more inhuman theology reigns and the elect are few and the world deemed good, it is greeted with sour face and fear-clutched heart and unnatural grief.

Parkman met young Marquand in a picture gallery, and, made homesick by the sight of mountains, "was not sorry to find an acquaintance and countryman where I supposed I was alone." They went up on the cathedral roof together, and saw all Milan laid out before them "like the skinned specimens of anatomy in the Florentine museum." Parkman was vastly impressed by the sixty-four hundred statues which adorned the sides of the church, the countless marble spires, and fruit and flowers carved everywhere in the white marble of the great structure. From the roof they descended to the crypt, to see the tomb of Milan's patron, St. Carlo Borromeo, reputed to be the richest in the world. It was of pure rock crystal from the Alps, set in silver and adorned with sixty images of solid silver:

> The saint lies embalmed within, as plainly visible as if nothing intervened—clothed in his pontificals, with golden images—the votive offerings of princes—crucifixes of emeralds, and other splendid ornaments arranged about his body—*à la* Indian. The chapel is completely encased in silver, wrought to represent the events of the saint's life.

But time had become a valuable commodity to Parkman, and with a final glance at the cathedral, "which, like St. Peter's, improves on acquaintance—but not to the same degree," he set off the next morning for Lake Como, on whose banks he recorded his last impressions of Milan in his journal, including a solemn detailed comparison of St. Peter's and the Duomo. But his eyes were already at work observing new scenes:

> I have seen nothing at home or abroad more beautiful than this lake. It reminds me of Lake George—the same extent, the same figure, the same crystal purity of waters, the same wild and beautiful mountains on either side. But the comparison will not go farther. Here are a hundred palaces and villages scattered along the water's edge and up the declivities. There is none of that shaggy untamed aspect in the mountains—no piles of rocks, grown over with stunted bushes, or half-decayed logs fallen along the shore. There are none of those little islands, covered with rough and moss-grown pine trees, which give a certain savage character to the beauties of Lake George. All here is like a finished picture: even the wildest rocks seem softened in the air of Italy. Give me Lake George and the smell of the pine and fir! But now I am at the foot of the Splügen, and the Alps all around, covered with snow, their sharp summits just losing the red tinge of the evening. Not long since the lake was all in a glow; but now it is like a sheet of lead, and the western mountains have become

dark as night. The path I have chosen is by far the sublimest and most savage of all; and it is little frequented. Tomorrow I shall be where I have wished to be for years.

But after all the Splügen disappointed Parkman: "scarce any part of it was superior to the Notch of the White Mountains." It took sixteen hours to cross the pass from Colico on Lake Como to Andeer, a little village in the midst of the mountains. No carriage could travel through the glaciers and everlasting snows near the summit, so passengers and luggage were drawn over this stretch on small sleds, pulled by the carriage horses. "The snow was fifteen or twenty feet deep in some places, and the horses waded and plunged through it as they might." But nothing more exciting than the overturning of the baggage sled occurred, and Parkman noted with clear disappointment that, "as for the danger of avalanches, no one has been hurt by them these five years." The view was desolate and grand, one expanse of glistening white covering everything except the pinnacles at the summit and the ragged forests of black pine that straggled up the lower slopes. But the road itself was so enormously high that the traveler was brought too near the peaks to appreciate fully their magnitude.

His disappointment vanished as soon as he had traversed the pass. Beyond, in the bottom of a valley, lay the village of Splügen, a decided contrast to the Italian villages so familiar by now to Parkman. And it seemed like home to emerge from forests of spruce and fir which lined the steep gorge in which the road ran, and find a sawmill and piles of lumber along the banks of a river, though the river was the Rhine. Bridge and houses were of wood, as in New England, although their projecting eaves gave a far more picturesque effect than that of a Yankee mountain village. In two hours more he reached Andeer, "a place not less wildly situated, and reached by a road winding through a succession of most savage ravines close by the Rhine, which foams and roars among the rocks and fir trees like an imprisoned wild beast." Here Parkman determined to remain several days, while he explored this country which appealed to him so much. His bad heart seems to have been forgotten until it obtruded itself:

Nothing could surpass the utter savageness of the scenery that you find by tracing up some of the little streams that pour down on all sides to join the Rhine—not a trace of human hand—it is as wild as the back-forests at home. The mountains, too, have the same aspect. There is one valley where a large stream comes down to join the main river, a mile from Andeer. Last night I followed it for a mile or two, back into the mountains—not Cooper himself could do it justice. The river was a hundred feet below in a ravine, where it lashed from side to side and bounded sometimes in a fall of fifty or sixty feet—the green headlong water, the white foam, and the spray just visible through the boughs of the distorted pines that leaned over the abyss. There was in one place a peasant's hut of logs, but it seemed only to increase the sublime effect of the wilderness. I got down to the bed of the river, and leaped out to some rocks near the center. It was nearly dark—long after sunset. What with the deafening thunder of the stream—the gloom that began to involve the shaggy branches of the yellow pines that leaned nearly across the gulf, and the stiff and upright spruces that sprang from every crevice of the rock—there was something almost appalling in the place. Above the tops of the trees rose mountains, like ours of New England, covered with fir trees wherever one could cling in the crevices of the steep cliffs. And in another direction the more distant peaks were white with snow, which retained its glistening brightness long after the moon had begun to cast a shadow.

Here was a change, with a vengeance, from the Italian beauties of the Lake of Como! I sat on a rock, fancying myself again in the American woods with an Indian companion—but as I rose to go away the hellish beating of my heart warned me that no more such expeditions were in store for me—for the present, at least—but if I do not sleep by the campfire again, it shall be no fault of mine.

He was able to fulfill this vow by the most rigorous of all his wilderness expeditions, the Oregon Trail trip, just two years later. He was not easily balked of his desires.

Parkman passed the following day in the valley of Ferrara, "one of the wildest and loneliest in the Alps, and accessible only by a bad footpath"—this despite his unpleasant reminder of heart trouble the day before. His description of the place is notable:

> The river comes down at the bottom, which the sun scarcely ever touches. The mountains rise on each side many thousand feet, broken into crags and precipices, with streams falling down them in all directions, scattering into white mists before they reach the bottom. The spruce trees are sprinkled all over the cliffs, wherever there is a crevice to cling in; some gigantic pines stoop across the river, and fairly seem to quiver with the tremendous roar of the water. All is solitary and still as death except the noise of the river; yet you cannot sit on one of those rocks and watch the green and furious water, glancing between the trunks and branches below, without fancying that you hear sounds and voices about you. I never knew a place so haunted by the "those airy tongues that syllable men's names."

He returned to Andeer, which he liked for reminding him so much of home, with its wooden barns and large square white houses and its little Calvinist meeting house, "something like one of ours," standing on a rise in the midst of the village. He noticed the women at work in the fields, spreading manure with wooden forks, and wrote: "Would to Heaven our women did the same, if it could make them as strong and hardy." There was one drawback to this mountain paradise: it was a German canton and Parkman lacked any means of communication with the ruddy-cheeked mountain girl who had charge of the inn in the landlord's absence. He tried Italian, but she understood not a word; then they entertained each other with alternate bursts of English and German:

> Sometimes a bright gleam would shoot across her face, as a word similar to one of her own language struck her ear. This suggested an expedient; so I began to pronounce the English names of all the things I wanted, using all the synonyms I could think of. I thus managed to make out a very good meal, though the items

of it were decided by the accidental coincidence of their names with the Swiss.

The landlord, upon his return, proved capable of speaking Italian, and this cumbersome method of ordering meals by lingual resemblances could be discarded. During his second day at Andeer, Parkman wandered in the Via Mala, "a place by nature more savagely wild than the valley of Ferrara; but not so solitary, as it is the sole outlet by which Andeer and its neighboring villages communicate with the rest of the world." It is here that the Rhine escapes from the Alps, forcing its way through a ravine about a foot wide and immensely deep, with the opposing cliffs as bare and raw as if they had been split apart by a wedge. The road follows the water course, crossing and recrossing the bed of the stream, which lies like a narrow white ribbon far below. Tributary torrents pour down from the cliffs, turning to mist as they fall and forming a rainbow when the sun strikes them.

Regretfully Parkman turned his back on the high Alps and descended through the valleys of the Grisons, where the scenery was no less magnificent, though of a different character. At Coire he found his first German inn, and was much taken with the ease, good nature, and spirit of equality which he found there. Then he went on to Zurich by way of Lake Wallen, which he traversed on a steamboat whose puffings were hoarsely echoed from the abrupt precipices along the shores. It was a dark and cloudy day, and the mountain tops were hidden in clouds, but by the time they reached the foot of the lake the weather cleared, and Parkman took one last long look at the mountains and mourned that he was to see no more of the Alps. He found an Italian softness in the scenery that now unfolded itself as he passed through this highly cultivated and fruitful region. Zurich seemed to him a beautiful town: "clean and neat, with all that air of newness and fresh paint that Dickens attributed to Boston." It strongly reminded him of home: "the same intermingling of white houses with blossoming apple and pear trees —the same grass plots and wooden fences—nay, at intervals the same old dingy barns of rough boards." The German talent for *Gemütlichkeit* appealed strongly to Parkman, and he marveled as he watched his fellow-travelers light their pipes, stretch out their legs and unbutton their coats, and make themselves thoroughly at ease: "Here was none of the painful dignity which an Englishman thinks it incumbent upon him to assume throughout his travels—no kneepans aching with the strain of tight-strapped pantaloons—no neck half severed by the remorseless edge of a starched dickey." And the republican spirit was evident and pleasing to Parkman, after the official-ridden Austrian states he had passed through. Through an error his passport had been visaed for Zurich alone, instead of for Zurich and Basel, but it was not even called for on the journey. In the diligence he fell into conversation with a polyglot German gentleman eager to try his English, "so that I enjoyed the novelty of a companion." At the diligence office in Basel he got into difficulties until this fellow-traveler offered his services as interpreter, but at the palatial Hotel of the Three Kings he found a waiter who spoke a little English. He liked Basel:

> Here in Basel you find none of the palaces and none of the dirt of an Italian city. No soldiers, except those of the garrison of the citadel and of the gendarmerie; no beggars; no spies in the cafés; no vexatious questionings of suspicious officials; no anxious scrutiny into passports or rummagings of baggage. The people walk about the quiet streets with solemnity on their faces and pipes in their mouths. Fat ruddy female faces are seen at all the windows of the steep-roofed houses, where an arrangement of mirrors enables them to see what passes below, without seeming to be on the watch.

He had seen similar devices before, for such was the favorite instrument of the Yankee social inquisition.

It was Sunday, and Parkman attended the service in the large square meeting house, conducted by a parson "in all the dignity of Geneva bands and gown." He also visited the Catholic church and became aware of a difference:

> The Catholic Church holds its head scarce so high as at Rome. I saw the people coming out from Mass—a stream of ugly, contented, and healthy visages. You did not see, as at Rome, a poor

devil in rags, bursting with diseases and a walking menagerie of fleas, kneeling before an altar that shines with massive gold and silver, and dipping his shriveled fingers into a font of holy water carved most exquisitely out of the richest marbles. The rough beams of this church were plainly visible—two dingy candlesticks and some bunches of flowers were the richest decorations of the altar—and the holy water was contained in a common copper kettle. But the people were strong, ruddy, and clean: the women looked like Amazons (though not amazonian in the etymological sense).

That evening he saw the burghers of Basel walking in the fields outside the town, watching the rifle matches, or regaling themselves with bread and cheese.

Much as he liked Basel, he felt obliged to press on the following day, so he took the train to Strasbourg, which he found uninteresting, and then traveled by diligence again to Paris. At first sight the French capital seemed an ocean of housetops, and he was impressed that it took an hour to reach the diligence office once they had passed the city gate. As soon as he was free he went to the Tuileries, the Palais Royal, the Boulevard des Italiens, and the Place Vendôme. It did not take him long to decide that this was the Athens of modern Europe, "let envious Englishmen sneer as they will." His uncle was out when he called, and Parkman was out when his uncle repaid the visit. But his resourceful relative left a note, in true Parisian fashion, "directing me to be at a celebrated café at a certain time where he was to be distinguished by a white handkerchief in his hand." The meeting was successful and uncle and nephew went off to a ball on the Champs-Elysées. For the following fortnight Parkman was so caught up in sightseeing and amusements that he completely neglected his journal until, while waiting at Boulogne for the Channel boat, he was able to recall his experiences:

I have been a fortnight in Paris, and seen it as well as it can be seen in a fortnight. Under peculiarly favorable circumstances, too, for it was the great season of balls and gaieties, and I had a guide, moreover, who knows Paris from top to bottom—within and without. I like to see a thing done thoroughly. If a man has a mind to make a fool or a vagabond of himself, he can do it admirably in Paris; whereof I have seen many instances. If a man has a mind to amuse himself, there is no place like it on earth: diversions of every character, form, and degree waiting for him at every step: let him taste them—then get into the diligence and ride away—or stay and go to the devil. You find there the same amusements variously seasoned to suit different tastes; if you have a fancy for the poetic and the romantic, you can have that; but if you want to make an absolute beast of yourself, without varnish or gilding, it can be done to most admirable perfection.

There is some evidence that Parkman enjoyed himself a bit too thoroughly in Paris, for he records that the white cliffs of Dover left him unmoved, "being afflicted with a colic." He also was so tired that he slept through the boat's arrival at Folkestone and had to be aroused a half hour later by the captain, after all the other passengers had left the ship. Despite this "most shameful fashion" of approaching England, he was glad to be in the "mother country." The next day, he rode up to London on the railroad:

A tremendous wind was blowing with an occasional puff of sleet and fine rain, sending a chill into our very bones. The passengers' noses turned blue—nobody spoke a word—two or three pulled out respirators from their pockets, and all crouched down together in the open cars and drew cloaks and shawls close about them. Our northeasters may do their worst; they cannot match that wind.

So thoroughly had Parkman perused Dickens that he thought he had been in London before, for there, in flesh and blood, were all the characters that figure in *Pickwick:*

Every species of Cockney was abroad in the dark and dingy-looking streets, all walking with their heads stuck forward, their noses turned up, their chins pointing down, their knee joints shaking as they shuffled along with a gait perfectly ludicrous, but indescribable. The hackney coachmen and cabmen, with their peculiar phraseology, the walking advertisements in the shape of a boy completely hidden between two placards, and a hundred others seemed so many incarnations of Dickens's characters. A strange contrast to Paris!

To Parkman the two cities were no more alike than the dining room of London and the elegant restaurant of Paris:

The one being a quiet dingy establishment where each guest is put into a box and supplied with porter, beef, potatoes, and plum-pudding. Red-faced old gentlemen of three hundredweight mix their "brandy-go" and read the *Times.* In Paris the tables are set in elegant galleries and salons, and among the trees and flowers of a garden, and here resort coats cut by the first tailors and bonnets of the latest mode, whose occupants regale their delicate tastes on the lightest and most delicious viands. The waiters spring from table to table as noiselessly as shadows, prompt at the lightest sign; a lady, elegantly attired, sits within an arbor to preside over the whole. Dine at these places—then go to a London "dining room"—swill porter and devour roast beef!

England's food and drink were not mother's milk to one who had climaxed the grand tour with a fortnight of Paris in May under the guidance of a knowledgeable uncle. He went to the Haymarket Theater to see Charles Matthews in a play of his own, and though he noted that "such admirable acting I never saw before," he found the theater a plain and simple little place, "scarce larger than our departed Tremont," and very unlike the great theaters of Rome and Naples, La Scala, and the Paris Opéra. He judged that the drama was on its last legs, since all the other old London theaters had turned to opera.

One disappointment came upon another. George Catlin's Indian Gallery was on view at the Egyptian Hall on Piccadilly, and a crowd of spectators, servants, street peddlers, cabmen, boys, and pickpockets about the door gave circumstantial evidence of Catlin's success. But on going in, Parkman found that the true point of attraction was Tom Thumb, the celebrated American dwarf, who had stolen the thunder of the Indian collection. Parkman was forced to listen to "the little wretch singing 'Yankee Doodle' with a voice like a smothered mouse, and prancing about, on a table, *à la* Jeffery Hudson, with a wooden sword in his hand." Only a few portraits of Indian chiefs, a few hunting shirts, and some arrows were left on the walls—the rest of the rich and valuable collection, which Parkman had seen in Boston, having been packed up—Catlin not suffering "the fruits of his six years' labor to rot in the dampness to gratify a few miserable cockneys."

St. Paul's was to Parkman "without exception the dirtiest and gloomiest church I have been in yet." He found the favorite English comparison of it to St. Peter's wholly ridiculous. But he thought the spectacle from the ball at the top of the cupola a most wonderful one, though he preferred a mountain view, of unbroken forests stretching in every direction as far as the eye could see, to this endless panorama of roofs and steeples, half hidden in smoke and mist; the filthy river running like a common sewer through the midst; and the stench of coal smoke that polluted the air. It was foggy and sleeting, in this "genial month of May," and Parkman grew thoroughly out of sorts with London and the Londoners:

> The smoke that you could see streaming in the wind from ten thousand earthen chimney-pots mingled with the vapors, and obscured the prospect like a veil. It was an indistinct but limitless panorama. The taller church spires alone rose above the cloud into a comparatively clear atmosphere, and they could be seen faintly far off on the horizon, to show how far this wilderness of houses reached. Now, thought I, I have under my eye the greatest collection of blockheads and rascals, the greatest horde of pimps, prostitutes, and bullies that the earth can show. And straightaway all the child's-book associations of London rose before me—the Lord Mayor's show "all so grand" and the host of narrow, stupid, beef-eating civic functionaries; and the unmatched absurdities and self-conceit of Cockneyism. "Was there ever such a cursed hole?" I thought, as I looked down on the smoky prospect.

The thing that most impressed him at St. Paul's was a cobwebbed and dusty stone-vaulted room where hung, "already rotten and half dropping from their staffs," the flags that were carried at Nelson's funeral.

As he walked endlessly through the teeming streets, he found an interesting mixture of vulgarity and helplessness in the swarm of ugly faces—"meager, feeble, ill-proportioned, or not proportioned at all, the blockheads must needs put on a game air and affect the man of the world in their small way." He saw not one handsome woman in fifty miles of walking, and he observed that although elsewhere Englishmen were tall, strong, and manly, here the crowd resembled the outcasts of a hospital. He found amusement in being mistaken for one of the pickpockets with whom the streets swarmed:

> Walk out in the evening, and keep a yard or two behind some wretched clerk, who, with nose elevated in the air, elbows stuck out at right angles, and the pewter knob of his cane playing upon his underlip, is straddling his bow-legs over the sidewalk with a most majestic air. Get behind him, and you see his dignity greatly disturbed. First he glances over one of his narrow shoulders—then over the other—then he edges off to the other side of the walk, and turns his vacant lobster eyes full upon you— then he keeps his hand over his coat-tail—and finally he draws forth from his pocket the object of all this solicitude in the shape of a venerable and ragged cotton handkerchief, which he holds in his hand to keep it out of harm's way. I have been thus taken for a pickpocket more than a dozen times tonight—not the less so for being respectably dressed, for these gentry are the most dandy men on the Strand.

After seeing so many miserable specimens of humanity he was glad to meet George Atkinson, the brother of his sister's husband, in Westminster Abbey, "the most interesting church I was ever in." They went up the river to Richmond together in a boat whose decks swarmed with a Cockney pleasure party. They had a fine day for their excursion, "by a miracle," and Parkman found the

Thâmes Valley beautiful. Upon their return, Hyde Park was full of carriages of the nobility, and Regent Street was swarming with thousands of people and filled with the "heavy stunning din from the wheels of carts, omnibuses, cabs, and carriages careering along in both directions at full speed, but without confusion and accident." Still more typical of London to Parkman was the Strand at night:

> The sidewalks are crowded with as dense and active a throng as in the daytime—more than half of whom are women on their nightly perambulations. The glare from the shops makes all as bright as sunlight. A watchman stands in his cloak at every corner. Strong bodies of the police are continually marching in order to and fro, with loaded clubs hung at their sides.

Eight days of this teeming human hive were enough for Parkman and, sending on his trunks to Liverpool, whence his steamer sailed, he set out for the north by railway. He got off at Darlington, and took the stage for Carlisle in order to see the border country which Scott's romances had made so familiar to him. He had trouble in securing passage "from the difficulty in understanding the damnable dialect of Yorkshire." On the way he passed Dotheboys Hall—"*Nicholas Nickleby* ruined not this establishment alone, but many other schools with which the vicinity abounds"—Barnard Castle, and the Tees, where Parkman burst out with an oath at being so unexpectedly introduced to the scenery of Scott's *Rokeby*. He dined at Penrith and went on, with the Cumberland hills off to the left, hiding among them the lakes and the home of Wordsworth. He got an enthusiastic account of the beauties of the Lake Country and its hills from an old farmer, "who had wandered over them all out of a very unusual admiration of the picturesque." This talkative soul then gave an account of the hills' geological formation, diverged to geology in general, then to chemistry, then to metaphysics and religion, and finally to the breeding of cattle. The next day Parkman set off at four in the morning for Abbotsford, "being in the region where one thinks of nothing but Scott and of the themes which he has rendered so familiar to the whole world." A raw cold wind came sweeping down from the Cheviot hills, the sky was obscured with stormy clouds, and the line "The sun shines fair on Carlisle walls" seemed highly inapplicable, for "The ancient fortification looked sullen and cheerless as tottering battlements and black crumbling walls beneath a sky as dark and cold as themselves could make it." But the sun came through as Parkman went his way; and the dark heathery sides of the Cheviots, the bright rapid streams that poured down from the glens, and the woods of ash, larch, and birch along their courses appeared to full advantage. By the Esk, Liddel Water, the Teviot, Branxholm Castle, Ettrick Forest, Minto Crag, and Yarrow he passed to the Tweed and Abbotsford on its banks, among the forests which Scott had planted himself. Parkman left his luggage at the inn at Galashiels and visited Abbotsford, Melrose, and Dryburgh—and considered "the day better spent than the whole four months I was in Sicily and Italy."

He had only three days to spare for this country, which appealed strongly to him, and so he rose at six and went to bed at ten and was on his legs the whole interval. He found quarters not far from Abbotsford in a stone cottage by the Tweed, kept by an old lady who remembered Scott's return from the Continent and his funeral. She summed the great man up thus: "He was an awful dull and heavy-lookin' mon to be sic a grand writer." Parkman's request for books brought forth a Testament, the Psalms of David "done into English verse for the service of the Scottish Kirk," and a volume of sermons by the Reverend Simeon McCabb. The landlady, whose visitors were usually salmon fishermen, then produced a bottle of whisky, remarking: "Mayhap it wad mak ye sleep better." It certainly did no harm, for Parkman was up at daybreak and fished the Tweed for two hours before breakfast. He hated to leave this spot, but he was pressed for time:

I like the Scotch—I like the country and everything in it. The Liverpool packet will not wait, or I should stay long here, and take a trout from every "burnie" in the Cheviot. The scenery has been grossly belied by Irving and others—it is wild and beautiful—I have seen none more so.

He took the coach from Galashiels to Edinburgh, where the fine situation and magnificent scenery of the Athens of the North very much surprised him. The view from Calton Hill he solemnly pronounced to be the only city view that deserved to be called sublime. He enjoyed the contrast between the old and new towns on their parallel ridges, the new putting Regent Street to shame architecturally, and being beyond comparison as to neatness and quietness; the old making a fine appearance in the mass despite its dirt and squalor, with the castle rising far above the lofty stone houses of High Street. The name of Walter Scott was on everybody's lips, and each time Parkman asked the name of some street, hill, wood, or island, the reply would be a word as familiar to him as his own name. The old booksellers of Edinburgh had many tales of Scott to keep his memory green, and after they were gone the magnificent monument on Princes Street, then being erected, would serve to mark his fame. In one bookshop Parkman saw a love-letter written by Burns to a married lady, whose son had no scruples about selling it to a dealer, though his mother's name was written out in full! Parkman walked up Arthur's Seat to the spot which Scott and James Ballantyne used to frequent as boys, reading and inventing romances together, and saw Auld Reekie many hundred feet below, half veiled in smoke with the castle rising in the distance. There he had viewed the regalia of Scotland, and recalled the scene when the chest where they had been hidden for many years was opened in the presence of a party of literati and ladies. One frivolous fellow lifted Robert Bruce's crown to place it on the head of a simpering young girl, but blushed scarlet and laid it down when Scott exclaimed: "No, by God!" Parkman noted sagely: "There is a power in a little profanity when it comes from a moved spirit; and is not affected like the oaths of a consumptive apprentice with a cigar in his mouth, who lisps Hell and Damnation because he thinks it sounds manly." He saw the house above the Canongate where that old ranter John Knox lived, with an image of him preaching at its corner. "This the people hold in great reverence. A scurvy-looking population they are!" And he mused on the chances of history, which had reduced the old town houses of the Scots nobles to tenements populated by "squalling tomcats, and yelling children, old hags with frilled caps, ruffian men, and young ladies to correspond." In Holyrood House he saw Queen Mary's apartments, with Darnley's armor lying on a table and the floor stained with Rizzio's blood. And one night he attended the opera of *Rob Roy*, with Mackay playing Bailie Nicol Jarvie in the manner which had won him a present from Scott. Reluctantly he left Edinburgh, "altogether a most interesting place," and passed a day in Glasgow, where he could find nothing worth looking at save the Tolbooth. The nearness of the Highlands was tantalizing, but he had not time to go there, since he had to catch a steamer for Liverpool on the evening of the day he arrived in Glasgow. The trip was made in the company of a hundred passengers, seventy or eighty cattle, and a large flock of sheep, all of whom became sick during the voyage. Liverpool was reached in twenty-four hours, and to Parkman it was much as he expected, dismal and smoky. He had sent his trunks in care of Baring Brothers and had to invoke the aid of the Liverpool partner of the firm before he could induce the guardian at the storehouse to part with them, "the only instance in the course of my journeyings where I have met with too much honesty."

Much to his disgust, he had to remain several days in Liverpool, waiting for his packet to sail, and he cursed the alteration in the sailing schedule which "forced me to throw away on this disgusting city time which I might otherwise have spent in the Highlands." He fell in with Colonel Winchester and his son and a Mr. Green, whom he had met in Rome, and with the latter went to a fête at the Zoological Gardens. There were at least a dozen American skippers in the crowd, and some old friends of Parkman in the form of a black bear, a cougar, and a Canadian wildcat, who glared through the bars of their cages with fury at the fireworks which marked the occasion. That evening he spent over a bowl of punch concocted by two Irish friends, with Green seasoning the concoction with his dry wit, which reminded Parkman of Dan Slade's, "whom he actually surpasses in stature, being six feet four inches high."

The next day he went aboard the *Acadia*, amid a tumult of visitors, last-minute presents and messages, and all the bustle of a ship about to sail. Despite the racket Parkman liked Liverpool better when seen from a ship's deck and half concealed behind a forest of masts. Soon they got under way and dropped down the Mersey, saluted by a fort and replying, to the consternation of the ladies, from two brass guns. It took two days to pass Cape Clear, fighting against head winds and a choppy sea. Most of the sixty-five passengers remained below, "for the sight of dinner had become an abomination. There was nothing but groaning and vociferations through the long ranges of staterooms." But soon the general sickliness disappeared, and Parkman saw more of his fellow-passengers, who included English, Irish, Scotch, French, Germans, and Americans, as well as half a dozen Canadians. Many of them, once they got on their feet, managed to keep eating all day long, for the table was set five times a day and under the terms of passage anything was to be had when called for. Others played cards or discussed the merits of their respective countries. The English clung together in a tight little knot, discussing their wine or military matters, for most were officers going out to Canada. The "damned Yankees" were scattered everywhere, and ranged from gentlemen down to "some vulgar and conceited traveling agent from New York."

The manners and customs of the sister races afforded some striking contrasts, which Parkman noted with amusement. His friends would stretch themselves out at length upon the deck in calm weather, wrapped in plaids or cloaks. Soon they would be joined in the same inelegant comfort by other Americans, who provided "a fair representation of the Yankee Nation." Meanwhile the English officers stiffly paraded about the ship, with a hauteur that heightened noticeably as they passed the sprawling group of Americans, who detected a tendency to lip-curling and disdainful whispering in their aloof shipmates. The situation was too good to be wasted:

Green bawls out to the Colonel's son: "Billy, you don't understand how to be comfortable. Here, let me show you how to enjoy yourself like an American and a freeman," so he lifts one of his long legs up to Billy's head and reaches the other out to the railing of the deck. "Well! I swow!" says another. "You do things first rate, I calculate, and no mistake. *We* don't live under a despotic government, I guess!"—and this man tries to emulate Green by stretching both feet across his neighbor's lap. "Yes," says the next man, "freedom's the word—to all but the niggers! I wish we kept those cattle in the north—a good thing to exercise a man on, of a cold morning, and give him an appetite for breakfast. I'd lash mine until they roared again." "I'd roast mine alive," says another, taking out a penknife to pick his teeth, "if they didn't behave." "I'd raise a breed for the doctors," adds another; "they sell well, and it doesn't cost anything to raise them, because the thinner the body is, you know, the better it is to dissect."

All this being uttered in a loud voice, the Englishmen could not help hearing. Unlike some of their countrymen, they began at last "to smell a rat"—so casting a look of disdainful ire on the grave countenances of the Americans, they descended with stately steps to the lower deck.

The same cleavage characterized the passengers at night, when they gathered in little groups for conversation over punch, wine, or porter. The English kept to themselves, and had only contemptuous glances for the noisy Americans, Scots, and Irish. Two of them did not mix even with their compatriots: the Bishop of Newfoundland, on his way out to take charge of his diocese, buried himself in a volume about his new see; and another, who always appeared in full dress with an ear-sawing starched collar, sat by himself drinking a bottle of wine, looking neither to right nor left, though on rare occasions he invited the Bishop's chaplain to take wine with him.

Parkman was reminded of a young American he had met in Paris who was possessed of the same unreasoned hatred of Englishmen which the pirate Morgan is said to have felt for Spaniards. He glared at Englishmen on the street as if they were mortal enemies, and insulted and played tricks on them at every opportunity. At masked balls he made the most of the circumstances to steal their partners or to make them ridiculous, "and then he would assail them with sneers and jests which would have got him into a scrape at any other place than a masked ball." Evidently Parkman had

absorbed some of this Anglophobia, which in any case came naturally to him, for he lost no chance to poke fun at his English shipmates. His account of the Sunday services on shipboard is typical:

> On Sunday the Bishop of Newfoundland preaches us sermons
> which the meanest freshman in Harvard ought to have been
> ashamed to have written. The Bishop (who—with reverence to
> his lordship, be it said—seems not to be gifted with any extraor-
> dinary share of common sense, whatever his spiritual gifts may
> be) takes great delight in lengthening out his precious liturgy as
> far as possible, repeating the creed and the prayers for the gov-
> ernment and the royal family several times. He does not deign
> to regard the two-thirds of his auditors who are neither British
> subjects nor Episcopalians.
>
> His lordship is a great enemy of the temperance reform, and
> relates with great satisfaction the story of a pewter mug which
> was presented to him by the "publicans" for preaching a sermon
> against it. It is a sin, he says, to teach men to do for their worldly
> interest that which they ought to do purely for the glory of God.
> It may, he says, produce results apparently good, but it "im-
> plants a bad principle"—and the evil effects are at some future
> day to be made manifest.

A distant iceberg took the company's mind off the oddities of
their fellow-passengers, and the more nervous sat up all night in
dread of catastrophe, but "None occurred," wrote Parkman suc-
cinctly. The sea became calm for the first time, and the ship made
better speed. One morning Parkman smelt the land breeze and an
hour or so later the coast of Nova Scotia was visible, although soon
obscured by fog and cloud. Yet far off on the horizon could be seen
a long line of highlands with forests and patches of open soil. "As
the state of the atmosphere changes, and its refractive power becomes greater or less, this false coast rises higher above the horizon
or sinks down below it." With this entry echoing Professor Treadwell's Harvard lectures on physics, the journal of the European
tour closes. At the foot of the page is written "June 17"; on that date
Parkman returned to the America which he was better equipped to
understand after his travels in Europe. During his months abroad,

he had never lost sight of his historical plans, and had learned much that helped to forward them. His book knowledge of European history had been reinforced by firsthand acquaintance with European civilization, and he now knew how different was that arising in America. In his solitary travels he had learned self-reliance and acquired the ability to get along with a wide variety of humanity. He had seen many sights and met many men; he was no longer merely a provincial patrician but something of a citizen of the world, none the less proud of his nation for having seen others.

8: America Through New Eyes

[*For*] *the traveler in Europe,—Art,*
nature, history combine. In America
art has done her best to destroy na-
ture;—association [has added] noth-
ing.

F.P., DIARY, 1844

THE first excursion that Parkman made after his return to
Boston was to the Concord Fourth of July celebration. His impatient temperament was vexed by the delays of the Boston &
Fitchburg Railway, and he admired the good humor of the people
in the cars. A group of young men amused themselves by singing
songs and telling jokes, and Parkman was slightly annoyed to find
a former schoolmate among the leaders, remarking: "In spite of
the coldness attributed to the Am[erican] character, he seemed to
play the *rowdy* with all his heart and as if he considered it the
height of glory." At the celebration itself, for which great crowds
had assembled, he noticed the extraordinary cheerfulness, polite-
ness, and accommodating spirit, which resulted in "perfect order
in the most difficult evolutions of the day," such as a hundred soldiers could not have brought about in Europe.

This occasion gave him an opportunity to examine with fresh
eyes the nature of his country and of its people. For all his dislike
of those not of his own class, the verdict was a remarkably favorable
one. His European travels had given him a better appreciation of
what it was to be an American:

> Some young men exhibited a good deal of humor and of knowl-
> edge in their observations—and I remembered that this is *our*
> *lowest class*. This orderly, enthusiastic, and intelligent body is
> the nearest approach to the peasantry of Europe. If we have
> not the courtly polish of the European upper circles, the absence
> of their stupid and brutal peasantry is a fair offset.

✿   ✿   ✿   ✿

I saw two drunken men. One, at the dinner, was immediately pushed out, with expressions of vexation and contempt. He made long speeches at the door to the crowd. A tall, thin, black-browed Yankee had pushed him out and was disposed to assume the bully over him, but finding his position in that capacity rather absurd, he began to change his bullyism into a half-amused air and tone. "Now don't ye be provoking me to strike," he said, " 'cause if I should, I should make a leetle daylight shine through you in no time"—turning with a triumphant consciousness of superiority to the bystanders, to see how they would be amused by his treatment of the drunken man.

An old farmer exhibited a sprightliness not very common among Yankees. He danced about with great activity, giving his advice aloud on all topics, in a humorous strain—when the train was coming slowly up, he shouted out: "Fetch a log there and block the team."

Students of H[arvard] do not on all occasions appear much better than their less favored countrymen, either in point of view of gentlemanly and *distingué* appearance or in conversation.

Parkman was fresh from a greater school than Harvard, and Cambridge *mores* were no longer the immutable law to him. He remained a Brahmin, and would until his death, but he had begun to understand the ways and natures of men other than the elect of the Hill.

He saw everything through new eyes. The social world of Boston and Cambridge now seemed characterized by simplicity and absence of forms—indeed, he thought an Englishman would say by provincialism—and he observed weightily: "A species of family admits familiarities which could not be borne elsewhere." He found the little Boston world full of the discussions of Fourierism by the "she-philosophers of W[est] Roxbury." He had little sympathy with the Brook Farmers, however: "Their speculations and the whole atmosphere of that haunt of 'new philosophy' were very striking and amusing after seeing the manners of Paris and London—the entertainments and pleasures and the workings of passions which they in their retirement seem scarce to dream of." His superiority now was that of sophistication, rather than of pride of birth. He had developed his already keen interest in human character, and cheerfully dissected his friends and classmates. Here is one such thumbnail sketch:

"Old Snow"—his careless abandonment—his tobacco chewing —his admiration of George [Cary]—his hatreds—his indifference and laziness—his want of foresight—his violent expressions of friendship.

A ship without a rudder—a good fellow, but on the way to wreck and worthlessness.

Despite all the sights he had seen in Europe, he had not lost his love for the New England countryside. This was something bred in his bones, and he never lost it in all his seventy years. He was just as much of New England as any white barn of a meeting house on a hill among the dark pines; his face grew more and more like the land he loved: the firm prominent chin, like a rocky headland on the Massachusetts coast; the ridges and furrows of his countenance like the hills that rose up from the shore, higher and higher until they lost themselves in the ranges; the eyebrows like the savage forests that arched over some precipice; and the eyes as clear and vital as any mountain lake among the clouds. These are the words he wrote upon his return to this land he loved:

England has her hedges and her smooth green hills, robed with a sense of power and worth, strengthened and sanctioned by ages—but give me the rocky hillside, the shaggy cedar and shrub-oak—the wide reach of uncultivated landscape—the fiery glare of the sun among the evening clouds, fling[ing] over all its wild and ruddy light. All is new—all is rough—no charm of a familiar countryside. Fierce savages have roamed like beasts amid its rugged scenery—there was a day of struggle, and they have passed away, and a race of indomitable men have supplanted them. The day of struggle was short, yet its scenes of fear and blood are not without a horrid romance, and well does the rugged landscape recall them to mind.

It was fitting that the young man who could thus hymn his birth-place, on the eve of his graduation from Harvard College, should live to fix those struggles enduringly on the printed page, and thus preserve the memory of a land which has been tamed by time and the work of many men, but still retains at heart its savage character.

It was not the sight of the land alone that gratified this returned traveler. The accents of New England fell strangely and pleasingly upon an ear that had become used to the soft explosions of Italian speech, the harsh gutturals of German, the quick smoothness of French, and the many strange ways of the English and the Scots with the language he had thought his own. His notebook for July and August of this year is full of little scraps of talk that delighted his ear:

The spring at the granite ledge near Pine Hill. "It's chock-full of animils"—a host of frogs leaped in—"Is the water good?" I asked. "Well, I guess it ain't the best that ever was."

On July 17 he made an excursion on the boat to Nahant, in a company which differed in silence and intelligence from the Cockney party with whom he had traversed the Thames. There was a man from Ohio with a model beehive, who denounced the millers for using a sort of trap to catch bee moths. When asked what hurt the millers did, the Ohioan exploded: "Hurt! Why, when they've killed about nine-tenths of the bees in the United States, and spoilt every hive in Ohio state, I should think they might be doing hurt, shouldn't you?" And then there was a traveled fool, who gave his occupation in the bar book as "Cosmopolite." This fellow observed that some improvements were "very credible to the town"—of which he was a native. Parkman noted with disgust that he aped English dress and manners. The type is still common in New England. In high dudgeon with a party of "heroes of the counter" and their ladies, Parkman rented a rod and went off to fish, receiving only a gruff "Thank yer" from the owner when he overpaid him. He had forgotten that New England does not take kindly to tipping. The regional canniness amused him when he sought the advice of local Waltons about the ways of the fish:

"Have you ever seen any about here?" "No, not *about here*, I ha'nt." Query: Had he anywhere?

The only thing that really displeased him was the "disagreeable whining manner" of some "vulgar Yankee girls."

He could not bear the city any longer, and scrawling a note on the flyleaf of his little notebook: "Third Wednesday of August—be at Cambridge"—for his graduation from Harvard—he set off on an expedition through western Massachusetts, among those Berkshire Hills that he had observed longingly from the railroad cars two years before. He traveled light, with a knapsack containing "three shirts, two stockings, flannel drawers, fishing apparatus, powder and shot, and *History of B[erkshire]*." Though he does not mention the presence of "Satan," his favorite gun, the powder and shot presuppose its part in this solitary expedition. At a Springfield inn he had a brush with the independent Yankee of the hinterland, not reduced to the subservient attitude of the farmers about Boston. Though Parkman was annoyed at not being called at a set time, and rebuked the man, the latter "stood right up to it—giving shot for shot." Parkman noted approvingly, "No English cringing," and also observed that the landlord did not indulge in any European bowing to his guests. Farther on his way he encountered further evidence of the take-it-or-leave-it attitude of Yankee tavern-keepers; for at Chester Factory the landlord sat cross-legged on his chair, taking no notice of the arriving guest, but when Parkman asked if the landlord was in, replied: "Yes, here I be."

At Chester Factory he took the stage for Stockbridge. The driver was a Yankee misanthrope whom Parkman studied with some curiosity:

> A fellow with hollow eyes and peculiar sullenness and discontent on his features. He had traveled all over the state, sometimes driving and sometimes singing at cows, but usually following his inclinations. Nothing pleased him. He hated the country, the road, and everything else. He had engaged on it for a year, but intended to get away at the first opportunity. He hated hard labor; and set such a value on his services that he refused to be coachman to a southern gent. who offered him $15 when he de-

manded $25. He intended never to marry, but liked "training with the girls." We passed the house of a man who was rich for the country, having about $20,000. "I suppose he likes this place," said the driver, looking up with contemptuous discontent, and giving his horses a switch under the bellies. He says he could be rich in a month, if he chose to try, but "he always wanted to take comfort, and have nothing to think on when even'g came; working in the daytime was enough for him."

* * * *

The driver turned to me with a surly envy and said he "guessed I warn't used to hard labor." The lazy rascal envies all who can live without labor. As we were driving on, I remarked on the beauties of the road. "*Humph!* Wouldn't you like to live here!" I inquired who were the occupants of a certain house. "Paddies" —with exquisite surly indifference. "Where does that road lead?" "Don't know"—in the same tone.

In this cheery company Parkman traveled over some of the most beautiful hill country in New England. He was still the student, notebook in hand, jotting down little bits of information about the customs of the region. He learned that dances were held occasionally in the villages, despite the disapproval of the Methodist ministers who largely ruled in this region and were transferred every two years, to avoid too great intimacy with their parishioners; that they received contributions and presents in addition to their salaries; and that the people were in the habit of coming to tea at the minister's, sending or bringing the materials of the meal. He continued his study of hotelkeepers, observing:

An American landlord does not trouble himself to welcome his guests. He lets them into his house and sits by quite indifferent. He seems rather to consider himself conferring an obligation in anything that he may do for them.

Lee he found full of factory girls, who disturbed him so much that he scarcely slept all night: "The very devil beset me there. I never suffered so much from certain longings which I resolved not to gratify. . . ." At last he reached Stockbridge, noting more soberly that "Maple and beech have followed the fir of the original growth" and that "The railroad has lessened the value of land by the influx of western produce. These towns never sent produce to Boston and do not now—the expense of R.R. transportation is too great."

Like many another traveler since, Parkman reveled in the antiquities and the antiquarians of Stockbridge, which remains perhaps the most beautiful and most interesting of old New England towns. He went about, collecting legends and pumping the older villagers for their memories of frontier days, and filled the pages of his notebook with what he thus learned:

> An old man at the church told me that the original meeting house where Sergeant preached stood on the green in front. About half a mile off is the site of the church of 1784 where, in the mound on which it was built, were found a number of Indian bodies. An old man, present when the graves were opened, said that they were heaped confusedly together, without instruments of any kind with them. Perhaps they were flung there by the whites after Wolcott's fight in [King] Philip's war. The Stockbridge Indians had a burying ground, the care of which they consigned, on leaving the place, to old Mr. Partridge, who keeps it carefully for them. It is in the village, and seems to contain a large number of bodies.

❖   ❖   ❖   ❖

> The old Negro * at the church. He remembered all about the Indians and exchanged recollections with the old man aforesaid. He had been a soldier in W[ashington]'s army. He had four children in the churchyard, he said, with a solemn countenance; but "These are my children," he added, stretching his cane over a host of little boys. "Ah, how much we are consarned to fetch them up well and virtuous, etc." He was very philosophical, and every remark carried the old patriarch into lengthy orations on virtue and temperance. He looked on himself as father to all Stockbridge.

❖   ❖   ❖   ❖

* Agrippa Hull (1759–1846), a resident of Stockbridge from his sixth year. He

Went up Monument Mt.

House of Jones. His kindness and obliging disposition. He had two large bowls of ash knots—a beautiful material—made by the Indians. The largest is used only for making wedding-cake. Also a mortar of a piece of the trunk of a maple, made by the Indians for his grandfather. The pestle was of stone. The conch which was used to call the Indians to church now calls his household to dinner. His brother, Mr. Stephen Jones, is a great geologist and very talkative. I got of him a chisel and two arrowheads.

But Parkman got more from the aged Dr. Oliver Partridge than from anyone else he encountered during his stay in Stockbridge. He filled ten pages of his notebook with the doctor's observations, though one is crossed with the later comment: "Rather doubtful, like the rest of the old man's stories." Parkman found the sage of Stockbridge in his combination laboratory and bedroom, amid a clutter of old tables, bookcases, shelves of medicines, and pharmacist's scales:

He is about ninety-four; and remembered Williams well, whom he describes as a large stout man who used often to visit his father and take him on his knee, and once went out the door and blew a trumpet to amuse him. He says he remembers the face as if he saw it yesterday, especially the swelling of the ruddy cheeks.

His father, Colonel Partridge, was in the service, and despised Abercrombie as a coward. The Dr. remembers seeing a thousand of Abercrombie's Highlanders at Hatfield or some other town where they were billeted. Abercrombie was always trembling with fear of Indians and sending out scouts about camp. When Howe fell, Partridge, the Dr. says, was at his side, and his lordship said: *"This army has no leader and is defeated."*

On one occasion Abercrombie ordered 800 rangers to be detached. Partridge or some other officer drew them up in a cornfield, directing the short men to stand on the hills and the tall

enlisted in the army in 1777 and served more than six years, four of them as Kosciusko's body servant.

ones in the hollows. The British officers were struck with admiration at the uniform height of the men.

*   *   *   *

Amherst he considers a very different man from A[bercrombie]. When he had landed and set down before Ti[conderoga], he offered a great reward to any spy who should explore the works. Three men at length offered themselves, an Indian, a half-breed, and an Irish ranger named Morrison, who died in Stockbridge and from whom the Dr. got the story. Amherst reminded them of the peril of the service, but they resolved to venture and, passing down the outlet in the breech-clouts of Indians, they landed under the walls. Passing on, in a violent rain, they found the first sentry in his box. Him the Indian killed and scalped, and, directing Morrison to remain there, the other two proceeded. They served another sentry in the same manner, till they arrived to where there was a flag, with another sentry, who was also killed. They then withdrew, and had only reached the beach when they heard the drums beat to relieve the sentinels. Morrison could not run as well as the others, so they seized hold of him to help him, and dragging him behind they got into the woods and hid. They soon heard guns fired as the relief guard came to the first sentry box, followed soon by two other successive discharges as the other dead bodies were discovered—and they heard noise and firing for some time in the direction of the fort. When they came to camp, the Indian showed the scalp to Amherst, who refused to believe on such evidence that they had gone so far into the works, on which the Indian unfolded from his body the flag which he had taken on killing the third sentry—indisputable evidence. The general ordered some rum, and promised the reward in the morning. In the night the fort was evacuated. Morrison took credit to himself as the cause, and old Dr. P., admitting his claim, promised him doctoring gratis, in consideration of his service to the country.

The Dr. tells some familiar ancedotes of Williams, and says that Konkapot and some other Indians accompanied him to the war. He remembered nothing of the affair of William Henry.

Such tales as these were meat and drink to Parkman, whose imagination was inflamed by the French and Indian Wars in which the father of this ancient had fought. History came alive as the old doctor rambled on, for time and repetition had not spoiled his stories. Parkman was carried away by enthusiasm as he listened; once the magic of the storyteller had ceased to exert its spell, the young student became skeptical of the authenticity of these remarkable relations. But he doubtless preserved a warm spot in his heart for the old man who had made it beat faster with such tales.

Parkman went on to Great Barrington, with his head still full of Dr. Partridge's stories. One in particular he found it hard to forget. Old Colonel Partridge's rangers were firing their guns in the woods about camp:

"What, what!" says the gineral (thus he tells the story). "We shall have the Injuns on us if you let your men go on so." "Your lordship," says he, "don't know nothing about our kind of fighting. We fire our guns off for the Injuns to hear, and when we see them coming we shoot 'em."

In a barroom at Great Barrington Parkman encountered an old Revolutionary soldier who displayed this same spirit. The record of this chance meeting is singularly vivid, as the old man himself evidently was:

. . . An old man with a sunburnt wrinkled face and no teeth, a little straw hat set on one side of his gray head—and who was sitting on a chair leaning his elbows on his knees and straddling his legs apart—thus addressed me: "Hullo! Hullo! what's agoin' on now? Ye ain't off to the wars a'ready, be ye? There ain't no war now as I knows on, though there's agoin' to be one afore long as damned bloody as ever was fit this side o' hell." He proceeded to inform me that he was an old soldier and always fought on the side of Liberty. He swore like a trooper at every sentence. He cursed the temperance reform which has run mad all over Berkshire. Someone speaking of a girl's uncle—"Uncle, is it? Uncle ain't the thing. You must look farder up"—and then laughing between his toothless gums. "Ther ain't none o' them things

nowadays, now the temperance folks says you mustn't," remarked a man. "You mustn't," said the old farmer, "G-d d-m
you mustn't."

He then began to speak of some of his neighbors, one of whom
he mentioned as "that G-d damnedest sneakingest, nastiest
puppy that ever went this side of hell." Another he likened to a
"sheep's cod dried," another was "not fit to carry guts to a bear."
His features were remarkably bold and well formed, but thoroughly Yankee, as also were his positions. "That d----d rascal's
brother," said he, pointing to a man near him, "played me the
meanest trick you ever seed," etc. The man was rather amused.

So was Parkman; for all his class consciousness he enjoyed a thorny
character of this sort far more than he did the "ripe scholar" of
Yankeeland, of whom he later wrote: "The products of his mind
were as pallid as the hue of his face, and, like their parent, void
of blood, bone, sinew, muscle, and marrow." His admiration was
reserved for the warrior rather than the priest, the man of action
rather than the man of books, and though ill health made him a man
of books when his soul cried out for action he devoted those books
to chronicling the deeds of men of action with a vividness rare in
the whole body of the written word.

Parkman went southwest from Great Barrington to Mount Washington, the most isolated mountain village in Massachusetts. After
getting a scrappy dinner at a farmhouse, he visited the "Bash-a-
bish" Falls, which offered a spectacle after his own heart:

Rocks covered with pine, maple, yellow birch, and hemlock
sweep round in a semi-circular form, the water plunging through
a crevice in the middle. The cliffs stretch away above, thick set
with vegetation—you see but a small patch of sky from the deep
gorge. The basin at the foot of the falls is filled with foam, and
the stream escapes downward in a deep gulf, full of rocks and
shadowed by the trees of the opposite mountain declivity.

As Parkman rested by the side of the road, a little boy came along
carrying a kettle of vinegar. Parkman engaged him in conversation
and learned that he lived near the head of the falls, but was soon

going to move "a great ways"—another westward-bound New Englander. Parkman showed the boy how to fire his gun and thus won his friendship. Together they clambered up a steep path to the summit and entered a lonely valley. One house was visible at the foot of the narrow valley, beside the brook which ran through it before flinging itself over the cliffs into the deep gorge out of which they had just climbed. There was an old ramshackle barn and some overgrown potato fields, but second-growth birch and maple pressed close to a new log house. By a mill dam Parkman waded the stream, carrying the boy, after a woman had appeared on the other side and vainly tried to lay a plank across as a bridge.

The woman immediately began to apologize for her bare feet, saying that she had mistaken me for her cousin and was so glad to see an acquaintance in that place that [she] had "run right down to see." She showed me her house, which was remarkably neat, with a little sheltered porch before it and a rude garden fenced with the outside slabs of boards from the mill. There were plenty of ducks and geese about. She did not wish to give me lodging as she was alone, her husband being gone, but she sent "Abel" to the spring for water, killed a duck, and gave me an excellent supper. "I warn't never rich," she said, "but I ain't always lived in a log hut." The place she stigmatized as a "hell on earth," which she was going to leave as soon as possible. She described her terror when sitting alone she hears the footsteps of a man about the house. Once, she says, she thought, nothing of it, but now, in that lonely place, it frightens her. A wildcat from the mountains has infested the house and stolen her ducks and hens. She has seen it, and one night, hearing the hens cackling, she went out, though in great terror, and made a fire to keep it off.

After getting this first-hand impression of frontier life, Parkman went to the other house in the valley to spend the night. This place belonged to a Mr. Murray, "a broken tradesman," and his Dutch wife. That evening Parkman studied the worn old man, as he sat smoking his pipe and talking between whiffs, and commented on the establishment:

The room where I slept contained various relics of departed prosperity: a handsomely curtained bed—images and French toys on the mantel. A table with books, vases, pamphlets, and a *basket of cards* upon it. His girls' dresses were hung up around, with a few maps etc. The furniture, though a little old, evidently belonged to his better day, and these various articles contrasted queerly with the hearth of rough stones and the rude white-washed fireplace, filled by way of ornament with pine and hem-lock boughs.

Murray, beset by dunning creditors, was pleased with the place, "because it is *retired*," and declared that he had had enough of company and wanted seclusion. Parkman got the other half of the story when he returned to Mrs. Comstock, his hostess of the previous night, for breakfast. Mrs. Murray's echoing of her husband's words provoked this truly feminine comment from Mrs. Comstock: "I should think Mrs. Murray might wait until she *feels* what she says, and not pretend to be so Christian-like and humble, when we all know she don't like the mounting no more than I do." If Mrs. Comstock had a sharp tongue, she had a generous heart, for she refused to accept payment for the meals she had furnished, and Parkman was obliged to cloak the money as a gift to young Abel. Then he went on his way, casting a last look at the falls from the top of the rock.

He turned northward, making thumbnail sketches of the inhabit-ants as he went and always on the alert for historical materials. At Lebanon Springs he met a man who said he had some journals of his father, "which contain, for what he knows to the contrary, notes of his services in Rogers's Rangers, when a young man." Here, across the border in New York, he found the makings of another agrarian revolt, like Shays's Rebellion in the Berkshires a few years before.

The Patroon's (or the *Patteroon's*) tenure is in peril. The tenants refuse to pay rent. I went to Stephentown to see the gathering for resistance. All along the road occurred boards with "Down with the rent!" and flags in the village and the gathering place, which was on a hill, at a mean tavern surrounded by a group of houses. The assembly was of the very lowest kind. The barroom full to suffocation, and vilely perfumed. One old man sat and talked for a long time. He had been with Indians and kept remarking on their good qualities, which remarks were received with great applause. The chief actors were to appear in the disguise of Indians. There was another old fellow who had been with the Indians and kept constantly talking of their friendship for him, perfuming all near with the stench of his filthy rotten teeth. Another fellow had been at Plattsburg, and distinguished himself by the vileness of his appearance and conversation. Another old fool, with a battered straw hat and a dirty shirt for his only upper garment, kept retailing his grievance, lashing himself into enthusiasm and exclaiming: "Down with the rent!" The Indians at length appeared and went through some meaningless maneuvers. A hole in a block of cast iron was charged with powder, and a plug being driven down hard into it, it was repeatedly fired. After a while, it was attempted to come to business. A few of the more decent squatted themselves on the bank of grass before the platform erected for the directors, but were listless and inattentive, while the directors, who managed the whole affair, nominated deputies from the different districts to arrange the matter. Those loudest in their noise were not of the number on the bank. The voice of the old man with the straw hat could be heard declaiming, and sharply exclaiming: "Down with the rent!" while the rest were eating or watching the clumsy and absurd movements of the "Indians."

Other towns of the Patroon's domain have also revolted, and his feudal tenure, so strangely out of place in America, has probably lived its time.

I have never seen a viler concourse in America.

So much for Parkman's sympathy with the democratic movements of his day.

He turned back into Massachusetts and headed north for Williamstown and North Adams. At the Hopper he paused to write a vivid bit of description which would have pleased Edward Channing, his master in rhetoric. Then he visited the site of Fort Massachusetts, on a wide meadow surrounded on every side by hills, with the Hoosic some six or eight hundred yards distant and a ridge of Saddle Mountain visible behind a high forest-covered hill. Here a garrison of fifty men under Ephraim Williams had been stationed to defend the frontier in 1746, only to be overwhelmed by French and Indians under Rigaud. There was something about the place in its loneliness that moved him:

> The crows caw loudly among the woods. Under an apple tree is a broken headstone with a fragment of inscription, where the bones of the officer who was shot—bones now in the W[illiam]s college—were found. The bullet was in the spine.
> It is a beautiful situation this fine day.
> French hatchets have been found here beside Indian weapons of stone.
> Horse radish planted by the soldiers grows here quite abundantly.

From old Captain Edmund Badger of North Adams, Parkman received an Indian hatchet and gouge as mementos of the place. The captain, like Stephen Jones of Colonel Jones's family and "the country Professor Hopkins," impressed Parkman by his passion for geology, which was shared by the old farmers of the region. Loftily he observed that "geology is a science of peculiar attraction to this class of people all the world over—witness the old Farmer whom I met in England." The "country professor" was the first exponent of geological and botanical field trips in America and the founder of the Hopkins Astronomical Observatory, the second of its kind in this country. But evidently Albert Hopkins lacked the impressive façade regarded as essential for scholarly repute in Parkman's day at Harvard. From Captain Badger, Parkman obtained much historical information. He was shown a copy of Colonel Williams's final will, and was told that the colonel's real home was in Deerfield, though he had a house in Stockbridge. Parkman was rather taken with the captain, although amused by his rustic ways:

> Captain B., an old member of the legislature, a great geologist, has been about with me discoursing on marble quarries, manu-

factories, etc., with his old hat pulled down over his eyebrows, his dingy coat hung on his shoulders, and his cane in his hand. He is, of course, practical in all his views of things. He has a number of stones in an old kettle which constitute his collection.

In Williamstown Parkman had a four- or five-hour talk and tea with General Hoyt, an "unquestionable authority." From him he learned much of Major Rogers, Sir William Johnson, Putnam, Montcalm, Marin, Dieskau, and other great figures of the French and Indian Wars. One story particularly appealed to him:

> . . . A man of Deerfield named Catlin, in the Rangers, told him that he was conducting a train of wagons to Abercrombie's army at the Lake [George]. Between Ft. Ed[ward] and Bloody Pond, he saw a crow picking the dung in the road, which ran through a low swampy place. He was in front of the wagons, and thinking no danger, thought he would shoot the crow. So bending under the bushes, he crept along the side of the road, to get a shot. The crow would not suffer him to approach, but flying up and realighting drew him on some distance from his men, and at length flew away. He was now on a rising ground again, when a tremendous yell and fire of musketry burst forth below him. The train, in the low part of the road, were fired on by a party, who did not touch him, although he had passed close to the muzzles of their guns. He immediately escaped to the station at Half-Way Brook, but most of his men were killed.

Parkman's interest was beginning to focus on Robert Rogers, and General Hoyt's statement that he had journals and letters of great interest and a *"complete unpublished life of Rogers"* led him to make a jubilant entry: *"Nil desperandum."* History got into the saddle after this absorbing interview, and the account of the excursion breaks off here, except for a purple patch or two of descriptive writing. For the rest, the little green pocket notebook is packed with references to books, magazines, papers, maps, and a long précis of a French manuscript supposed to have been written by Dieskau when he returned to France. Parkman found time, however, to note down one final classic of New England speech which evidently fell upon his ears when he stopped at a farmhouse for a meal: "Should have given ye a pie today, but ain't got no *timber* to make 'em."

Soon after his return to Boston, he went out to Concord to witness a muster of the militia on September 13. He gave a vivid sketch of the affair in the first pages of a new brown pocket notebook:

> Muster at Concord—on a hill, with the tents with provisions for the companies on one side, and the booths, peddlers, oyster stalls, bookstalls, etc., on the other. Several companies of rangers, in frocks and with rifles. The tall artillery sentinel—the gambling at the tavern, the congregation in the barroom. George P[arkman(?)]'s follies.

Evidently he was embarrassed by his companion's behavior, for he followed this passage with a note about "That remarkable constraint [to] which the presence of a person of inferior sense, acuteness, and energy will sometimes subject one far his superior." A truly cousinly remark! He was evidently in bad temper this September—perhaps tired from his arduous tour of the Berkshires, for after a few notes on historical books and papers the journal goes on with the irritated account of how his intentions toward the female sex were misunderstood one evening:

> Some men are fools—utter and inexpressible fools. I went over to Dr. B[igelow]'s last night to call on Miss ——. Heaven knows I am quite indifferent to her charms, and called merely out of politeness, not caring to have her think I slighted her. But the Dr., in the contemptible suspicion that he is full of, chose to interpret otherwise. William Train was there, whom I allowed to converse with Miss P. while I talked with the Dr.'s lady. The Dr. watched me, although I was not aware of it at the time, till happening to rise to take a bottle of cologne, out of a mere whim, and applying some of it to my handkerchief, the idiot made a remark, in a meaning tone, about *"long walks"* in the evening injuring me. He soon after asked me to take a glass of wine, saying that it would make me *feel better.* He whispered in my ear that Train *would go soon,* and I had better stay. What could I

do or say? I longed to tell him the true state of my feelings, and above all what I thought of his suspicious impertinence. I left the house vexed beyond measure at being *baited* as a jealous lover, when one object of my indifference to Miss —— that evening was to prove to her and the rest how free I was from the influence of her attractions. Is it not hard for a man of sense to penetrate all the depths of a blockhead's folly, and to know what interpretation such a fellow will put on his conduct? I sent him a letter which I think will trouble not a little his jealous and suspicious temper.

If it had not been for his morbidly reticent nature, Parkman might have been amused by the doctor's obvious desire to favor the course of true love. Instead he got himself into a childish state of indignation and sulkiness, and took it upon himself to judge his elders out of the vastness of his self-complacency. For all his physical and intellectual charm, he must have often been a rather unpleasant young man at this period, before trials and tribulations knocked the smugness and superiority out of him.

During his first year at the Law School he took considerable interest in unorthodox religion, and attended many sectarian gatherings—though as a none too friendly observer. A few days after this social incident, he went out to Watertown with Henry White to attend a Millerite meeting. His account of it gives a good idea of the spiritual stirring of New England at this period against the old orthodoxy of Calvinism and the new orthodoxy of Unitarianism. It was the age of the sects, when Protestantism split and resplit into the almost three hundred cults which now call themselves Protestant, though they have departed far from the parent religion.

At a private house a dozen or so of men and oldish women were seated silently about the room. We sat down, and for a long time the silence was interrupted only by sighs and groans. At length a big stout fellow struck up a hymn which was fervently sung by all. Then they dropped on their knees, while another prayed aloud in a hearty and earnest manner, responded to by sighs, exclamations, and cries of Amen. Several other prayers were made. One large, broad-faced, stupid fellow was a long time getting under way, but grew at last very loud and fervent. A woman joined immediately in a voice still more rabid. Then there was silence. A moment after the large man by the table rose slowly and, fixing his eyes on vacuity, exclaimed: "How bright the vision! Oh, how long shall this bright hour delay?" I at first thought this a burst of enthusiasm—it was no such thing, but a quotation from Dr. Watts. The fellow went on with more quotations, gathered from far and near, describing the glories of heaven, etc. There was a good deal of spiritual pride about this man. He evidently thought himself a full match for any clergyman at expounding scripture, and gifted with a large share of grace. I set him down as a vain proud fanatic, of a cold nature. Of course he was speaking from the immediate impulse of the holy spirit within him, and his discourse was rambling and bungling enough. He said he once went out west, and described *à la* Yankee the difficulties he encountered, and drew a parallel between his journey and the Christian heavenly journey. He then spoke of Christ, giving a sketch of his life, and remarking that though he might have "associated with the popularest men of his time," he preferred persecutions. He said that all true Christians must be persecuted, as he told a minister at Boston; if they were not persecuted they were not Christians. "Well, now, I tell you what it is, brothers and sisters, and *friends,* these here ministers, the popularest men of their day, ain't Christians," etc. He thought that a blazing stake would be set up here in Watertown, to persecute the true believers—"Yes, I do, and that are within three months, too."

The enthusiasm of the poor devils is excited amazingly by the tricks played on them. He exposed their doctrine—Christ was to take the form of flesh—heaven was to be *"located"* on earth —and then he drew a bungling picture of the heaven.

Several speakers followed him. One woman modestly remarked that it was easy to endure the cross and the stake, and suchlike great evils, but it tried the Christian's soul when it came to parting with little ornaments and dresses. The Bible champion corrected some of her quotations as she went on. When she sat

down, he said that for "them that hadn't got grace inside of them
it *was* hard, as Sister Stone said, to part with little worldly trifles
—but if one has truly got the spirit of God, and is persecuted
and shunned, and despised by men, he don't want no more to do
with them things. If a man or a woman sticks to his jewels, it's
a sign he ain't got grace, but goes by rule, like them that preach
in meeting off of notes, etc., etc., etc.

With screams, ejaculations, and prayers, the meeting was going on when we left.

This discourse was a frontal assault on the position held by Dr.
Parkman and the other eminent Unitarian divines of Boston, and
for all his growing lack of sympathy for Boston's new state religion,
Francis Parkman had no sympathy with such lowly cults as Millerism. At this stage of his life he seems to have been something of a
pantheist—certainly the most reverent of his notes deal with nature. When weary of Blackstone and the company of law and theology students, and the others at Cambridge, he wandered out
into the woods which still could be reached in a few minutes' walk
from the heart of the town. But one day, in a melancholy frame of
mind, he found that nature echoed his mood instead of restoring his
spirits as it usually did:

Nothing is more cheerful and bright than the clear sunny days
of autumn, when the woods have changed—but it is a dull and
chilling sky—all is cold and cheerless. Blue jays are screaming
and occasionally a squirrel chirrups. The shrubs have grown
dark and dull with last night's frost, and the cold puffs of air
shake them in a melancholy manner. The pines along the edge
of the clearing, the piles of wood, the rocky hill with its various-
colored shrubbery and rough and broken growth of wood along
its top, all wear the same gloomy aspect. A white spot on the
dull sheet of cloud marks where the sun should be.

Evidently his unwilling apprenticeship to the law weighed heavily
upon Parkman on this Novemberish day. No doubt he found it unfortunate that, according to Burke, "more Blackstones were sold in
the colonies than in England,"

The caustic mood was still on him when he went to see the pageant of "Cornwallis" at Brighton on October 18. He found little to be admired in the spectacle:

I was there before the militia had gone off. Some had the large skirted coats of revolutionary officers, some wore battered helmets, some three-cornered hats, some nothing. They had every variety of weapon, from blunderbuss to rusty saw; and were of all ages and sizes. A more ragamuffin assemblage I never saw.

"Officers to the front!" exclaimed the general on his horse. The long line of ragamuffins, who stood leaning on rifles or muskets in every variety of outlandish costume, looked as if they had never an officer among them, but at the word, a number of fellows straddled out from the line—with yellow breeches and red coats; or with false beards and dirty shirts, armed with axes, swords, or guns. These marched up to the front and faced gravely towards the general. "*Gentlemen* officers," he began, etc. The address over, the officers withdrew, and the music struck up, at which the whole line of ragamuffins got under way, and marched straggling off the ground, just as the sun went down.

In the space in front of the tavern was the usual congregation of idlers and loafers—with a gang of Indians firing their guns and yelling close by.

Parkman was a young man hard to please that fall—his great dissatisfaction with everything stemming, no doubt, from his unwillingness to study law, a course he had adopted at his father's insistence. He did not like his friends; he did not like his girls; he did not like nature; he did not like the "lower classes"—and to round out the list he penciled a bitter portrait of a rising Boston family, who had acquired wealth too recently for his patrician taste —though the shirt-sleeves were only two generations back in his own family:

The family of ——. He himself is a generous, open, hospitable, kind-tempered man, of vulgar birth and education, who has got an enormous fortune. His delight is in liberality, and he scatters money like water. His lady—a very dull and vulgar personage—

is chiefly solicitous to make a display of the "tasty" and "genteel." They have a score of half-gentlemen hangers-on around them. The house is furnished with an elegance that would better fit a palace. —— has brought from Europe a splendid collection of pictures, which he has not the cultivation to appreciate, but delights to listen to their praises. He has statues, splendid articles of *bijouterie* from Paris, some of which are most anti-republican in character, and piled together with a profusion akin to that of a warehouse. The damask curtains, the artificial flowers, the wax candles, and the numberless and regal ornaments give his rooms a most remarkable aspect.

His children, who play at whist with the aforesaid hangers-on all the evening, are much petted, and provided with lapdogs. ——, his son, educated in Paris, is particularly weak and senseless, placing the height of human glory in dissipation, in which he has of course indulged, though scarce sixteen. The mother and children are, indeed, all very weak and ill-informed; but the cordial hospitality and kindness of —— may make up for all, though [he] is quite in want of tact and discrimination, as might be expected.

Consideration of this *nouveau riche* family evidently moved Parkman to more general reflections on society in America. Relieved by the efforts of his grandfather from the necessity of earning a living, he had little use for the businessman, who was gradually becoming the most important figure in American life as the minister lost the dominant position that had been his since the first Puritans landed in Massachusetts. Parkman had little use for the general run of clergymen, whom he sometimes characterized by such sharp terms as "vermin" and "weasels," but that dislike gave him no greater fondness for the new ruler of American life:

Where in America is to be found that spirit of sport and bluff hearty enjoyment that is seen in English country gentlemen and others? Business here absorbs everything, and renders people incapable of every other pleasure.

Officers of the army and navy are sometimes an exception. There is an old retired navy surgeon at Medford, who lives with his dogs and his guns like an English squire, enjoying himself in the same hearty manner. Business, too, swallows much that is noble. The somewhat chivalrous sentiments, the reference of all things to the standard of a gentleman's honor, a certain nobleness (though it may be joined with debauchery and blackguardism) is found among the officers of armies.

Our businessmen, on the other hand, have narrowed away all this. Thoughts bent on practical gains are not pleasant to contemplate, no matter how much virtue may accompany them.

Aside from keeping his patrician eye open for such general tendencies, Parkman filled his notebook with little sketches of character and incident. He was consciously attempting to learn the writer's trade, as well as to acquire the scholarly background necessary for the great task he had set himself. These undeveloped notes are tantalizing; what there is of them is sharp and promising, but it is now impossible to fill up the gaps in Parkman's mental shorthand, as in this instance: "The theological discussion at the Medford barroom between Wait the blacksmith, James the Irishman, and the Whig who had been invited to drink a glass of champagne with Dudley Hall." The argument sounds promising, but we shall never hear it.

In the files of the *Knickerbocker Magazine* for 1845, however, may be found Parkman's first published work, a half dozen lively sketches in prose and verse, based upon incidents of early frontier life. These "blood and thunder chronicles of Indian squabbles and massacres" mirror his preoccupation with history when his attention was supposed to be concentrated on law. From reticence or a desire to avoid parental censure of such frivolity, Parkman adopted the pseudonym of "Captain Jonathan Carver, Jr."—the original Carver, a far-wandering adventurer, being credited with the authorship of the celebrated *Travels through the Interior Parts of North America*. Lewis Gaylord Clark, the *Knickerbocker's* editor, soon penetrated his new contributor's disguise, since Parkman had misspelled his pen name. But Clark wrote in most kindly terms to the literary tyro, calling his work "worthy of Cooper's pen" and urging him to keep on writing.

Parkman used his classmates at the Law School as unconscious models for his thumbnail sketches of character. He was learning the trick of significant detail; some of these brief portraits are singularly vivid:

Jan. 8, 1845. One of the most amusing characters of our table is Bigelow, a man so nervous and excitable that he has no self-restraint, and is constantly advancing strange propositions with a most absolute air. This morning he was inveighing against the "aristocracy" of the cadets, but his more usual expression is that of the most unmitigated contempt for "clodhoppers." Tonight he pitched upon "counter jumpers" as the subjects of his animadversion, roundly declaring, rolling back his head and bringing his fist down upon the table, that there was not a respectable counter jumper in Boston. Cobb remarked that Mr. Lawrence had extolled to him the character of that respectable class, on which Russell remarked tha[t] Mr. Bigelow's acquaintances were probably from the inferior ranks of counter jumpers. "That's a damned imputation! I defy any man here to say that I ever associated with counter jumpers—least of all, Mr. Russell, those whom it is your pleasure to denominate, in so highflown and grandiloquent a style, the *lower ranks* of counter jumpers," etc.

    ❦   ❦   ❦   ❦

Brooks: "Law! Damn it, I never knew anything like it. Why, I can't take up a book without it puts me to sleep. I don't know what in the devil made me take law—it's horrid! Greenleaf met my father the other day and told him I was making fine progress: what does he know about it? Father swallowed it all; I wish Greenleaf would hold his tongue; I swear, it's horrid."

    ❦   ❦   ❦   ❦

Law School Debating Society. Batchelder brought in numerous books from which he read for three-quarters of an hour, and made besides a most loose and ridiculous speech. He seems an instance of a man who is suspicious and timid from *running* or *snubbing* in private conversation, but will talk on forever, feeling a perfect independence, in the debating club where no one interferes with him.

Lee of Louisiana spoke in the negative of the question, which was that of nullification.

Hoadly of Ohio, whom I have often remarked for a wretchedly sickly, and feeble-looking person, spoke in the affirmative. His voice was like a lion's; and a supernatural energy seemed to animate his yellow faded features and give them an expression of fierce resolution.

Hooper of South Ca. also spoke in the aff[irmative]. He is a very gentlemanly southerner: pale, long-haired, well-formed and well-dressed: apparently haughty, proud, and aristocratic. He spoke with great fluency and not without taste, and was eminently courteous and stately in his manner.

Thayer of Mass. took a *common sense view* of the matter— every one of that assembly was *presumed to know* various things which he mentioned: the members of the convention were *at least* men of ordinary abilities, etc. A weak Yankee.

Even Parkman's oldest friends were not spared a taste of the acid in which he now seemed habitually to dip his pen, and the great as well as the lowly of the academic world came in for their share:

The thin, large-nosed man who tried to know everybody—took the Prex's cloak, with an "how-de-do, Mr. Quincy," and whom the Pres., with his usual felicity, cut.

There are also two personal reflections, the first of which suggests that someone suggested to Parkman that his pride and sense of superiority were offensive, while the second hints at the cause of Parkman's attitude:

"Pride goeth before destruction, and a haughty spirit before a fall"—think of that!

＊   ＊   ＊   ＊

Is a man a coward because he feels less than himself in a crowd?

For the rest, there are a few purple patches on nature, some notes of a visit to his classmate Snow in Fitchburg with Joe Peabody, and

an irreverent account of the Navy Club parading about in costume.
The most interesting entry of the first six months of 1845 deals
with a public meeting in Boston:

> May 30, 1845. A great meeting of the Fourierites in Tremont
> Chapel. Most of them were rather a mean set of fellows—several
> foreigners—plenty of women, none pretty—there was most cor-
> dial shaking of hands and congratulations before the meeting be-
> gan. A dirty old man, four feet high, filthy with tobacco, came
> and sat down by me and was very enthusiastic. He thought Mr.
> Ripley, who made the opening speech, "one of the greatest men
> our country can produce." Ripley was followed by a stout old
> man, in a sack, who had previously been busy among the au-
> dience welcoming, shaking hands, etc. He spoke with his hands
> in his pockets, and gave nothing but statistics, in a very dry, un-
> interesting manner. It surprised me to see these old fellows, who
> looked like anything but enthusiasts, attached to the cause. Hor-
> ace Grant [Greeley]—the editor from N.Y.—spoke in a very
> weak indecisive manner, seeming afraid of himself and his au-
> dience. He, however, gave some remarkable details of the work-
> ing of the "present system of society" as illustrated by the work-
> ing classes of N.Y.
>
> Brisbane and Dana followed in a pair of windy speeches, and
> Channing was beginning a *ditto* when I came away. They say
> that there is a system of laws by which the world is to be gov-
> erned "harmoniously," and that they have discovered those laws.
> F. Cabot was there, looking much more like a lunatic or a beast
> than man.

This gathering of the Transcendentalists, including many men
whom we now consider the greatest of the day, was a mere side-
show to Parkman, a collection of freaks and oddities. He had no
sympathy with the spiritual and intellectual currents of the day,
and was completely detached and unaware of them. He was of the
old order in New England, and intended that it should remain as
he had always known it.

As soon as he could put aside the law books for the summer,
Parkman left Cambridge on a historical research expedition which

took him through Pennsylvania, northwestern New York, and the Great Lakes region. This was not adventure for adventure's sake, but a sober fact-finding journey, which filled his notebook with references to books, magazines, and various living authorities who might be expected to clear up some vexed point of his proposed history of Pontiac's conspiracy, the great rising of the Indians against the whites at the close of the Seven Years' War. He left Boston on July 8, 1845, going first to New York and then to Philadelphia. He gathered a few references in New York, but was seemingly more impressed by a woman he encountered in Union Park,

> who had dreamed of chairs, and then, on another night, of glass tumblers; and, as she looked on the workmen at the fountain, felt a presentiment that she was destined to make her bread by means of it—so she bought chairs and a pitcher and glasses for water and lets them out for the people, as in the Champs Elysées. She also remarked upon the girls who make the park a place of assignation—spoke of the inconstancy natural to mankind—and was plainly up to snuff.

From Philadelphia, where he had letters of introduction to present from his teacher Jared Sparks, he went on to Lancaster, for he was anxious to find out all that he could about the Paxton Men's activities in 1763–64.

In Lancaster he joined forces with his historical correspondent, Simon Stevens—whose name he had not yet learned to spell, but whose brother Henry was to supply him with historical materials for many years, as a London bookseller. This Pennsylvania Dutch region seemed like another land to the New Englander, and he noted its oddities in detail:

> The people chiefly Dutch—among them a number of Mennonists, with long hair and beard. All the people here are strong and hearty as any men I ever saw—seem to take life easily—have open and hearty manners, but are represented by Stephens as particularly close and miserly—as ignorant and stupid also; knowing nothing beyond their farms, and, in the management of these, following the manner of their forefathers. The land here is very

rich, producing excellent wheat—there are a number of very rich people living in a very plain manner here. Lancaster City is said to be the richest in the state. According to Stephens, this little place contains four distinct and separated circles of society.

Through this rich countryside he and Stevens rode out to Paradise to visit Mr. Redmond Conyngham, who had collected a great store of information about the Indians and local history. The way took them not many miles from the home of the "Protestant monks," as Parkman called them, at Ephrata. The small, well-built houses of stone, with their very large and queerly shaped barns, impressed him by their strangeness. At Paradise they stopped at the whitewashed stone house of Mr. Whitmer, who welcomed them with hearty courtesy, though dressed like an ordinary laborer, and asked them to spend the night, which they were glad to do:

I was presented to his wife and daughter, who sat on the "stoup," after which the old gentleman hoped we would spare him the trouble of "bucking up"—he being evidently too lazy. We found his house stored with marine and mineral curiosities, etc., he being a virtuoso after his fashion, and—a miracle for a Dutchman —a dabbler in science!

Going to Mr. Conyngham's, who gave me much information on the Inds. we returned and found two young ladies, who quite deserved the title, invited to meet us. Having taken supper, during which the old gent. thrust in his head, and with a hearty grin, exclaimed ironically to his daughter, who poured out the tea: "Hulloa, Laura, don't these fellers mean to be done eating pretty soon? They'll starve us out of house and home." Having taken supper, we took a walk with the girls by the side of Peckway Creek—a small and not very clear stream close by the house. Our apartment was quite sumptuously furnished—Stephens says the old man is worth $40,000—but S. exaggerates.

Found my classmate Baker a schoolmaster here.

Returned to Lancaster in the morning—visited the famous jail—explored the yard and the rooms—the *reputed* scene of the massacre. The prisoners are sometimes afraid to enter No,

13 or 14—which tradition points out (falsely?) as the place—
no blood visible (!).

On the eighteenth he went on to Harrisburg, walking that evening
by the Susquehanna, a "most broad and majestic stream—full of
islands—with a fine prospect of mountains beyond—waters that
ripple over a stony bottom, making a deep low murmuring." He
saw a group of Dutchmen playing quoits, and found their faces
singularly free of "Yankee care and thought." But he liked these
"stout specimens of flesh and blood," and found them a remarkable contrast to the "puny Philadelphians." From Harrisburg he
went to Williamsport by canal boat—a form of transportation new
to him—none too sorry to leave behind him such a center of Loco-
focoism as the capital: "Several men in the offices were true representatives of their party—blackguards of the first water, though
one or two were quite gentlemanly men."

From Williamsport he continued to Trout Run by a miserable
railroad. Grand Island, not far from Williamsport, was known to
him as the goal of Colonel Armstrong's expedition against a band
of frontier-harrying Indians. There the river was flanked by high
hills, while below were wide intervales. Between Trout Run and
Blockhouse he passed through a wilderness of mountains, without
clearings, and found the scenery more to his taste than the "low
and disagreeable set of fellows" in the stage. Dining at Blossburg,
"a mining place—very small—very rough—very dirty—and very
disagreeable," he went on in the rain by rail to Corning. Beyond
Blossburg, along Tioga Creek, the settlements were chiefly Yankee,
but that redeeming fact did not make up for the discomforts of the
train and "the drunken swearing puppy in the cars," who first
amused and then disgusted Parkman. He spent the night at Corning, and in the morning came to Seneca Lake, where he took the
steamboat at Jefferson. Reaching Buffalo, where he saw some
Seneca Indians in the street, he took the crowded Detroit steamer,
which had on board:

    . . . A host of Norwegian emigrants—very diminutive—very
ugly—very stupid and brutal in appearance—and very dirty.
They appear to me less intelligent [than] and as ignorant as the

Indians. Besides these, a motley swarm of passengers of all nations.

He found the shores of Lake Erie low and monotonous, and little
else noteworthy about the voyage. But Detroit proved more pleasing, and he was struck by a group of Indians:

> . . . the little squaw—the old one with her continual grin—the
> old man with nose poxed away—and the rest. They had got a
> kettle of rum and were drinking it. They were miserably weak
> and slender. Evidently their only enjoyments were eating and
> drinking. They laughed and were very happy over their liquor.

So much for what white civilization had done to Pontiac's people
in less than a century.

With this observation Parkman got down to serious business:
making notes of the topography of the region and the chief scenes
of his proposed history—Hog Island, Ile à la Pêche, Presque Isle,
Lake St. Clair, the St. Clair River, Lake Huron. After spending a
night in Detroit he went on up Lake Huron to Mackinaw, plaguing
the captain of the steamer into identifying all points of interest
along the way. Mackinaw won his heart at once:

> The place is the picture of an ancient Canadian settlement—
> the little houses in Canadian style—some of them log, with roofs
> thatched with bark—the picket fences of rough sharpened stakes
> that surround them all—the canoes and Ind. huts on the shore
> give them a wild and picturesque air. Wild-looking half-breeds
> in abundance—a group of squaws and children, wrapped in their
> blankets, sat on the steps of a store—one little Canadian—three-
> quarters savage—had a red shawl tied round his head, red leg-
> gins, gay moccasins, and a blanket coat—another, who looked
> out from between his straight black locks with a wild and par-
> ticularly vile expression, was staring at the steamer.

This was the type of wilderness outpost which furnished the background to so much of the history that young Parkman was going
to write. He thrilled to the environment at once, as others have
thrilled since, reading his descriptions of such places. Parkman

came just in time, for, as he observed, "the fur companies are used up—Mackinaw is no longer an outfitting place—the voyageurs' occupation 's gone." But for some years yet Mackinaw preserved the old-time air, though its original function was lost.

Parkman was fortunate in his guide to Mackinaw, Lieutenant Henry Whiting of the Fifth Infantry, then stationed at the post. That first Sunday he showed the Sugar Loaf to Parkman, who had already walked around the shore of the island before breakfast, noting the "banks of limestone frequently jutting in rough spires, feathered with shrubs, from the midst of a thick growth of arbor-vitae, birch, and maple that cover the steep and high banks, while the white and waterworn masses are strewn along the water's edge." Near the Sugar Loaf was old Fort Holmes, on the highest point of land, commanding the present fort, and close to this, on the descent below, was Skull Rock where the trader Alexander Henry hid during the massacre in 1763. Parkman found the houses odd, thatched as they were with elm bark and built of square and whitewashed logs. Whiting characterized the French Canadian for him as "good-natured—jovial—lazy as far as regular work is concerned, but extravagantly fond of wandering about, fishing, etc." Captain Martin Scott, Whiting's superior, recalled for Parkman's benefit his memory of having seen bones in the cave at Skull Rock, before it had been filled up by the Indian boys at the mission, "each of whom, as he visited the place, threw a stone in."

Parkman made a journey by boat to Sault Sainte Marie, with a letter from Whiting to Henry R. Schoolcraft, the famous authority on the Indians, and wrote a careful account of the lay of the land for future reference. It was odd, in the midst of this wilderness, to meet a Mr. and Mrs. Arnold of New Bedford, who had a Miss Chandler and James Lawrence in their party and the atmosphere of New England about them. But Parkman did not allow this encounter with his old world to interfere with observation of one new to him:

The channel soon widens and loses some of its picturesque character, though some highlands and precipices appear. Two Ind. lodges of bark on the shore. Suddenly we turned into a narrow winding passage where, towards evening, the scene was as wild and beautiful as any I ever saw. This was not many miles from the Sault. At the Sault everything full of copper speculators. Found, with the party aforesaid, lodgings at the Baptist mission house—Mr. Bingham's. Conversed with him on the Inds.—hope he is not a fair specimen of Ind. missionaries: he is stupid and ignorant, and said to have no influence. Protestant missionaries generally are said to be without power or respect.

Ft. Brady—a square stockade with blockhouses at the corners.

The inhabs. of the Sault are chiefly Canadian and half-breeds —always dancing and merrymaking—who live in houses resembling those at Mackinaw.

Ind. lodges, some round, some peaked, on the bank of the Rapids. All Ojibway. Lodges covered with pukivi mats and birch-bark, the former very thick and warm. Saw Inds. fishing in the Rapids.

Mr. Arnold failed in his attempt to get the ladies a paddle down the rapid. Lawrence and I went down together. A half-breed, educated at the Mission at Mackinaw, named Joseph, directed the canoe. (The Chippewa birches are all large—they have small wooden canoes.) Joseph was remarkably intelligent. I afterwards conversed with him. All the Inds., he said, knew of Manabosho, and he mentioned several of his exploits, as recorded by Schoolcraft—also those of Paupukeewis, whose name he mentioned with a laugh. He spoke of fasts, love philters (which he said were universally in the hands of the young women), charms, etc., etc. He evidently believed much of them himself, and cautioned me against ever letting an Ind. girl to whom I might become attached get possession of one of my hairs, as she would then have it in her power to do me some mischief. He boasted to have once defeated a spell cast on a man by a conjurer.

Mr. and Mrs. Jones, copper speculators grown elevated by prospects of wealth—the latter coolly introduced herself at Bingham's—on scarcely any pretext—to Mrs. Arnold—and then presented her husband. She has been up to Copper Harbor, an exploit which increases her self-confidence and complacency. She gives her opinion as to where forts should be built, etc.

We returned to Mackinaw by the channel we came by— scenery appearing no less fine than before.

Through his friend Lieutenant Whiting, Parkman here made the acquaintance of Robert Stewart, who had played a leading part in the founding of Astoria. From Stewart he obtained some well-founded criticism of the "army of mystery books" about the Indians that he had been reading avidly amid the calm of Cambridge. Stewart thought the Christian Indian Tanner's book of much value: that he dictated nothing but what he believed to be true, but was sometimes self-deceived by the relics of his superstition and his savage imagination, and a victim of his former habit of telling stories until he himself believed them. Stewart cited the instance of an Indian who firmly believed that he had changed himself into a rattlesnake. He was less kind to the great Schoolcraft:

> Mr. S. thinks that Schoolcraft's *Algic Researches* are a superstructure of falsehood on a true foundation—that having once caught the tone and spirit of the tales, he multiplied them *ad libitum*—though he thinks many of them are genuine.

Captain Scott had promised to send Parkman to Old Mackinaw with a boat crew of soldiers, but was so bent on getting up a picnic of his own that he seemed little inclined to fulfill this promise. So Whiting engaged an old Canadian, François Lacroix, who with his two sons carried Parkman and himself over in a fishing boat. They explored the ruins of the old fort, ate dinner there, and turned back. The Canadians used a quick easy stroke, but it was not quick enough to keep them from being caught in a storm:

> . . . Before we left the land the thunder was growling from a huge pile of black clouds to the southward, and before we were half over, a long flash leaped from the edge of a black curtain of thundercloud down to the dark waters at the horizon and then the thunder bellowed over the waste. The shore of Michigan was obscured by white mists and rain—then Bois Blanc

grew dim also—the old fort too was veiled, and it evidently rained there, though away to the north the long undulating shore of Pt. St. Ignace was easily seen, and the nearer white cliffs and green shrubbery of Mackinaw. At last the drops fell fast upon us—another thunderclap bellowed over the water— old François laughed and put on his *chapeau*, and we pulled hard for the town. As we skirted the shore the Canadians stood at the doors of their huts in the rain looking at us. Passing between an old wreck and the shore, the swells, which ran high in the straits, nearly capsized Whiting, who stood in the boat. At length we gained the beach—the boat was hauled up—and we found the picnic party had abandoned their purpose, though the storm was passing, and a fine *arc-en-ciel*, as François said, rested on the water to the southward.

There were plenty of indications that Mackinaw had long been a great resort of the Indians. In the fort there was a box of bones which had been collected from various caves and crevices about the island—some had been found during this very August storm by a soldier taking refuge from the rain, under a rock, though most came from the Skull Rock cave. And the Indians still were very much in evidence at Mackinaw:

> Last night the Inds. in the lodges on the beach got drunk. I heard them singing for a long time in a mournful maudlin fashion, repeating the same words, and varying the song with what seemed to be boasts or narratives of exploits. The same monotonous music rose from half a dozen lodges that stood in line together.
>
> This morning I found a group sitting among the ruins of a hut which they seemed to have pulled down about their ears. They were still drunk, singing and laughing. One of them was a remarkably handsome squaw with a good-looking young man, with his leggins and bare thighs, at her side. There was another drunken fellow coiled up singing on the ground. Then a tall thin savage-looking old fellow came along and seated himself in the midst. They turned rum out of a bottle into the cover of a

tin pail, and tried to drink it raw, keeping up a constant laughing and maudlin merriment.

From Mackinaw Parkman went to Palmer, Michigan, in search of some historical papers he had heard about. Since it was Sunday, he attended church, but derived little profit from the occasion, save the sight of a pretty face in the choir. The clergyman was "a vile-looking fellow, tall and sallow, with a loud voice and a bad, obtrusive face." Parkman had little love for the flower of his own caste, and none at all for the mediocrities who filled the frontier pulpits. He got more church than he had bargained for, since a thunderstorm came up and detained the little congregation within doors for some time after service. The time was passed in singing psalms—an occupation for which Parkman had no great fondness. He found more congenial company at Brown's Tavern, where an "intelligent fellow" told him much of mines and steamboats.

But his purpose in visiting Palmer was to examine six trunks of papers which had belonged to Lieutenant McDougall, who had been a prisoner of Pontiac during the siege of Detroit. He spent a disagreeable day at this task, in a large room of a Mr. Whitman's house. The women of the house were at work there making carpets, and Parkman found the silence oppressive. To break it, he asked the older woman what she wanted for a fine engraving of George Washington which he found among the papers. She declared she would not take a dollar for it, but another woman came in "who, smitten with jealousy, tried to get a gift or a *swap* of it, but it would not do." After overhauling this immense mass of papers, he returned to the tavern and soon was in bad temper with a "dyspeptic man who insisted on helping himself to such morsels as suited him (with his own knife and fork). He had nursed himself till he had reached a state of egotistic selfishness."

Parkman returned to Detroit by the steamer *Red Jacket,* passing the time pleasantly with a Canadian gentleman in conversation about the islands of Thunder Bay. He crossed over to Windsor in Ontario to visit M. François Baby, descendant of one of the early French traders at Detroit, whose establishment consisted of a fine old brick house, with a hall strewn with "books, guns, neglected tables, old clocks, chests of drawers, and garments and Indian equipments." A little Negro girl and a strange-looking half-breed were sunning themselves among the hens and hogs in the backyard. From Windsor he went on to Sandwich, remarking on the little square porches in front of the old Canadian houses, and the local custom of always riding at a canter. He noted details about the construction of canoes, finding the large Chippewa type the "perfection of the thing," and also got his first sight of the Mackinaw boats, which he was to see a year later carrying furs down the Platte from the Rockies. He visited the venerable old Huron Church above Sandwich, where he found an assemblage of the little Canadian carts. But it seemed to him that the people here had caught English manners and "their French complaisance has disappeared." In search of a Mr. Askins, related to another early trader, he stopped at an English-looking cottage, but when the door was opened one glance told him that it was not the house he sought:

> The owner was an officer—his sword hung with his garments in the hall, and hard by were his gun and fishing rod. A fine pair of antlers lay on the windowsill of a little projecting room that seemed his study. So much for English tastes.

Finally he found Mr. Askins, "a little dried-up *distingué* man," who expressed much interest in Parkman's purpose and talked incessantly, but "almost unintelligibly from his front teeth being knocked out." Parkman, none the wiser for the sputter of talk, was ushered forth with a profusion of compliments in the best tradition of the race to which Mr. Askins's mother, a Campeau, belonged.

Parkman went back down Lake Erie to Buffalo by boat, taking careful notes on the topography of the country. Landing in a hubbub of noise and confusion, he continued to Niagara, where he put up at the Cataract, "a bloated noisy house—a set of well-dressed blackguards predominated at table":

> One fellow—very good-looking—I particularly noticed. He sent the waiter with a bottle of champagne to a friend of his at another table, who coolly helped himself and then proceeded to

fill the glasses of some ladies near him out of his friend's bottle. At this the latter's face became heavily overshadowed; he reddened with vexation, played uneasily with knife and fork, and turning to a neighbor remarked that he "always knew —— for a damn mean fellow, but *that* was a little *too* sneaking." So he bowed across the table and sipped his glass with great gravity. When the bottle which had got into such dangerous hands was returned to him, his face wonderfully brightened. Poor fellow! He had come with a half-year's clerk's salary to be gay and live fast for a week at Niagara: it was hard that his earnings should be drunk up in that unceremonious fashion.

Parkman's prolonged travels had left him prey to dyspepsia and consequent melancholy. He looked at the great cataract, but did not "feel in the temper to appreciate it or embrace its grandeur." Completely a victim of the "blue devils," he contemplated nature's wonders and man's inanity:

An old woman who, for the pure love of talking and an itching to speak to everyone, several times addressed me with questions about she knew not what, [which] filled me with sensations of particular contempt, instead of amusing me as they would have done had not my stomach been disordered. I sat down near the rapids. "What's all this but a little water and foam?" thought I. "What a pack of damned fools," was my internal commentary on every group that passed—and some of them deserved it. But, thank Heaven, I have partially recovered my good humor, can sympathize with the species, and to some degree feel the sublimity of the Great Cataract.

How many of the visitors here deserve to look on it? I saw in the tower a motherly dame and her daughter, amid the foam and thunder and the tremendous pouring of the water. "Oh, Ma!" (half-whispered) "He's looking at us! There, I've torn my sash; I must go home and pin it up, etc." Old Niagara pours bellowing on forever, as it has poured since the beginning of time, and generation after generation of poor little devils of human beings play their little pranks and think their little thoughts around him. He roars on undisturbed, while age after age of the manikins look at him, patronize him with their praises, and go to the devil before his eyes. What does he care for their pranks, their praises, or their fault-finding? His tremendous face never changes; his tremendous voice never wavers; one century finds him as the last did, in his unchanging power and majesty.

But he had not come to Niagara to write Channingesque phrases about what was referred to by his Negro guide as "The Seven Wonders of the World, sir!" but to have a look at the Devil's Hole, the scene of one of the worst massacres of the French and Indian War. Visiting the place in a violent August rain, he thought it the perfect spot for an Indian massacre. The great cliffs that lined the river were here notched away, leaving a deep gorge, "with sheer savage limestone fencing it on three sides, and the river on the other." He stood on Platform Rock and looked down into the gulf filled with a mass of thick vegetation: it was here that the ambushed were forced over the precipice to fall more than eighty feet to their death. Parkman viewed the scene with a tactician's eye, and it impressed him mightily, more than the Falls themselves. But one could not visit Niagara and avoid the sights, so Parkman zealously inspected all the various views of the Falls, and concluded that none in the world could match that from Table Rock. But he was amused, nevertheless, by an "old withered, hollow-eyed, straight-backed Yankee peering at the Falls, with a critical scrutiny, as if he was judging of the goodness of a bank-note."

Having had his fill of overpowering scenery, Parkman took the Lewistown Railroad as far as Syracuse, making topographical notes on Fort Niagara, Oswego, and Lake Salina. At Syracuse he hired a horse and rode to Onondaga Castle, the home of the Five Nations, descending into the valley near sunset. He found the prospect of the wooded hills, the rich flats, and the little stream Onondaga "very beautiful and romantic." It was all familiar to him from Bartram's description, which he found would answer for the present day with only a few changes. He acquired a guide by the judicious gift of cigars, and was shown the council house, where the Green Corn Dance was soon to be celebrated: "It was a long plain, one-story building, containing only one large room, with a fireplace at each end, benches placed around, a brass horn to convoke the people, and a large turtle-shell rattle to keep time to the dance." By more presents of cigars and pipes, he got the Indians in good humor, but found them nevertheless "the worst people in the world to extract information from: the eternal grunted *yas* of acquiescence follows every question you may ask them without distinction." One old fellow proved more talkative, and seemed to remember the partitioned council house described by Bartram, but Parkman concluded in despair: "It is impossible to say, however, whether he really did so."

Leaving Onondaga behind, he went on past the site of Fort Stanwix, Oneida, and German Flats, finding that though the Mohawk Valley had no pretensions to sublimity it formed a rich and picturesque landscape, which appealed to him—"I am getting a stronger relish for quiet beauties." Having made careful notes on the country he was going to write about, he turned his attention to his fellow-travelers on the train:

> The lawyer with the sharp nose, thin face, and small mouth. His vehement narratives about himself, and the singular contortions of countenance with which he enforced them.
>
> The noisy and vulgar party of girls, who sat on the backs of the seats and filled the car with their cackling. The old fool of a woman, their mother, who rivaled the accomplishments of her daughters. Is not a *half-educated* vulgar weak woman a disgusting animal? When there is no education at all, and no pretension, the matter is all very well—where high education and good sense are united, it is very well indeed; but the half and half genteel—damn them!

A man and woman were run over and killed by the cars at Schenectady—Parkman used the incident twelve years later in altered form in his novel. One of his fellow-passengers was incited to fury, and with clenched fists threatened a man whom he took for a member of the railroad company: "I accuse you for a murderer! By God, I'll have the law on you—I want to know who you are. I want to know if you are a gentleman, etc." And on this note of violence

Parkman re-entered, by way of the steamer from New York, peaceful New England, where only the mild excitements of a Hasty Pudding dinner, a class supper, and other Commencement festivities occupied his attention until the Law School reopened. Though Parkman completed the law course and took his degree, history was his dominant concern during the months that followed. In the middle of January 1846 he made a brief trip to New York and Baltimore for research purposes. Under the double burden of law and historical studies, his sight showed signs of collapse, and using this circumstance as an argument, he won his father's consent to the greatest of all his preparatory expeditions, the Oregon Trail trip, on which he set off in March.

Part Two

THE OREGON TRAIL
1846

9: A Patrician on the Oregon Trail—I

*We little thought what the future had
in store.*

F.P., *Oregon Trail*, 1872

AMERICA'S march to the Pacific was well advanced when
Parkman made his Oregon Trail trip in the spring and summer of 1846. The old frontier of the Mississippi was crumbling away
as the nation pursued its Manifest Destiny westward and in less
than half a century doubled its extent. The national state of mind
is best expressed in the eloquent words of Herman Melville:

> God has predestinated, mankind expects, great things from our
> race; and great things we feel in our souls. The rest of the na-
> tions must soon be in our rear. We are the pioneers of the world;
> the advance guard, sent on through the wilderness of untried
> things, to break a new path in the New World that is ours. In our
> youth is our strength; in our inexperience, our wisdom.

The Jacksonian revolution, none the less a revolution for having
been fought at the polls, had brought the West and the South to
power at the expense of New England and the Atlantic seaboard.
As the remnants of the Federalists and the Whigs met defeat after
defeat at the polls, the country turned its face westward and
founded first an inland empire and then a continental one. The
great movement came to a climax in the middle forties with the
annexation of Texas, the Mexican War, the conquest of California
and the Spanish Southwest, and the settlement of the Oregon
boundary.

In the forties the trickle of hunters and traders and missionaries
who had followed the routes blazed in the earlier years of the
century by Lewis and Clark, Pike, Long, Bell, and Smith became a
swelling stream of emigrants and settlers, driven westward by the
ruinous effects of the panic of 1839, by the growing industrializa-
tion of the East which went against their independent grain, by

fever in the Illinois and Missouri bottomlands, by the desire to find a safe haven for their faiths amidst growing intolerance, by the lust for more land and more lucrative trade. John C. Frémont— the "Pathfinder" who actually was only a path-popularizer—re-explored the overland routes to Oregon and California and Mexico long used by the mountain men; the *Report* of his first and second expeditions in the early 1840's, ably written in collaboration with his wife, the talented daughter of Senator Thomas Hart Benton of Missouri, was printed by the ten thousand by order of the Senate and the House, read widely and discussed still more widely. It was a book of incalculable influence on its period: it did much to open the sluice gates and swell the stream of western emigration into a torrent. There were only a hundred American men, women, and children in Oregon in 1840; less than a hundred in California; and fewer still in the Southwest. Yet in six years' time these regions became part of the United States, and their American population had increased more than fortyfold. Over the rough trails from Independence, Missouri, the gateway to the West, the emigrants came in their thousands each year, bearing their few belongings with them, inflamed by roseate dreams of a new life in the new world of the West, and driven by that obscure urge to push on into the land of the setting sun which is the history of this country. Eighteen hundred and forty-seven saw the high-water mark of the Oregon emigration, with nearly three thousand new settlers pouring over South Pass into the Pacific Watershed; the great trek of the Mormons to Salt Lake, which established the fortunes of the Latter-Day Saints and the state of Utah; and increased emigration to California. All this lay ahead when young Francis Parkman was on the Oregon Trail in 1846, but the signs of things to come were plain. Some two or three thousand souls, two-thirds of them bound for Oregon, the rest for California, traveled the Oregon and California trail in that year; and while Parkman amused the Indians on Laramie Creek with rude fireworks made from leaves of Frémont's book, that brash adventurer was prematurely declaring the Republic of California and hoisting the Bear Flag at San Francisco. Barely a month later Commodore Sloat sailed into Monterey and annexed California to the United States, and having surprised himself by his daring in fulfilling his instructions, he retired and turned over his command to Commodore Stockton. Meanwhile General Zachary Taylor was advancing deep into Mexico and winning the victories of Palo Alto, Resaca de la Palma, and Monterrey, which paved the way for Winfield Scott's breaking of the Mexican power in the Southwest in the following year.

A young man, self-dedicated to the service of history, probably never had better opportunities to observe at first hand history in the making. To complete its kindness to one already a darling of fortune, fate threw Parkman into the company of many of the great men and great movements of the West in that era: of the great Oregon emigration of 1846, of the ill-fated Donner Party which perished in the High Sierras that winter, of the fomenters of the California uprising which brought the flag to the Pacific, of old Pierre Chouteau the co-founder of St. Louis, of Thomas Fitzpatrick, "Broken Hand," the greatest of the mountain men; of Daniel Boone's grandsons, of Louis Vasquez, partner of Jim Bridger and great scout and hunter in his own right; of Colonel Stephen Watts Kearny who led the dragoons of the Army of the West into Mexico that same summer, and in the previous year had marched over most of the route that Parkman followed; of the Mormons seeking a New Jerusalem and a haven from the persecution of the Gentiles; of Paul Dorion, the son of the half-breed voyageur who had accompanied Lewis and Clark's expedition to the Columbia River and the Pacific as far as the South Mandan villages, and who had shared the rigors of Wilson Hunt's journey to found Astoria.

What use did the young Boston patrician, already blessed with the means and leisure to take the trip, and the temperament and training necessary to meet the rigors of western life, make of these remarkable opportunities? The answer, a surprisingly disappointing one under the circumstances, has up to the present been found in the pages of *The Oregon Trail,* Parkman's first and best-known book. A more satisfactory answer may now be found in the diaries from which that book arose, which are far more revealing than their author knew as he penciled his observations into the little books by the campfire, in the rude comfort of some fur-trading establishment, or in an Indian lodge in the Rockies. Since the book was dictated to his companion on that journey, Quincy Adams Shaw, while Parkman was taking the water-cure at the Brattleboro Spa in Vermont in a vain attempt to regain the health and sight which he had shattered on that arduous trip, it is not surprising that these three little notebooks, bound in leather and marbled boards, complement the published work with much additional material and constitute a narrative far more readable and absorbing than the famous book which was derived from them, but was diluted triply by the circumstances of its composition. Here is the West in 1846, written down as it passed before the eyes of a student of the wilderness, and of a historian who had as yet written no history, but had already attained some mastery of the craft of writing, and powers of observation rare in one so young. These slim volumes, with their pencil scrawl faint on the faded blue paper, went westward by train, stage, and river steamer from New York to St. Louis, then up the Missouri to Independence and Westport, the great emigrant jumping-off places for Oregon and Santa Fe and California; then in saddlebags across the prairie and the plains and up the Platte to Fort Laramie, then into the foothills of the Rockies with a wandering village of Indians, then south under the shadow of Long's and Pike's Peaks to the Pueblo and Bent's Fort, and then back along the Arkansas to Westport by the Santa Fe Trail.

Parkman was both too young and too typical a Bostonian to be an objective observer. Therefore it is well to examine his own make-up before examining his observations. The very circumstances that enabled him to take the trip handicapped him as an observer of historic events. Thanks to his strenuous wilderness expeditions during his college years, he was an excellent rider and a good shot, and not unaccustomed to physical hardship. Nevertheless the twenty-three years of his life had been easy ones, and, for all his love of the outdoors, had been passed more among books and in luxurious surroundings than among men engaged in the struggle for existence against great natural and economic odds. The record of *The Oregon Trail*, however, bears out Parkman's observation in later life that "a gentleman of the right sort will stand hardship better than anybody else . . . that a trained and developed mind is not the enemy but the active and powerful ally of

PAGES FROM THE OREGON TRAIL
NOTEBOOKS

Parkman's firsthand notes on Indians and Santa Fe traders—the raw materials for The Oregon Trail. *The reproduction at the top is the exact size of the original page.*

constitutional hardihood. The culture that enervates instead of strengthening is always a false or partial one."

Parkman withstood the rigors of life on the Oregon Trail, which cost the lives of many of the emigrants and ruined the health of more, but the trip brought about the breakdown of a constitution already injured by overzealous efforts to strengthen it. Parkman went west to rest his eyes, strained by too much study; he returned with them weakened still further by exposure to the pitiless glare of the sun and the harsh alkali dust of the plains, and with an impaired digestion, the insomnia to which he was to be a lifelong victim, and the arthritis that crippled him and prevented him from ever leading again the strenuous life he loved so well. It must never be forgotten in reading *The Oregon Trail* that during much of the expedition it describes Parkman was a sick man, kept going only by his constitutional tenacity and strength of will—increased by the necessities of his immediate circumstances—and that its lively pages were dictated by an invalid unable to use his eyes for reading and writing and obliged to husband his physical and nervous strength with the utmost care. That is one reason why the diaries are invaluable, for two of the three volumes were largely filled with notes before sickness overtook Parkman, and their tone was not affected by the hypochondria to which he soon after fell a victim. There are few references to illness in the diaries, though there are many in the book.

Perhaps the most serious single handicap that Parkman had as a student of the West was the very inherited wealth that made the trip possible. The means that enabled him to devote two-thirds of a year to a journey, simply for adventure, recreation and study, which so many were making in order to live, blinded him to the profound social forces which were at work in the West in 1846. His companion, Quincy Adams Shaw, was interested chiefly in the opportunities the expedition furnished for adventure and good hunting. Parkman shared these interests, but he also had a scholarly object:

I went in great measure as a student, to prepare for a literary undertaking of which the plan was already formed. . . . It was this that prompted some proceedings on my part which, without a fixed purpose in view, might be charged with youthful rashness. My business was observation, and I was willing to pay dearly for the opportunity of exercising it.

These words, written a quarter of a century later in a new preface to *The Oregon Trail,* perhaps lays too much emphasis on Parkman's seriousness of purpose at the time. It is clear that his passion for adventure, for the wilderness, and for a life as different as possible from that which he had been leading as a Harvard student and the son of an eminent Unitarian divine of Boston, was quite as influential in driving him westward as his desire to observe the Indians in their own surroundings before they were spoiled by contact with the whites. He was a young romantic, fired by much reading of Scott's and Cooper's tales and Byron's poems to rebellion against the "invincible commonplace" that had overtaken the East. He did not choose to lead the soft life of luxury he might have led in Boston; but he had not abandoned the ideology of his class and environment. Boston and Harvard had made him an aristocrat and considerable of a snob, contemptuous of the new democracy of the "rabble" and heedless of the forces at work in the West. He was committed by tradition, training, and taste to the preservation of the old Federalist-Whig order, which was already well on its way to ruin. The extent of his social and historical blindness is best indicated by his own report of a conversation with Shaw as the cousins were on the last part of their trip:

I remember that, as we rode by the foot of Pike's Peak, when for a fortnight we met no face of man, my companion remarked, in a tone anything but complacent, that a time would come when these plains would be a grazing country, the buffalo give place to tame cattle, farmhouses be scattered along the water courses, and wolves, bears, and Indians be numbered among the things that were. We condoled with each other on a prospect so melancholy, but we little thought what the future had in store. We knew that there was more or less gold in the seams of these untrodden mountains; but we did not foresee that it would build cities in the waste and plant hotels and gambling houses among the haunts of the grizzly bear. We knew that a few fanatical outcasts were groping their way across the plains to seek an asylum from Gentile persecution; but we did not imagine that the polygamous hordes of Mormon would rear a swarming Jerusalem in the bosom of solitude itself. We knew that, more and more, year after year, the trains of emigrant wagons would creep in slow procession toward barbarous Oregon or wild and distant California; but we did not dream how Commerce and Gold would breed nations along the Pacific, the disenchanting screech of the locomotive break the spell of weird mysterious mountains, woman's rights invade the fastnesses of the Arapahoes, and despairing savagery, assailed in front and rear, vail its scalplocks and feathers before triumphant commonplace. We were no prophets to foresee all this; and, had we foreseen it, perhaps some perverse regrets might have tempered the ardor of our rejoicing.

No prophet indeed, and singularly blind for one whose admitted business was historical observation. The signs of the great transformation of the West were there, but Parkman could not read them.

The expedition originated in the fertile brain of Quincy Shaw, a great lover of travel and hunting. Coolidge Shaw, his brother and Parkman's cousin, wrote to the latter from Rome, where he was studying for the priesthood:

Quin writes me that he hopes to have your company on his westward trip—I should like to be of the party.

It is rather a pity that this hope was not realized, for the presence of an embryo Jesuit might have lent a more earnest spirit to the expedition. Certainly Parkman's book would have been of more interest if he had followed the scheme proposed for the journey by Coolidge Shaw:

By the way, the Bishop of Oregon [Blanchet] has just left here; it is a pity that you can't go as far as his settlement on the other side of the Rocky Mountains to see how finely they're getting along there. I proposed to Quin to become a Catholic & then a priest, & cut off there & convert the Indians, when he'd see enough of wild & hard life to satisfy him tho-roughly, I reckon. But the young gentleman seemed rather to "sniff" at the notion, as I supposed he would.

In any case Quincy Shaw's plan needed no urging to enlist Parkman in it. His intention of writing the history of the Old French War had now enlarged until it constituted a history of the American forest and of the American Indian. To write that history an intimate knowledge of the primitive savage was essential. In the West alone could that knowledge still be gained at firsthand, for the Indians of the East had become extinct, tamed, or had been transferred to western reservations. On the plains and in the Rockies the Indians still lived much as they always had, and casual contact with mountain men and traders had not altered them. For some years still the tribes, except for the Comanches, were to remain on the whole well disposed to the whites who were gradually usurping their magnificent heritage. Not until after the Civil War were they conscious of being crowded out, and so driven to those bloody wars which made Sioux and Comanche names as dread as ever Mohawk and Iroquois had been in the East.

The cousins were to meet in St. Louis to outfit for the expedition. Parkman took a circuitous route in order to obtain further information for that history of Pontiac which already filled his mind, though it was not to see print for another five years. He was in New York at the end of March, where he met a Mr. Kay, a Fourierite Philadelphia bookseller, "a queer combination of worldly shrewdness with transcendental flightiness"—Parkman had not changed his poor opinion of the "she-philosophers of Brook Farm." Evidently he patronized this idealist, being full of that excessive superiority of young men fresh from Harvard, and he further noted:

> The little contemptible faces—the thin weak tottering figures —that one meets here on Broadway, are disgusting. One feels savage with human nature.

The next day he saw Mr. Schoolcraft, the great authority on the Indians, and gathered some bits of lore about the Indian character, which he carefully noted down. On April 1 he was in Harrisburg, where the river was just subsiding after a spring freshet. The sight of a man lounging on the river bank—what better occupation in the spring?—led him to the sage rhetorical question: "Is it not true that the lower you descend in education and the social scale the more vicious men become?" Sound doctrine for a young Boston patrician of Federalist notions. The next day he was in Carlisle, having crossed the Susquehanna in a flatboat filled with "quiet, stupid, stout Dutch," whom he found a striking contrast to a corresponding group of Yankees. Parkman was by no means an American: he was a Yankee, who felt at home only in Yankeeland, and disliked the ways and manners of all outlanders. He was still in many respects a very provincial young man, despite the liberalizing effect of his travels. The trouble with the Pennsylvania Dutch, he finally decided, was that "their minds were gone to sleep." He traversed the Cumberland Valley, noting the main features of the landscape, with particular attention to relics and landmarks of General Bouquet's campaign in 1763. He lingered for another day at Carlisle, jotting down his impression as if in a foreign country: "The population here is said to be chiefly of English and Irish descent. The men at the tavern seem to be chiefly lawyers, and are of decent appearance."

On April 3 he reached Chambersburg, after passing through low hills which rose gradually to the northern and southern ranges of the Blue Ridge. He reached Pittsburgh on the sixth, after an uncomfortable journey in the crowded stage. The coach had left at midnight and at dawn he was high in the mountains above Loudon, overlooking the Cove Valley. The place names now were familiar to him from much reading of border-warfare accounts; he underlines them as he notes them down, and one can almost hear the music they made in his ear: Tuscarora Mountain, Sidling Hill, Bloody Run, Bedford, Wills Mountain, Dunnings Creek, Ligonier. And he adds: "This was, I suppose, the identical road cut to meet Braddock's road in 1755, and the same by which Bouquet passed." He found that very few people in the neighborhood of Bushy Run had ever heard of the battle, and no one could show him the scene of it. Before leaving Pittsburgh, he visited the scene of Braddock's defeat, and with the smugness and the infinite wisdom of young

Harvard he observed: "It is as described by Sparks." Nevertheless Parkman made a thorough examination of the ground, carefully noting down the details for later use in *Pontiac*. The place moved him: it brought the past into the present, for bones still littered the battlefield. And it pleased him that his guide refused any reward for his trouble; for that refusal seemed to show a certain reverence for historically hallowed ground. With Mr. Richard Biddle he visited Bouquet's redoubt and the remains of Fort Pitt.

In the course of his fieldwork he came to the conclusion that the Pennsylvania countryfolk were very fine physical specimens, but "dull and stupid":

> One of the stage-drivers completely realized my idea of an Indian trader—bluff, boisterous, profane, and coarse. As I watched him, I could not help recurring to certain female friends and wondering how beings so opposite in all points of person and character could belong to the same species.

It was hardly fair to set a backwoods stage-driver up for comparison with the belle of Keene who then held Parkman's affections, but young men in love have done stranger things before and since. Parkman continued in a sophomoric philosophical mood:

> "Human nature is the same everywhere"—so says everybody, but does not education make most essential distinctions? Take a Wordsworth, for instance, and how little will you find in him in common with the brutish clods who were my fellow-passengers across the Alleghenies? Or take any ordinary man of high education, and what sympathies can he have with such?

In short, take Francis Parkman, Jr., A.B., Harvard, fresh from the Law School and strong on intellectual pride. But he had acquired enough of the scholarly attitude to follow this smug observation with: "Read some good history of Penna., and observe out of what combination of nations and religions the present population sprang."

He passed down the Ohio in a steamboat, rubbing shoulders distastefully with "gamblers and ragamuffins," There was also a

free and easy New Yorker on board, who struck up an acquaintance
with him by remarking at some delay: "I shan't see my wife tonight." Parkman learned that this fellow had been "neglected in
his youth and through a susceptible turn of mind had, according
to his own account, plunged into every kind of excess. About six
years ago he 'got religion'—and he lately married. . . . He is on
his way to see his new wife in Cincinnati." Such confidences were
outrageous to a reticent Bostonian, particularly when forced upon
him by a onetime railroad engineer. Parkman was moved to attempt his first generalization about the West:

> The English reserve or *offishness* seems to be no part of the
> western character—though I have had no opportunity of ob-
> serving a gentleman of high standing. I observe this trait in my-
> self—today, for instance, when a young fellow expressed satis-
> faction that he should accompany me to St. Louis, I felt rather
> inclined to shake him off, though he had made himself agreeable
> enough.

To a lover of the wilderness, all was fair in nature and only man
was vile—or at least suspect:

> Spring is beautifully awakening as we descend the Ohio—a
> hundred shades of green are budding out along the steep declivi-
> ties; and round the scattered houses are peach trees in rich
> bloom. It is pleasant to look upon all this, after contemplating
> the deformity of minds and manners that prevails hereabouts.

As he passed down the river, the banks grew lower and lower, and
the bottomland wetter. The forests rose from the very margin of
the water, whose wide expanse was broken here and there by an
island.

At Paducah three flatboats full of West Virginian emigrants came
on board. They had spent a month descending the Holston River
to the mouth of the Tennessee in their homemade boats. The boats
were like floating houses, and Parkman judged them to be the same
as those originally used in navigating the Ohio. The men were good-
looking and hardy, though smaller than the Pennsylvanians:

Some were dressed in red rifle-frocks, and they tell me that Indian leggins are still occasionally used in the Valley. All their domestic implements had an old-fashioned air—chairs with bottoms of ash-slivers—gourd dippers—kettles—anvil-bellows —old bureaus—clothing—bedding—frying pans, etc., etc., were rapidly passed into the steamer. Several old long-barreled flint-lock rifles followed. Conversing with these men, I found them intelligent and open, though apparently not much educated. They were going to Iowa.

And shortly Parkman was on the Mississippi, gazing at its rapid muddy current and the low forest-covered banks which had witnessed the passing of La Salle and the Jesuit missionaries, and of many more of the great figures of the past who haunted his brain. Perhaps his jubilation at this attainment of one goal brought about a general rise of spirits, for he seemed free for the first time of the depression that he called "the blue devils," and able to admit that in some respects the West might be superior to the East:

> The men of the emigrant party are manly, open, and agreeable in their manners—with none of the contracted, reserved manner that is common in New Englanders. Neither have the women, who are remarkably good-looking, any of that detestable starched lackadaisical expression common in vulgar Yankee women. The true philosophy of life is to seize with a ready and strong hand upon all the good in it, and to bear its inevitable evils as calmly and carelessly as may be.

The morose New Englander had already been impressed by the happy-go-lucky way of the West.

Parkman's good fortune stood him in good stead, for he had an encounter with the white hope of the Whigs and the only political leader who might halt the advance of Jacksonian democracy. Upon arrival at the Planters' House in St. Louis he found a crowd gathered around its door,

> and in the midst stood HENRY CLAY, talking and shaking hands with anyone who chose. As he passed away he asked an old man for a pinch of snuff, at which the mob was gratified; and the old

man, striking his cane on the bricks, declared emphatically that Clay was the greatest man in the nation; and that it was a burning shame he was not in the presidential chair. So much for the arts by which politicians—even the best of them—thrive.

Quincy Shaw had not yet arrived and Parkman found "infinite difficulty from contradictory accounts of the Indian country." In New York Ramsay Crooks of the Northern Division of Astor's American Fur Company had given him letters requesting all possible assistance from the company's western representatives; now Chouteau and Clapp of the Western Division overwhelmed him with their attentions. They provided him with a passport, reading:

St. Louis 25 April 1846

To any person or persons in our employ in the Indian County— This will be presented by our friends Mr. F. Parkman and Mr. Quincy A. Shaw, who visit the interior of the country for their pleasure & amusement, and whom we beg to recommend to your kind and friendly attention.

If these Gentlemen shall be in need of anything in the way of supplies &c., you will oblige us by furnishing them to the extent of their wants; as also to render them any & every aid in your power, of which they may stand in need.

Very truly yours, &c.
P. Chouteau Junr. & Co.
John Clapp

Signature of Mr. F. Parkman—F. Parkman
   do—Quincy A. Shaw—Quincy A. Shaw

Penciled on the back are Parkman's notes of mileages on the Oregon and Santa Fe trails, the great names jotted down as casually as the tame cities of a modern auto route, except for notes about where water might be found. Parkman stuffed this document into a fold of his pocket account-book, along with several calling cards, reading solely "F. Parkman." No Boston gentleman of Federalist stock could go adventuring among the Indians and trappers without such pasteboard tokens of gentility!

Weary after his arduous journey by train, stage, flatboat, and steamboat across half the continent, Parkman put aside all preparations for the expedition and crossed the river to Cahokia, to pass a beautiful spring day in that level country, "part forest, part prairie, the whole just awakening into life and bloom." Amid the herds of wild ponies who ran about, he rode over the prairie, struck by the strangeness of a region new to him:

> The forests here are not like ours—they are of a generous and luxuriant growth, and just now fragrant with a multitude of buds and blossoms, and full of the song of birds. They are fettered and interlaced by grapevines that overrun the whole, like so many serpents.
>
> Cahokia is all French. French houses, with their fat, projecting eaves and porches, little French horses—and a little French inn. Madame Jarrot's house is the chief establishment of the place. Calling on the old lady for historic[al] information, I entered a large hall, with a floor of polished oak—oak panels—a large fireplace, and two stairways in the rear leading up to the chambers. This hall was the reception room—the only part of the house I saw—but it smacked sufficiently of the Olden Time.

But St. Louis was as representative of the future as of the past. In 1846 it was humming with life, as the metropolis of the West, the home of the great American fur trade, and the outfitting center of emigrants bound for Oregon, California, and New Mexico—though that last role was fast passing to Independence.

Parkman encountered Passed Midshipman Selim E. Woodworth, U.S.N., here, "on his way to the Columbia River with dispatches. He has a wild plan of raising a body of men and *taking Santa Fe.*" Parkman, like many other Americans, had no notion of how deep a game President Polk was playing and what his real designs were. Those dispatches may have concerned the encouragement of American chauvinism in the Oregon region, still nominally British, or they may have existed only in the curious brain of this thirty-year-old officer on leave of absence and out for adventure. Woodworth, of course, had no part in the taking of Santa Fe later this same year by the Army of the West, for he was on his way to Oregon at the time, but he was active in the temporary California government early in 1847, and covered his name with ignominy by refusing to lead the Third Relief to the Donner Party, then marooned in the High Sierras and reduced to cannibalism, unless a sizable cash guarantee was made. Parkman met him twice again while in the West, and in each instance Woodworth was causing trouble characteristically by words rather than actions. Parkman's harsh judgment of the midshipman, who evidently had some notion of duplicating Frémont's career, seems to be borne out by the facts.

On April 19 Parkman interviewed old M. Cerré in his search for Pontiac material, and wrote a long entry in his notebook which reveals that he was still in a pseudo-philosophical frame of mind:

> How infinite is the diversity of human character! Old M. Cerré of nearly eighty—lively, bright, and active—the old man goes about rejoicing in his own superiority to age—wrapped up in himself, unobservant, impenetrable, impassive. His companion was the reverse—young, silent through bashfulness, observing all, feeling all, and constantly in hostility to external influences—though resolute and determined, acting ever under the burden of constitutional diffidence. How hostile is such a quality to a *commanding* character. It is the mind as it stamps its character on the *bearing* and *manner* that carries weight—the bold, unhesitating, confident expression has authority—not the forced, sharp, painful expression of resolution struggling against diffidence. Some men have a sort of power from their very vanity— they are too dull, too impassive to feel a repressive influence from other minds—and thinking themselves the greatest men on earth, they assume a part and voice that impose a sort of respect. Others there are who, with many of the internal qualities of command, can never assume its outward features—and fail in consequence. How wide and deep and infinitely various is human nature! And how the contemplation of it grows more absorbing as its features disclose themselves to view.

Having learned that Pontiac was killed near Cahokia, according to local tradition, he crossed the river again to the French settlement that afternoon, amid a crowd of Sunday merrymakers:

The country overflows with game. In returning I saw on board the boat some twenty sportsmen. Some had a dozen or two of duck slung together—others as many fish as they could carry, perch, bream, garfish, buffaloes, catfish, etc. The sportsmen were chiefly Germans. No wonder that the French at the old settlement led a merry life of it.

Fresh from his ramble in the lush countryside, Parkman noted down the contents of a letter from "old Mr. Thomas Fitzpatrick, the well-known hunter and frontiersman," written to Lieutenant James W. Abert of the Topographical Engineers in February of that year, containing his opinion of the origin of the western Indian tribes. Parkman largely adopted it, and the substance of his notes is given in the published version of *The Oregon Trail.*

Another day he rode out to Jefferson Barracks, the famous cantonment, and found the view from the hill above Vides Poches lovely:

The French settlers plant fruit trees everywhere amongst their picturesque-looking houses, and these were all in bloom. The French are content to live by the produce of their little gardens, knowing nothing and caring nothing for the world beyond their little village.

This observation is more than a little dubious, since the Great West was pioneered by the French of the Mississippi Valley towns, as the names of hundreds of rivers, mountains, and settlements indicate; since the fur trade of the West was developed to the point where it became attractive to John Jacob Astor by the able Pierre Chouteau, who lent his name to points as far north as Dakota and as far south as New Mexico, and by his French and half-breed *voyageurs;* and since the descendants of these intrepid adventurers still did the hewing of wood and the drawing of water for all expeditions to the plains and mountains. Parkman's life was saved on several occasions by two Frenchmen from St. Louis, and without their aid he never could have made the journey which first brought him fame. There may have been tame French settlers in the *ban-lieue* of St. Louis, but many of the fruit farms he saw were the refuges of men who spent many years on the prairie and in the mountains for the few months they spent in ease on their little farms near the western metropolis. Parkman had not yet learned the first principle of the historian's craft: that generalizations are easy and appealing, but usually false.

And he revealed here, in the first of many instances, his lack of insight into ways of life other than his own, and his arrogant pride in his Anglo-Saxon blood as opposed to other strains. It was to be many years before he partially escaped from this provincial attitude; he never succeeded in freeing himself entirely from it. Though he later had many French Canadian friends, he found his closest companions in Canada among Canadians of Anglo-Saxon blood. He was always slightly on guard against the Latin, whose ways he never came to comprehend with full sympathy, and this was perhaps his greatest handicap as the historian of the French in North America. One of the most remarkable features of his great achievement is that he succeeded so magnificently in his enterprise despite this deep-rooted bias.

From Thomas Fitzpatrick, who was not "old" but white-haired at forty-eight as a result of his rigorous experiences, he gathered more information about the social organization of the Indians of the West and of their customs in war and peace. He heard his first tall tales of the feats of the medicine men: in a few months he was to be a witness to similar phenomena. Impressed by Fitzpatrick's lore, Parkman refrained from judging him, as he judged many other acquaintances on this journey, summarily and rather callowly. On April 25 he penciled this entry:

> I have seen a strange variety of characters—Dixon, the nonentity—Ewing, the impulsive, unobserving, ardent Kentuckian, who lays open his character to everyone and sees nothing of those about him—the quiet, sedate, and manly Jacobs, his companion. These two are going to California.

On the following day, he rode out to pay an eleventh-hour visit to old Pierre Chouteau, the co-founder of St. Louis, who lived three miles out of the city:

Found his old picturesque French house in the middle of the woods—neat Negro houses, with verandas—bird cages hung in the porch—chickens chirping about the neat yards. The old man was not well and could not tell me much. He, however, described Pontiac as a man six feet high, of very commanding appearance, and whenever he saw him, splendidly dressed. He used to come to St. Louis on visits.

His son, Lignest P. Chouteau, told me the following, as coming from his father. Pontiac held a high command among Montcalm's Indians. He was killed at Cahokia, at the instigation of the English. The Spaniards requested his body and buried it at *St. Louis.* Mr. L.P.C. is to look into the church records for the mention of it.

In the diary this is no hint of the great nostalgic passage in *Pontiac* which seemingly arose from this meeting. Evidently Pierre Chouteau's recollections were more impressive in retrospect than at the time they were delivered, for Parkman later found "the magic of a dream and the enchantment of an Arabian tale" in them, and made this eloquent picture of the two St. Louis the old man had known:

> Where in his youth he had climbed the woody bluff, and looked abroad on prairies dotted with bison, he saw with the dim eye of old age the land darkened for many a furlong with the clustered roofs of the western metropolis. For the silence of the wilderness, he heard the clang and turmoil of human labor, the din of congregated thousands; and where the great river rolled down through the forest, in lonely grandeur, he saw the waters lashed into foam beneath the prows of panting steamships, flocking to the broad levees.

The parallel between the old wilderness—a bit of which Parkman observed in his ramble near Cahokia and which he recorded in a morbid passage of *The Oregon Trail*—in which creature struggled with creature for survival and might was right, and the bustling city in which emigrants were preparing for the long journey to Oregon, California, or Mexico, and traders were making ready their wagons for Santa Fe, escaped this dedicated observer, who did not recognize that this, too, was the battle for survival. He was glad to leave the turbulent western metropolis, with its jumbling of new and old and of many racial stocks, all touched by the new doctrine of equalitarianism, and hard driven by the need to find new fields for trade, farming, or faith. He was glad to exchange the city where Commerce and Gold were kings for the wilderness where man could still match himself against nature rather than his fellow-men.

On April 27 he and Shaw boarded the steamer *Radnor*, all their equipment having been embarked. There were a number of Kansas or Kaw Indians on the *Radnor*, and Parkman found the celebrated Indian gravity rather more *"vacant* than *dignified."* In the cabin there were other passengers whom he disliked more thoroughly, and one contemporary who symbolized the era:

> On board the boat are a party of Baltimoreans—flash genteel —very showily attired in "genteel undress," though bound for California. They make a great noise at table and are waited on by the Negroes with great attention and admiration. Also a vulgar New Yorker, with the mustache and the air of a Frenchman —bound for Santa Fe.
>
> A young man on board, from St. Louis, bound for Santa Fe, has one brother on the Atlantic, another on the Pacific, and a third on the Mississippi, while he is going to the del Norte. So much for American wandering.

The *Radnor* snorted upstream against the Mississippi's spring current of four miles an hour, and entered the Missouri in a dismal rain. Parkman was fascinated by the shifting picture along the river banks: cottonwoods and elms, limestone bluffs, lofty and noble forests, old trees completely enveloped in grapevines and young trees springing up where the river had changed its channel. Sandbars and snags were frequent—the *Radnor* ripped its bottom out on one of the latter that very fall—and the shifting channels demanded great caution and vigilance from the pilot. But the passengers were not alarmed, and amused themselves as best they might. The Kaw Indians were induced by a pint of whisky to be entertaining. Their chief went ashore in full paint, wrapped in a blanket and carrying a sword, to greet a white friend at Jefferson. One Indian sang while a fat Negro danced; others begged from the passengers, while still others played cards about the deck. Parkman was disgusted with these miserable specimens of Cooper's "noble savage."

On May 2 the *Radnor* reached the landing for Independence, where Parkman eagerly eyed the storehouses, the great Santa Fe wagons, the "piratical-looking Mexicans, employees of the Santa Fe traders, with their broad peaked hats—the men with their rifles, seated on a log, ready for Oregon." The gentlemen adventurers from Baltimore got gorgeously drunk, and one, in full dress, fell overboard. Parkman was concerned with more sober matters, and noted sagely: "Speyer, the Santa Fe trader, has an enormous number of goods on board." This trader was later alleged to have supplied the Mexicans with large quantities of arms and munitions during the war. Then Parkman walked a mile or two into the woods to stretch his legs and to free himself of feeling "a little hipped." He considered himself older and wiser than when he first ventured into the wilderness of northern New England five years before, as a Harvard freshman on vacation:

> The reawakening of old thoughts and feelings, recurring along with the whole train of subsequent observations and experiences, is very agreeable. I felt as I had felt many years before, but I was no longer the same man, either in knowledge or character.
>
> C.W. of St. Louis, who harnessed his mule into his wagon, and drove off for Santa Fe, bent on seeing [life]. He seemed about eighteen years old, open, enterprising, and thoughtless. He will come back a full-grown man.

On May 5 they reached Kansas, formerly known as Chouteau's Landing, where they put up at the log-house tavern of Colonel Chick on a bluff above the river, while in nearby Westport they completed their preparations for the expedition that lay ahead. Despite the beautiful weather, Parkman complained that he "felt hipped and wavering." But there was much to take his mind off his indisposition. The Kaw Indians went by, on their way toward their homes. Mules and horses wandered about in great abundance, for Westport was the place to outfit with cattle before taking to the trails. Parkman rode out from Westport to see a Sac encampment, but the tribe had already gone. He was consoled, however, by his first sight of the prairie:

> A great green ocean . . . for the forest terminates at this place, where also is the boundary of the state of Missouri. A lofty forest, all fresh and verdant in the spring—then a tract of shrubbery and crab-trees full of fragrant blossoms—and then the great level expanse of the prairie.

Over that wide ocean, which was not really level but rose imperceptibly like an inclined plane until it reached the mouth of South Pass, the gateway to Oregon and California, Parkman was to travel for a month and a half before he reached Fort Laramie.

This was Indian territory, and many of the eastern tribes had been established here by the government. Besides the Kansas, Parkman saw Shawnees, Delawares, and Wyandots. He carefully noted down their dress and dispositions, also their reputation among their neighbors of the frontier. Meanwhile he and Shaw decided to join forces with a British hunting party, who had been reluctant to set off by themselves into the Indian country. The party included Captain Bill Chandler of the British Army, his brother Jack, and a Mr. Romaine, possibly the same young Englishman who had accompanied Father de Smet into the buffalo country in 1841 with Bidwell's Oregon party. The Britishers were greatly disinclined to join up with the "Kentucky fellers" who were leaving almost daily for Oregon and California. Parkman and Shaw felt "no greater inclination for the company of the emigrants than they did," and so the two pleasure parties combined. It is an indication of Parkman's shortcomings as an observer of western life that he found the company of foreigners more congenial than that of the men who were making America out of the wilderness, and so missed the fellowship of the trail which might have afforded him some valuable historical insights. This Anglo-American alliance on the plains moved another traveler on the trail in this same year, young Edwin Bryant of Louisville, to record in his *What I Saw in*

California a rumor that a party of five Englishmen, "supposed to be emissaries of their government, had started in advance of us, bound for Oregon, and that their object was to stir up the Indian tribes along the route, and to incite them to deeds of hostility toward the emigrants." Thanks to his Boston and Harvard upbringing, the future great American historian was not only unable to endure the company of his compatriots, but was not even recognizable by them as an American.

Parkman went over to visit the emigrants' camp and encountered his St. Louis acquaintance:

> W[oodworth] seems to be making a fool of himself. . . . He is a great busybody and ambitious of taking a command among the emigrants. . . . Woodworth parades a revolver in his belt, which he insists is necessary—and it may be a prudent precaution, for this place seems full of desperadoes—all arms are loaded, as I have had occasion to observe. Life is held in little esteem. This place, Westport, is the extreme frontier, and has all its characteristics.

He noted with amused contempt the democratic spirit of the emigrants: "They were in great confusion, holding meetings, passing resolutions, and drawing up regulations, but unable to unite in the choice of leaders to conduct them across the prairie." There were more than a thousand emigrants encamped on the prairie outside Independence, and the town was booming:

> At Independence every store is adapted to furnish outfits—the public houses were full of Santa Fe men and emigrants. Mules, horses, and wagons at every corner. Groups of hardy-looking men about the stores, and Santa Fe and emigrant wagons standing in the fields around. While I was at the Noland House, the last arrival of emigrants came down the street with about twenty wagons, having just broken up their camp near Independence, and set out for the grand rendezvous about fifteen miles beyond Westport. What is remarkable, this body, as well as a very large portion of the emigrants, were from the extreme western states —N[ew] England sends but a small proportion, but they are

better furnished than the rest. Some of these ox-wagons contained large families of children, peeping from under the covering. One remarkably pretty little girl was seated on horseback, holding a parasol over her head to keep off the rain. All looked well, but what a journey before them! The men were hardy and good-looking. As I passed the wagons I observed three old men, with their whips in their hands, discussing some point of theology though this was hardly the disposition of the mass of the emigrants.

This was J. Quinn Thornton's party from Illinois, with which Edwin Bryant and the Donners traveled under the leadership of Colonel "Owl" Russell. Parkman regarded these theological-minded emigrants as exceptional, for he immediately added that all the emigrants were not of this type and "among them are some of the vilest outcasts in the country." He not only had no sympathy with Americans of another sort than his own—the party whose democratic debates amused Parkman so much was headed by former Governor Boggs of Missouri and included many notables of that state—he had no understanding of the forces that drove men westward:

> I have often perplexed myself to divine the various motives that give impulse to this migration; but whatever they may be, whether an insane hope of a better condition in life, or a desire of shaking off the restraints of law and society, or a mere restlessness, certain it is that multitudes bitterly repent the journey and after they have reached the land of promise are happy enough to escape from it.

On May 9, after a false start in which an unruly mule nearly flung the cart containing their equipment into the Missouri, they began their journey westward, having exchanged the culprit for a less unruly beast supplied by a grandson of Daniel Boone. The expedition consisted of four men with eight animals. Parkman and Shaw each had an extra horse in addition to the one he rode. Parkman's first-string mount, a "good horse for whom I paid too much," had been christened Pontiac, the second he called Hendrik. Both young men carried heavy pistols in holsters on their Spanish saddles, which were equipped with blanket and trail-ropes. Shaw also had a double-barreled shotgun and Parkman a fifteen-pound rifle. They wore red flannel shirts, buckskin trousers, and moccasins. Their guide and hunter, Henry Chatillon, rode an Indian pony, carried a knife and rifle, and wore the blanket coat, fringed deerskin trousers, and moccasins of the mountain man. Deslauriers, the French Canadian muleteer, drove the covered French cart—better known as a "mule-killer"—which contained a tent, provisions, ammunition, blankets, and a great quantity of presents for the Indians. In addition to the two mules that pulled the cart, a spare one was driven along in case of accident.

Parkman and Shaw seem to have been fortunate in their choice of retainers. Chatillon was a fine type of Westerner. The two youths fresh from Harvard, who tended to judge men by appearance, had taken an immediate liking to this "tall and exceedingly well-dressed man, with a face so open and frank that it attracted our notice at once," when they saw him in the St. Louis office of the Fur Company; and they were surprised to find that he wished employment as their guide. In this instance appearances were not misleading, for Henry Chatillon was a natural aristocrat, though he could neither read nor write—on the flyleaf of one of the notebooks Parkman wrote out his own and Henry's names, so that the latter could see what his signature looked like—and had an Indian wife and half-breed offspring. At thirty he was one of the best hunters in the Rockies and had earned his living on the plains and in the mountains since he was fifteen. Parkman found him upright, simple, kind-hearted, tactful, a good judge of character, brave beyond the mere bumptiousness of the average mountain man, and of a "natural refinement and delicacy of mind such as is rare even in women." As a son of the Puritans, Parkman deemed his French companion lacking in the "restless energy of the Anglo-American" and too much given to "an easy generosity, not conducive to thriving in the world." But greatly to his own credit, he concluded: "I have never, in the city or the wilderness, met a better man than my true-hearted friend, Henry Chatillon." Deslauriers, the muleteer, was a man of a lower type, stupid but cheerful, polite under

the worst conditions, and a loyal and indefatigable servant. Parkman thought him "a true son of Jean Baptiste." The choice of
traveling companions for the trail was an important matter, for as
Parkman observed at the end of the first day's march: "The vexa-
tions and deprivations of such a journey do indeed resolve a man
into his first elements—and bring out all his nature."

The party took two days to reach Fort Leavenworth where they
were to meet the Britishers, passing through the country of the
Delawares and Shawnees and having the usual difficulties crossing
the Kansas by ferry and accustoming their raw horses to being
hobbled. Parkman found the sight of the white walls of Leavenworth and the tents of his new friends most welcome. On May 12
he called on Colonel Stephen Watts Kearny at the fort and then
with Shaw rode over to the near-by Kickapoo village, which he
found disappointing.

All half-civ[ilized] Ind[ian] villages in wooded counties are the
same thing—straggling paths through woods and underbrush,
with here and there a log house—a creek winding through the
midst. Indians are most provoking beings. We addressed one
who was lying at full length in the sun before his house—he
would not give the least sign of recognizing our presence. We
got from the rest nothing but silence, hesitation, or false directions.

Thus checkmated as an observer at first hand, he turned with relief
to discussion of the Indians with the trader who lived among them:

. . . He characterizes them as ungrateful—the more they get,
the more they expect—and become suspicious in the extreme.
We were hot and tired, and the trader showed us into a neat,
dark, and cool parlor, where he gave us iced claret and an excellent lunch—a most welcome refreshment. His mistress, a yellow woman, brimful of merriment, entertained us with her conversation.

Parkman marveled at the civilized comforts of this outpost of
civilization, though he noted that "a pistol, loaded and capped, lay
on the mantelpiece; and through the glass of the bookcase, peeping

above the works of John Milton, glittered the handle of a very mischievous-looking knife." When he returned to the fort, he found Captain Chandler regaling Colonel Kearny with tales of past prowess as a steeplechaser and anticipated exploits as a buffalo-hunter. Parkman joined the group at Kearny's table and bade farewell to civilization with "the last Madeira—the last fruits that we shall enjoy for a long time." But for all that, he was willing enough to say "a long adieu to bed & board, and the principles of Blackstone's *Commentaries*."

At sunrise on May 13 the Anglo-American expedition was ready to jump off for the wilderness. It must have been a vastly impressive spectacle, for the Britishers were outfitted to the hilt:

> They had a wagon drawn by six mules, and crammed with provisions for six months, besides ammunition enough for a regiment; spare rifles and fowling pieces, ropes and harness, personal baggage, and a miscellaneous assortment of articles, which produced infinite embarrassment. They had also decorated their persons with telescopes and portable compasses, and carried English double-barreled rifles of sixteen to the pound caliber, slung to their saddles in dragoon fashion.

In addition to the three principals, Captain Chandler, his brother Jack, and Romaine, there were the two hunters Boisverd and Sorel, and a St. Louis muleteer named Wright. The livestock of the combined party amounted to twenty-three head. But for all their foresight, they had neglected one important particular: a knowledge of the route. Neither Romaine, who had chosen the new route (that followed by Colonel Kearny and his dragoons the previous summer to make a show of force at Fort Laramie), nor any other member of the party knew the trail, and after several hours' march they ended up in the Kickapoo village, only a short distance from their starting point and miles out of their way. The hospitable trader supplied directions and they made a bee-line across the prairie, which reminded Parkman of the wastes Mazeppa wandered over:

> Man nor brute,
> Nor dint of hoof, nor print of foot,

Lay in the wild luxuriant soil;
No sign of travel, none of toil;
The very air was mute.

Before sunset they struck the dragoons' trail, and, thanks to Chatillon's eye for the weather, were snugly encamped before a stormy night broke upon them. The thunder and the wolves who came up to the camp at night frightened the horses, and the captain, who was very solicitous about his animals, moved about in an old plaid, keeping watch.

The next day the first of many differences of opinion among the Britishers ended in their heavy wagon bogging down in a stream, and the whole party had to turn to to rescue it. Since the same thing happened four or five times a day for a fortnight, Parkman and Shaw soon wished they had chosen more lightly equipped companions. Impatient Parkman railed at their slow progress, an average of only ten miles a day. He found the prairie belt dreary and tame, eager as he was to reach the "great American desert" of the buffalo and the Indian. They saw no game for a fortnight and much mud; nothing more eventful than straying horses, stuck wagons, or broken harness and axletrees marked their progress. In the absence of game they were reduced to a diet of biscuit and salt meat; the water was poor; and they were much plagued by the sultry heat, by the daily thunderstorms, and by snakes and mosquitoes. Thanks to the perverse ingenuity of Romaine, they lost their way again, but fortunately were set right by some dragoons who had deserted from Leavenworth, and eventually they found themselves upon the trail made by a party of emigrants, rumored to be Mormons, who had set out earlier in the season from St. Joseph, Missouri.

Tribulation had produced friction between the two groups, and the flames were fanned by Shaw and Parkman's refusal to fall in with the captain's cherished scheme of proceeding in military order as a safeguard against hostile Indians, though they were not yet in dangerous country. But this St. Joseph Trail proved much better going than their previous course—they were now entering upon the true plains region—and they doubled their rate of progress as they passed over "a vast swelling prairie, with scarcely any trees in sight, where the advanced wagon looked like a mere speck on the green surface." At campsites they found the grass cropped close by the cattle of the "Mormons" who were only a week ahead of them on the trail. The heat was intense and they stripped off all superfluous clothing. There was no escape from the relentless sun as they rode on: "the expanse of prairie stretched for mile after mile without tree or bush—we ascended swell after swell and could see nothing but the vast green level." At last they found a clump of trees, indicating water, and Parkman tried a bath:

> The water was the same that we have had lately, only worse— quite warm and full of frogs and snakes—no current, but plenty of weeds and mud. We struggled through bushes, reeds, and mud till we came to a nasty pool, rich in mud, insects, and reptiles, where we washed as we could. Dor-bugs swarmed in the prairie and camp.

To complete their discomfiture, they found the next morning that all the horses had run off, and they had great trouble in rounding them up again. Under such conditions the rift between the two parties opened wider. They traveled separately now, only camping together, and that perforce because there were so few passable campsites. The Britishers' hunter, Sorel, was obviously dissatisfied about something, and refused to fall in with Chatillon's choice of stopping places at noon and night. Parkman observed: "The Englishmen kept on—the devil knows where," and it is quite clear from the context that he might well have added "or cares." Now it was the Britishers who were in haste and who wanted to push on the moment they had snatched some food, while Parkman's party preferred to rest themselves and their tired beasts at midday, having adopted the plains custom of "nooning." Parkman was growing bitter about Romaine, who seemed determined to have everything his own way.

The usual wild summer weather of the plains was intensified this season, and every evening brought a storm to add to the travelers' discomfort:

Last night we were awakened by tremendous peals of thunder, quite different from any in our part of the country—beginning with a tremendous burst, they ran reverberating around the whole firmament. The rain that followed was like a cataract, and beat through the tent in a thick drizzle, wetting everything. The lightning was very intense and brilliant. Lay by today until afternoon, when the restlessness of Romaine impelled his party to move. We, against our judgment, consented to follow, not caring to appear obstinate—so broke up camp and moved off. Intensely sultry and oppressive, and when the sun came out it was terribly hot. The sky was hung with clouds, and thunder muttered incessantly. As we rode, things grew worse, till the whole prairie and the grove grew almost black in the stormy shadow; and the lightning kept flashing vividly. The masses of cloud in front grew blacker and more ragged—the thunder more and more threatening, till both horses and men took alarm, and we all rushed forward in a medley, running or galloping, and the muleteers lashing and shouting. We wheeled round behind a line of trees—tore off our saddles—hobbled the frightened brutes—seized the tent, and thrust the pole into the ground. No sooner was this done than a sharp flash and a crashing peal came upon us, and the rain descended like a torrent. We do not know our position, but we are on the Mormon Trail, and probably within ten days of the Platte.

The next day, when it had cleared sufficiently to proceed, they struggled on over a wretched trail, ruined by the storm. The Britishers were in advance and discovered a cow which had wandered from the "Mormon" party ahead. After ineffectual attempts had been made to noose her, the captain drove her along like an extra horse. But a sudden gust of wind and rain made the horses stop and turn tail, and the cow took advantage of the moment to flee once more.

A rifle ball was sent after her ineffectually; and the captain, in defiance of the storm, cocking one of his huge buffalo pistols, galloped off in pursuit, and both soon vanished in the diagonal sheets of rain. Presently he and the cow appeared looming through the storm, the captain shouting to us that he had shot her. He rode behind her, driving her along, which was very easy as she was shot through the body. As we approached the woods where we were to encamp, something was seen that looked like a tent, on which the cow was allowed to fall into the rear, for fear of lighting on her owner: but the alarm proving false, she was driven to camp, and at last finished by Romaine, who shot two bullets into the poor devil. We feasted on her at night.

Parkman and his companions, like the emigrants, were fearful of the Mormons. At Independence they had heard a rumor that twenty-three hundred Mormons were about to set out from St. Joseph. Since the greater part of the emigrants were from Illinois and Missouri and already on bad terms with the Latter-Day Saints, a sharp conflict might result when "large armed bodies of these fanatics should encounter the most impetuous and reckless of their old enemies on the broad prairie, far beyond the reach of law or military force." Indeed the emigrants had asked Colonel Kearny for a dragoon escort as far as the Platte, but this request had been refused. Parkman was no more eager than the emigrants to fall in with the "fanatics" and kept a sharp eye out for their appearance. Actually only two small Mormon parties traveled the trail in this year, and the main body did not push west to Salt Lake until the following spring.

The trail was reduced to mud by the storms, and the Britishers' heavy cart was constantly getting stuck. Cheered by fresh meat and milk, Parkman and Shaw pushed on at the rate of twenty miles a day. They found another cow, which they drove along with them, and, camping by a stream which they supposed to be the Little Vermilion, they had "a most delightful bath in a deep clear pool, surrounded by beautiful woods full of birds, and at that time lighted by the setting sun." Around the campfire at night Henry Chatillon told of the ways of the fur trappers and traders, of the customs of the different Indian tribes, and Parkman began to feel that he was learning something of the subject that obsessed him. The next day, May 23, they reached the long-looked-for Big Blue, which was so swollen by the rains that they had to raft across:

> Romaine, with his usual activity, waded across to ascertain the depth. Plenty of wood grew on the banks, and in an hour or two the raft was made, the Canadians working like dogs, in the water and out of it. Romaine was as usual noisy and obtrusive, offending the men by assuming the direction of affairs of which he knew nothing. The fellow overboils with conceit. Got across, after a fatiguing work—dined, and advanced about five miles. Coming to camp by a creek, we saw wagons ascending a distant swell.

They encamped that night at the junction of the St. Joseph route with the old Oregon Trail, and after supper they heard laughter and voices coming across the prairie—the first signs of human life that they had encountered in eight days on the great empty sea of green. They had found newly made graves and other traces of the emigrants along the way, but this was the first party they had encountered, although the trail was much traveled in this year.

The next morning they overtook the great lumbering ox-drawn wagons, and the cattle driven along in their wake by "yellow-visaged" Missourians. Parkman judged that the men were torn by fear and dissension, and that the women were divided between regret for the homes they had left behind and fear of the savages and deserts and mountains that lay ahead.

> The wagons we saw were part of an emigrant party, under a man named Kearsley. They encamped about a mile from us, behind a swell in the prairie. The captain paid them a visit, and reported that the women were damned ugly. Kearsley and another man came to see us in the morning. We had advanced a few miles when we saw a long line of specks upon the level edge of the prairie, and when we approached we discerned about twenty wagons, followed by a crowd of cattle. This was the advanced party—the rest were at the Big Blue, where they were delayed by a woman in childbed. They stopped a few miles

farther to breakfast, where we passed them. They were from the western states. Kearsley had complained of want of subordination among his party, who were not very amenable to discipline or the regulations they themselves had made. Romaine stayed behind to get his horse shod, and witnessed a grand break-up among them. The captain threw up his authority, such was the hurly-burly—women crying—men disputing—some for hurry—some afraid of the Indians. Four wagons joined us— Romaine urged them, and thereby offended us. Kearsley is of the party.

The new additions to the party numbered ten men and one woman. Shaw and Parkman were not pleased at this addition to the expedition, which they thought would be burdensome, though they found no fault with the men, who were "rude indeed in manners, but frank, manly, and intelligent." As it happened, the Britishers' wagon broke down and it was a week before the hunting hare caught up with the emigrant tortoise. The fear of the Indians which had induced Romaine to make this unwelcome addition to the party was now more generally shared, and a watch was kept all night lest the thieving Pawnees make off with the horses and mules. A few days later they met two emigrants—one Turner and another —who had turned back without their rifles to look for strayed cattle, and were nearly robbed of their horses by six Pawnees, who fled at the approach of Parkman's party. When they came up to Kearsley's party again, they learned that he had mistaken a band of Pawnees for a buffalo herd. In fact the travelers were now crossing the Pawnees' main line of travel from their winter villages on the lower Platte to their southern war and hunting grounds. But they reached the dreary valley of the Platte without a brush with the Indians, though the latter were not in the best of tempers and had killed two stragglers from an emigrant train a few days up the trail.

They were anxious to reach the good hunting country of the Platte Valley, for their store of bacon was nearly exhausted. Chatillon and Sorel combed the prairie for antelope and prairie-hen, but without success for several days. Parkman, riding along in the intense heat, indulged in "an epicurean reverie":

> . . . Dreamed of a cool mountain spring, in a *forest* country—two bottles of champagne cooling in it, and cut-glass tumblers, full of the sparkling liquor. A wide expanse of perfectly flat prairie—rode over it hour after hour—saw wolves and where they had dug up a recent grave. Turkey buzzards and frequent carcasses of cattle.

They were still in doubt as to their position, though they knew that they were in the vicinity of the Little Blue, which they kept encountering from time to time. That evening they witnessed a beautiful prairie sunset:

> Immense masses of blue lurid clouds in the west shadowed the green prairie, and the sun glared through, purple and crimson. As we drew near the valley of the stream, a furious wind, presaging a storm, struck us. We galloped down in the face of it—horses snorting with fear. Rode to the ground—up went the tent and on came the storm.

At last the hunters' luck changed and they feasted on antelope meat. The prairie was littered with buffalo bones, indicating that a herd had been surrounded. The spirits of the party lifted; and as they moved rapidly to a camp near the Little Blue, the captain galloped wildly over the prairie in pursuit of a wolf.

On May 30 they reached the Platte at last, being farther on their way than they had thought. Antelopes were plentiful on the level plain, and they saw the low blue line of the Platte Buttes in the distance:

> Towards sunset, drew near the Buttes—a range of low, broken, sandy hills, and, after a long and gradual ascent, saw the Platte from the summit—apparently one vast level plain, fringed with a distant line of forest—the river ran invisible in sluices through the plain, with here and there a patch of woods like an island.

The Platte Valley was one of the great thoroughfares of the West, and they now encountered many other travelers. A solitary emigrant, looking for Turner, told them that Robinson's party was encamped three miles off; that Kearsley's wagons were in advance; and that a large hunting party of Pawnees was somewhere in the vicinity. That afternoon Parkman's party crossed a very large Indian trail. The next day the Pawnees, thirty in number, passed close to their camp:

> . . . A hunting party—no women, these being probably planting corn at the village. Rather mean-looking fellows, each with a bow and arrows, led horses loaded with dry meat. The chief walked behind—I gave him a piece of tobacco, which very much pleased him.
>
> When three or four miles from camp, overtook the emigrants —Robinson's party of about 40 wagons—who had just set out. Turner had got in safe. One fellow had inscribed his wagon "54°48′ "—a mean set, chiefly from the East. A very cold raw disagreeable day, with a violent freezing wind, which benumbed us—rain soon followed, which wet us through. Kearsley, with the 4 wagons that had joined us, was ahead about a mile. Disorder in both these parties.
>
> Went twelve miles and camped—miserably cold and dismal —wet through, with no means of getting dry—a set cold rain. Wrapped ourselves up as we could and went to sleep in the tent, while the emigrants went on.
>
> The Pawnees say that buffalo are two days ahead.

The valley of the Platte at first offered nothing but monotonous landscape and vile weather, instead of the excitement Parkman had hoped to find among its "wild beasts and wild men." Sultry heat gave way suddenly to furious storms of sleet and hail, driven by freezing winds, and Parkman thought of the uncertain New England climate as mild and equable by comparison. They spent four days traveling along the Platte before they saw their first buffalo, although they encountered many buffalo wallows and much of what Parkman delicately referred to as *bois de vache*, the firewood of the treeless plains. Only Chatillon was able to track down a buffalo, for the principals of the party, who had come so far to hunt the biggest game of the plains, were appalled by the roughness of the country and the atrociousness of the climate. The day after they sighted their first buffalo, they met their first "wild men": a convoy of Mackinaw boats carrying furs downstream to St. Louis under the direction of Papin, the *bourgeois* or boss of Fort Laramie:

> Returning, met Henry on his little pony Wyandot—he came to say that 11 boats were coming down the river from Laramie. Gave my letter to Q[uin] to be delivered, and rode back two or three miles after the wagons to get a letter H[enry] had given me, intended for Papin, the *bourgeois* of the boats. On my re-turn, found the boats lashed to the bank waiting—flatbottomed —with 110 packs each—one month from Laramie—aground every day, for the Platte is now low and is very shallow and swift at best. The crews were a wild-looking set—the oarsmen were Spaniards—with them were traders, F[rench] and Ameri-can; some attired in buckskin, fancifully slashed and garnished; and with hair glued up in Ind[ian] fashion. Papin a rough-looking fellow, reclining on the leather covering that was thrown over the packs.
>
> I saw Woodworth here—his party are close behind.
>
> Papin reports that the Mormons are a few miles ahead—that the Pawnees have taken 10 of their horses, and whipped one of their men into camp—that the Sioux have been out in force, and driven off the buffalo—all this alarms the capt[ain] exceedingly.

These encouraging items of news were too much for the captain, who became "very nervous and old-womanish," and fancied that Indians hid behind every hill they passed. But Parkman, perhaps out of sheer bravado, rode off alone into the hills the next after-noon, galloped after antelope, and then lay down on a barren ridge, and "contrasted my present situation with my situation in the convent at Rome." Actually there was more danger from wild animals than from wild men, as the party soon discovered. That night all the emigrants' cattle were driven off by the wolves, the cattle guard having fallen asleep, so in the morning Shaw, Parkman, and Chatillon went buffalo-hunting until the lost animals could be rounded up. Parkman became separated from the others in pursuing a herd of bulls, and rode for hours over the prairie, amid thousands of buffalo, antelope, prairie-dogs, burrowing owls, wild geese, and wolves. At first he headed westward, but decided that course to be wrong and turned north on a buffalo track which brought him out at last on the trail. His only comment on this experience was: "Awkward feeling, being lost on the prairie."

The party was much torn by dissension among its incongruous elements. Parkman observed on June 7: "The lagging pace of the emigrants—the folly of Romaine—and the old-womanism of the capt[ain] combine to disgust us. We are resolved to push on alone as soon as we have crossed the South Fork, which will probably be tomorrow." The next day brought new difficulties, for Sorel, Romaine, and two of the emigrants, who had gone hunting, got lost and did not return at nightfall. At nooning four members of the emigrant party ahead came into camp, and told of losing ten of their horses to a very large band of Indians, at whom they had fired, and also of having a hundred and twenty-three head of cattle, for which they were searching, driven off by wolves. Anxiety about the missing members of Parkman's party became acute, and the captain feelingly remarked; "It is a serious business traveling through this cursed wilderness." At the crossing of the south fork of the Platte, where they intended to wait for their lost companions, they found the large party of emigrants who no longer had enough cattle to carry them on and were in great distress:

> Nooned and made the fording—a picturesque scene—river half a mile wide and nowhere more than three feet deep—swift and sandy—had some little trouble. On the farther bank were collected a crowd of the emigrants—rather mean-looking fellows—much less respectable than those with us. Romaine and the rest came in just before, having followed the buffalo too far, and camped.

The travails of this particular party of emigrants were typical of the mishaps that beset those who traveled the Oregon and California trails. In the absence of oxen, driven off by the wolves, they had been compelled to abandon much of their baggage and provisions, and to yoke cows and heifers to the wagons. But they still went on, though the worst of their trip lay ahead. In commenting on the character of these unfortunates in *The Oregon Trail* Parkman revealed his limited understanding of the emigrant movement:

> Finding at home no scope for their energies, they had betaken themselves to the prairie; and in them seemed to be revived, with redoubled force, that fierce spirit that impelled their ancestors, scarcely more lawless than themselves, from the German forests, to inundate Europe, and overwhelm the Roman empire.

To young Parkman, fresh from his sheltered life in Boston, the men who made America out of the Great West were barbarians, to be compared to the savage hordes of Huns who devastated Europe. Yet he had a flash of insight into the great historical process of which he was a witness. It came not from the men, with whom he had nothing in common, but from the jetsam of the toiling ox-trains, which dotted the valley of the Platte:

> . . . The shattered wrecks of ancient claw-footed tables, well waxed and rubbed, or massive bureaus of carved oak. These, some of them no doubt the relics of ancestral prosperity in the colonial time, must have encountered strange vicissitudes. Brought, perhaps, originally from England; then, with the declining fortunes of their owners, borne across the Alleghenies to the wilderness of Ohio or Kentucky; then to Illinois or Missouri; and now at last fondly stowed away in the family wagon for the interminable journey to Oregon. But the stern privations of the way are little anticipated. The cherished relic is soon flung out to scorch and crack upon the hot prairie.

Parkman came of a class that held property more sacred than man himself, and only this abandonment of property could give him an inkling of the great drama that was being played out before his unseeing eyes.

Soon after crossing the South Platte, Parkman and Shaw determined to part with their fellow-travelers. They had grown weary of the autocratic ways of Romaine, and thought he endeavored to retard the party while they were eager to press on. Parkman had tired of the "peculiarly elegant stories" of the captain, of his Irish braggadocio and bluster which cloaked a certain timidity, and of Jack Chandler, who was merely a good-natured echo of his brother. They explained their decision to the captain, whose reaction was the stiff comment: "A very extraordinary proceeding, upon my word!" He clearly regarded the matter as desertion in the face of the enemy, though the American party numbered only four and the combined forces of the Britishers and the emigrants sixteen; and his farewell was a cool one.

> They seem to have thought that we were obliged to remain with them for protection. They say their party ought to be *larger*. Wright, the muleteer, plainly hopes in his heart that our horses may be stolen.

Freed at last of the encumbering alliance which had produced so much irritation on both sides, Parkman and Shaw made better time and soon overtook a large emigrant party farther up the North Platte, "camped in a circle—fires, tents, and wagons outside— horses within. The bottom covered with the cattle." At first the newcomers were mistaken for the van of the dreaded Mormons, but the emigrants were soon put right on that score. Parkman observed with pride: "They expressed much surprise that so small a party should venture to traverse that region, though in fact such attempts are often made by trappers and Indian traders." He heartily disliked the emigrants' curiosity, which was in fact part of the fellowship of the trail, and found it embarrassing to explain that he and Shaw were traveling for pleasure and not in hope of bettering themselves. Yet he summed up the emigrants as "a very good set of men—chiefly Missourians," "fine-looking fellows, with an air of frankness, generosity, and even courtesy, having come from one of the least barbarous of the frontier counties." It remains clear, nevertheless, that Parkman's passion for the wilderness did not include a taste for its pioneers.

The next day, as they were taking a nap while nooning, Henry

Chatillon awoke them with the announcement that people were coming:

> They were the van of the emigrants—first came a girl and a young man on horseback, the former holding a parasol—then appeared the line of wagons, coming over the sandhills. We saddled in a trice, pushed ahead, and kept on. The girl and her beau apparently found something very agreeable in each other's company, for they kept more than a mile in advance of their party, which H[enry] considered very imprudent, as the Sioux might be about.

The following afternoon they saw in the distance "a half-subterranean house," which a trapper named Frédéric, charged with the care of furs to be sent downriver in the spring, had made to winter in. Parkman was moved to comment: "What a devil of a solitary time!" and Henry entertained his employers with an account of the "blows-out" given by the Yellow Stone *bourgeois* in the spring when the trappers came in after their lonely winters. That evening they met a party of five men going down from Laramie, to whom Parkman gave some hastily scrawled letters to be mailed at the settlements, and then they pushed on a mile or two farther to camp with Roubideau's party. Parkman was impressed with the mark that the West had put on these returning pioneers:

> The Oregon men returning to the settlements—the vulgar-looking fellow in the white shirt and broadcloth pants, who gave me the acc[oun]t of the Oregon settlements and gov-[ernme]nt. His companions around their campfire. What a character of independence and self-reliance such a life gives a man!

The next day Roubideau left the emigrants and joined Parkman's party. That day they pushed on to Scott's Bluff, which greatly impressed Parkman:

> All these bluffs are singular and fantastic formations—abrupt, scored with wooded ravines, and wrought by storms into the semblance of lines of buildings. Midway on one of them gushes

the spring, in the midst of wild roses, currants, cherries, and a hundred trees, and cuts for itself a devious and wooded ravine across the smooth plain below. Stood among the fresh wild roses and recalled old and delightful associations.

On the following day, June 14, they had their first close contact with the plains Indians, for they met a whole Dakota Sioux village on the march. Its chief, Old Smoke, was a friend of Henry Chatillon, and so Parkman made his first study of the wild tribes under favorable auspices. He feasted the Indians on sweetened tea, buffalo meat, and biscuit—then passed the pipe. This noonday banquet was such a success that they were urged to visit Smoke's twenty lodges. Parkman found the Indian encampment a picturesque scene:

> The squaws put up temporary sunshades and scattered the packs and utensils about—the boys splashed in the river—the horses were picketed around. The shield and three poles hung up for each lodge—medicine—Smoke's was pure white. One old fat man rode along with us, professing great friendship for the whites, and boasting what he would do against the Crows, a party of whom are out.

On June 15 they nooned on a sandy bottom near Richard's fort on the Platte. This was the first opportunity Parkman had to observe life in a fur-trading establishment in the wilderness; and he made careful notes:

> Rode over the sand as far as a little unfinished log fort, in the midst of a sterile prairie, built by Sapi [Papin?]—log houses in form of a square, facing inwards—two Sioux lodges in the open area—corral behind, and plenty of shaggy little ponies feeding on the bottom. The *bourgeois*, Richard, received us politely and ushered us into a log room, with a rock fireplace, and hung with rifles and their equipments, *fanfaron* bridles, garnished buckskin dresses, smoking apparatus, bows & quivers, etc. The men lounging around on robes—passed the pipe—an Indian seated in the corner—Reynal filling the pipe in the chimney corner—a *voyageur* with hair glued in Indian fashion, lounging on a bedstead.

They returned Richard's hospitality by inviting him to take coffee at their camp; and having washed as best they could in the muddy waters of the Platte, and shaved for the first time in six weeks, they set off for the goal of their long journey across the plains, Fort Laramie.

Soon they caught a glimpse of Laramie Peak; then they passed Sybille and Adams's deserted fort; and as a prospect opened among the barren hills, they saw the clay walls and bastions of the fort on Laramie Creek, framed by arid and desolate ridges, with the seven-thousand-foot range of the Laramie Mountains as a grim and majestic background. Their first attempt to ford the swollen creek was a failure, and on a second, farther up, the swift current nearly carried their cart, mules and all, downstream. The proceedings were watched from the walls by a critical company, among whom Chatillon singled out such mountain notables as Bordeaux, Vasquez, Tucker, May, and Chatillon's great rival as a hunter, Simoneau. Finally they crossed safely, and rode up at last to the gate of Fort Laramie, become an actuality and no longer a mere name, after thirteen hundred miles of arduous travel which had taken them two months. They had traversed the states of Missouri, Kansas, and Nebraska, and penetrated into Wyoming.

10: A Patrician on the Oregon Trail—II

My business was observation and I was willing to pay dearly for the opportunity of exercising it.
F.P., *Oregon Trail*, 1872

PARKMAN and his party were received somewhat coldly at the gate of Fort Laramie by Bordeaux, who was acting *bourgeois* in the place of Papin, and took them for independent traders. It was not until their status as gentlemen adventurers had been explained by Chatillon and his statements had been supported by their passport from the St. Louis office of the Fur Company—which Bordeaux was unable to read himself and had to have read to him by Monthalon, the clerk of the fort—that the atmosphere began to clear. Meanwhile Parkman looked around this remote outpost of civilization with eager eyes, comparing what he saw with the tales told night after night around the campfire by Chatillon and Roubideau, both old mountain men to whom Laramie was another home:

Leading our horses into the area, we found Ind[ian]s, men, women, and children, standing around, *voyageurs* and trappers —the surrounding apartments occupied by the squaws and children of the traders. Fort divided into two areas—one used as a corral—two bastions or *clay blockhouses*—another blockhouse over main entrance. They gave us a large apartment, where we spread our blankets on the floor. From a sort of balcony, we saw our horses and carts brought in, and witnessed a picturesque frontier scene. Conversed and smoked in the windy porch. Horses made a great row in the corral. At night the Inds. set up their songs. At the burial place are several Inds. laid on scaffolds, and a circle of buffalo skulls below. Vasquez, Simoneau, Mont[h]alon, Knight, and other trappers are here.

❧   ❧   ❧   ❧

Fort Laramie. June 16. Prices are most extortionate. Sugar, two dollars a cup—5-cent tobacco at $1.50—bullets at $.75 a pound, etc. American Fur Cmpy. exceedingly disliked in this country—it suppresses all opposition, and, keeping up these enormous prices, pays its men in necessaries on these terms.

The fort has a double gate, at the main entrance under the blockhouse. When there was danger from the Inds. the inner gate was closed, the Inds. admitted to the space between, traded through an open window or orifice, opening from a large room now used as a blacksmith's shop.

Lodged in Papin's room and visited now and then by Inds., the fathers or brothers of the white men's squaws, who are lodged in the fort, and furnished with meat at the company's expense.

This morning Smoke's village appeared on the opposite shore, and crossed on their wild little horses—men and boys naked and dashing eagerly through the water—horses with lodgepoles dragging through squaws and children, and sometimes a litter of puppies—gaily attired squaws leading the horses of their lords —dogs with their burdens attached, swimming among the horses and mules—dogs barking, horses breaking loose, children laughing and shouting—squaws thrusting into the ground the lance and shield of the master of the lodge—naked and splendidly formed men passing and repassing through the swift water.

❖   ❖   ❖   ❖

Some who visited us kept looking with great curiosity at the circus pictures that Finch has nailed up in the room.

At their camp in the evening, the girls and children, with a couple of young men, amused themselves with a dance, where there was as much merriment and fooling as could be desired.

The emigrants' party passed the upper ford and a troop of women came into the fort, invading our room without scruple or reserve. Yankee curiosity and questioning is nothing to that of these people.

Parkman and Shaw lingered four days at the fort, resting after their trip, amused by the Indians and irritated by the emigrants.

In an attempt to beat the Fur Company's profiteering game, Shaw tried to bargain for some lead with the emigrants, but they were so afraid of being overreached that it was impossible to conclude any transaction with them. The emigrants were very much on their guard in these strange surroundings, and they could not understand the openhanded ways—and tall tales—of the fur traders and trappers. Bordeaux was much amused by "the suspicion and distrust of the emigrants, who are constantly asking questions and then refusing to credit the answers." Parkman, a close-fisted Yankee who kept his accounts to the last half-cent, was struck by the free ways of the mountain men:

> Gifts pass here as freely as the winds. Visit a trader, and his last cup of coffee and sugar, his last pound of flour are brought out for your entertainment, and if you admire anything that he has, he gives it to you. Little thanks expected or given on either side.

This, too, was the way of the Indians, though their appetite for presents was insatiable and the more that was given, the more they expected. Parkman's large store of trade goods for this purpose soon began to melt away.

After witnessing a begging dance, partaking of an "excellent" puppy feast given by Old Smoke, and swapping his horse Pontiac for Paul Dorion's little mare, Parkman, with Shaw and Henry Chatillon, set out up Laramie Creek to meet Tunica's * village with which Henry's squaw was traveling and which they hoped to join. Parkman had engaged an extra hand at the fort named Raymond, and their party also was accompanied by Reynal, the trader at the Sioux village they planned to visit, his squaw, and her two nephews.

> We made rather a wild-looking band. Reynal's squaw's property fastened by the lodgepole arrangement to a mule—herself riding a handsomely caparisoned mule, and her nephews galloping about on their horses, in full equipment of bows and arrows, etc.

On the second day, after an easy ride through beautiful country abounding in flowers and minerals strange to Parkman, they

* The Whirlwind in *The Oregon Trail.*

reached the Chugwater, on whose wooded banks they encamped near a prairie-dog village. Parkman pumped Reynal for information about the Indians and struck a rich vein of material. In particular Reynal explained to him the subdivisions of the Sioux and the lack of leadership which made the proposed war expedition against the Crows, and the gathering for this purpose at the mouth of La Bonté's Creek, so problematical and uncertain.

Restless as always, Parkman could not bear waiting in camp for the Indians to come up for the rendezvous, and he rode over to the fort several times for provisions and news. Smoke's village had departed, Michigan and Illinois emigrants swarmed about the fort, and Russell's party of emigrants—or at least its vanguard—had just arrived, "which, becoming dissatisfied with its pragmatic stump-orator leader, has split into half a dozen pieces."

Passed along the line of wagons, conversing with the women, etc. These people are very ignorant, and suspicious for this reason—no wonder—they are grossly imposed on at the store.

❊   ❊   ❊   ❊

The emigrants had a ball at the fort—in this room—the other night. Such belles! One woman of more than suspected chastity is left at the fort, and Bordeaux is fool enough to receive her.

May, his fiery, nervous temper, and his acct. of the French in the country.

June 28. Yesterday rode down with Paul Dorion, who wished to swap a wild horse, to Richard's fort. Found there Russell's or Boggs' company, engaged in drinking and refitting, and a host of Canadians besides. Russell drunk as a pigeon—some fine-looking Kentucky men—some of D. Boone's grandchildren—Ewing, Jacobs, and others with them—altogether more educated men than any I have seen. A motley crew appeared in Richard's rooms squaws, children, Spaniards, French, and emigrants. Emigrants mean to sell liquor to the Miniconques who will be up here tomorrow and, after having come all the way from the Missouri to go to the war, will no doubt break up, if this is done. Paul very much displeased, as well as the Canadians.

Returning to the fort, met a party going to the settlements to whom Mont[h]alon *had not given my letters.* Sent them by that good fellow Tucker. People at the fort a set of mean swindlers, as witness my purchase of the bacon, and their treatment of the emigrants.

News of two traders killed by Arapahoes—one just going up told me, remarking that he was bound to meet the same fate.

Despite this news, which did not promise well for Parkman's scheme of accompanying the Sioux into the Rockies on their proposed expedition against the Crows, and even made his party's present situation dangerous, he started back alone for the Chugwater camp late in the afternoon. He lost his way and it was not until long after dark that he saw the glimmering of the campfire on the bottom. He found Reynal alone at the camp—for Chatillon and Shaw had gone to bury the former's squaw, who had died while on the journey to join her husband—and in a state of some apprehension, for there had been gunfire in the vicinity during the day. On the large cottonwood tree which stood near the camp there was an unpleasant reminder of what they might encounter: "The bark is cut off for the space of a foot square and marked with 14 pipes and 14 straight marks, to indicate that a band of Crows had come down and struck *coups.*" Reynal was not eager to be the occasion of adding another mark to the tally. Henry's Indian connections stood his party in good stead, however, for they were informed from time to time of all Indian movements by his relatives.

Parkman chafed at the "most weary series of delays, arising from the utter uncertainty of the Indians' movements," and wondered how they stood the abject laziness of their life:

It is scarce tolerable to us, and yet it is theirs from year's start and to year's end. Bull Bear,* a young chief, famous for his intrepidity, ambition, and activity, lies kicking his heels by the fire like the rest.

On July 3 Tunica's village at last arrived, but was still undecided whether to go to the war rendezvous at the mouth of La Bonté's Creek or merely to hunt west of the Laramie Mountains, which Parkman called, after Frémont's map, the Black Hills. On the fol-

* Mahto-Tatonka in *The Oregon Trail.*

lowing day Parkman got at first hand a tale of great privation on
the plains:

> This afternoon three Inds. came to camp, bringing on a mule a
> wretchedly emaciated Negro. He was out 33 days ago with
> Richard, on Horse Creek—the oxen ran off—he went to look for
> them, and had been wandering in circles and starving ever
> since, without gun, knife, moccasins, or any knowledge of the
> country or its productions. We seated him in the midst of a circle
> of trappers, squaws, and children—the wretch could scarcely
> speak. The men consider his escape almost miraculous.

This incident brought a flood of accounts of similar experiences
from the party of trappers who had come down to the Chugwater
to fatten their horses on the fertile bottoms before starting off on
another trip to the beaver country. The restless Parkman noted:

> Their hunts occupy but two months or more—spring and fall—
> and for the rest of the time they are idling about the forts or on
> the prairie, eating, drinking, or sleeping.

These trappers brought news of Bisonette's arrival at the fort and
of a quarrel between Bordeaux and another man in which the former had shown himself a coward—Parkman, still bitter about Laramie, observing: "which I can easily believe."

He had lost interest in the whites, however, for now his longed-
for opportunity to study the Indians at first hand had come. He
covered pages of his notebooks with jottings about manners and
morals—"What abominable indecencies the best of the Indians
will utter in presence of the women, who laugh heartily"—customs,
legends, and such. On July 5 the camp was moved to the "Forks"
—probably Sybille Fork of Laramie Creek:

> A few old men went ahead and sat down, where they wished
> the line to stop—and when they stopped in the bottom, the camp
> was formed in a circle around them.
>
> We had, it seems, a narrow escape a few days ago. The tracks
> seen on Chug. by Reynal and H. proved to be a party of Crows,
> as the Sioux have just found some bones and corpses flung from

their scaffolds. They were some thirty in number, and probably missed our camp in the morning fog.

Saw the dance of the Strong Hearts in the village this morning —great frolic and buffoonery.

This afternoon a war parade in full dress—sat in the shade of Reynal's lodge and looked at it—listened to the constant joking and trickery of the squaws—tasted sundry messes of pommes blanches and venison placed before us—saw a domestic quarrel, where the rebellious squaw pulled down the lodge, packed her horse, and rode off, while the husband looked quietly on. The warriors were in full dress—a miserable old squaw squalled after them from a lodge door, exciting them to glorious exploits —as one of them rode from the ring, a crier proclaimed his name, and published his renown before the whole village.

On the sixth Parkman rode over to Bitter Cottonwood Creek on the North Platte with the trappers, to meet Henry's friend Bisonette and go with him to La Bonté's. While they were nooning a party of emigrants appeared, and two Indians of the trapper Morin's lodge went off to beg from them:

The whole line of emigrants stopped nearly an hour, made them coffee, and gave them bread—such is their timidity and perplexity and want of management and regulation. The Inds. are getting more and more importunate in their demands upon them.

What with the endless delays, boredom, and a touch of dysentery, Parkman was in a state in which he could find little good to say of either Indian or trapper. The following observations have little of his beloved Cooper about them:

An Ind.'s meanest trait is his unsatiable appetite for food and presents. They are irrepressible beggars, and at meals, no matter how slender the repast may be, chiefs and warriors surround us with eager eyes to wait for a portion, and this although their bellies may be full to bursting. If one wishes to see an Ind. village, send a notice that you will feast, and they will come a two days' journey for the sake of your cup of coffee. What a life! where the excitement of an enjoyment so trifling can tempt them to such pains-taking. In fact the greater part of a trapper's or an Ind.'s life is mere vacancy—lying about, as I am now, with nothing to do or think of.

On the seventh two of the trappers, Rouleau and a one-eyed Canadian named Seraphin, departed for the mountains, and another party of mountain men, headed by Chatron, came in from the fort with word that Bisonette would not arrive until tomorrow. But on the following day he still did not put in an appearance, and Parkman rode on up the Platte to Horse Shoe Creek—"swift water, limpid as crystal"—and the following day to the mouth of La Bonté's Creek, where he found "no Inds.—no buffalo—but plenty of flies." He fumed again at the utter laziness of camp life, but all he could do was to wait and listen to the trappers' tales. One concerned a recent whirlwind courtship on the plains:

> Jeangrus met a party of emigrants, from whom some trapper from the fort stole a woman, as they camped night before last. He approached with two horses—met the fair one at the edge of the camp—mounted her and vanished.

On the tenth he came to the bitter conclusion that there would probably be no muster of Indians at La Bonté's, "as there certainly were no buffalo"; and after discovering that Shaw did not wish to rejoin the Indian village and accompany it into the mountains, he "resolved to go alone, that my object may not be wholly defeated." This decision, seemingly so lightly arrived at, is a revelation of Parkman's quality. Rather than be balked in his purpose, he determined to set off with but one companion into the heart of a wilderness filled with savages ripe for trouble, though he was already a sick man and there was no prospect of finding the food and rest he needed.

The following day Parkman set out with Raymond, equipped with a little flour and tea and a haunch of antelope. Henry went to look for Shaw's lost horse, while the latter remained to accompany the cart to Horse Shoe Creek, where he planned to camp before returning to Laramie. Parkman's entries for the day read like a log-book of the plains:

Steered about south. Prairie scorched and arid—broken with vile ravines and buttes—plenty of agate, jasper, etc.—gigantic grasshoppers and crickets—scorched pines along the sides of the ravines—a good place for grizzly bears. Nooned on Horse Shoe Creek, and, striking the Oregon Trail, reached at night our former camp on Bitter Cottonwood.

July 12. Raymond saw an antelope, and went to shoot it. The animals were hobbled, but, tormented by the flies, ran suddenly off, Paul Dorion's mare breaking her hobbles. I followed in vain. Raymond, returning, ran up the high butte, and saw them careering over the prairie. He followed, and did not return for about four hours, when he came in with them, having followed them to the Little Fork of the Laramie—ten or twelve miles. He had had no water, and that which he drank upon returning was immediately vomited. His appetite was gone, but I made him some tea, and let him rest. In his eager pursuit, he left his rifle on the ground, and we had much difficulty in finding it in the afternoon. I had good reason to be anxious during his absence, as I did not know exactly where Q. was encamped, and every day's delay made it more difficult to find the Ind. village.

While crossing Laramie Creek itself they picked up the trail of Tunica's village, but sudden storms coming down from the mountains made following it difficult. Thus they spent several days:

Nooned and set out on the trail—it led toward the mts., but such was the nature of the arid, barren, stony ground that only here and there the faint trace of a lodgepole was visible, as it passed over some ant-hill, or clump of prickly pear—or sometimes a stone would be turned over by the kick of a horse. Intensely hot. Followed slowly all the afternoon, losing the trail repeatedly. Saw a heavy smoke rising from a valley this side Laramie Mt. Lost the trail at last and encamped in a hollow bottom, where Laramie comes swiftly out of the hills, and where our own fire would be invisible.

The next day they came upon the traces of lodgepoles and then upon a campsite, where the small number of fires indicated that they were upon the trail of only part of the village. They followed a bare and scorching valley into the Laramie Mountains where it was necessary to lead the animals, and then descended "into a succession of little grassy and well-watered nooks among these black and desolate hills." Then, after passing over a hot and barren prairie, they came to a succession of defiles among "fine abrupt mountains," which reminded Parkman of Dixville Notch:

Bare cliffs above—beautiful woods below—a clear stream glancing in their shadows over a bed of rock—and all alive with birds like Mt. Auburn. It was a place to repay a week's travel.

Parkman's heart always leaped when he came among high hills, and he shook off here some of his boredom and weariness and discouragement. From time to time they came upon campsites, so they knew that they were still on the track. But the savage nature of the region was symbolized by several little forts, rudely made of interlaced logs and branches.

In the afternoon we ascended a narrow and most romantic pass —the stream, in its bed of rocks, by our sides, a dense foliage around us, and lofty beetling cliffs above. Larkspur and a sort of aster were among the numberless flowers—pleasant mementos of civilization in such a wilderness. In a basin among rugged hills at the head of the pass, the Inds. had encamped again, and a little farther on we did the same. (Absinthe everywhere.) Just emerging from the hills, saw several bulls on a distant butte.

July 15. Started, and soon got on a prairie where the traces were totally lost—a wide stony expanse, tracked with buffalo. Medicine Bow Mts. in the distance. After some weary and anxious hours, found the lodgepole marks, again to lose them. They pointed, however, towards the head of Laramie Creek, and thither we resolved to follow them. A number of little lakes, where wolves, antelopes, and large plover were congregated. Tried in vain to kill some, our meat being nearly gone. Were fast approaching a region quite dangerous on acct. of Snakes, Gros Ventres, and Arapahoes. Raymond advised return. Resolved to advance till night, and, soon after ascending a butte, saw the circle of lodges, with the bands of horse, close by the bare banks of Laramie. Thanked God that my enterprise was not defeated.

The trader Reynal came out to greet the latecomers and quartered Parkman upon Big Crow. The village had disagreed and split up, Tunica's faction going one way and Bad Wound's another. After the lean rations of the last few days, it was good to be invited to feast after feast—the village was full of fresh meat—and so, soon after his arrival, Parkman was seated in Reynal's lodge with a large group, eating and discussing the cause of thunder, a storm having just come up:

> The Sioux, like the northern tribes, say that the thunder is a bird, flying over the firmament, and that once an old man saw it descend and flap its wings on a lake which caused the lightening.

Parkman found even this portion of the village still divided among itself. Some of the young men were desirous of raising a war party, while others were content with gambling, smoking, and eating, and watching the squaws play ball. Big Crow gave a feast for more than twenty guests, perhaps with the hope of the village coming to a decision through a powwow of the principal men:

> Old Red Water, the fast friend and imitator of the whites, spoke at some length, expressing his gratitude. I answered, Reynal interpreting. Feast distributed by soldiers, chosen for such purposes, whose awards, says R., never give dissatisfaction. R., on the instigation of the Eagle Feather, took the occasion of this meeting to enforce the expediency of moving tomorrow after the buffalo; Eagle Feather seconded him, and remarked that, since Bull Bear's death, there had been nothing but divisions and separation among them—they were a body without a head. Others gave their opinion, but there was no decision—a completer democracy never existed. When all was eaten, Red Water sang his song of thanks, made another speech, and then intimated that the company ought to leave breathing room to the whites—on which they went out.

Parkman stood on bad terms with Reynal, whose "insatiable avidity to get hold of whatever he sees" displeased him, but became fast friends with old Red Water, one of the leading men of the village. From him he gathered many legends and bits of Indian lore: of the cricket which when picked up in the hand always turns his long horns in the direction of the buffalo; of the white beaver he saw in a lodge into which he had crawled while hunting—the old man considered the beaver and white men the wisest of all animals, and was convinced that they were the same; of his shooting an arrow clean through a buffalo cow, though well past sixty years of age; and of his unwillingness to tell his tales—"it is against his medicine, for they are about to go to war, and it is not good to talk much at that time." Another Indian, a young brave named White Shield, soon became Parkman's friend, though his motives were less disinterested than Red Water's, for he was a born beggar. White Shield was the leader of the war party whose plans had still not crystallized, a sore throat being sufficient excuse for him to put aside all thought of it for the present.

In a day or so, the village went buffalo-hunting on Laramie Plains, since new skins were necessary for lodge-coverings, but Parkman was "too languid to hunt with spirit." The hard ride on slim provisions in pursuit of the village had made him a semi-invalid. On the morning of July 23 Reynal reported that he had dreamed of strangers arriving, as had also a young Indian. Parkman was startled when Seraphin and Rouleau, who had left him at Horse Shoe Creek, soon appeared, on their way to the Medicine Bow country after trapping in the Laramie Mountains.

All the Inds. here try to dissuade them, saying that, since the death of Boot and May, the Arapahoes have grown very audacious, having got over their first terror, and call the whites dogs, saying that none of them shall leave this country alive. They laugh at the government and the dragoons. The trappers are resolved to go on. There is considerable danger in the immediate vicinity of the camp, from the Snakes.

* * * *

Rouleau and Seraphin set off this morning on their dangerous exped. Rouleau says if he only had one more horse he would

not go—this is his present necessity for continuing his dangerous trapper life. He whistles, sings, and laughs with the utmost
gaiety, and rides off with as careless a heart as if bound back to
the fort.

Since the buffalo skins had been cured, and the camp become
insufferably dirty, the village moved back up the creek, to get the
meat cached at the former camp and to cut lodgepoles in the hills.
That night a quarrel broke out in the camp among members of the
different Indian societies, which threatened to become deadly but
blew over. At the alarm old Red Water rushed out of his lodge,
gun and bow in hand, but tripped and sprawled on the ground,
much to Parkman's amusement. In another day they returned to the
Laramie Mountains:

> Camped in a narrow grassy spot among the rough hills—a most
> picturesque scene. Lodges no sooner up than, with characteristic
> hurry, forth poured half the population to get the lodgepoles,
> trotting, running, and scrambling on their horses, with dogs,
> colts, and all, along a rude narrow valley. Squaws in full attire,
> twinkling with their ornaments and laughing. Two deer sprang
> up—Reynal fired—jumped from my horse to do the same—
> instantly the whole helter-skelter procession was sweeping by
> me. A suitable place was found, squaws and men were all at
> work. Left the two men and wandered up the mts.—a hunter's
> paradise—signs of game incredibly thick—cold streams—rocks,
> pine, and spruce—all had the air of my old friends, the mts. of
> N.E. Strawberries—larkspur—robins—bumble-bees. Mts. very
> abrupt, precipitous, and broken. Saw beaver dams in returning.
> Sat down in the lodge to a hearty meal of buffalo meat, purveyed
> by Red Water, in the absence of my host, his son.

Parkman felt well enough next day to go hunting in the mountains
with Reynal, but had little luck. The village hummed with activity
as lodgepoles were trimmed, and *shongsava*, the red willow bark
used by the Indians to dilute tobacco, was gathered by the brook.
The next day Parkman climbed a high rocky mountain a few miles
from camp:

On the way, where little streams came down, cold as ice, among the stones and moss, and everywhere about the rocks, were scattered the Ind. boys, looking for berries or small game. They destroy all that comes to hand—young rabbits, ducks, prairie-cocks —everything; and this is their education. A savage prospect from the summit—lodges in the green valley like a circle of white specks.

Dozed away the afternoon in Reynal's lodge, thinking of things past, and meditating on things to come. Here one feels overcome with a irresistible laziness—he cannot even muse consecutively.

❀   ❀   ❀   ❀

As the pipe passed the circle around the fire in the evening, there was plenty of that obscene conversation that seems to make up the sum of Ind. wit, and which very much amuses the squaws. The Inds. are a very licentious set.

On July 30 they broke up camp and moved on toward the pass in the mountains. Just before reaching the camp ground, they saw a large number of mountain goats on the slopes above. Parkman and Raymond led a party of Indians in pursuit, scrambling over rocks and ravines until tired out, when they returned to their tethered mounts and thence to camp in the plain below. The Indians succeeded in so perplexing the agile beasts that they brought several within range of their wretched guns. Raymond and Reynal followed one wounded sheep and pelted her to death with stones in a ravine, but the meat proved to be tough and old. Several more frightened flocks could be seen from the camp.

As the camp broke up this morning, set out with Raymond among the hills for a hunt. Killed an antelope. The White Shield followed, for a share in the spoils. Arrived in camp in time to join the circle of old smokers in the middle. A noble spring of water not far distant—a great basin of rocks, fringed by soft water like crystal, many feet deep, and cold as ice. Escaping, soaking through the soil or creeping almost invisibly down the grassy ravine, it formed many rods below another basin, still larger and deeper—equally clear, but not so cool—a natural bathing-tub and a luxurious refreshment in the intense heat.

Aug. 1. Fairly among the mts. Rich grassy valleys—plenty of gooseberries and currants—dark pine mts.—an opening that tempted me to ride up into it, and here in the cool pine woods I recalled old feelings and old and well-remembered poetry. Climbed a steep hill—on the left the mts. and the black pine forests—far down the bare hills, and threading the valley below came the long straggling procession of Inds.

At noon the village camped in a grassy nook, where horses, dogs, men, women, and children crowded together. The men sat smoking, while the women worked on the new lodge-coverings and the children scampered among the steep rocks. Early the next morning Parkman set out in advance of the village, remembering his engagement to meet Shaw at Laramie. But sport interfered. Raymond wounded a black-tailed deer at two hundred yards; Parkman broke its shoulder at three hundred; and young White Shield followed it into a deep dell and finished it. They were delayed by butchering the deer, and joined the village's line of march instead of being far in advance:

> They were straggling down a deep and narrow gorge—rocks and pines—a confused, noisy, and wild procession. The mts. in front were all on fire, and have been so for weeks—a boundless and cloudlike volume of smoke obscured the whole landscape in front, except here and there the jutting ridges of bold cliffs and bristling pines, or the paler outline of more distant heights, just visible through the veil. High and stern crags on every side. But soon we descended into a milder region—one of valleys and little streams; where plenty of wild fruit grew, which the children gathered.

Thus they came down from the mountains onto the scorching prairie which Parkman found "hot as the devil." After plunging head, arms, and feet into water holes and smoking and eating, Parkman and Raymond took final leave of their Indian friends and set off for Fort Laramie, accompanied by a young brave who refused to camp at the first place proposed because two dead men were buried there. Setting out before daybreak from their old camp on the Chugwater, they reached the fort early on August 3, two days later than the appointed rendezvous, and were eagerly welcomed by the rest of the party. Shaw had been there for more than a fortnight, and was becoming uneasy about his cousin's fate. With great feeling Parkman remarked: "A civilized breakfast not to be sneezed at!" Full of biscuit, salt pork, and coffee—very welcome after an exclusive diet of unsalted meat—Parkman stretched out on a pile of buffalo robes and spent the rest of the day reading Byron.

Taking little time to recuperate from his arduous weeks with the Indians in the mountains, Parkman and his party set off southward the following afternoon, bound for the Pueblo and Bent's Fort. A trapper named Rouville and his Paiute squaw joined the party, since they wished to meet Bisonette along the way. Either the men or the horses were tired out, for they proceeded at the rate of only ten or twelve miles a day. There was little water—often it was necessary to scratch holes in the sand to find a mere swallow —and the only food the region afforded was wild cherries. They crossed Goshen's Hole—"a damned dry place, full of ravines"— and after three days they reached Horse Creek, where they found Bisonette, Sybille, Paul Dorion, and forty Sioux lodges of Tunica's village, as well as some Cheyennes. That evening they had horse races in which "the *ci-devant* circus rider Rouville" starred. Parkman was amused by the contrast between the Yankee and French temperaments, but did not let his amusement interfere with his business of pumping the trappers for information about the Indians. The mountain men were beginning to worry about the Indians this year, and to blame their belligerency on the emigrants. The Pawnees, for example, had held up Finch, killed Bradley in June, held up Bisonette, tried to rob Turner, stolen horses, whipped an emigrant into camp—and then, far from being repentant, had "told Rouville that they would rob and kill every white who passed through their lands." The Sioux said that the Pawnees had been committing outrages for years and no dragoons had come to punish them, so they meant to do the same. The Sioux were "never so turbulent as this year"—few of them had witnessed Kearny's show of force the previous year at Laramie, "being afraid to come," and those who had were dissatisfied that there had been no giving of presents. The Sioux had a bad record this year, too:

> [They] declare that if the emigrants continued to pass through, they would rob them and kill them if they resisted. Broke up the pots and pans of the emigrants who feasted them. Robbed Sublette and Reddick, and fired upon them. Robbed Bonny. Robbed a party of eight wagons at Independence Creek in July.

The Arapahoes had been alarmed after killing Boot and May in the spring, but, when no dragoons appeared, grew insolent and declared that no whites should ever leave their country alive.

From Sybille and Bisonette Parkman gathered more Indian lore. From the latter he learned that the Indian speeches which had so impressed him were always prepared in advance of the occasion:

> Bisonette once caught the Sioux *rehearsing* the speech they were to make to Col. Kearny on the visit they expected from him this summer. One of them personated their American father.

While at this camp Parkman had the opportunity to hear more Indian oratory. Bisonette gave a feast of coffee, corn boiled with grease, and a concoction of pounded cherries, grease, and flour:

> First a speech from him, telling them to make more robes than they had made last winter. A reply from the orator, followed by a broad intimation that they had now better begin to eat—at which an old "soldier" poured out the coffee, which was at once gulped down. Then the corn preparation was devoured—then the other mixture. Lomalomie, the "Hog"—the sick Tunica gorging like the rest—the Cheyenne guests served by the soldier with a treble share—the Crow prisoner. Pipe circulating constantly. Concluding speech of thanks from the orator.

One evening the Strong Hearts of the Sioux and Cheyennes did their dance. This association, like other Indian societies, drew its members from several tribes. The dancers passed from lodge to lodge, dancing at each, "the object being a present—a begging dance."

On August 8 a Missouri Indian, the Stabber, came into camp from the Arkansas, bringing "vague reports of troops passing up and of a victory over the Spaniards." Parkman, cut off from the civilized world for months, was irritated by the vague and unconnected way in which this obviously important news was retailed. On the ninth the camp broke up, and Parkman's party pushed on to Spring Creek. The region was rich in wild cherries, on which Tunica's lodges had been living, since they did not dare to cross the Laramie Mountains to obtain buffalo meat. Then they went on over a hot and dry prairie by Pole and Crow Creeks and thence to the mouth of Cache la Poudre on the South Platte. On the evening of the twelfth they caught a glimpse of "the very high mt. called Vasquez's Peak," but the following morning the air was not clear enough to distinguish it. They crossed the Platte, killing an immense rattlesnake as they went, and followed the river southward, nooning near St. Vrain's Fort—"deserted—entered it—two bastions—built of 'doughbies'—fast tumbling into ruins—fine situation." They camped that night by the river, near Vasquez's Fort. On the fourteenth, a very dry, hot, and smoky day, they passed Upton's Fort—also deserted—and camped again that night on the river, where the trail left it and crossed to Cherry Creek. They found fresh traces of a large Indian village, which they thought to be the dreaded Arapahoes. Then they went on, passing close to the site of Denver, to Cherry Creek, which was dry, like so many of the streams at this season, so that they had to dig waterholes. There were cherries, plums, black currants, and gooseberries in abundance, however, to make up for the lack of water. They followed Cherry Creek to the point where the trail crossed over the divide to the waters of the Arkansas. On the seventeenth they caught sight of the snow-covered summit of Pike's Peak; and Chatillon killed a straggling buffalo bull, whose meat proved too rank and tough to eat. Their animals were sickly, so they made an easy stage and camped at the head of Kiowa Creek.

August 18. Nooned on Black Squirrel Creek, after traversing a fine piece of pine woods. In the afternoon, a thunderstorm gathered upon the mountains. Pike's Peak and the rest were as black as ink. We caught the edge of the storm, but it had passed by the time we arrived at Jamie's Camp, where several little streams were tumbling down to the bottom in waterfalls. Before night the black shroud was lifted, and a bright sunset greeted us.

August 19. As we left camp, there was promise of a warm and clear day, but white wreaths of cloud soon gathered about the mts., reminding one of Byron's description of Luli and Pargo. The white snow patches—the ravines and the black forests were obscured and revealed by turns—it was a sublime and beautiful sight.

The weather cleared by the time they nooned at the Fontaine Qui Bouille, which they thereafter followed, but that afternoon they were caught in a tremendous thunder and hailstorm. As it passed, a fine double rainbow stood out against the deep black and purple of the clouds. On the twentieth they saw the valley of the Arkansas, and soon after the squat mud wall and cornfields of the Lower Pueblo came into view:

The Pueblo is in a beautiful bottom. Found Richard there, being prevented by the war from going to Taos, till the troops make a way. News of the victory at Matamoros—of Kearny's march to Santa Fe—and of the road being full of troops.

The Pueblo built like a rude trading fort. But two or three men and a few Spanish women there. Richard entertained us hospitably in the little mud room, the best in the fort, and gave us a good supper on the floor.

The Mormons that came across with him are on the other side encamped for the winter, and perhaps longer, and on the 21st we rode over to see them. Found them at work upon their log houses, but they suspended their labors to talk with us.

*   *   *   *

Some of them completely imbued with the true fanatic spirit—ripe for anything—a very dangerous body of men. One of them had been wounded by a grizzly bear in coming here. A great many more are said to be on their way up the Arkansas.

So much for the Latter-Day Saints, in the opinion of the young Bostonian.

On August twenty-second Parkman set out eastward down the Arkansas for Bent's Fort (near La Junta, Colorado), which he reached on the twenty-fifth. All the grass about the fort had been eaten by the animals of the Mormons and the troops of Kearny's Army of the West, whose 1600 men were supplied by 1556 wagons and 20,000 oxen, mules, and horses. Several sick officers and soldiers were at the fort, which was in charge of one Holt, both Bents being absent. From them Parkman learned that the Army of the West, which had left for Santa Fe three weeks before, had suffered many casualties on its way up the Arkansas, from the heat and from excessive use of water. He judged that "the military ardor of the invalids had chiefly evaporated." Parkman passed a burning hot day at the fort, reading newspaper accounts of the Matamoros affair, and listening to a wiseacre's opinion that the Spaniards would evacuate Santa Fe without fighting. Actually, this had already happened on the eighteenth, thanks to the fifth-column activity of Magoffin the trader. On the twenty-sixth Parkman sent Deslauriers ahead with the cart, while he and Shaw and Chatillon remained to dine at the fort with Holt and young St. Vrain. They dismissed Raymond here, and picked up recruits for the homeward—and most dangerous—leg of their journey: a volunteer named Hodgman, down with brain fever and "a very 'slow coach' "; two men from California, one an Iowan named Munroe and the other a Boston sailor whom Parkman first knew as Ben and later as Jim Gurney; and a homesick Missouri emigrant from Bridger's Fort, Ellis by name. The commissary officer at the fort furnished Hodgman with provisions but would not trust him with a gun. On the first day's ride Hodgman gave an indication of his quality by having much trouble with his mule—for the rest of the trip he was to involve himself in one difficulty after another, to the amusement or irritation of his fellow-travelers. But the sailor at once showed himself to be "very ready and active" and a real addition to the party.

During the afternoon Chatillon caught three stray dragoon horses, "in very low condition, and bitten by the wolves." Poor as they were, these beasts were a welcome addition to the worn-down animals of the party. The worst was taken by Ellis, Parkman and Shaw retaining the others. This was the first of many signs of military use of the Santa Fe Trail, for an army, particularly an untrained one, leaves much jetsam in its wake. Parkman found time to record features of the country new to him—soap plants, tarantulas, lizards—and to sum up two of his new companions:

> Hodgman, good-natured but helpless, has been clerk on Mississippi steamboats for eight years—has rubbed through the world for thirty—and is a boy yet. How much a man may see without learning!
>
> Ben, the sailor—his stories of California horses and horsemen.

Keeping always close to the Arkansas, they pressed on at good speed. On the afternoon of the twenty-ninth they met Magoffin's train of rakish Santa Fe wagons, and learned that both buffalo and an Arapahoe village were near by. The wagoners told also of Pawnees having killed a man named Swan, who was buried by his friends, then dug up, and scalped by the Indians, and then reburied by Magoffin. On the thirtieth they encountered an ox-train of clumsy government wagons, and were assured that the trail was dangerous. Parkman did not like the looks of this contingent— "Raw, smock-faced boys, and of a sickly appearance"—and was inclined to disregard the warning. Hodgman lied his way into getting sick rations from Coates, the master-driver, who advised Parkman that Ewing had killed one of a band of Pawnees who sought to steal his party's horses, that the Indians were out for vengeance against the whites, and urged the eastward-bound party to make all possible speed between the Caches and the Pawnee Fork.

The following afternoon Parkman saw the Arapahoe village on the opposite bank of the Arkansas, and, thinking it best to put up a bold front, crossed over with Chatillon and Shaw to meet them:

> Hodgman, thinking the whole party was going, was clamorous for my pistols, and wished to put on his cap and uniform to strike

terror. Some young men who were guarding their numerous horses went with us. Village all in a stench with meat. Squaws busy with skins. Sat before one of the chief lodges, holding our horses fast, and the curious crowd soon gathered around. Bad faces—savage and sinister. In complexion, form, size, and feature inferior to the Sioux. Their faces formed a complete wall around us. Distributed a few presents—traded a shield, trail-ropes, etc.—took out some awls and had the women called to receive them. They came screaming with delight—very ugly and dirty, like the men. The whole village, lodges and all, was in keeping with the inhabitants. Near sunset, rode through the long grass and across the Arkansas to camp, where a few Inds. had arrived before us. Hodgman was engaged in trading a robe with them, and behaved so ridiculously, or rather insanely, that he amused us all. Jim made great fun of him. H. traded one of the horses we found for a mule.

At night the wolves set up a most mournful and discordant howling which lasted all night. There was little sleep in the camp —the men were anxious for the horses—H. was sick—Hodgman was fidgety and restless—and I was kept awake by the burning pain of my poison—the horses, too, tramped incessantly through the camp. Hodgman woke me out of a nap with a story that he had seen an Ind. in a white robe drive off the horses, which were just out of sight. Went out to see, and on the way he talked so vaguely and strangely that I perceived the fever had not left his brain. It was, I suppose, nothing but his fright.

On the first of September they began to see buffalo in plenty, though at first only bulls, which were not good eating. At nooning they saw the Arapahoes across the river pursuing a herd of cows. Saddling hastily, they splashed across the shallows, just "in time to see the ground strewed with carcasses and the process of butchery begun." They had not gone a mile on their way when the prairie in front was suddenly black with buffalo:

Q. and I put after them, driving them up the hills on the right. The mare brought me upon the rear of a large herd. In the clouds of dust I could scarcely see a yard, and dashed on almost blind,

amidst the trampling of the fugitives. Their rumps became gradually visible, as they shouldered along, but I could not urge the
mare among them. Suddenly down went buffalo after buffalo,
in dust and confusion, into an invisible ravine some dozen feet
deep, and down in the midst of them plunged the mare. I was
almost thrown, but she scrambled up the opposite side. As the
dust cleared, I fired—the wounded beast soon dropped behind
—I plied him with shot after shot, and killed—not a cow—but
a yearling bull!

Tonight the bellowing of the bulls supplied the place of the
howling of the wolves.

The next day they advanced a dozen miles among the buffalo, and
killed sufficient of them to provide a supply of meat for the journey. They met some wagons belonging to a trader, and two companies of Monroe and Platte City Volunteers, "most unmilitary
fellows."

The execution wreaked among the buffalo by this small party
gives an idea of why the great beast of the plains soon became extinct:

Sept. 3. H. killed yesterday four cows, and today meat is drying
all round our camp. Hodgman is taken with an astonishing flow
of spirits and rattles away in the most amusing fashion. Shot an
old bull in the back, as he came up from the river—his death
agonies were terrific. Shot another in the afternoon. H. killed a
number of cows, and Q., who was with him, by laying behind
one of them, killed 5 bulls as they approached. A long line of
buffalo stretched over the prairie, beyond the river. The roaring
and fighting of the bulls were incessant.

They dried only a small fraction of the meat they had brought
down: the rest was left to the wolves, and to the turkey buzzards,
hawks, and crows, with here and there an eagle, who soon hovered
over the gutted carcasses. They had to push on, because of the
stench of rotting meat, and as they went they fired at bulls, tumbling them into the dust and going on without even examining
the prey. On the sixth they met two more companies of Colonel

THE BUFFALO HUNT

One of Frederic Remington's Illustrations for The Oregon Trail, *which earned Parkman's hearty approval for their faithful picture of the old West.*

From *The Oregon Trail* (1892 edition), by permission of the publishers, Little, Brown & Co.

Sterling Price's Missouri Volunteers, "a set of undisciplined raga-muffins." On the eighth the St. Louis County companies came up:

> . . . Much less raw in appearance than the former. They had lost horses, and bought some of us. Their questioning was most pertinacious and tedious. Our amusement is plaguing Hodgman, whose good nature is imperturbable—equal to his gluttony and helplessness. In the afternoon picked up three stray horses of the Volunteers, saddles and all! We are within 50 miles of Pawnee Fork.

The following day they rounded up three more horses and met a train of trading wagons, passed a large Indian trail, and saw several Pawnee forts. That afternoon, following the traders' advice, they decided to abandon the main trail along the river and take to the Ridge Road, where they would be less likely to be surprised by Indians. They rode twenty-five miles without water the next day, and then found only mud in a ravine two miles from the trail. But just at this moment they encountered more of Price's regiment of mounted infantry, including Captain Garrison, the commissary officer, who told them of good water three or four miles farther on, where a large detachment was encamped.

> . . . As we descended the hollow where the water lay, saw the opposite shore covered with wagons and footmen, and the water itself surrounded by white tents, cattle, and wagons drawn up in order. These were other companies of Price's regt., the Mormon battalion commanded by Col. Smith, and wagons of Mormon emigrants. There is, it seems, a general movement of the Mormons to California. The battalion consists of 500 men, who have volunteered as soldiers, taking this method of emigrating. We encamped lower down the little stream and were soon surrounded by the inquisitive throng.

Here they lost all the volunteers' horses they had picked up along the way, for the beasts were claimed by their rightful owners, much to the disgust of the finders, "especially Jim, who parted very reluctantly with his mare." But a little later they caught three stray mules. They pushed on to a creek some three miles from Pawnee

Fork, where they paused to rest their almost worthless animals and to observe with pleasure the first signs of the settlements. On the twelfth they crossed Pawnee Fork with its deep channel running among the plentiful trees, a welcome sight after the arid plains. They camped on the Arkansas, halfway to Walnut Creek, and at dark a train of twenty-eight government wagons came up and corralled on the road. Hodgman rode out to beg from them:

> Upon his hailing the wagons from afar with *Camp ahoy,* he was frightened almost to death at seeing the whole force turn out and level their guns at him. They thought he was a band of Indians raising the war whoop—were as frightened as he—and came very near shooting him. He behaves on all occasions very foolishly and childishly.

The next day they met still another wagon train before nooning at Walnut Creek, where they found grapes and walnuts. And as they camped that night on the big bend of the Arkansas, where the trail left the river, a train of Sutter's wagons came up. The trail had become a much traveled highway, thanks to the war.

The next day, as the party cut across country to Cow Creek, Parkman and Chatillon went buffalo-hunting in the great heat and just as they were returning, hot, thirsty, and unsuccessful, to camp, they came upon a herd of cows. But before they could fire, a tremendous volley came from the bushes along the creek, where a dozen government wagoners had stationed themselves for a still hunt, and frightened the herd away. The wagoner Nimrods were "a very disorderly set, and quite set at defiance the authority of Brown, the master-wagoner." That night on Cow Creek they found grapes and plums, and, best of all, a spring of fresh water. They had been drinking for days from mudpuddles. On they went, crossing creek after creek, and finding dead cattle and broken wagons littering the road. Parkman celebrated his twenty-third birthday as they nooned at a mudpuddle. But the character of the country soon changed entirely as they left the plains and came into the rich greenness of the fertile prairie belt. Prairie-hens abounded and the streams were swift and well timbered. It was no longer necessary to stand guard at night, and with the need for unity over, the incongruous party split up. On the eighteenth Munroe, Jim, and Ellis went ahead, after Ellis had had a row with Shaw, and Parkman saw no more of them till they reached Westport. Hodgman, nicknamed Tête Rouge for his luxuriant red hair, was afflicted with innumerable ailments, notably sore feet, and they could have spared his company, too. At Diamond Spring, they met wagons which, to Parkman's disgust, had taken three weeks to cover the short distance from Fort Leavenworth. On the twentieth they reached Council Grove, whose beautiful meadows and woods delighted Parkman's soul. Here an enterprising blacksmith had set up shop and was doing a roaring trade repairing wagons. The woods gave Parkman a foretaste of the settlements; he had had enough of the plains, and pined for the lush New England countryside. The next night they camped at Dragoon Creek, after doing twenty-one miles. Here they met some wagons, whose drivers hailed them:

> "Whar are ye from, Californy?" "No." "Santy Fee?" "No—the mountains." "What yer been doing thar? Tradin'?" "No." "Trappin'?" "No." "Huntin'?" "No." "Emigratin'?" "No." "What *have* you been doing, then, God damn ye?" (very loud, as we were by this time almost out of hearing).

To the last Parkman was irritated by people who did not mind their own business. The easy friendliness of the West had not relaxed his chill Bostonian reticence.

At Rock Creek, after a thirty-mile stage on their jaded animals, they met Folger, Lee, and Upton of Bent & St. Vrain Company, who were in advance of a wagon train. The next morning they met the train, with which were St. Vrain himself and a brother of Catlin's friend, Joe Chadwick. On the twenty-fourth Hodgman left them, much to their satisfaction, and headed for Fort Leavenworth; and on the twenty-sixth Parkman and Shaw slept again under Colonel Chick's roof at Kansas after passing through the beautiful Shawnee farm country, "the foliage just touched with the hues of autumn." In Westport they had met Jim Gurney and Munroe again, as they sold off their outfit before going on to Kansas. On Sunday they rested at Colonel Chick's, and on the following day went over to Wyandot City to see the government payment to the Indians for the improvement of their Ohio lands. Parkman found these tamed Indians sickly-looking, and judged very few of them to be full-blooded. And on October 1 they boarded the steamer for St. Louis, only to get stuck on a sandbar.

> There is a gang of slaves below. Two of them are chained together. Another fellow, with an immense mouth, is beating the banjo, and a dance is going on with the utmost merriment. None are more gay and active than the two fellows chained together. They seem never to have known a care. Nothing is on their faces but careless, thoughtless enjoyment. Is it not safe to conclude them to be an inferior race?

> The mind is its own place and of itself
> Can make a Heaven of Hell, a Hell of Heaven!

With this passing and stereotyped comment on the issue which was to convulse the nation in the next decade and a half, and to play a large part in changing the West which Parkman had come to know during these rigorous months into something which he neither knew nor cared to know, the Oregon Trail diaries conclude. He had gone to the West to grow in wisdom; he returned wise in matters of detail, but still blind to the basic elements of a region whose first explorations he was to chronicle when he was older and less set in his patrician prejudices against the democratic ways of the West. He paid too high a price for what he got out of his expedition, for he went back to Boston a sick man, who was to become sicker still in the long dark years that lay ahead, before he fought his way back to health and fulfilled his great youthful scheme.

It is one of the tragedies of our literature, which has always been characterized by unfinished or unwritten masterpieces, that Francis Parkman was too ill to work up for himself, as he might have done, the rich record of his great triangular journey through the heart of the West. The penciled notes in the little marbled books were too faint for his failing eyes to read, so Quincy Shaw read them to him and then took down his dictated rewriting of them. Much was lost in this double filtering process, and more in the revision of the manuscript by the staid and proper Charles Eliot Norton— of all people! But the essence of the great work that was never written is still in those three little notebooks, and one can write it for oneself in reading them.

Part Three

THE DARK VALLEY

1847–1865

You have gone vicariously through the dark shadow and the dark valley. Blessed are they who have the solace of an active mind and a busy hand when the night comes and the blight falls.

E. G. SQUIER TO PARKMAN, 1866

11: Entrance of the Enemy

*The prospect before him was by no
means attractive, contrasting somewhat pointedly with his boyish fancy
of a life of action and a death in battle. Indeed, the change from intense
activity to flat stagnation, attended
with an utter demolition of air castles, may claim a place, not of the
meanest, in that legion of mental tortures which make the torments of the
Inferno seem endurable.*

F.P., LETTER to ELLIS, 1864

AT THE beginning of 1846 Parkman had amassed the materials
for his history of the conspiracy of Pontiac. He had read all
there was to be read on that subject; he had ransacked libraries
and attics over a good part of America in search of documents; he
had visited the principal scenes of the action. His reliance, though,
was "less on books than on such personal experiences as should, in
some sense, identify him with his theme." He had obtained these
experiences by the long series of wilderness journeys which cul-
minated in the Oregon Trail trip. Few historians have set about
their lifework with so thorough a preparation—but then few historians have determined the nature of their work at the age of
eighteen. But Parkman had made one fatal error, which cost him
dear and almost ruined his career. He saw it clearly enough in
1864, as he looked back on his early life: he had entered on "this
long pilgrimage with all the vehemence of one starting on a mile
heat." When weaknesses of constitution made themselves evident,
he had unwisely crushed them, and so confirmed them. The troubles
began to make themselves felt during his Law School years, when
he burned the candle at both ends by studying history as well as
law:

His faculties were stimulated to their best efficiency. Never, before or since, has he known so great a facility of acquisition and

291

comprehension. Soon, however, he became conscious that the impelling force was growing beyond his control. Labor became a passion, and rest intolerable, yet with a keen appetite for social employments in which he found not only a pleasure, but, in some sense, a repose. The stimulus rapidly increased. Despite of judgment and of will, his mind turned constantly toward remote objects of pursuit and strained vehemently to attain them. The condition was that of a rider whose horse runs headlong, the bit between his teeth, or of a locomotive, built of indifferent material, under a head of steam too great for its strength, hissing at a score of crevices, yet rushing on with accelerating speed to the inevitable smash.

Portents of that inevitable smash soon appeared. He began to be troubled by a weakness of sight, which increased with ominous rapidity during his second year of law. He recoiled from the thought of studying through the eyes of another—though his sisters thus helped him with his work during the winter of 1845–46—and he determined to rest his failing vision while obtaining the firsthand view of Indian life which he deemed essential to his purpose. But this kill-or-cure remedy of the Oregon Trail trip was too harsh, and while in the West he was seized by a complication of disorders which nearly brought "both him and his scheme to an abrupt termination." A starvation diet and the exercise of the strong will which was his greatest asset enabled him to subdue the threat: "On a journey of a hundred miles over a country in parts of the roughest, he had gained rather than lost strength, while his horse was knocked up and his companion disconsolate with a painful cough." He could not adopt the airs of an invalid while with the Sioux, "since in that case a horse, a rifle, a pair of pistols, and a red shirt might have offered temptations too strong for aboriginal virtue." And when he was almost too weak to sit in the saddle, he found the tonic of the chase enabled him to hunt buffalo over broken country. He thought the sport good, and he held that, "to tame the devil, it is best to take him by the horns."

But he found he had to pay the price of his rash remedy when he returned home and the stimulus of danger was removed. His

dysentery cleared up with civilized diet, but his sight grew worse
and new afflictions fell upon him:

> To the maladies of the prairie succeeded a suite of exhausting
> disorders, so reducing him that circulation at the extremities
> ceased, the light of the sun became insupportable, and a wild
> whirl possessed his brain, joined to a universal turmoil of the
> nervous system which put his philosophy to the sharpest test it
> had hitherto known. All collapsed, in short, but the tenacious
> strength of muscles hardened by long activity. This condition
> was progressive, and did not reach its height, or to speak more
> fitly, its depth, until some eighteen months after his return.

Nothing more dismaying than invalidism, which he had always
particularly scorned, could have befallen Parkman. He had "profound respect for physical strength and hardihood, when joined
with corresponding qualities of character." He had done everything
in his power to strengthen his physique—and now it broke down
and left him more helpless than those who had never taken exercise or given a thought to their bodies. This was indeed a hard fate
for one who had

> a special aversion for the Reverend Dr. Channing, not for his
> heresies, but for his meager proportions, sedentary habits, en-
> vironment of close air, and female parishioners, and his preach-
> ments about the superiority of mind over matter, for, while I had
> no disposition to gainsay his propositions in the abstract, it was
> a cardinal point with me that while the mind remains a habitant
> of earth, it cannot dispense with a sound material basis and that
> to neglect and decry the corporeal part in the imagined interest
> of the spiritual is proof of a nature either emasculate or fanatical.

Parkman was a fanatic of the opposite camp, one who lashed and
spurred the body too vigorously in pursuit of physical hardiness.

In this crisis, of whose seriousness not even his family was at first
aware—for his nervous symptoms were not apparent and he was
not the man to make much of them—he found two alternatives
before him. One was an impulse "to return to the Rocky Mountains,
try a hair of the dog that bit me, and settle squarely the question

to be or not to be." The other, which his family favored and he adopted in November 1846, was to go to New York and study in a law office, while subjecting his eyes to the attentions of Dr. S. R. Elliott of Staten Island, who had cared for his sister Carrie the previous year, and numbered among his patients at West New Brighton a representative collection of Bostonians: Charles A. Dana, George Ripley, Longfellow, the Reverend Charles Lowell and his son James, Professor Youmans, and some of Parkman's Shaw cousins. So off to New York he went, furnished by his uncle Shaw with letters of introduction to "old family friends and prominent merchants," and urged by his father to sit under his friend, the Reverend Mr. Bellows, at whose board he ate his Thanksgiving dinner. Abandoning the customary Bostonian stopping place, the Astor House, Parkman lodged at Delmonico's Hotel and nominally occupied himself with law in the courts and in the office of Mr. Lord on lower Broadway.

He was by no means a friendless stranger in a strange town. His cousin Charles Parkman was a student at the Union Theological Seminary over on Eighth Avenue; many of his college friends passed through or lingered in the city; Quincy Shaw, Charles Dabney, and Charles Eliot Norton among them. Whole families came down from Boston to visit, for the tradition of escaping from the Bostonian atmosphere for a breathing spell of freedom in New York was already well established. And since the economic center of the country had already begun to shift from New England to New York, many Boston businessmen, among them his father's friend, Gardiner Howland, had established themselves in the new commercial capitol. Their homes were open, of course, to young Francis Parkman, and it is clear that he allowed neither his illness nor his legal occupations nor his historical investigations to rule out a considerable amount of social life. In the spring he was forced to give up this pretense of following the career which his father had favored, and was obliged to devote himself entirely to the cure at Staten Island. At first Dr. Elliott had said a cure would be a matter of two months. When January came and Parkman's eyes were worse, he still said the case was curable, but put no time limit to the treatment. Before reaching this pass, Parkman began to write

The Oregon Trail by dictation—a procedure of which he soon caught the knack and found "as easy as lying." But the book lost much of its vitality in the triple distillation as Parkman listened to Sarah or Quincy Shaw or another volunteer read his notes aloud, then framed his sentences mentally, and dictated them. Reading the installments as they came out in the *Knickerbocker* (the first in February 1847)—for Lewis Gaylord Clark remained true to "Captain Jonathan Carver, Jr." and thought the *Trail* "the best yet" —you can almost see Parkman slowly winning mastery over the new technique and making it his instrument. After the first few installments, the quality improved so much that the chapters were put up in the lead or second position of each number of the *Knickerbocker*. Clark spun the serialization out until February 1849, for *The Oregon Trail* had caught many new subscribers, whom he was loath to lose through its conclusion. But the effort of composition—perhaps the practice of visualizing mentally the words and phrases he dictated, as Dr. George M. Gould suggests in his interesting discussion of Parkman's illness—made Parkman's eyes worse, and he was condemned to complete repose, "to me the most detestable of prescriptions." Fuming against this treatment and his helpless inaction, he saw eventually that his only chance of successfully accomplishing his chosen purpose in life "lay in time, patience, and a studied tranquillity of spirit, and I felt extreme disgust that there was nothing for it but to renounce past maxims and habits and embrace others precisely the opposite." To make things harder for him, some of his classmates were going off to the Mexican War to win glory by the sword, as he had always wished to do, and nearly twenty years later he recalled "with what envious bitterness I looked at a colored print in a shop window representing officers and men carrying a field battery into action at the battle of Buena Vista."

After a period of bitterness and despair, he resolved that anything was better than inaction, and against the advice of his physicians, who threatened him with disaster for his folly in disregarding their instructions, he cautiously set about the composition of *The Conspiracy of Pontiac*, for which the materials had already been collected. His account of this gallant attempt in the autobiographical letter of 1864 is one of the most moving of literary confessions:

> The difficulty was so near the impossible that the line of distinction often disappeared, while medical prescience condemned the plan as a short road to dire calamities. His motive, however, was in part a sanitary one, growing out of the conviction that nothing could be more deadly to his bodily and mental health than the entire absence of a purpose and an object. The difficulties were threefold: an extreme weakness of sight, disabling him even from writing his name except with eyes closed; a condition of the brain prohibiting fixed attention except at occasional and brief intervals; and an exhaustion and total derangement of the nervous system producing of necessity a mood of mind most unfavorable to effort. To be made with impunity, the attempt must be made with the most watchful caution.
>
> He caused a wooden frame to be constructed, of the size and shape of a sheet of letter-paper. Stout wires were fixed horizontally across it, half an inch apart, and a movable back of thick pasteboard fitted behind them. Paper for writing was placed between the pasteboard and the wires, guided by which, and using a blacklead crayon, he could write not unlegibly with closed eyes. He was at the time absent from home, in Staten Island, where, and in the neighboring city of New York, he had friends who willingly offered their aid. It is needless to say to which half of humanity nearly all these kind assistants belonged. He chose for a beginning that part of the work which offered fewest difficulties and with the subject of which he was most familiar, namely, the Siege of Detroit. The books and documents, already partially arranged, were procured from Boston and read to him, at such times as he could listen to them, the length of each reading never, without injury, much exceeding half an hour, and periods of several days frequently occurring during which he could not listen at all. Notes were made by him with closed eyes, and afterwards deciphered and read to him till he had mastered them. For the first half-year, the rate of composition averaged

PARKMAN'S DESK AT CHESTNUT STREET AND THE WRITING GUIDE HE
USED WHEN HIS SIGHT WAS POOR

By courtesy of Miss Elizabeth Cordner.

about six lines a day. The portion of the book thus composed was afterwards partially rewritten.

His health improved under the process, and the remainder of the volume—in other words, nearly the whole of it—was composed in Boston, while pacing in the twilight of a large garret, the only exercise which the sensitive condition of his sight permitted him on an unclouded day while the sun was above the horizon. It was afterwards written down from dictation by relations under the same roof, to whom he was also indebted for the preparatory readings. His progress was much less tedious than at the outset, and the history was completed in about two years and a half.

He had been told that brainwork was poison for one in his condition: years later he remarked wryly that "the dose was homeopathic and the effect good." Within a year after beginning work, he found himself able to put in two hours or even more a day. How maddening such piecemeal composition and tortoise-like progress must have been to one whose spirit burnt like a flame within the shackles of the flesh, Parkman leaves us to imagine. In this patient battle against the illnesses which he grouped under the title of "The Enemy" he found a contest which tried his fighter's heart. But he never ceased to regret that the battle was fought in the study and not in the field; that he held "the pen with a hand that should have grasped the sword."

At Dr. Elliott's his cousin Sarah Barlow Shaw was his chief assistant. It was she who wrote his letters for him when his eyes were at their worst, and it was she who gave his family firsthand accounts of his condition on her occasional visits to Boston. A Mr. Levi Thaxter of Watertown—later husband of the poetess Celia of the Isles of Shoals—served for a time as a paid pair of eyes, reading over to Parkman the material he needed to have fresh in his mind. Up in Boston Caroline and Mary Parkman copied away industriously in their brother's interest. Meanwhile Henry Stevens was sending books and papers from London, and Benjamin Perley Poore, who had collected historical documents for the Commonwealth of Massachusetts, sent bundles of copies from the Archives of the Colonies in Paris. Since the history of "the American forest and the American Indian at the period when both received their final doom" had never before been written, it had been necessary for Parkman to search, or have searched, a vast amount of material buried in government archives or in obscure private records. By his own confession, the collection of the necessary documents was "the most troublesome part of the task," of whose enormity he gave some idea in his preface to the book:

> These consisted of letters, journals, reports, and dispatches, scattered among numerous public offices and private families, in Europe and America. When brought together, they amounted to about three thousand four hundred pages. Contemporary newspapers, magazines, and pamphlets have also been examined, and careful search made for every book which, directly or indirectly, might throw light upon the subject. I have visited the sites of all the principal events recorded in the narrative, and gathered such local traditions as seemed worthy of confidence.

In these few words, Parkman summed up the task which took the better part of five years. Jared Sparks, his former history professor and now President of Harvard College, opened many doors to him, but Parkman's own obvious zeal and enthusiasm opened as many more. From General Lewis Cass he got a valuable collection of papers dealing with the siege of Detroit by the Indians. Henry R. Schoolcraft, E. B. O'Callaghan, Lyman Draper, W. L. Stone, Brantz Mayer, O. H. Marshall, and many other historical students contributed materials for the work. The project was truly a heroic task, for Parkman had to make his own way:

> The field of the history was uncultured and unreclaimed, and the labor that awaited me was like that of the border settler, who, before he builds his rugged dwelling, must fell the forest trees, burn the undergrowth, clear the ground, and hew the fallen trunks to due proportion.

The arduous task of sifting the materials was begun and accomplished when Parkman was denied the use of his eyes for either reading or writing. His amanuensis repeatedly read aloud from the documents, notes and extracts were made, and then the narrative was written from dictation. When the long task was done, under these seemingly paralyzing conditions, Parkman was able to write:

> This process, though extremely slow and laborious, was not without its advantages; and I am well convinced that the authorities have been even more minutely examined, more scrupulously collated, and more thoroughly digested, than they would have been under ordinary circumstances.

He did not ask the critics' mercy because of his personal difficulties, but proudly made these public as assets rather than liabilities for his chosen work.

One of the factors that made it possible for him to grind away at *Pontiac* despite almost insuperable odds was the favorable reception of *The Oregon Trail*. The East was fast developing an interest in the West, and Parkman's book offered a colorful picture of the West as seen through eastern eyes. Its faults passed unnoticed, and it was praised to the skies in the *North American* by Francis Bowen, who in the same review casually dismissed Edwin Bryant's much more solid and informative work, *What I Saw In California*. Of course the *North American* was written by and for the Boston elect, of whom Parkman was one—indeed he soon became a contributor to that august organ of New England opinion—but in other quarters he also got an unusually good press. Richard Bentley, the London publisher, became enthusiastic about the work and brought out an English edition, but unfortunately the English reading public did not share his opinion or that of the reviewers, and few copies were sold. The New York Historical Society conferred an honorary membership on Parkman early in 1847, probably partly for the *Trail* and partly for his researches on *Pontiac*. Even Dr. Parkman, who had not taken his son's chosen profession seriously, was forced to admit that the *Trail* was "admirably written" and that he took pleasure in hearing of the success of his son's "lucubrations." He found with paternal pride that Francis had become famous, and wrote to tell him so:

Last week Elly [Parkman's brother, John Eliot] came into town and, having a half-day's leisure, strolled over to the Navy Yard at Charlestown. As he was looking around, as boys love to look, an officer met him and asked him his name, and, finding it Parkman, he asked him further, if he was any relation to the gentleman who wrote articles in the *Knickerbocker*. Elly told him that he was his brother, which, as you know, was no more than true.

The officer then said, "Come with me, and I will show you all there is to see; for I am glad to know a brother of the writer of those pieces. He writes well, and I read *The Oregon Trail* with great pleasure."

He then took Elly all over the Yard, and when he had showed him fully all that was to be seen, he invited him into his own room and, among other things, showed him the numbers of the *Knickerbocker*, which he said had given him so much pleasure.

I confess, my dear Frank, I was much gratified by this, but I should not be studious to write it out at length, did I not feel, that, under your trials and inability to do as much as you desire, you are entitled to know that what you have done, and still can do, is fully appreciated. It is a consolation, when some of our plans are interrupted, to know that others have so well succeeded, and I congratulate you on having accomplished so much, and successfully, amidst great discouragements.

But despite such pleasant tributes, Parkman rebelled against the slow course of Dr. Elliott's cure, and sometime in the late summer of 1847—probably early in September—he went to Brattleboro, Vermont, to take the water-cure at Dr. Wesselhoeft's famous establishment. The Brattleboro Spa was a popular resort for Bostonians, who were not particularly noted for their health at this period. The letters from Parkman's family are overrun with the references to the sudden death of this or that young friend of the family and the everlasting illnesses of the elders. Parkman's own brother-in-law, William P. Atkinson, was a firm believer in the merits of the water-cure and for some months had urged Parkman to try its effectiveness: "I feel confident it wd restore you with less pain and far more satisfaction to yourself than any other way, if indeed it is not the *only* way left to you." Atkinson felt that the water-cure had saved his own life, and he urged Parkman to consult the novelist Bulwer's account of how the cure had helped him. Parkman needed little urging to abandon Dr. Elliott's wearisome treatment, and he joined his brother-in-law at the Spa and remained there until late in the year. At least Brattleboro furnished a taste of the country that he loved and in happier days had wandered widely over. But this great plan of William Atkinson's, like all his other great plans —he seems to have been a perfect Micawber of a man, to the despair of his practical Parkman relatives—came to naught, for Parkman was no better for his stay at Brattleboro, aside from having his spirits raised by the change of scene and the company of Quincy Shaw, who helped him there to produce more installments of the *Trail,* which was now appearing every other month in the *Knickerbocker.* So, late in the fall, he returned to Dr. Elliott's establishment on Staten Island, where he remained for most of the next year. The Brattleboro experience evidently made little impression on him, for its only echo is in some scenes of his autobiographical novel, *Vassall Morton,* which appeared nine years later.

Parkman's health grew worse by fits and starts, despite the attentions of Dr. Elliott. In July 1848 he wrote hopefully to Charles Eliot Norton: "My health is now, I think, decidedly changing for the better. My position is anything but comfortable, but I begin to flatter myself that I have only to hold fast for a while and the world will brighten once more around me." Norton had made an excursion to Niagara—Parkman rallied him for being not quite "Yankee enough to do up the job in two hours, one for dinner and for seeing the Falls"—and Parkman wrote longingly: "If I get out of this scrape, I should like to go up to Lake George and thereabouts with you sometime; and spend a week or two in fishing among the islands there." But two months later he had to write:

Staten Island, Sept. 12, 1848

My dear Charley,

Thank you for your two kind letters, to the first of which I should have answered sometime ago, had I not been out of town —up at Catskill—where I went to get rid of an attack akin to my old enemy of the prairie. I met with partial success, but my system has been greatly deranged again, and old symptoms revived with most unwelcome activity.

The condition of my head has in consequence caused me at times suffering most intolerable, so that I have found no relief except in lying flat on my back without thought or motion. My best chance of recovery is in perfect idleness, for every effort of mind increases the difficulty. Patience, I suppose, is the only medicine; and a most hateful one to me it is.

With regard to your very friendly offers to read the proofs of *The Oregon Trail,* I think I may very thankfully accept them. Putnam will publish, in January or February, a good edition with illustrations by Darley, who is now at work on P.'s new edition of Irving. He would bring it out sooner, but his hands are more than full at present. This month I sent no chapter to the *Knickerbocker,* because I want the book to be out before the appearance of the last chapter, for fear of piracy. If P. can make a satisfactory arrangement to that effect, there will be an English edition also.

I am glad to hear that you have not abandoned your literary pursuits, and hope before long to see the results upon the pages of our ancient and respectable quarterly. Put a little pepper and allspice into it—it will not harm its respectability, and perhaps will make it more welcome to the taste of some of its readers.

I have heard with much regret that your sisters have been suffering from illness and am glad to learn of their improved health. Pray give my best compliments to them and to your father and mother, and assure them of my respectful regards. Don't let Ned Dwight work himself to death. He is engaged in a great scramble after usefulness, which he can reach with much less effort. Can I do anything for you here? If so, you may command my services—and believe me, with sincere regards,

Yrs truly

F. Parkman

He passed part of that fall again in Brattleboro, but early in November was obliged to leave "post-haste, on account of the cursed condition of my eyes which suddenly relapsed into a state quite as bad certainly as they have been, and so painful that it was folly to endure it when there was any chance of being relieved." So back to Staten Island he went, where Dr. Elliott told him his eyes were out of danger so long as he submitted to treatment. After a month of Staten Island Parkman wrote Norton that he was "sick of the business, however, and shall go to Boston; my eyes may go to the devil if they like; but I'm tired of this place & no threats of consequences will keep me here longer." In March 1849 he reported to Norton that "my eyes are very fair, though otherwise I am rather below par." Parkman had recently given his friend E. G. Squier, an anthropologist who was much interested in the Indians, a letter of introduction to Norton, after warning him that Norton might seem "starchy" at first meeting and warning Norton that Squier was something of a rough diamond. However, the pair got on well together, and Squier was even accepted into the bosom of the august Andrew Norton's family on later visits to Boston and Newport. A common interest in ethnology united Squier and Norton despite their great differences of manners and background.

All Parkman's slender store of working ability was now concentrated on *Pontiac*. He had determined to write this book, which was the last in chronological order of the series he had in mind, as if fearful that he might not live to produce the books which were to tell the story of New France from the first French settlements in the sixteenth century down to the English conquest in 1760. Pontiac's conspiracy was the last great flare-up of the Indian power which had been used for their own purposes by both French and English; with its collapse, the history of the Indians as a major force in the continent was at an end. In the preface to the sixth edition, Parkman remarked: "I chose the subject of this book as affording better opportunities than any other portion of American history for portraying forest life and the Indian character, and I have never seen reason to change this opinion." His interpretation of the conspiracy was revolutionary: no historian had penetrated through the murk of reminiscence which hung over the French and Indian Wars and the pre-revolutionary period of our history to mark out the salient features of the period. Parkman was the first to see that the effect of the English conquest of Canada was to change the political aspect of the continent, freeing the interior from military despotism and giving it to ordered democracy. He was the first, too, to see that the conquest spelt the doom of the Indians, who might have long postponed disaster under the easy-going French rule. They were well aware of the danger of exter-mination under English rule, and fought fiercely under a great and daring leader to avoid it. *Pontiac* is the story of that fight.

The book is a remarkable performance as the first effort of a young historian, quite aside from the handicaps which beset its author. There is a striking sureness of technique, and an ease in the use of the vast collection of materials at his disposal which shows how well he had prepared himself for his task. Though he relied more on secondary sources than was later his custom, Parkman found little to change in the book when revising twenty years after its first appearance, although the discovery of the Bouquet and Haldimand papers threw new light on several points. Despite the careful revision that he gave to all his books from time to time, most of *Pontiac* remains as it was written originally. If only one of Park-man's histories can be read, this is perhaps the best choice, for it is at once a summary and the crown of the great epic of *France and England in North America*. The first chapter is a sweeping treat-ment of the Indians east of the Mississippi in all their aspects—a thoroughly competent summary of what was known about the Indian at this period. The second chapter sketches the broad out-lines of the French and English colonial systems in America. The third deals with the early relations of these three great forces in their struggle for the possession of the continent, and the fourth summarizes the conflict between the rival colonies down to the fall of French Canada. These chapters constitute a brilliant his-torical synthesis which at once outlines the field that Parkman was later to cover in detail and prepares the way for the careful account that follows of the great Indian uprising whose effects were felt from Mackinaw to the Virginia frontier. It is one of the great books of American historical literature, and better than any other single volume it orients the reader in the pre-revolutionary history of America.

There is an amazing firsthand quality about the book, which others of the series lack. In it Parkman made more use of oral tradition than in any other work, and he also drew many illustrations from his own experiences with the Indians. The first was possible because he had talked to the sons and grandsons of men who had fought in these border wars. He had sought out the son of John Elder of Paxton: he had talked with François Baby of Windsor, the son of Pontiac's friend; and in old Pierre Chouteau of St. Louis he had met a man who had known Pontiac himself. He was also writing about events which took place only eighty years before he began investigating them. Many of the scenes he described had not altered much in that space of time, and his rich imagination eliminated readily such changes as the years had made in the sites he inspected. And more than any of his books, *Pontiac* deals with the forest and the Indian, and it was only a few years since Parkman had wandered through the one and lived with the other. It was not a question, as it was later, of clothing the bare bones of history—documents and records—with flesh and blood: it was more a matter of recollection of matters he himself knew at first or second hand. He had wandered the border in many parts of the country and become intimate with settlers in the wilderness, and so he was able to write vividly and realistically of border life. He had done his groundwork at almost the last possible moment, for the Indian character was changing rapidly under white pressure, and so, too, was the border way of life. It was no longer to be man against the wilderness, but economic forces, which used men as ruthlessly as they used nature, spoiling both for those who came after. The machine age was at hand, and the old framework of society was being overturned to meet the needs of the new industrial system. Preoccupied with the old order, a hundred years behind his time in his thoughts, Parkman at first did not notice the revolution; when it forced itself upon his attention he found no good in it and turned his back upon it as far as he could.

After his return to Boston, Parkman carried on his work on *Pontiac* in the attic of his father's Bowdoin Square house, whose gloom was welcome to his light-shy eyes. The writing went faster than he anticipated: at the outset, in 1848, he had figured that four years would be required for the task, but in March 1850 he was able to send part of the completed manuscript to his old history professor, Jared Sparks (to whom he later dedicated the book) for a verdict, and felt free to count on finishing the book before the year's end. The reply was encouraging, even if Sparks, as a member of an older order of historians, felt that Parkman had not indulged in enough moralizing:

Cambridge, Mar. 19/50

My dear Sir,

I return your MS., with many thanks for the pleasure I have derived from the perusal of your highly interesting narrative. It affords a striking picture of the influence of war, and religious bigotry, upon savage and semi-barbarous minds. Putting all things together, however, there is no possible apology for the atrocious acts of the Paxton Men. There could not be a stronger case of deliberate and cold-blooded murder. The provocation and surrounding circumstances afford no ground of mitigation of so inhuman a crime. It is one of the great lessons of history, showing what passion is capable of doing when it defies reason, & tramples on the sensibilities of nature, to say nothing of the high injunctions of Christianity. Although you relate events in the true spirit of calmness & justice, yet I am not sure but a word or two of indignation now & then, at such unnatural & inhuman developments, would be expected from a historian, who enters deeply into the merits of his subjects.

With best wishes for the success of your enterprises, I am,

My dear Sir,

Sincerely your friend,

Jared Sparks

Francis Parkman, Jr., Esq.

In June Parkman put the manuscript into the hands of his life-long friend, the Reverend George E. Ellis, the editor of the *Christian Examiner* and the author of some colonial biographies, as his agent in placing it for publication. Jared Sparks provided a letter vouching for his acquaintance with Parkman's historical studies— "I doubt if any writer has bestowed more thorough research, or has more completely investigated his subject"—and paying tribute to the "spirited style" and "good judgment and discrimination" of the portions of the manuscript he had read. Mr. Ellis promptly offered the work to the Harpers, who said they would be glad to consider it, although from the first they thought Parkman should follow in the footsteps of Prescott, Motley, and Ticknor and have the work stereotyped at his own expense, subsequently submitting the proofs to publishers and getting their offers for its printing and sale. The Reverend Mr. Ellis was a determined man, and he harried the Harpers by three visits during one hot August week in pursuit of their verdict, which was that they would not care to assume all the risk of publication, being "apprehensive that the work, highly respectable as it is, will not meet with a very rapid or extensive sale." Their reader had reported on *Pontiac* in these terms:

Parkman's History of the Indian Wars
treats of a period of American history, of secondary importance in itself, but interesting in its general connection with the settlement of this country. The subject is handled with very considerable ability—in a manner highly creditable to the industry, intelligence, & literary skill of the author. The narrative is lively, and often graceful—the rules of historical perspective are well observed, and the whole effect of the picture is pleasing and impressive.) It will worthily fill a niche among the standard works of American history. At the same time, I do not anticipate for it a remarkably brilliant reception. This is forbidden both by the subject and the style. It will be a stock book, commanding a steady sale, and finding a place in all well-assorted libraries. It will require a good deal of effort to push it into general circulation among the people.

While Mr. Ellis was conducting these negotiations, Parkman was already visualizing his book in a "decent and scholarlike dress," two volumes in the format and type of Prescott's *Mexico*. He also offered Mr. Ellis a bewildering choice of clumsy titles, none of which would have gone on the spine of a book:

As to the title, the following occurs to me, which however I don't greatly admire:

"A history of the War with Pontiac & the Indian Tribes of North America in their combined attack upon the British Colonies after the Conquest of Canada."

I like best the one that first occurred to me; & I think that Johnson's dictionary will bear me out in the use of the word conspiracy:

"A History of the Conspiracy of Pontiac & the struggle of the North American Indians against the British Colonies after the Conquest of Canada."

How will this do—"The War with Pontiac (or Pontiac's War): a History of the Outbreak of the Indian Tribes of America against the British Colonies after the Conquest of Canada."

Eventually the book was stereotyped at Parkman's expense, and published in Boston by Little and Brown, and in London by Richard Bentley, under the title of *History of the Conspiracy of Pontiac, and the War of the North American Tribes against the English Colonies after the Conquest of Canada.* It made a large octavo volume of more than six hundred pages, and even so a note was added that "More than half the documents intended for publication in the Appendix have been omitted, from an unwillingness to increase the size of the volume." The book was published in America in September 1851; the English edition appearing about a month earlier, in order to secure copyright there. The anonymous reader for Harper's was right in his judgment. The book had a *succès d'estime,* but it never sold more than a few hundred copies a year. Bentley succeeded in disposing of only 153 copies of an edition of 500 in the first year. He attributed the lack of success to "the *subject* possessing in itself comparatively little interest *here,* to what it naturally would in the United States; and secondly to the title." This last he intended to remedy by rechristening the work "The War in the Wilderness," or "Romance of Indian Warfare," or "The Conspiracy of Pontiac against the Colonists of North America." He confessed that he was disappointed by the book's reception, "having read the work with great interest," and he hoped that a new title would "induce people to look at the book, and then I feel sure they will read to the end." Such words were balm to the author's heart, and doubtless made up for the thoroughly discouraging statement of account which accompanied Bentley's note.

From Parkman's fellow historical workers came letters which doubtless cheered and encouraged him to continue the course he had mapped out for himself. To Brantz Mayer in Baltimore, who shared with Parkman the affliction of eye trouble as well as the passion for historical research, the young author sent a copy of the work with the following covering letter—one of the few in which he mentions his difficulties to someone outside of his personal circle:

Boston Sept. 12, 1851

My dear Sir:

I have just sent you by Harden's express a copy of the *Conspiracy of Pontiac*, as a slight acknowledgment of the assistance and sympathy for which you made me your debtor during the progress of the work. I trust your eyes are better than when I last heard from you. Mine are behaving badly and keep me a prisoner in bright weather—the effect of too much exposure. I have grown used to it, however, like the eels in the proverb. One of our chief lawyers here, Judge Sprague, has managed to distinguish himself in his profession without them, and walks the streets with blue spectacles and a green umbrella. Hoping to hear good accounts from you of the condition of your sight, I remain, my dear sir,

Yours with great regard,

F. Parkman, Jr.

Brantz Mayer, Esq.

Ten days later he received the following graceful reply:

Baltimore, 22 September 1851

My dear Sir,

I am doubly indebted to you for your beautiful gift and the kind allusion in your preface, which I hardly deserved. I lost no time in reading the *History of Pontiac's Conspiracy,* and although

I have not quite finished it, I can no longer ungraciously delay the expression of my delight and gratitude.

Your work has, in truth, impressed me as the first history of North American events, pertaining to our race, which combines *perfectly* a philosophical spirit of investigation with a dramatic power of narrative.

Especially have I been charmed with your groupings of Indian Nations, tribes, and characteristics, as well as the ease with which you glide into your story after laying this introductory foundation which is the key of the splendid Tragedy.

I think you may tread as proudly and confidently of enduring remembrance in the History and Literature of the English Race as Gibbon did on that memorable night when he laid down his pen after writing the last lines of the *Decline & Fall*, and walked to and fro within the copse of his garden at Lausanne. At your early age this is a great gratification; and, should it please God to restore you once more to a perfect command of your eyes, it will doubtless stimulate you to unfold another leaf from that mysterious past in which I am sure you must have caught glimpses of many a golden legend whilst searching for Pontiac and his people.

I regret to say that my eyes are not much improved, but they are yet strong enough to see and welcome friends. As you are now at liberty, I hope you will direct your steps southward; and whenever you do so, you must not fail to tarry a few days with me in Baltimore, where I presume I shall remain the whole of the coming winter.

I am truly your friend,
Brantz Mayer

F. Parkman, Jr., Esq., Boston

Such a tribute as this must have done much to make up for Parkman's black hours, when progress in his chosen work, much less success, seemed out of the question.

Lyman Draper, the tireless investigator who never felt satisfied enough with his researches to sit down and write the books he planned to base upon them, congratulated Parkman on his work

—in which, true researcher that he was, he found one or two details wrong—and urged him to deal with Sir William Johnson in his next book. Old Stephen Williams of Deerfield, from whom Parkman had gathered information about his famous forebear of Fort Massachusetts fame, wrote to propose an exchange of a copy of *Pontiac,* of which he had heard many good things, for one of his own genealogical productions, since he was regrettably short of funds. The book satisfied those who knew something of the period and were acquainted with the difficulties involved in treating it. Mr. Ellis completed his good offices to his young friend's work by writing a long laudatory notice in the November *Christian Examiner.* But it was even more flattering to young Parkman to receive the following penetrating criticism from his old traveling companion Theodore Parker, the great liberal minister of the day, perhaps the most widely read man in America, and a literary power in Boston of the forties and fifties:

Boston, 22nd Dec. 1851

Dear Sir,

I have lately read your work on Pontiac with much pleasure. I have gained a good deal of information from a book which relates to a period & a place where I had not studied the Indians much. On the whole it seems to me that the book is highly creditable to you—to your industry, & your good sense. But you will be likely to get praise enough, & asked me to speak discriminatingly of the work, so I will write down the things ʳ hich occurred to me in reading the book & in studying some parts of it. I will speak of the substance, the arrangement, & the style; of the *timber,* the *plan,* & the *finish* of it.

I. Of the *Substance,* that is the *Sentiments & Ideas.* You evidently have a fondness for the Indian—not a romantic fondness, but one that has been tempered by sight of the fact. Yet I do not think you do the Indian quite justice; you side rather too strongly with the white man & against the red. I think you bring out the vices of the Indian with more prominence than those of the European—which are less excusable. The treachery which you criticize in the Indian was to him no more a violation of any sentiment or idea that he felt or knew than it was for a Briton to fight with powder & balls. This treachery is not specific of Indians; but generic of all races in a low state of development. It seems to me Pontiac was much more excusable than the Paxton Men, the Owens & the like. It seems to me that the whites are not censured so much as they deserve for their conduct toward the Indians in 3 particulars: 1. in the *matter of Rum*, which the Xian [Christian] brought to the savage; 2. in the *matter of women*, whom the Xian took from the savage as concubines & then deserted when the time came; 3. in the matter of *treachery & cruelty* which the whites so often displayed.

I have thought you are a little unjust to the Quakers. But here I have so little direct & positive knowledge that I hesitate in my judgment. One thing is curious in history:—the Teutonic Race in all its 3 great divisions—the Goths, Germans, & Scandinavians—is naturally exclusive & loves to exterminate the neighboring tribes. On the other side, the Celts & Greco Italian stock assimilate with other tribes. The history of America shows the same thing in the conduct of the English & the French toward the Indians. It would have enriched your work a little to have called attention to that fact—not generally known. It always enriches a special history to drop into it universal laws or any general rules of conduct which distinguish one nation from another.

The facts of history which you set down seem generally well chosen. The historian cannot tell all; he must choose such as, to him, most clearly set forth the Idea of the nation—or man—he describes. Bancroft chooses one set of facts, Hildreth another—& how different the N.E. of Bancroft from H.'s N.E. So much for the material—which is mainly good *timber*—now a word of the *frame & plan*. So

II. Of the *Distribution* of the Parts. The title indicates that the *conspiracy of Pontiac* is the chief theme. But in the book itself it seems to me this is not exactly so, that other things are not quite enough subordinated to the main theme, so as to give unity to the whole book. The *Barn* is a little too near the house, & the *shed* a little too prominent for the general *effect* of the house itself. This appears as you look over the table of contents, when

Pontiac & his scheme are not the central object about which the rest is grouped. So (the book lacks the dramatic unity which is necessary for the artistic treatment of such a subject. Pontiac does not appear so important in the titles of the chapters as the title-page seems to demand. Then the book lacks a sufficient conclusion & ends too abruptly. You do not tell the effect which his death had on Indian affairs. A special history like this requires at the end a general summary with the philosophical reflections which have grown out of the historical treatment of the theme.

It seems to me it would have been better to have divided the matter something after this line:

Introduction containing all the general matter relative to the Indians, their origin, geographical distribution, language, arts, agriculture, domestic, political, & religious institutions. This is now too much scattered about the book.

Book I. History of the Indians in their connection with the Europeans—up to the time of the general rising.

Book II. History of Pontiac & his efforts to overcome the Europeans.

Book III. Result of the movement on the Indian people—& its effects on their subsequent history.

Then it seems to me there would have been more & more obvious unity in the Book; now it seems as if the materials had been collected without a definite aim, & that the plan was not quite complete till the Book was done. So much of the *plan* & *frame*. Now a word of the *finish*. So

III. Of the style of the book. Some passages in it are very well written; in general the style is good, simple, natural, easy. But there is a general lack of severity of style—for which the great master of Roman history is so remarkable. Some passages remind me of Melville & Headley—whom you would not like to be like. There is a lack of what is characteristic. This appears:

1. In the description of *places.* You do not tell what kind of trees, &c., there were, only trees—leaving us to grasp whether they were pines or palms, bushes or cork-trees.

2. In the description of *persons,* the book lacks portraits. Wolfe is well done, so is Montcalm (the account of Braddock is well

done). But the picture of Pontiac is not adequate to his important place in the history. It strikes me that Johnson is not very well done. Some passages are left too imperfect. It seems as if you got vexed with the thing & struck out a little recklessly, to hit or miss as it might happen. The style of the book often indicates haste—as do almost all American books—like everything else we do.

Dear sir, is not there a list of faults for you? Yes, more than all your critics in the Reviews, I suppose, have found with you. But if I did not respect you—& think you capable of better things than you have done yet—I should not go to the trouble of pointing out all these faults. You seem to have chosen literature for your profession, & history for your special department thereof, & I do so love to see literary conscientiousness applied to explain the meaning of human history and convey its lesson to mankind, that I have taken the pains to point out particular things in which your Book might have been made better. You have already received so much commendation that it is not necessary I should go into the pleasanter business of telling you how many things I like in the book.

Believe me,
truly yours,
Theo. Parker

Francis Parkman, Jr., Esq.

Parker, great reader that he was, put his finger on many of the weak points of the book. There is a striking absence of generalization, and such little as there is seems rather jejune and callow. The construction of the narrative, suspending as it does the siege of Detroit half-way through, going off to follow the events of the war in other sectors, and then returning to complete the account of the siege, is notably awkward. But it was a difficult task to make a coherent account of a war fought on so many fronts, and to give unity to a narrative of events which had little more than a tenuous connection. And since Parkman had to frame the book in his mind and could not plan it out on paper, it is not surprising that he fell into this fault. Also, unsure of his power to complete the scheme of works which existed in his mind, he had crammed too much background material into his account of Pontiac's conspiracy, thus laying himself open to Parker's charge that the contents of the book did not fairly fall under the title he gave to it.

Parkman took his friend's criticism with good grace. In his reply he convinced Parker that the latter was wrong about the Quakers, and defended himself ably against the charge that he had been too hard on the Indians. He also brought out his set pieces of characterization of persons and places, but Parker remained adamant in his opinion that the book failed in that particular as "a general thing." Replying to Parkman's answer, Parker pointed out that "Cooper always fails in this; Cervantes never. Longfellow blunders in this & that matter in his Golden Legend, making Walther von der Vogelweide, who died before 1228, worship in a church of Erwin von Steinbach, who did not begin his work upon it till 1277, &c." Parkman learned this lesson thoroughly, and in his notes henceforward paid particular attention to the minutiae of the persons and places he dealt with. For all its severity, Parker's criticism was far more useful than the empty observations of the *North American* reviewer, who was content to echo Parkman's critical observations and paraphrase his narrative. Brantz Mayer had given him the encouragement and hope necessary to continue his labors despite the difficulties that beset him; Theodore Parker, making no allowances for those difficulties, challenged him to go on and do greater things. It is difficult to say which letter was most helpful to Parkman; certainly either was worth all the rest of the flood of congratulations, commendatory notices, and praise that swept up to Parkman's door in the first few months after his first historical work appeared—which flood probably served no better purpose than to console him for the book's lack of commercial success It was to be many years before Parkman made as much out of his books as they cost him to write; he was fortunate, amid all his handicaps, in being blessed with a secure enough financial position to continue his labors regardless of how little they brought him.

12: The Dungeon of the Spirit

> *From a complete and ample experi-*
> *ence of both, I can bear witness that*
> *no amount of physical pain is so in-*
> *tolerable as the position of being*
> *stranded and doomed to lie rotting for*
> *year after year. However, I have not*
> *abandoned any plan which I have ever*
> *formed and I have no intention of*
> *abandoning any until I am made cold*
> *meat of.*
>
> F.P. TO E. G. SQUIER, 1849

IN the spring of 1850, Parkman thought his victory over "The Enemy" so far assured that, after an engagement of a year, he married Catherine Scollay Bigelow, daughter of Dr. Jacob Bigelow, one of the most prominent Boston physicians and a great lover of the White Mountains, to which he had devoted several botanical expeditions as a young man. The marriage took place in May, and the newlyweds established themselves for the summer in a little cottage, "small, snug, and comfortable," on Dorchester Avenue, Milton Lower Falls. Writing on June 15 to Charles Norton, who was then traveling in Europe, Parkman thus described his life:

We have woods about us, dark enough for an owl to hide in; very fair society, not too near to bore us, & what is quite as much to the purpose, a railroad to place us within arm's reach of town. This kind of life has one or two drawbacks, such as the necessity of paying bills, and the manifold responsibilities of a house-holder, an impending visit from the tax-gatherer, and petitions for the furtherance of charitable enterprises which, as I am informed, the son of my father will not fail to promote.

❋   ❋   ❋   ❋

I have a reader for an hour or two, and when it is not too bright, play the amateur farmer, to the great benefit of my corporeal man. Kate is generally my amanuensis, as perhaps you may see by this handwriting. *Pontiac* is about three-quarters through, & I hope will see the light within a year. I think it will make two volumes with maps, plans, et cet. I calculated at start- ing it would take four years, which, at the pace I was then writing, was about a straight calculation, for I was handsomely used up, soul & body on the rack, & with no external means and appliances to help me on. You may judge whether my present condition is a more favorable one. I detest being spoony or an approximation to it, so I say nothing, but if you want to under- stand the thing, take a jump out of hellfire to the opposite ex- treme, such a one in short as Satan made when he broke bounds & paid his visit to our first parents.

In Milton he passed a happy summer, aided in his work by his wife and her sister Mary Bigelow. The peace of what Squier called Parkman's "classic retreat" was disturbed only by a five o'clock in the morning visit from the Indian Copway, who had a scheme for settling the Indians which Parkman considered "a flash in the pan, or rather no scheme at all." It seemed to him that Copway had too much to say about "the forest gentlemen, nature's noble- men, etc., but very little about the regeneration of the tribes." On September 22, before leaving Milton to spend the winter at Dr. Bigelow's on Summer Street, Parkman wrote again to Norton, giving an account of his activities:

It is a fortnight since your letter came to hand, and I have been too busy to answer it; rather a new condition of things for me, but the fact is all the time which I could prudently give to work has been taken up in carrying forward my book so as to be ready for publication next spring.

      ✿   ✿   ✿   ✿

I wish with all my heart that you could be here, as you kindly wish, at the forthcoming of my book; but a copy shall be put by for you. I find it seriously no easy job to accomplish all the de- tails of dates, citations, notes, et cet., without the use of eyes. Prescott could see a little—confound him, he could even look

over his proofs—but I am no better off than an owl in the sunlight. The ugliest job of the whole is getting up a map. I have a
draft made in the first place on a very large scale. Then I direct
how to fill it in with the names of forts, Indian villages, &c., all
of which I have pretty clearly in my memory from the reading
of countless journals, letters, et cet., and former travels over the
whole ground. Then I examine the map inch by inch, taking
about half a minute for such examination, and also have it compared by competent eyes with ancient maps and drafts, then I
have the big map reduced to a proper size. I have got to the end
of the book and killed off Pontiac. The opening chapters, however, are not yet complete. I have just finished an introductory
chapter on the Indian tribes, which my wife pronounces uncommonly stupid. Never mind, nobody need read it who don't
want to. Mr. George Ellis stands my friend, has read the manuscript through and likes it. Nobody else has seen it. I shall stereo-
type it myself and take the risk. Pray Heaven the newspapers
& reviews may have tender hearts. All depends on them nowadays. Merit must speak out trumpet-tongued or else it's all of no
use. Ten men in New York earn their daily bread by the trade
of literary puffing; but woe is me, I have nothing in my pocket
to give them, and wouldn't give it if I had. . . .

The young historian may be forgiven for concealing from his friend
the fact that the Harpers had rejected his book. And when it came
to the point of publication, Parkman was not averse to salting away
a few friendly notices in the leading journals through the goodwill of E. G. Squier, even if he was unwilling to bribe the professional puffers. For all his idealism, Parkman had a very sharp head,
and occasionally the commercial acumen of his merchant grandfather cropped out. Aware that he had to create an audience for
the history he wanted to write, he was not above rigging the critical
reception of his books as best he could, despite his scorn of George
Palmer Putnam's "sly publisher's trick" upon the reading public in
adding "California" to the title of *The Oregon Trail.*

In town Parkman found *Pontiac* went more slowly, and he began to plan on publication in the fall of 1851, but he finished the
book during the winter. With *Pontiac* completed and in the process

of being stereotyped, Parkman wrote some reviews for the *Christian Examiner* of two of his friend Squier's books, a long notice of *Indian Antiquities in North America* in the May number and a short one of *The Serpent Symbol* in the July issue. That summer he was established on Cottage Street in Brookline. Parkman found moving the crowning evil among the tribulations of life, and was glad to be "snugly shaken down at last" and free to divide his time "between antiquities, agriculture, and educating a dog." May and June were passed in final reading of the proofs of *Pontiac,* and during the summer he wrote letters to Squier arranging for notices and puffs of the forthcoming work. To Norton went this letter:

Boston, June 25, 1851

My dear Charley:

Bowen wrote me this morning that you intended, on his application, to review *Pontiac* for the *N.A.* This is a kindness somewhat unexpected. I took the book to Bowen, upon which he observed that he must have a review of it and mentioned you as the person best fitted to do it. I don't know how it was but I had a sort of instinct that you were busy this summer in writing something or other and accordingly I demurred at his troubling you with the proposal.

The other day after seeing you, finding that my conjecture was right, I wrote to Bowen not to propose the job to you as you had other work in hand. It appears, however, that he had already written. I owe you, my dear Charley, double thanks for your friendly intention, and only hope that will not interfere with any other plans.

As for the remaining proofs, maps, etc., I shall be able to forward them in a few days. The execrable job of stereotyping is not yet quite through but I am looking forward to a speedy deliverance from the printer's devils, on which occasion I shall sing, Oh, be joyful. Give my kindest remembrances to your family and believe me,

Your obliged friend,
F. Parkman, Jr.

Norton evidently was helpful in several roles on the occasion of the publication of his friend's first historical work, for late in July

Parkman was thanking him for correcting the proofs, and apologizing that all his corrections might not figure in the English edition, since that batch of proofs had had to be sent off by an earlier steamer. Parkman was in town, complaining about the "infernally hot" weather: "I wish to heaven I were a fish or a lobster—anything to get out of a warm air bath at a temperature of ninety. Three toads perished today in my garden—stewed to death under the stones where they ensconced themselves."

Despite the fact that he might consider himself entitled to a vacation after two and a half years of work on *Pontiac,* once that book was out of the way he began to clear the ground for the series of books of which it was to form the crown. A letter to Squier gives some indication of the new difficulties that beset his way:

Boston, Sept. 17, 1851

My dear Squier:

Yours of the 13th came to hand yesterday; I commiserate your situation and wish you a prosperous deliverance. Quill-driving in the Tartarean weather of last week is too serious a matter for a joke and as for the thirty pages of proof, they will serve to expiate all your past sins, and form a handsome balance against any which it may please you to commit in future. I think Littell will insert extracts. I met him the other day and, with your matter in view, dropped a hint to that effect, so send along your sheets and if he won't listen to reason, I will find some editor who will.

Being just out of one scrape, I am plunging into a worse one. *Pontiac,* thank Heaven, is off the stocks. When the next one will be, I don't know, but suppose my hair will be gray first. Go to work at consulting fifteen hundred books in five different languages with the help of a schoolgirl who hardly knows English and you will find it a bore; add to this the infantile music in the next room * and you will agree that my iniquities have as good a chance of being atoned for as yours.

Yours very faithfully,

F. Parkman

* His first child, a daughter christened Grace, was born during this eventful summer.

P.S. A word in the ear of the *American Review* would not be amiss. He has my book. Just give him a hint to use it with propriety.

But he had reckoned without "The Enemy," who soon made himself felt again, the more vigorously for having left his victim alone for a time, as if to humble Parkman of any pride in his triumph with *Pontiac*. His own account of this new crisis in his second autobiographical letter is perhaps the best:

I then began to gather materials for the earlier volumes of the series on France and England in North America, though, as I was prevented from traveling by an extreme sensitiveness of the retina which made sunlight insupportable, the task of collection seemed hopeless. I began, however, an extensive correspondence, and was flattering myself that I might succeed at last when I was attacked with an effusion of water on the knee which subsided in two or three months, then returned, kept me a prisoner for two years, and deprived me of necessary exercise for several years more. The consequence was that the devil who had been partially exorcised returned triumphant. The evil was now centered in the head, producing cerebral symptoms of such a nature that in 1853 the physician who attended me at the time, after cautious circumlocution, said in a low & solemn voice that his duty required him to warn me that death would probably follow within six months; and stood amazed at the smile of incredulity with which the announcement was received. I have known my enemy longer than he, and learned that its mission was not death, but only torment.

Five years later, another physician [Brown-Séquard]—an eminent physiologist of Paris, where I then was—tried during the whole winter to discover the particular manifestations of the insanity which he was convinced must needs attend the symptoms he had observed, and told me at last what he had been about. "What conclusion have you reached?" I asked. "That I never knew a saner man in my life." "But," said I, "what is the chance that this brain of mine will ever get into working order again?" He shook his head and replied: "It is not impossible," with which I was forced to content myself.

Between 1852 and 1860 this cerebral rebellion passed through great and seemingly capricious fluctuations. It had its ebbs and floods. Slight and sometimes imperceptible causes would produce an access which sometimes lasted with little respite for months. When it was in its milder moods, I used the opportunity to collect material and prepare ground for the future work, should work ever become practicable. When it was at its worst, the condition was not enviable. I could neither listen to reading nor engage in conversation, even of the lightest. Sleep was difficult, and was often banished entirely for one or two nights during which the brain was apt to be in a state of abnormal activity which had to be repressed at any cost, since thought produced the intensest torture. The effort required to keep the irritated organ quiet was so fatiguing that I occasionally rose and spent hours in the open air, where I found distraction and relief in watching the policemen and the tramps on the Malls of Boston Common, at the risk of passing for a tramp myself. Towards the end of the night this cerebral excitation would seem to tire itself out, and gave place to a condition of weight and oppression much easier to bear.

Since "The Enemy" took two full decades from Parkman's working life, at a period when his powers should have been at their best, it is worth examining the further details of his illness that he gives in the earlier autobiographical letter:

All the irritability of the system centered in the head. The most definite of the effects produced was one closely resembling the tension of an iron band, secured around the head and contracting with an extreme force, with the attempt to concentrate the thoughts, listen to reading, or at times to engage in conversation. This, however, was endurable in comparison with other forms of attack which cannot be intelligibly described from want of analogous sensations by which to convey the requisite impressions. The brain was stimulated to a restless activity, impelling through it a headlong current of thought which, however, must be arrested and the irritated organ held in quiescence on a penalty to avert which no degree of exertion was too costly. The whirl, the confusion, and the strange undefined torture attending this condition are only to be conceived by one who has felt them. Possibly they may have analogies in the savage punishment once in use in some of our prisons, where drops of water were made to fall from a height on the shaved head of the offender, soon producing an effect which brought to reason the most contumacious. Sleep, of course, was banished during the periods of attack, and in its place was demanded, for the exclusion of thought, an effort more severe than the writer has ever put forth in any other cause. In a few hours, however, a condition of exhaustion would ensue; and both patient and disease being spent, the latter fell into a dull lethargic stage far more supportable. Excitement or alarm would probably have proved wholly ruinous.

These were the extreme conditions of the disorder which has reached two crises—one at the end of 1853, the other in 1858. In the latter case it was about four years before the power of mental application was in the smallest degree restored, nor, since the first year of the confinement, has there been any waking hour when he has not been in some degree conscious of the presence of the malady. Influences tending to depress the mind have at all times proved far less injurious than those tending to excite, or even pleasurably exhilarate, and a lively conversation has often been a cause of serious mischief. A cautious vigilance has been necessary from the first, and this cerebral devil has perhaps had its own uses as a teacher of philosophy.

Meanwhile the Faculty of Medicine was not idle, displaying that exuberance of resource for which that remarkable profession is justly famed. The wisest, indeed, did nothing, commending the patient to time and faith; but the activity of his brethren made full amends for this masterly inaction. One was for tonics, another for a diet of milk, another hydropathy; one scarred him behind the neck with nitric acid, another drew red-hot irons along his spine with a view of enlivening that organ. Opinion was as divergent as practice. One assured him of recovery in six years; another thought that he would never recover. Another, with grave circumlocution lest the patient take fright, informed him that he was the victim of an organic disease of the brain, which must needs dispatch him to another world within a twelvemonth; and he stood amazed at the smile of an auditor who neither cared for the announcement nor believed it. Another, an eminent physiologist of Paris, after an acquaintance of three months, one day told him that, from the nature of the disorder, he had at first supposed that it must be in accordance with precedent attended with insanity, and had ever since been studying him to discover under what form the supposed aberration declared itself, adding, with a somewhat humorous look, that his researches had not been attended with the smallest success.

The nature of Parkman's illness has never been adequately diagnosed, despite these vivid case histories written by the patient himself and a relative wealth of information from other sources as to its manifestations and the methods adopted to cope with it. It is too important in his life to be dismissed without inquiry, although that inquiry may lead to no more valuable results than previous attempts of the sort. It is clear that the trouble centered in the condition of the eyes, for with the decline of Parkman's sight the other symptoms, which on the surface seem neurotic, made themselves evident. The water on the knee, and the subsequent arthritis or rheumatism, are clearly a result of the rigors of his life on the Oregon Trail trip and the earlier wilderness expeditions. He himself has admitted that he used none of the precautions that hardened woodsmen were accustomed to take, and that he drove himself harder on these excursions than was wise, in an effort to attain his Spartan ideal. For the rest, his own theory of a hereditary mental disorder is not probable, although it is possible in the light of his sister Carrie's and his brother John's milder difficulties, and a nervous breakdown which his father underwent in 1845, and from which he was cured by a pleasure trip to Europe in the summer of that year. It is probable that Parkman inherited certain neurotic tendencies. But the clue seems to lie in the eyes, as Dr.

George M. Gould postulated in his consideration of Parkman in *Biographic Clinics*. The study of ocular affections has progressed remarkably since Dr. Gould considered Parkman's case, but the results of that progress seem largely to bear him out. A leading modern oculist has confirmed the opinion that Parkman's condition was "undoubtedly one of very severe eyestrain." It is difficult, of course, to make a diagnosis of a dead man, but in the opinion of this specialist the eyestrain was "due to a marked incongruity of the ocular images, such as aniseikonia, which is a difference in the size and shape of the ocular images, in view of the fact that no muscular unbalance nor severe refractive error existed." All Parkman's symptoms may be explained on this basis: his aversion to bright light, his headaches, his sufferings in doing close work, and his feelings of mental confusion and disorder. Aniseikonia is a disease whose nature and treatment have only recently been fully explored, and it is possible that modern oculists might have spared Parkman much of his pain and his wasted years. It would be well, however, not to reject entirely Parkman's view that his inactivity, enforced by the condition of his leg, had something to do with his difficulties. It is clear that he was a highly strung individual to whom action was a necessity. Enforced confinement and brooding over his illness—painted in the worst possible light by the best available opinion—are enough to account for some of the neurotic symptoms. Your hearty individual, glowing with conscious good health, often offers less resistance to disease and is more prone to hypochondria than one who is more accustomed to indisposition and more willing to accept invalidism. For all his hatred of invalidism, Parkman could not keep his mind off his troubles, and thus probably made them worse. He was able, too, to indulge his indispositions; for no economic necessity drove him to conquer them. He was surrounded for most of his life by adoring women relatives, who pampered him and followed his least whim as law. Such a situation is not the healthiest for a person with neurotic potentialities, and these Parkman clearly had, for all his strength of mind and character. The record he has left us of his mental life suggests that he had a slight manic-depressive tendency; the periods of intense activity, followed by periods of complete inaction, fit in with this theory. But theory it remains, for a psychological analysis of a person dead these fifty years is even more tenuous than a medical one. But the two diagnoses may well be taken for what they are worth, in view of the fact that they go far to explain the illness which was so prominent a feature of his life and had such important effects upon his work.

One of the most interesting results of his illness is the way Parkman compensated for the inactivity that was forced upon him by his lameness. At first he tried to get outdoor exercise by riding, but soon that became impossible for him. Then his compensation took the form of excursions of the intellect. The vividness of his descriptions of action is famous, but no one has pointed out why his accounts of the epic journeys of the early French explorers and missionaries have a firsthand quality. Parkman had made such journeys before illness struck him down, and he made them again in his mind, as he framed these accounts in the twilight of the garret to which his intolerance of light confined him. In January 1852, after the water on the knee had made its first appearance and reduced him to indoor life, he published a long critical essay on Cooper's works in the *North American,* as if he were turning to books for the action that was denied him. It is an interesting essay, for Cooper, with Scott as a close second, was his favorite novelist, and Parkman was to supplant Cooper as the painter of frontier life and the Indian to the American reading public. He overturned Cooper's highly literary concept of the "noble savage"—one who had lived with the Dakota Sioux had few illusions left as to Indian nobility of character—but he owed much to Cooper. First of all Cooper had formed an audience for works dealing with pre-revolutionary American history. His romances gave readers a vague background familiarity with the French and Indian Wars and with the chief characters of Parkman's histories. Cooper had also brought back a certain vigor and native character to the budding American literature, which too long had suffered the domination of minds such as Washington Irving's, which drew their substance from across the Atlantic and had established a neo-Goldsmithianism as the highest standard of writing. Parkman, like Cooper, was articulately American, and more than a little jealous of British

influence and literary dominance. But still more important was another influence of Cooper on Parkman: the latter so saturated himself with the *Leatherstocking Tales* and absorbed so much of their
technique that he was able to make his histories quite as lively
reading as Cooper's best romances. From this discipleship Parkman learned the trick of describing action in words as vivid as the
deeds themselves. Few American writers had yet learned that trick,
and certainly no American historian before Parkman. Indeed Parkman is still frowned on in some historical circles as being too readable to be sound; though more pedestrian historians have had difficulty in finding flaws in his facts and in his interpretations. In
Parkman's time Gibbon was the bright star of historical writing,
and readability had yet to become, with the entrance of the Teutonic tradition of minutely thorough—and dull—scholarship, a
major crime against the sacred muse of history.

From the publication of *Pontiac* in the fall of 1851, Parkman's
health grew gradually worse until his illness reached a crisis in
1853, though in 1852 he was well enough to accept President
Sparks's appointment of him as a member of the Harvard Committee for Examining in History, thus giving, as the president put
it, "encouragement to your favorite study by your countenance
and aid." In the latter year he spent some months undergoing a
water-cure at Northampton, and was so feeble that he had to be
carried about. The following two years were a dark period, spent
largely shut up in his house. With the death of his father in 1852,
Parkman inherited an adequate income, and in that year he
bought three acres of land on the banks of Jamaica Pond and built
himself a small but comfortable cottage there. This house was his
summer home during the rest of his life, and it was there that he
died. For twelve years after his father's death Parkman spent his
winters in his mother's house at No. 8 Walnut Street on Beacon
Hill, at the head of Chestnut Street, for the family disposed of the
great mansion in Bowdoin Square soon after Dr. Parkman's death.
The size of that dwelling may be indicated by the fact that it subsequently served as a Federal courthouse. These years of illness are
the most domestic period of Parkman's life. His only son Francis
was born in 1853 and another daughter, Katherine, in 1858. But

young Francis died in 1857, and heart-breaking as that event was to his father, it had even a stronger effect on his mother, who never rallied from her sorrow. Catherine Scollay Parkman died the following year after giving birth to her third child, and Parkman's domestic life crashed to ruins with that event, which came at the same time as—or more probably caused—his most serious breakdown. His iron character seems to have broken beneath the double blow of the loss of his son and his wife in two successive years, and his family and friends feared for his sanity. Indeed, he was given up by them, and they expected to hear of his death in Paris, where he had gone in the winter of 1858–59 to consult a brain specialist and to recover his powers, if possible. Again his work came to Parkman's rescue, and while the eminent Dr. Brown-Séquard was studying him covertly for symptoms of insanity, he was investigating the government archives and arranging for copies of the documents and maps that fell into the field of his proposed historical series.

This period of illness and despair from 1851–59 saw the production of but one book, and that a romance, not a history. *Vassall Morton,* Parkman's only novel, was published in 1856 by Phillips, Sampson and Company of Boston. Though it had a certain critical success as a promising first novel—George William Curtis called it the best of recent American novels, though he added: "Mr. Parkman's literary position provokes a demand, not of comparative, but of positive, excellence in any work he undertakes, and his novel does not satisfy that demand"—it never attained a second edition, and Parkman never wished to have it included in his collected works—indeed he never referred to it in later years. From the literary point of view his decision was justified, for the book has many beginner's faults: the first part lacks movement, the plot is transparent, there are few dramatic scenes, the dialogue is wooden, and the characterization is stated rather than developed. But from the critical point of view the book is extremely important, since it is highly autobiographical. In it Parkman makes heavy use of his Boston and Harvard, European, western, and New York experiences. The hero, from whom the book derives its title, is clearly Parkman himself, or rather Parkman's ideal of himself: a high-spirited attractive young man, an idol of the ladies though not a lady's man, a good shot and horseman, a man obsessed by a craving for action who remains manly despite all the blows that fortune showers upon his head. The minor characters may be readily identified among Parkman's circle of friends and acquaintances; in many respects it is a *roman à clef.*

In both plot and style the influence of Parkman's favorite authors —Byron, Scott, and Cooper—is clearly marked. Vassall Morton is a rich young man of assured social position in Boston, who graduates from Harvard at the opening of the tale. He is in love with Edith Leslie but her father wishes to marry his daughter to a weak and unscrupulous though clever classmate of Morton's, Horace Vinal, who promises to restore the family fortunes. When Edith insists on becoming engaged to Morton, Colonel Leslie exacts a promise from Morton that he will go abroad for a year. He does so, and in Paris he encounters his unscrupulous rival, who equips him for a proposed excursion through Austria with letters of introduction to the leaders of revolutionary conspiracies against Austrian rule, representing them as prominent men of affairs and scholars. Upon presentation of these letters Morton falls into the net of the Austrian police, and is shut up in a prison fortress as a political prisoner, after a threat of execution by the firing squad has failed to win his supposed secrets from him. Eventually, after years of moldering in a dungeon, he makes his escape to Switzerland, where he is befriended by an English gentleman, whom he had met while in the West some years before, and who enables him to return to America by way of Italy. Upon arrival in New York he learns that Edith has recently married his rival, Vinal, since hope had been abandoned for Morton after his strange disappearance. But Morton falls in with the scoundrel who forged the letters of introduction and is now blackmailing Vinal. He buys the incriminating evidence, and crushes his rival by laying bare the whole plot. Edith overhears this revelation, and, appalled by what has happened, separates from her husband, who finally flees to Europe and is lost at sea while attempting to make good his disappearance.

The somewhat lurid Victorian melodrama of this plot at first glance does not offer anything of particular interest in a study of its author. But a close reading of the book reveals how much of himself Parkman wrote into this romance. The hero's long captivity is a symbol for Parkman's illness. Many reviewers commented on the extraordinary realism of Parkman's account of the thoughts and moods of a prisoner, which is not so extraordinary when it is considered that its author had known the miseries of confinement for eight years, and had suffered all the tortures of the Ehrenburg in his mind, while debarred from the life of action which was meat and drink to his temperament. The hero's delight in winning his freedom and wandering over the Alps, rejoicing in his liberty to move among the mountains, although with the constant dread of discovery and recapture always hanging over him, is an expression of Parkman's hope that he himself might at last win freedom from "The Enemy" and be able to wander once more among his beloved mountains, though he suspected that "The Enemy" would always be threatening another visitation which would confine him again. Parkman had obeyed the injunction to write of what he knew at first hand, and the liveliest portions of the tale arise directly from his own experiences of the decade before he composed the work. Whole passages are taken over with few changes from the notebooks of his European tour, and almost all the action can be paralleled in one period or another of Parkman's early life. Only in the invented portions of the novel, which are few, does the story limp badly and become completely incredible. The ideas of his hero are those of Parkman himself, and nowhere else, save in a few fugitive newspaper and magazine contributions on such issues of his lifetime as the Civil War, female suffrage, and universal education, is there to be found so clear a statement of Parkman's views and general philosophy.

Parkman's ideas did not alter perceptibly from the 1850's, when he wrote *Vassall Morton*, to his death in 1893—largely because of his extraordinary isolation from the intellectual life of his own time through illness and the closely guarded security provided by his means. These ideas are revealed in *Vassall Morton* in some detail. Basic in Parkman's character was manliness, and here is his own definition and ideal of it:

That unflinching quality which, strong in generous thought and high purpose, bears onward towards its goal, knowing no fear but the fear of God; wise, prudent, calm, yet daring and hoping all things; not dismayed by reverses, nor elated by success; never bending nor receding; wearing out ill fortune by undespairing constancy; unconquered by pain or sorrow, or deferred hope; fiery in attack, steadfast in resistance, unshaken in the front of death; and when courage is vain, and hope seems folly, when crushing calamity presses it to the earth, and the exhausted body will no longer obey the still undaunted mind, then putting forth its hardest, saddest heroism, the unlaureled heroism of endurance, patiently abiding its time.

And how if its time never comes?

Then dying at its post, like the Roman sentinel at Pompeii.

To this ideal he approximated his own life.

Morton, meditating in his Austrian dungeon, offers more of Parkman's ideas on the nature of man:

When I was a boy I pleased myself with planning that I would study out the springs of human action, and trace human emotion up to its sources. It was a boy's idea—to fathom the unfathomable, to line and map out the shifting clouds and the ever-moving winds. De Staël speaks the truth—"Man may learn to rule man, but only God can comprehend him." View him under one aspect only. Seek to analyze that prevailing passion, that mighty mystic influence which, consciously or unconsciously, directly or indirectly, prevails in human action, and holds the sovereignty of the world. It is a vain attempt; the reason loses and confounds itself. What human faculty can follow the workings of a principle which at once exalts man to the stars, and fetters him to the earth; which can fire him with triumphant energies, or lull him into effeminate repose; kindle strange aspirations and eager longings after knowledge; spur the intellect to range time and space, or cramp it within narrow confines, among mean fancies and base associations? In its mysterious contradictions, its boundless possibilities of good and ill, it is a type of human nature itself. The soldier saint, Loyola, was right when he figured the conflicts of man's spirit by the collision of two armies, ranked under adverse banners; for what is the spirit of man but a field of war, with its marches and retreats, its ambuscades, stratagems, surprises, skirmishings, and weary lifelong sieges; its shock of onset, and death grapple, throat to throat? And whoever would be wise, or safe, must sentinel his thoughts, and rule his mind by martial law, like a city beleaguered.

How to escape such strife? There is no escape. It has followed hermits to their deserts; and it follows me to my prison. It will find no end but in that torpor and decay, that callousness of faculty, which long imprisonment is said to bring, but which as yet I do not feel. Perhaps I may never feel it; for strive as I will to prepare for the worst, by inuring my mind to contemplate it, that spark of hope, which never, it is said, dies wholly in the human heart, is still alive in mine. And sometimes, of late, it has kindled and glowed, as now, with a strange brightness. Is it a delusion, or the presage of some succor not far distant? Let that be as it may, I will still cling to the possibility of a better time. Whatever new disaster meets me, I will confront it with some new audacity of hope. I will nail my flag to the mast, and there shall it fly till all go down, or till flag, mast, and hulk rot together.

This is close self-analysis, cloaked in fictional terms. The spark of hope which kindled within Parkman in 1855, as he wrote this book, was doomed to be extinguished: for his triumph over his illness of the past two years was to be enjoyed for but two more years, before his little domestic world was to be shattered and he was to suffer the most severe attack of "The Enemy." But his flag remained nailed to the mast, and, despite the gloomy opinion of his doctors and his dearest friends, he lived until flag, mast, and hulk rotted together.

Into what depths of despair he had already sunk, when oppressed by "The Enemy," is adequately indicated by Morton's remarkable soliloquy on his confinement:

"Fools and knaves are at large; robbery and murder have full scope; vanity and profligacy run their free career; then why is honest effort paralyzed, and buried here alive? There are those in these vaults—men innocent of crime as I—men who have been an honor to their race—who have passed a score of years in this living death. And canting fools would console them with saying that 'all is for the best.' I will sooner believe that the world is governed by devils, and that the prince of them all is bodied in Metternich. Why is there not in crushed hope and stifled wrath the swelling anguish and frenzy and despair, a force to burst these hellish sepulchers and blow them to the moon! It is but a weak punishment to which Milton dooms his ruined angel. Action—enterprise—achievement—a hell like that is heaven to the cells of the Ehrenburg. He should have chained him to a rock, and left him alone to the torture of his own thoughts; the unutterable agonies of a mind preying on itself for want of sustenance other. Action!—mured in this dungeon, the starved soul gasps for it as the lungs for air.

"Action, action, action!—all in all! What is life without it? A marsh, a quagmire, a rotten stagnant pool. It is its own reward. The chase is all; the prize nothing. The huntsmen chase the fox all day, and when they have caught her, fling her to their hounds for worthless vermin. Alexander wept that he had no more worlds to conquer. What did it profit him that a conquered world lay already at his feet? The errant knights who roamed the world with their mistress's glove on their helmet, achieving impossibilities in her name—which of them could have endured to live in peace with her for six months? The crusader master of Jerusalem, Cortés with Mexico subdued, any hero when his work is done, falls back to the ranks of common men. His lamp is out, his fire quenched; and what avails the stale, lackluster remnant of his days?

"Action, the panacea of human ills; the sure resource of misery; the refuge of bad consciences; a maelstrom in whose giddy vortex saints and villains may whirl alike. How like a madman some great criminal, some Macbeth, will plunge on through his

slough of blood and treachery, frantic to dam out justice at
every chink, and bulwark himself against fate; giving conscience
no time to stab; clinching crime with crime; finding no rest; but
still plunging on, desperate and blind! How like a madman some
pious anchorite, fervent to win heaven, will pile torture on torture, fast, and vigil, and scourge, made wretched daily with
some fresh scruple, delving to find some new depth of self-
abasement, and still struggling on, unsatisfied, insatiable of
penance, till the grave devours him! Human activity!—to pursue
a security which is never reached, a contentment which eludes
the grasp, some golden consummation which proves but hollow
mockery; to seize the prize, to taste it, to fling it away, and reach
after another! This cell, where I thought myself buried and
sealed up from knowledge, is after all a school of philosophy. It
teaches a dreary wisdom of its own. Through these stone walls
I can see the follies of the world more clearly than when I was in
the midst of them. A dreary wisdom; and yet not wholly dreary.
There is a power and a consolation in it. Misery is the mind-
maker; the revealer of truth; the spring of nobleness; the test, the
purger, the strengthener of the spirit. Our natures are like grapes
in the wine press; they must be pressed to the uttermost before
they will give forth all their virtue.

"Why do I delude myself? What good can be wrung out of a
misery like mine? It is folly to cheat myself with hope. This hell-
begotten Austria has me fast, and will not loosen her grip.
Abroad in the fresh world, fortitude will count for much. There
one can hold firm the clefts and cracks of his tottering fortunes
with the cement of an unyielding mind; but here it is but bare
and blank endurance. Yet it is something that I can still find
heart to face my doom; that there are still moments when I dare
to meet this death-in-life, this slow-consuming horror, face to
face, and look into all its hideousness without shrinking. To
creep on to my end through years of slow decay, mind and soul
famishing in solitude, sapped and worn, eaten and fretted away
by the droppings of lonely thought till I find my rest at last
under these cursed stones! God, could I but die the death of a
man! De Foix—Dundee—Wolfe. I grudge them their bloody

end. When the fierce blood boiled highest, when the keen life was tingling through their veins, and the shout of victory ringing in their ears, then to be launched forth into the wilderness of space, to sail through eternity, to explore the seas and continents of the vast unknown! But I—I must lie here and rot. You fool, you are tied to the stake and must bide the baiting as you can. Will you play the coward? What can you gain by that? You cannot run away. What wretch, when misery falls upon him, will not cry out: 'Take any shape but that'? In the familiar crowd, in the daily resort, how many an unguarded face masks a wretchedness worse than this, some shrunken, cankered soul, palsied and world-weary, more hopelessly dungeoned than you. Crush down your anguish, choke down your groan, and say: 'Heaven's will be done.'

"Muster what courage you may. Not those spasms of valor that make the hero of an emergency, and when the heart is on fire and the soul in arms, bear him on to great achievement. Mine must be an inward flame, that warms though it cannot shine; a fire like the sacred Chaldean fire that must never go out; a perpetual spring, flowing without ceasing, to meet the unceasing need."

In his dungeon of the spirit Parkman had learned the lessons of life that are to be learned only by someone who has passed through the dark places and the hard ways. He had learned the highest kind of courage, and his spirit had been tempered in the hottest fires. Of the author of this masterly portrayal of the despair of confinement, one can only remark, as Van Wyck Brooks has done: "*Eccovi,* this child has been in hell."

And when at last Parkman escaped from his dungeon, he found, like Morton, that

. . . The years of his imprisonment had not been the dead and barren blank which he had inclined to think them. His mind had ripened in its solitude, and the studies which he had before followed with the zeal of a boy, more eager than able to deal with the broad questions which they involved, he could now grasp with the matured intellect of a man.

Parkman, like Morton, had laid down his plan of life while in college and adopted one maxim to which he held fast: "Never to abandon an enterprise once begun; to push on till the point is gained, in spite of pain, delay, danger, disappointment—anything." In 1855, after almost a decade of illness and discouragement, he could follow that maxim with the remark:

> Some years ago I entered upon certain plans, which have not yet been accomplished. I have been interrupted, balked, kicked and cuffed by fortune, till I am more than half disgusted with the world. But I mean still to take up the broken thread where I left it, and carry it forward as before.

And so he did, though it was to be six years more before he was restored sufficiently in health to proceed with his chosen lifework.

Parkman recognized the value of the difficulties that lay in his way, even while he was suffering them. Under their burden he developed a Stoic ideal of life:

> None but a child or a fool will seriously regret any shape of experience out of which he has come with mind and senses still sound, though it may have changed the prismatic colors of life into a neutral tint, a universal gray, a Scotch mist, with light enough to delve by, and nothing more.
>
> One's life is a series of compromises, at best. One must capitulate with Fate, gain from her as much good as may be, and as little evil.
>
> And then set his teeth and endure. As for myself, though, if gifts were portioned out among mankind in equal allotments, I should count myself, even now, as having more than my share.

Immediately arising from this discussion is a statement of his lack of belief in equality—one of the popular ideas of his day:

> "Every ideal of mortal equality is a great fallacy; and all the systems built upon it are built on a quicksand. There are mountains and valleys, deserts and meadows, the fertile and the barren. There is no equality in human minds or character. Who shall measure the distance from the noblest to the meanest of

men, or the yet vaster distance from the noblest to the meanest of women? The differences among mankind are broader than any but the greatest of men can grasp. With pains enough, one may comprehend in a measure the minds on a level with his own or below it; but above he sees nothing clearly. To follow the movements of a great man's mind, he must raise himself almost to an equal greatness."

"A hopeless attempt with most. Everyone has a limit."

"But men make more limits for themselves than Nature makes for them."

From this aristocratic notion of mankind derived Parkman's politics, which all his life remained those of his Federalist grandfather. In a conversation of Morton with his democratic friend Dick Rosny, Parkman puts his own views into Morton's mouth:

"Democracy is under the weather, just now, Dick."

"Just now, I grant you. What with log cabins and hard cider, and coons, the enlightened people are pretty well gammoned. Before you know it, democracy will be upon you like a load of bricks. Why, what can you expect of a party that will take a coon for its emblem? I saw one chained up this morning in the yard of Taft's tavern, a dirty, mean-looking beast, about half-way between a jackal and an owl. He looked uncommonly well in health, and could puff out his fur as round as a muff. But when you looked close, there was nothing of him but skin and bone; exactly like the Whig Party. He put up his nose and smiled at me. I suppose—damn his impudence—he took me for a Whig. That coon is going into a decline. It won't be long before he is taken by the tail and tossed over Charles River bridge; and there he'll lie on the mud at low tide, for a genuine emblem of the defunct Whig Party, and a solemn warning to all coon worshipers."

    ✿   ✿   ✿   ✿

"Democracy is tall enough to take care of itself. I wear that ring; but it don't follow that I stand on my ancestry. You needn't laugh; the case is just this. If the blood in my veins makes me stand to my colors where another man would flinch, or hold my head up where another would be sprawling on his back; if it gives me a better pluck, grit, go-ahead; why, *that's* what I stand on—*that's* my patent of nobility. What the deuce are you laughing at? The personal quality—don't you see?—and not the ancestry."

"If you stand on personal merit, you'll be sure to go under before long. The democracy are growing as jealous of that as of ancestry, or of wealth either."

"Why, what do you know about politics? You never had anything to do with them. You are no more fit for a politician than for a fiddler."

"I'm glad you think so. If I must serve the country in any public capacity, I pray heaven it may be as a scavenger sooner than as a politician. Who can touch pitch and be clean? I'll pay back your compliment, Dick. You are a great deal too downright to succeed in public life."

"I'll find a way or make one. But I tell you, Colonel"—and a shade of something like disappointment passed over his face—"if a man wants the people's votes, it's fifty to one he's got to sink himself lower than the gutter before he gets them."

"Yes, and when the people have turned out of office every man of virtue, honor, manliness, independence, and ability, then they will fling up their caps and brag that their day is come, and their triumph finished over the damned aristocracy."

"You are an unbeliever. You haven't half enough faith in the people. Now I put it to your common sense. Isn't there a thousand times more patriotism in the laboring classes in this country —yes, and about as much intelligence—as in the rabble of sham fashionables at Saratoga, or any other muster of our moneyed snobs and flunkies?"

"Exceptions excepted, yes."

"War to the knife with the codfish aristocracy! They are a kind of mongrel beast, expressly devised and concocted for me to kick. I don't mean the gentlemen with money; nor the good fellows with money. I know what a gentleman is; yes, and a lady too, though I do make stump speeches, and shake hands all around with the sovereign people. No, sir, it's the moneyed snobs, the gilded toadstools that it's my mission to pitch into."

Parkman disliked the rabble of fashionables at Saratoga as much as his friend did; he was hard on the *nouveau riche* (there is a sharp portrait of such a Boston family in the novel); he despised the Americans who traveled in Europe to raise their social standing, "who swear by Europe and hold the soil of America dirt-cheap. You can see with half an eye what they are—an uncommonly bad imitation of a bad model." He was no Anglophile, unlike so many members of the "codfish aristocracy," no victim of what he called the "John Bull mania, which is the prevailing disease of Boston in high places and low." He was an American, but not a democrat or a believer in democracy. He thought he was an aristocrat; he was that only by temperament, for his social philosophy was that of an oligarch, who believed that the best people came to the top by making the most money. Yet he despised commerce and trade, since his grandfather's commercial success had enabled two generations of his family to live like aristocrats; he hated utilitarianism; and he felt no moral necessity to earn his own living. He was bitter about the fact that budding industry was beginning to defile his beloved New England countryside; that there was "no sanctuary from American enterprise." He was an admirer of the Middle Ages because of their "vital ideas of religion towards God and devotion towards women." He found their religion, often accused in the New England of his day of being nothing but a mass of superstitions, "not more gross and vulgar than the spirit-rapping superstition, the last freak into which this age of reason has stumbled. And as for the other idea, the fundamental idea of chivalry, we are beginning to replace it with woman's rights, Heaven deliver us!" Chivalry to him was like Don Quixote, "who stands for it—fantastic and absurd enough on the outside, but noble at the core." Despite his penchant for the age of chivalry, he did not prefer it to the nineteenth century—at least consciously:

"No, the reign of shopkeepers is better than the reign of cutthroats. But the nineteenth century has no right to abuse the Middle Ages. The best feature of its civilization is handed down from them. That feeling which found a place in the rough hearts of our northern ancestry, half-savages as they were, and gave to their favorite goddess attributes more high and delicate than any with which the Greeks and Romans, at the summit of their refinement, ever invested their Venus; the feeling which afterward grew into the sentiment of chivalry, and hand in hand with Christianity has made our modern civilization what it is—that is the heritage we owe to the Middle Ages, and for which we are bound to be grateful to them. It is a flower all the fairer for springing in the midst of darkness and barbarism; and now that we have it in a kinder soil, we can only hope it is not fast losing its fragrance and brightness."

He saw clearly that his philosophy had something of the medieval in it, but he was unaware that that fact was one of his assets in writing sympathetically of the great effort of a feudal civilization to colonize a new continent in that pattern which to Parkman, consciously, was to be despised by comparison with the more modern English pattern of life.

George William Curtis made a shrewd guess when he stated in *Putnam's Monthly* that *Vassall Morton* had "a sketchy character, as if it had been thrown off in the intervals of severer studies." So it had been, but its sketchiness is also due to Parkman's inability at the time to work for anything more than brief periods. The fragmentary, outline character of the novel, with its short chapters, is a good index of Parkman's powers in 1855. A history could not well be composed by fits and starts, so Parkman tried his hand at the easier form, ironically adopting as the epigraph of the book Boileau's:

> Ecrive qui voudra! Chacun à ce métier
> Peut perdre impuniment de l'encre et du papier.

It is clear that he never took the book too seriously. It was an effort to keep his hand in as a writer while engaged in the long process of assembling the materials for his great historical project—particularly since that tedious task was frequently interrupted by the recurrent crises of his illness. Parkman also had a great fondness for novels. The records of the Boston Athenaeum, of which he became a proprietor in 1853 and a trustee in 1858, show that he took out many romances, particularly during the periods when his health prevented him from devoting all his energies to historical work. His early fondness for Scott and Cooper left him with an established appetite for fiction, and one of the few pleasures left him was to listen to the reading aloud of novels by one of his family circle. It was natural that he should try his hand at composing a romance, and doubtless the reliving of his experiences in his mind, as he adapted them to his purpose, provided an escape from his present troubles. He was one of the greatest borrowers among the proprietors of the Athenaeum—only Edward Everett Hale and his own cousin George Francis Parkman, who shut himself up in his Boston and Newport houses after the murder of his father by Dr. John Webster in New England's most lurid scandal of the period, exceeded his record. Aside from the historical works that he withdrew for reference, there is a wide range of reading preferences. One of the most curious is a long-enduring fondness for travel books, as if Parkman assuaged his desire for action by armchair travel. Molière he never wearied of, and he read Corneille and Tasso eagerly. Rabelais was a great favorite, as were Hakluyt and Purchas. Biographies of the great—notably Milton, Napoleon, Washington, Richelieu—seem to have been grist singularly adapted to his mill. He was widely read among the more serious French authors: Saint-Simon, Sainte-Beuve, La Rochefoucauld, Cousin, de Staël, Voltaire. Irving seems to have been one of his favorites among American writers; Dryden, the romantic poets, Ruskin, and Arnold among the English. Sismondi's *History* was taken out time after time, as was Michelet. Parkman's own books were mainly historical works; it was a working library of some 2500 volumes, for he did not believe in large private collections.

Except for a trip to Montreal, Ottawa, and Quebec in October and November 1856, in which year he enjoyed better health than at any other time during this long period of illness, Parkman's historical work seems to have consisted largely of reading and correspondence, from the publication of *Pontiac* in 1851 to 1861, when he was able to resume writing. It was now even more difficult than in the case of *Pontiac* to seek out the essential materials for the history of half-forgotten chapters in the American colonial past. The necessary books were exceedingly rare and hard to come by; most of the documents were in the disordered archives of the French government, but many others were scattered in public and private libraries in France, England, and Canada. Parkman found the task of collection "abundantly irksome and laborious." He was helped by the recent action of the states of New York and Massachusetts, and of the government of Canada, in acquiring from Europe copies of documents relating to their history. A little group of researchers had entered the field just before Parkman set about his work, and they freely gave him their assistance. Among the most notable of them was Dr. Edmund Bailey O'Callaghan, an Irish-born physician exiled from Canada for his part in the Papineau Rebellion of 1837. He fled to Albany and took up the practice of medicine there, but soon became interested in early New York history. His two-volume *History of New Netherlands* (1846–48) was so successful that he was appointed to edit the state's old records, a task which occupied him for the next twenty-two years. He was a man of prodigious energy and breadth of knowledge—he had studied in Dublin, Paris, and Quebec—and he had a passion for accuracy, a quality then rare among antiquarians. Parkman considered his *Documentary History of the State of New York* a "work which did honor to all concerned in it." He opened a correspondence with O'Callaghan in 1849, since at that time it became necessary for him to obtain copies of documents in Albany. From a formal exchange of requests the correspondence ripened through the years into a friendly exchange of research discoveries and personal news. The following letter gives a good indication of Parkman's activities at the time it was written:

Boston, June 19, 1856

My dear Sir:

Though I have not heard from you since my last, & though I have nothing in particular to write about, I don't like to let a pleasant correspondence lie in abeyance—so snatch a leisure moment to scrawl this. I am devoting all the very limited eyesight and other needful appliances that I can command to French

American history. I learn from Mr. Faribault, of Quebec, that there are in Canada 23 vols. of documents. I have a friend in Paris delving for me to find more. Your Ninth Volume is invaluable. May the eyes of your legislators be opened that they may carry on so generous an enterprise to its full consummation! By the way, I thought that the Post Office had played me a trick not very rare with it, and failed to bring me a note from you touching a memoir on Champlain; but I found some time since that I had charged it unjustly. The note was carefully filed away with others upon similar matters. It reached me in the spring of 1853, at a time when I was very ill and in no plight to give it the attention it deserved. During that time—unhappily a long one —when I was forced to suspend historical studies, I amused myself with writing a story. Possibly you may have seen and smiled at the publisher's advertisement of it.

Pray, what is the address of Mr. Shea, author of the *Catholic Missions?* I wish to correspond with him.

Believe me, dear Sir,

Always sincerely yrs,
Francis Parkman

John Gilmary Shea, with whom Parkman opened a correspondence in this year, was the first American Catholic historian of note, and a pioneer worker in Parkman's own field. He was, curiously enough, an almost exact contemporary of his rival, being born a year later than Parkman and dying a year earlier. He had spent some years in the Jesuit novitiate, but left the order and subsequently devoted himself to the study of early Indian missions. His first work, to which Parkman refers in the letter to O'Callaghan, was the *History of the Catholic Missions among the Indian Tribes of the United States, 1529–1854.* He also published new editions of the narratives of many of the early missionaries and explorers, and summed up much of the matter that Parkman was concerned with in his *History of the Catholic Church in the United States.* His point of view, of course, was to become distasteful to Parkman as the latter developed more of an anti-Catholic bias, but the two remained correspondents for many years, and Parkman freely acknowledged his great debt to Shea in the introduction to *Pioneers of France in the New World*. Parkman had found the Jesuits "very reserved" when he had inquiries made about their early records in Rome, and he had access to only a poor text of the *Jesuit Relations* and a few miscellaneous manuscripts in regard to them. It was convenient to have in Shea a friend close to the Society. Other ecclesiastics proved more helpful. Father George Fenwick, of Holy Cross College, and Bishop Fitzpatrick of Boston freely gave him assistance and offered him the use of the libraries they controlled. Father Felix Martin, S.J., of St. Mary's College, Montreal, and the Grand Vicar C. J. Cazeau of Quebec were among the Canadian clerics who assisted his researches. Since the writing of the history of the French period was in Canada largely a prerogative of the clergy, Parkman had a large clerical correspondence, which increased as the years went on. As early as 1856 he was writing thus to the Abbé Ferland, the Laval University historian:

Boston, Sept. 10, 1856

Reverend Sir,

It gives me great pleasure to find myself in communication with a gentleman so well versed in a subject which I have, I may say from boyhood, regarded with the utmost interest. The early history of Canada is so full of dramatic incident, and noble examples of devoted heroism, that it is a matter of wonder that American writers have, until lately, so little regarded it. For my own part, I shall spare no effort to place it in its just light.

I am glad that the Canadian government has procured copies of documents in the French archives. Can you inform me whether these are understood to comprise *all* relating to Canada in the offices of Paris? If so, I shall be spared a visit to France. I mean to spend a part of the winter in Canada in search of material, and hope, among other things, to find a copy of your *Notes sur les Registres,* and of your critique on Brasseur, of which I have hitherto failed to gain possession.

I need not say that I shall hold myself greatly your debtor if you can give me any suggestions which may aid me in my inquiries after material. There is no more important period in Canadian history than that of the civil and ecclesiastical organization, after the colony passed out of the hands of the "Hundred Associates." Any papers bearing upon this period would be particularly valuable.

Your *Notes*, I trust, will be continued. I have seen only the first number, & this is of so much value that a suspension of the publication would be very much to be regretted.

I have the honor to be,

Very respectfully yours,
Francis Parkman

Monsieur l'abbé Ferland

Among his other Canadian correspondents at this time were Louis-Joseph Papineau of Montebello, Jacques Viger of Montreal, and G. B. Faribault of Quebec, who were all concerned with the history of their forebears and had formed collections of works on New France.

In December 1858 Parkman was accepting George Bancroft's offer to mediate with Archbishop Hughes of New York about making available papers, which he believed to be at Rome, relating to the Jesuit and Franciscan missions in Canada and Louisiana. In November of the following year he was again writing Bancroft to intercede in getting him an opportunity to consult the *Lettres de Marie de l'Incarnation,* the one or two copies of the book of which he knew being "fast locked up in convent libraries," and another book, Juchereau's *Histoire de l'Hôtel-Dieu de Québec,* which "being chiefly in unaccommodating hands, I fear I must go to Canada to consult it." The rise of the Know-Nothings to complete power in Massachusetts had probably made the Catholic authorities in Boston less accommodating to heretical inquirers. Parkman's correspondence of this period indicates how helpful the established historians of his day—Bancroft, Sparks, and Palfrey—were to the young tyro. In addition to their help and that of fellow-workers of his own generation, the means inherited from his father enabled him to keep a small corps of researchers at work for him in foreign capitals. Henry Stevens was at his disposal in London; Ben Perley

Poore in Paris; C. F. Fairbanks, and later Hector Bossange, in Rome; and Buckingham Smith, the Legation Secretary, in Madrid.

One of these agents, Ben Perley Poore, took advantage of his client. The story is an unpleasant one, but since it illustrates the nature of Parkman's difficulties and of his character, it cannot be passed over. In 1845 or 1846 Parkman engaged Poore, "with whom he had a previous slight acquaintance" through Jared Sparks, to collect documents bearing on the conspiracy of Pontiac. Since 1844 Poore had been the agent for Massachusetts in the collection of documents bearing on the colonial history of the state. He accomplished this task and Parkman's first commission satisfactorily. In the spring of 1851 Poore accompanied Parkman to the State House in Boston, and read the headings of the copies there to him, for at this time Parkman was unable to read a line. Parkman asked how many manuscript records relative to the early history of America there were in the Paris archives which had not been included in either this collection of Poore's for Massachusetts or in Brodhead's for New York. Poore estimated them at 10,000 folio pages and accepted Parkman's commission to get them copied. The task was to be done sometime in the future, as Poore was then editor of a Washington newspaper. Poore declared that there was a clerk in the Bureau de la Marine in Paris, who was like himself a Free Mason and would probably consent to send him the original documents from the archives, which Parkman could then have copied at lower cost in America. Parkman naturally objected to this shady scheme, and made an agreement for five hundred pages of copies, which were to be ready in six months. About Thanksgiving 1851 Parkman suffered the return of illness which confined him to his house for several years. That winter Poore came to see him, asking for an advance of $200 and offering his own maps and books as security. He reported that the work had been delayed, but that he had learned of a great number of other documents bearing upon the subject. He offered to undertake copying these, reducing his price from fifty to twenty cents a page. Parkman agreed and advanced the $200. He heard little from Poore for several years, but was too ill to concern himself with the matter. In the spring of 1853 Poore appeared with three large volumes of copies, which would soon be complete, and asked for $250 more. In 1855 he brought the books again, and Parkman looked them over, though unable to read the documents themselves. He was pleased with the work, and offered to pay twice the agreed price and did so. At that, Poore still owed him about $100 from the various advances, but Parkman did not press him for payment. Early in 1856 Parkman told John G. Palfrey about the collection of copies and offered them to him for his use. Palfrey looked them over and reported to Parkman that Poore had "deceived both you and the Commonwealth," since three-quarters of the copies were duplicates of those in the State House collection. Parkman immediately broke off communication with Poore and put the matter into the hands of a lawyer. It was too much to have his kindness and tolerance of Poore's delays repaid in this scurvy fashion, and he went after the swindler with vigor. But Poore was always penniless, and no recovery could be made. Parkman consoled himself by giving Poore the worst sort of reference when other historians consulted him about the merits of his former Paris agent as a copyist. The essential hardness and Puritan vindictiveness of Parkman's character were revealed by his long prosecution of Poore, as by another incident, many years later, when he was taken advantage of by a historical swindler. The end of the Parkman-Poore story came almost twenty years after, when Parkman was pulling every available wire in an attempt to lobby through Congress an appropriation for the publication of Pierre Margry's collection of documents on La Salle. A bigwig to whom he had written advised him that the one man in Washington who could see the matter through was an official of the Government Printing Office—none other than Major Ben Perley Poore! Parkman's reaction is not recorded, but undoubtedly there was an explosion in Boston that day.

Despite such heart-breaking incidents—seven years of possible study of the French sources had been wasted by Mr. Poore's ingenious scheme—Parkman kept at the laborious job of collecting his materials. He also was engaged in digesting them as best he could, never being able to use his eyes for more than five minutes at a time during the whole period, and often entirely dependent upon a reader. Most of the material was in seventeenth-century

French, and he considered himself fortunate when he could get a reader who understood even modern French. The documents, barbarously mispronounced and half unintelligible, were read to him over and over again, until he had caught their meaning, had significant passages marked in the curious system of symbols he used for this purpose, and had stored his memory with the important points. This slow process underwent a long interruption in the winter of 1858, when he suffered his most severe nervous collapse after the death of his wife. He could not bear the sight of the scenes of his once happy domestic life, and went abroad to Paris, hoping there to recover his health and his desire to work. He passed that winter in the Hôtel de France et de Bath, under the care of Dr. Brown-Séquard, while his sister-in-law, Mary Bigelow, took charge of his two motherless daughters at home. The trip, the new life, and the proximity of the vast archives which he knew were a treasure house for his work stimulated him to pick up the pieces of a life which had seemed ruined by the loss of his son and wife and the collapse of his health. Within a few months after his arrival in Paris he was investigating the archives, using a hired reader as a pair of eyes, and making his own arrangements through the banking house of Monroe and Company—he wanted no fly-by-night agents after his experience with Poore—for copies to be made and forwarded to him when he returned to America. It is more than probable that his devotion to his work saved his mind at this period. He was close to the end of his strength. For ten years fate had done its worst with him, bringing down still severer misfortune upon his head after every lull in his battle with "The Enemy," and crushing his hopes of at least finding personal happiness in life, if he was to be debarred from the work he wanted to do.

13: The Way Back

After it became clear that literary work must be indefinitely suspended, I found a substitute in horticulture, and am confident that I owe it in good measure to the kindly influence of that gracious pursuit that the demon in the brain was gradually soothed into comparative quiet.

F.P., LETTER TO BRIMMER, 1886

AFTER spending the winter in Paris, Parkman returned to Boston in 1859 in no better health than he had left it. This was the worst period of his illness; he was unable to do so much as to sign his name, and "it was about four years before the power of mental application was in the smallest degree restored." Aware that he had to rebuild his shattered health if he were to continue with his work, he set about the task, resolutely as always, by spending as much time out of doors as he could, working in his garden. On his summer place at Jamaica Plain he built a greenhouse, and with the aid of several gardeners set about transforming his property into a flower-lover's paradise. As in his historical work, he had to make use of unhandicapped assistants, but he directed everything himself. Farnham, the official biographer who served briefly as his secretary, pictures him in his garden:

When able to walk, he would go at a rapid gait from place to place, and sit down on a stool carried for the purpose; he would then do some of the lighter work, such as sowing seeds, planting borders, weeding, and cultivating. He often cut the grass of the borders when sitting in his wheelchair, and used a rake or hoe in this inconvenient attitude. Sometimes the sensitiveness of his eyes prevented him from being out of doors in the sunlight; yet in spite of all such opposing conditions, he soon became so well known among his friends and neighbors as a successful grower of flowers that the Massachusetts Horticultural Society elected him as a life member.

Between 1859 and 1884, the years in which he devoted special effort to horticulture, he won three hundred and twenty-six awards from that society, in addition to serving on its library committee for nine years, as its vice-president for three years, and as its president for three years. Even this avocation, taken up when it seemed that life held little more for him, was pursued with the intense energy typical of the man.

Parkman now passed the winters with his mother and sisters in their Walnut Street house, and the summers with them at his own Jamaica Plain home. In the winter he digested all the gardening manuals and treatises that the Athenaeum afforded, and during the growing season he applied the principles mastered in this study. In 1866, only seven years after he first took an interest in gardening, he published *The Book of Roses,* which was long regarded as the best guide to the cultivation of that flower. As early as 1861 his fame as a horticulturist was so firmly established that his neighbor, Francis L. Lee of Chestnut Hill, on enlisting for the Civil War, turned over to Parkman a small collection of Japanese plants recently purchased in Yokohama by Dr. George B. Hall. This was the first collection brought directly to America from Japan, and included the double-flowering apple, which later became known as the Parkman Crab; retinispora, *Thuja dolabrata,* rhododendron brachycarpous, *Andromeda japonica,* the double-flowered wistaria, and bulbs of the *Lilium auratum,* which Parkman brought to flower before anyone else in America or Europe. Developing this rich collection made Parkman's reputation as a horticulturist. His greatest horticultural triumph was the *Lilium Parkmanni,* a hybrid crimson auratum, which was the result of much careful and laborious experiment. But he was chiefly known as a rosarian, and is said to have had more than a thousand varieties of roses in his garden. Charles Sprague Sargent hailed him as "one of the first Americans to cultivate a collection of roses on scientific principles . . . his example has done more, perhaps, than that of any other man to raise the standard of rose-growing in America to its present excellence." Though Parkman specialized in the hybridization of lilies, he also brought out new varieties of iris, delphinium, peony, and poppy. He was one of the first Americans to grow herbaceous plants, and his garden was always full of interesting shrubs, bulbs, and hardy perennials.

Parkman's triumphs as a horticulturist are the more remarkable because he had no scientific training and by nature lacked the temperamental characteristics of the true gardener. It was galling to him to be puttering about his garden in a wheelchair while his classmates were fighting in the Civil War. One reason that he adopted the pursuit was that it provided him in some degree with the activity which his temperament craved. He could not bear invalidism, and when some friend commiserated with him on his difficulties, he exploded with a "Damn it all, I'm not feeble!" He may have been reconciled to his gardening by a recollection of his earliest piece of writing, the essay on "Studies of Nature":

Nature affords for our contemplation subjects from the minutest to the most grand. We may study the animalcule contained in a drop of water, or observe the motions of the planetary bodies as they revolve in their unchanged orbits. No class of pursuits affords so vast a variety of subjects and none is capable of awakening a deeper interest. Nature cannot be exhausted. . . .

We are all born with an instinctive fondness for the beauties of nature. We all take pleasure in viewing a lofty mountain, a fertile valley, or a clear stream. . . . But suppose a man who has made nature his study, who, while searching into the great laws that govern her, has not neglected the tribes of living and inanimate objects to which she is indebted for life and beauty —suppose him to be placed where we were, and to be looking upon the same objects. The black and precipitous rocks which lie piled in confusion above him remind him of the period when that mountain emerged from the plain impelled by some irresistible subterranean power. He notices the deposits which through successive ages have accumulated about its base, and compares the present appearance of that valley, enlivened by grazing herds and sparkling rivulets, with its aspect in former ages, when it perhaps formed the bed of a stagnant lake, the abode of monsters, now happily extinct. The plants and animals about him next engage his attention, and in observing their appearances and watching their motions he finds an inexhaustible source of innocent gratification.

"But," say some, "of what use are such pursuits, or what man of sense can take pleasure in studying the habits of a paltry insect, or in classing and arranging an insignificant shell?" I answer that whatever tends to increase our knowledge of the globe we inhabit is of use, and that objects which appear to be too trifling to be noticed may, at some future day, be found of great benefit to mankind. . . .

Why, then, should the Naturalist be accused of spending his time in useless pursuits? Use of which we have no idea may yet be made of his researches, and in the meantime there is no pursuit more innocent, more interesting, or more agreeable than the study of Natural History.

Parkman could no longer climb the lofty mountain, wander the fertile valley, and paddle the clear stream, as he once happily had done, but at least he could observe nature in his backyard and win his way back to health by studying its mysteries. Not only did he thus gain "innocent gratification," but he steadied a nervous system brought near the breaking point by a long series of strains, and rested eyes exhausted by too much poring over old books and manuscripts. But he was not content with such rewards, and went on to make researches quite as remarkable in their own field as his historical ones, and to make the results of those researches available to the world. In addition to writing *The Book of Roses,* and a notable Bussey Institution Report on the hybridization of lilies, he contributed more than thirty articles to the *American Journal of Horticulture* over a period of five years, on a wide variety of subjects. These are largely straightforward technical discussions and reports of experiments, admirably clear. The paper on the hybridization of lilies gives some idea of the immense care and patience which Parkman devoted to his horticultural experiments. But to the general reader the most interesting of Parkman's horticultural writings remains *The Book of Roses*, which despite its author's flat statement in the introduction—"The object of this book is to convey information"—is a work of considerable charm, some part of which is no doubt due to the perfect period-piece woodcuts which ornament it. Though the book was designed as a manual for use, Parkman's love for what he called the Queen of Flowers made him burst out occasionally in lyric passages of praise. Perhaps the most interesting section to the non-horticulturist contains Parkman's philosophical reflections on breeding, in which his social ideas are mirrored in his horticultural ones:

> Like all things living, the world of mind or of matter, the rose is beautified, enlarged, and strengthened by a course of judicious and persevering culture, continued through successive generations. The art of horticulture is no leveler. Its triumphs are achieved by rigid systems of selection and rejection, founded always on the broad basis of intrinsic worth. The good cultivator propagates no plants but the best. He carefully chooses those marked out by conspicuous merit; protects them from the pollen of inferior sorts; intermarries them, perhaps, with other varieties of equal vigor and beauty; saves their seed, and raises from it another generation. From the new plants thus obtained he again chooses the best, and repeats with them the same process. Thus the rose and other plants are brought slowly to their perfect development. It is vain to look for much improvement by cultivating one individual. Culture alone will not make a single rose double, or a dull rose brilliant. We cultivate the parent, and look for our reward in the offspring.
>
> The village maiden has a beauty and a charm of her own; and so has her counterpart in the floral world—the wild rose that grows by the roadside. Transplanted to the garden, and, with its offspring after it to the fourth and fifth generation, made an object of skillful culture, it reaches at last a wonderful development. The flowers which were in the ancestress single and small become double in the offspring, and expand their countless petals

to the sun in all the majesty of the Queen of Flowers. The village maid has risen to regal state. She has lost her native virgin charm; but she sits throned and crowned in imperial beauty.

Now, all the roses of our gardens have some wild ancestress of the woods and meadows, from whom, in the process of successive generations, their beauties have been developed, sometimes by happy accidents, but oftener by design. Thus have arisen families of roses, each marked with traces of its parentage. These are the patricians of the floral commonwealth, gifted at once with fame, beauty, and rank.

*　　*　　*　　*

There are different kinds of culture, with different effects. That which is founded in the laws of Nature, and aims at universal improvement, produces for its result not only increased beauty, but increased symmetry, strength, and vitality. On the other hand, it is in the power of the skillful florist to develop or repress whatever quality he may please. By artificial processes of culture roses have been produced, beautiful in form and color, but so small that the whole plant, it is said, might be covered with an eggshell. These are the results of the ingenious florists of China and Japan. The culture that refines without invigorating, belongs, it seems, to a partial or perverted civilization.

The concluding sentence echoes Parkman's statement elsewhere of his belief in the superiority of the educated man to the boor, even in matters of physical endurance. The social ideas expressed in this passage are those of a Federalist oligarch, scornful of the *nouveau riche* and of the mob, and sublimely confident of his own powers and those of his class. Many years later Parkman took the stump in opposition to universal education and universal suffrage. Like the Bourbons, the codfish aristocracy never learned anything and never forgot anything. And like the Bourbons, they fell before the mob that they despised.

When the Civil War broke out, Parkman railed more than ever at the fate which barred him from taking part in the strife, and left him "holding the pen with the hand that should have grasped the sword." More than at any other period he interested himself in the events of his own time, and during the early years of the war he wrote nearly a dozen letters to the Boston *Daily Advertiser* on issues of the day. These are among the few instances in which he set down his ideas on political and social topics, as well as on the greatest historical event of his own lifetime. His conception of the war and of the stage in the nation's development which it marked, is clearly revealed in his communication to the *Daily Advertiser* on September 4, 1861, after the overconfident Union forces had met their first crushing defeats and English recognition of the Confederacy had become a possibility:

Every day the gravity of the nation's position seems more and more impressed on the minds of the people. Enthusiasm is giving place—at least it is to be hoped so—to a deeper and intenser purpose. All is at stake; the die is cast, we must do or perish. The peril, the solemnity of the hour cannot be too earnestly pondered. It is well to survey our stormy horizon, not in despondency and trembling, but in the firmer spirit of one who observes his ground, takes account of his dangers, and forearms himself against the worst. Our house is divided against itself. Our own blood has risen in arms against us, and we grapple for life or death with a fraternal foe, the most restless and warlike of mankind; ambitious, aggressive, and now maddened with an insane hate. With such an adversary there is no safety but in conquest. He or we must be humbled. If we but act the part of men, the conflict is one of no doubtful issue; but it is one which may tax our strength and constancy more than the less momentous struggle of the Revolution taxed those of our fathers. Nor is southern treason our only danger; for if those among ourselves who have neither conscience to feel the course of right, nor manhood to feel the course of honor, nor wit to feel the course of safety—if the counsels of such should prevail, then indeed would all be lost. The nation might hide her dishonored head and wait in ignominy the sure steps of her dissolution.

This might seem enough, but this is not all. Other storms are threatening in the outer darkness. There are contingencies, not probable, perhaps, but only possible, which it behooves us to consider and confront. The commercial interest, with its profits cut off, and the aristocratic interest eager for the ruin of republicanism, might, in case of a new reverse to our arms, or protracted war, bring foreign interference into the contest. If we listen to the dictates of a foreign power, or of all foreign powers combined, and suffer ourselves to be turned from our great enterprise, there is but one result—disintegration, decay, contempt, ruin. But if we stand to our work, doing that which truth and human liberty demand of us, then the whirlwind and the storm will be our portion. Yet let us not hesitate, or shrink for an instant from the stern alternative. Marathon would grow dim before the splendor and majesty of such a conflict, and the heroic tale would ring through unborn centuries how, to vindicate the right, a nation of freemen stood against the world in arms.

Our position is a solemn and critical, but not a melancholy, one. Perhaps, even, it is one not to be lamented. There is close analogy between the life of nations and of individuals. Conflict and endurance are necessary to both, and without them both become emasculate. Rome grew colossal through centuries of war. Out of the agony of civil strife came constitutional liberty to England, and vigor and unity to France. The individual is rare and the nation never yet seen which the continuous smiles of fortune could not weaken or pervert. Our own unmatched prosperity has wrought its inevitable work. We are a *parvenu* nation with the faults and follies of a *parvenu*. Rising with astonishing suddenness to wealth and greatness, we have not always been noted for the modesty or the dignity with which we have filled our new position. A too exclusive pursuit of material success has notoriously cramped and vitiated our growth. In the absence of a high interest or ruling idea, a superficial though widespread culture has found expression and aliment in a popular literature commonly frivolous and often corrupt. In the absence of any exigency to urge, or any great reward to tempt it, the best character and culture of the nation has remained for the most part in privacy, while the scum of reckless politicians has choked all the avenues of power. Already, like a keen fresh breeze, the war has stirred our clogged and humid atmosphere. The time may be at hand when, upheaved from its depths, fermenting and purging itself, the nation will stand at length clarified and pure in a renewed and strengthened life. It behooves us, then, less in fear than in hope, to bide the tempest; for among its blackest clouds shines a star of promise.

It was said of Washington that in the Revolution he was slow to draw the sword, but having drawn it, he threw away the scabbard. The North has been slow to draw the sword, but the steel is bare at last, and now let her, too, throw away the scabbard.

This communication reveals a curious combination of ideas and prejudices, couched in terms of speech rather than the printed word. In the intensity of his feeling Parkman makes the eagle scream in support of free republicanism in the best tradition of the platform eloquence of the day. Yet the third paragraph preaches a gospel not too far removed from that of the Nazis in our own time: war is better than peace, the blood bath is better than the decadence of peaceful civilization, the *Herrenvolk* must fight to the finish against the encirclement which threatens ruin to its primitive virtues. And there is a veiled expression of Parkman's conviction—later to be expounded in detail in another such communication, and implicit in his historical works—that it is the individual, the leader, who controls the course of history and determines the fate of nations. There is also an unfortunate suggestion of the utterance of the armchair patriot about this letter, but it must not be forgotten that Parkman would infinitely have preferred taking part in the strife to preaching the holy war. But he was barred from personal participation in the battle; he could only beat the drum on the sidelines of the fray.

Parkman's concern with the leader principle is mirrored in a letter he sent both to the *Daily Advertiser* and to the New York *Evening Post* early in January 1862. His special kind of republicanism, not democratic but Federalist, is clearly evidenced:

As well an army without generals as an imperiled nation without its counselors and guides. Where, then, are they? Why is mediocrity in our high places, and the race of our statesmen so

dwindled? Schools, lyceums, and newspapers have not engen-
dered them. A half-culture, shallow if not unsound, has spread
far and wide; but the high traits of a trained and finished manhood have grown rarer and rarer yet. The people have ceased to
call for them and they have well-nigh ceased to appear; for here,
as in things less vital, demand and supply act and react with an
inevitable and deadly reciprocity. The people have demanded
equality, not superiority, and they have had it—men of the people, that is to say, men in no way raised above the ordinary level
of humanity. In degrading its high offices, the nation has weakened and degraded itself. When log cabins, raccoons, and rail-
splitting became rallying cries of potent influence on the course
of elections, the fact was mournfully significant.

When the President declared that every volunteer regiment
raised at his summons could furnish men fit to conduct the government, in that strange assertion he spoke the popular mind;
great men were a necessity only in the days that are past and
gone; we have outgrown them; we, the people, are sufficient to
ourselves; to us all things are possible. The people are and ought
to be the masters; but a wise master will choose skilled and faithful servants, and prize them at their worth. They have chosen to
be served, not by patriotic statesmen, but by dexterous politicians, fluent demagogues, or at least by men who, whatever their
merit, could never by any attributes of a conspicuous superiority
disturb a perverted self-love or confute the maddest theory of
universal equality.

A high culture has not been in request. It is scarcely too much
to say that it has of late been banished from the arena of public
life; and thus shut out from this great field of exercise and stimulus, our best culture has become in great part nerveless and
emasculate. If the people will learn that no expansion of territory, no accumulation of wealth, no growth of population can
compensate for the decline of individual greatness; if they can
learn to recognize the reality of superior minds; and to feel that
they have need of them; to feel, too, that in rejecting and ignor-
ing them they prepare the sure though gradual ruin of popular

government—that beneficent lesson would be cheaply bought by years of calamity and war.

Much of this letter sounds like an echo of Vassall Morton's debate on democracy with Dick Rosny. Parkman, like the rest of what Rosny called the "codfish aristocracy," could only hark back to the past without being able to cope with the present or to anticipate the future. The beginning of the end of the Brahmins' control of Boston was at hand, partly because of an astigmatism that could not recognize in Lincoln, the rail-splitter, the time's equivalent of Washington and Jefferson. The Brahmins ran too much to the Hamilton type, and like him were distrusted by their plebeian contemporaries whom they ignored, not choosing to attempt to understand them. For all Parkman's mouthing of the doctrine that the people ought to be the masters, he clearly inclined to Hamilton's belief that "the People are a Great Beast." The Civil War brought out the best qualities of the Brahmin type; the emergency and the principles at stake enabled them to forget thir fastidiousness and play public roles. There were many others besides Parkman's kinsmen Robert Gould Shaw, Theodore Parkman, and Henry Ware Hall (to whom he dedicated a book published in 1865) among Boston's young men who saw the crisis and threw themselves whole-souled into it. But once the war was over, too many, like Henry Adams, felt that there was nothing left for them to do in Boston that had not been better done by their ancestors, and so wasted what might have been useful lives. Parkman hoped that the war would rouse the ruling class from its decline; instead it spelled its doom, and into the sacred precincts of the very citadel of the codfish aristocracy, the State House, brought a still meaner class of politician. After the war a new type of businessman was in the saddle, and he found it convenient to have his creatures, who could be bought and sold, in public office.

The whole problem of leadership was much in Parkman's mind during this year, as it was in the minds of many in the North, as the Union forces struggled through a series of disasters and unrealized victories under incompetent leadership. On October 14,

1862, Parkman again took up the matter in the columns of the *Daily Advertiser,* under the title of "Why Our Army Is Not the Best in the World." He found that the rank and file of our army, drawn from the "most valuable classes" of our people, had no match in the world, and that, if the Union had produced no Napoleon, it had "at least six or eight generals of whom no nation need be ashamed." But he thought the greatest number of subordinate officers were not fitted at all for command:

> He is a worthless officer who can only command the obedience of his men because military rules give him power to enforce it. The fallacies of ultra-democracy cannot be safely applied to the organization of armies. The leader ought to be at least as good a man as he who follows, and yet many an officer in Federal pay might with great propriety change places with half the privates who obey his mandates. Village demagogues, city "b'hoys," and the like are the last men to be entrusted with the honor of the nation and the lives of her soldiers.
>
> It is much to have a leader who is afraid to run away, who knows what the point of honor means, and on whom the brand of cowardice would bring results more terrible than death. It is much to have a leader in whom his soldiers can recognize one who by nurture, by associations, by acquirements, by character, has an inherent claim to their respect. Such there are, and not a few, and we may congratulate ourselves that nowhere has the proportion of such been greater than in the regiments of Massachusetts. Yet here, as elsewhere, there is woeful abundance of a different element, and hence have come neglect, inefficiency, disorder, drunkenness, defeat, shame. . . .
>
> It is not in managing to pass an examination in the drill-book but in the intrinsic character and spirit of the man that the most essential requisites must be sought. Our social influences have not been favorable to the development of such requisites, but they are to be found among us, nevertheless; and to use them and develop them to the utmost is a paramount necessity if the nation is to have a real military strength—if every war is not to drain her of men and money to an extent wholly disproportioned

to results achieved. Such men are to be found in all the intelligent classes of our society. Education—using the term in the comprehensive sense which includes the influences which spring from favorable associations and surroundings—can never fail to produce them. New England nurture has been of anything but a martial stamp, and yet she has drawn a most efficient, faithful, and brave body of officers from the ranks of her educated young men. We look with hope to see a military element infused into all our schools and colleges. It is not for us to enlarge on these topics. Democracy has learned the weak points of her armor. At least she has ample means to learn them. In peace, as in war, she cannot dispense with competent and right-minded leaders. If she demands them, they will come in time. If not, her future is black with disaster.

A year later, on June 30, 1863, Parkman again amplified his views on the question of leadership, which was still the great problem of the Union forces. By that time he found some truth in the southern argument that the aristocrat would win out in the end over the shopkeeper, no matter what the odds. He pointed out that history shows that "Luxury and commerce have sometimes emasculated a warlike people," and found that the predominant spirit of trade in the North had done "widespread and deadly mischief." But still more he was inclined to blame the politicians who meddled with military appointments, less eager to win the war than to prevent the rise of reputations, won on the battlefield, which should eclipse them. From commander-in-chief down to the lowliest regimental officer, army appointments, promotions, and demotions were all too often, in the early stages of the war, based upon political considerations. Parkman was quite justified in concluding this outburst with the comment: "The armed slaveholder, backed by the passion, ignorance, and blindness which he has drilled to do his work of treason, is a perilous enemy, but less insidious and less dangerous than the selfish politician."

It is clear that Parkman took more of an interest in politics during the Civil War than at any other time during his life. On October 17, 1862, a few days after pointing out the weak spots of democ-

racy's armor, he contributed an article to the *Advertiser* which dealt
with the false conservatism that would make peace without settling
the issue and hymned the beneficial effects of the war:

Eighteen months of war have wrought ruin enough; and there
is more in store; but like thunderstorms in a thick and fever-
burdened air, the war has been a fearful minister of good. The
weeks that preceded the final outrage at Fort Sumter are never
to be forgotten: menace upon menace, insult upon insult; demands outrageous alike to God and man, urged with an unheard-
of insolence and passively received, till it seemed that all manhood, all honor, all conscience had fled the nation, and that she
would drain the cup of her abasement to the uttermost dregs. It
was the climax towards which many years had tended. More and
more the mean and bad elements of the nation had risen in influence. Material interests and base political rivalries ruled us.
There was no limit to their exactions, and seemingly no limit to
concession and sacrifice in their behalf. . . .

Who can forget ever the day when from the spires and domes,
windows and housetops, the stars and stripes were flung to the
wind, in token that the land was roused at last from deathly
torpor? They were the symbols of a new life, portentous of storm
and battle, yet radiant with hope. Our flag was never so glorious.
On that day it became the emblem of truth and right and justice.
Through it a mighty people declared a new faith—that peace,
wealth, ease, material progress were not the sum and substance
of all good. Loyalty to it became loyalty to humanity and God.
The shackles of generations were thrown off. We were a people
disenthralled, rising from abasement abject and insupportable.
An electric life thrilled to the heart of the nation, and they who
had stood aloof, in despondency and scorn, from the foul arena
of party strife, now with an eager and buoyant alacrity offered
their breasts to the cannon. Women, with sympathies bounded
till now by the circles of private life, threw into the conflict lives
more valued than their own. Shall these sacrifices be in vain?
Shall that bright hope be the herald of the opening day, or was
it but the sinister gaping of the clouds that portends a thicker

night? Must we again be the vassals of outrage and wrong, entangled in the same wretched work of compromises and compliances? Shall all that is noble in our national life again be borne down and smothered, and the bats and owls of society again flock from their hiding places, triumphant and clamorous? To buy a transient and hollow peace, a brief interval of material prosperity, shall faith, honor, conscience, loyalty, all that makes the soul of a nation, be choked and starved into annihilation, and shall this ruin be wrought in the name of Conservatism? It would be a wholesale crime, as unavailing as monstrous. It would be a suicidal folly. To the eye, the mockery of a cure,

> While rank corruption, mining all within,
> Infects unseen.

It would make a desert and call it peace. The safety of the nation lies in being true to herself. A true peace must be hewn out with the sword. We fight against incarnate wrong, and come what may, we must crush it.

Parkman was not the man to lose heart because of early reverses —or he would have become a suicide years before this—and in this one instance he went against the sentiment of his class and caste, or at least a good proportion of them. He was led to consider that class fairly objectively for the first time, and he recorded his reflections in another letter to the *Advertiser* in July 21, 1863, on "Our Best Class and the National Politics":

We mean our cultivated class, rich or not rich. We do not mean the untaught or half-taught offspring of the rich, a class than which none among us is more insignificant. Those we mean are few in number and very weak in political influence.

In other free countries the culture of the nation is a strong and vital member of the body politic, giving and receiving life from the national veins; in despotisms it is the most dreaded foe of the despot, the center of the national aspirations, the core of the national heart. With us the case is reversed. Our cultivated class, from the fact of its culture, is in a great measure thrown aside from the broad and turbid current of our national life. It has been blamed for this, charged with inertness, squeamishness, and the like, but only with a very partial justice. Volition governs individuals, but the character of classes is simply a question of cause and effect.

In the main this political nullity—for it is little better—comes of a vigorous and good stock; partly from that "Brahmin caste" which, as one of its members tells us, has yielded a progeny of gentlemen and scholars from the days of the Puritans; partly from the practical energy which has raised itself to place and fortune. It gives us admirable lawyers, excellent physicians and divines, good literary men, good men of science, here and there a finished scholar, here and there an artist, with accomplished dilettanti, intelligent travelers, and well-bred gentlemen. And though it has long ceased to play any very active part in the dusty arena of political turmoil, its patriotism was not dead, but only dormant. Witness Ball's Bluff, Shiloh, Cedar Mountain, and Antietam, Fredericksburg, Gettysburg, and the Peninsula, and the memory of those who at the blast of war rejoiced that at last they could serve their country without shame. Witness the necrology of Harvard University. Of her graduates, dead the past year, and under the age of forty, thirty-five out of forty-three died on the battlefield or from the wounds and diseases of war. Numbers more will bear its marks to their graves; and had all borne themselves as they, treason ere this would have groveled in the dust.

The well-instructed class has been jostled from political life far less by its own shortcomings than by the action of our political machine. Small rewards in infinite number, the spoils of office, have called up an infinite swarm of small men, hungry, eager, clamorous, banded together in vast combinations, playing into each other's hands, and looking askance at those who will not utter their shibboleth. What can a handful do against a host in a country where the bought vote of the unlettered boor can neutralize the vote of the wisest and the best? Fall into the ranks or leave the service; here is the virtual demand of all these vast aggregations in which, under the covering mantle of a professed principle, self-interest and petty ambition hunt their game. The necessities, the exactions are too repugnant, the prize too small. Deplorable enough that the places of trust of a great nation should carry so little honor, confer so little social consideration; but by a swift and ominous progress we have come to that ominous pass where "the post of honor is a private station." Not that the political swarm think so. The prize in their eyes is a glittering lure, and the solid spoils a bait to be scrambled for in every posture of moral and mental gymnastics. Human nature has not changed much since the birth of Adam. It is vain to expect any body of men to display much alacrity to reach an object which must be pursued through weariness, disgust, and nausea, and when obtained is not worth keeping. We mean that most of the ablest and best-instructed minds of the nation, entering upon political life, would sow not only without pecuniary gain, but at a pecuniary sacrifice, and would reap in return little but the satisfaction of doing a much needed service to the country. There are a few of the best culture who have entered, and for a time remained in public life from little other consideration than patriotism simple. Their influence is a drop to the ocean, a cheaper quality than theirs will pass current in the political exchange. They are matched with as good talkers, as good declaimers; better managers, more practiced, adroit, and pliant. In short they have found themselves in an element foreign and disagreeable to them, and have generally withdrawn after a time, consoling themselves that they have done their part.

This cultivated class is sometimes charged as relatively weak and unpractical. To a partial degree the charge is true. No class in the country has more natural elements of force, but these are not and cannot be fully developed. It lacks a career. All below it are impelled by stimulants and tempted by opportunities such as no other country can supply. Fortune, position, reputation are within the possibilities of the humblest, and thousands upon thousands are straining nerve and muscle to ascend those heights to whose summits—though none of the loftiest—distance and the unknown still lend their mighty enchantment. The farmer's son dreams of the palatial mansion and the merchant prince and the Demosthenes of the village debating club behold in a vision the glories of the Senate Chamber and the White House. Here is the inspiration of a lifetime. Each stoutly fights his way to the surface of the vast and shallow expanse, but here he must stop. Neither he nor his children after him can go farther. They must remain where they are, or sink again towards the bottom.

But the man with whom the fancied splendors, so potent at a distance, are robbed of every rag of their illusion, shares none of this invigorating and fertilizing stimulus. Special careers, and good ones, are open to him. He may give himself to the professions—as, for example, to the law, though without the prospect of the vast political and social elevations which in some other countries reward the successful jurist. In the so-called learned professions, however, this class has found its chief field of activity and acquitted itself well and honorably. In science and letters it has played a creditable part. For the pursuits which have as their object, directly and simply, the accumulation of money it has shown little inclination. The full development of manhood, however, is not to be found in any one of these special pursuits; neither in the law, when separated from the practical application of its great principles to great affairs; nor in literature; much less in science. Despotisms fear literature; they encourage science as a harmless escape for a dangerous mental activity. Literature draws her strongest vitality from the pulsations of the great national heart; and let us most earnestly hope that those who best represent her may always be found, as they have been found since the outbreak of this great war of principles, in an intense and vital sympathy with those pulsations.

Twice again in this month of July 1863 Parkman wrote long letters to the *Advertiser,* one on the same theme, entitled "The Chiefs of the Nation," which dealt with democracy's need for "men to represent her, men to lead her, not swarms of interwrithing worms to batten on her entrails." He concluded this passionate exhortation thus:

"Let the best rule," is the maxim of aristocracy. "Let the best serve," is the maxim of the only healthful and permanent democracy. Who are the best? They are gone; their race is died out.

Surely as effect follows cause, for half a century they have withered and dwindled away. The race, we mean, of legislators and
statesmen, minds trained to apply great principles to practice,
to grapple with great affairs, to guide the nation with a wise and
temperate vigor along the giddy heights of that grand destiny
which awaited her, and perhaps awaited her in vain. When will
such men return? When a deep and abiding sense of our deep
need of them has seized and possessed the national heart, when
the fallacies that have deluded us so long shall be thrown from
us as debasing and perilous illusions, and the national mind rises
to a true conception of republican freedom.

The other and more important letter, headed "Aristocrats and
Democrats," developed his view of the war as a struggle between
southern oligarchy and northern democracy: "A head full of fire, a
body ill jointed, starved, attenuated, is matched against a muscular colossus, a Titan in energy and force—full of blood, full of courage, prompt for fight, and confident of victory. Strong head and
weak body against strong body and weak head; oligarchy against
democracy." He opposed the small group of slaveholding aristocrats, "the leaven of the whole fermenting mass," who had become
adept in politics in the battle to maintain their power, to the politi-
cally leaderless and inexperienced North, made up—according to
the southern view—of merchants and politicians controlled by self-
interest and low ambition, and besotted abolitionist fanatics. Knowing these classes, the southern leaders thought they knew the northern people. They saw how: "The eagle soared on our banners; the
crow, the buzzard, and the owl clamored in our council halls. But
they never dreamed how, under a surface of froth and scum, the
great national heart still beat with the pulsations of patriotic manhood. The error has been their ruin." Parkman concluded with a
profession of faith in democracy's eventual victory, accompanied
by reservations which reveal his own oligarchic turn of mind:

Oligarchy and democracy, the strong head and the strong body,
cannot live side by side. In war we can in time master them. In
peace every advantage will be with the concentrated will, the
trained and subtle intellect. Our safety is in the destruction of

their system and the purging of our own; in the development and use of the statesmanship latent among us, and long kept latent by the perverted action of our political machinery. An incalculable waste of wealth, time, life, and honor would have been spared us, had the servants of the people been worthy of their trust.

The political gospel which Parkman thus preached was an outmoded one that had no appeal to the popular mind. With the exception of Lincoln, the Civil War produced no such great men as he had anticipated would arise from the conflict. Grant was no Washington, and only Lee among the Confederate leaders approximated to the stature of the revolutionary heroes. It is significant that Lee was the champion of the losing cause: "Marse Robert," the aristocrat of the highest type, went down to defeat before the embattled shopkeepers led by Grant, the plain man of the people. Whether Parkman at length saw that it was futile to shout against the wind is not certain, but at any rate he renounced his newspaper exhortation. After July 1863 he contributed only one more letter to the *Advertiser,* and that was a factual report of conditions in the Confederate prison camps as experienced by his brother John Eliot, who was captured while serving in the fleet blockading Charleston. It is clear, from this account, that the notorious Andersonville was not the only Confederate prison where conditions were nearly unbearable.

The abandonment of interest in issues of the day may, however, more probably be assigned to Parkman's resumption, after nearly seven years' inactivity, of his historical work. In 1861 or 1862 his ability to work returned in some measure, and he set about the composition of the first work in the great series that he had planned. The new book, *Pioneers of Old France,* dealt with the earliest explorations of North America and told the story of the first Spanish and French settlements. Parkman evidently quickly recovered his powers, for he contributed advance chapters of the history to the *Atlantic* in July, August, and November 1863, and again in November 1864. In the latter month he also published in *Harper's* an account of his vacation experiences with Henry White in 1842, under the title of "Exploring the Magalloway." The article, which was unsigned—as were most of the other contributions—is a fictionalized revision of his diary. His development in narrative ability and characterization is marked when the two versions are compared. By this stage in his career he had learned the tricks of the writer's trade, and had formed a personal style which is easily recognizable in this anonymous account of a youthful excursion. It is also clear from the tone of the article that Parkman was pining for the wilderness once more, and that it now seemed possible that sometime in the future he might make another such expedition, though for the moment he had to content himself with reliving past experiences. Unquestionably his health—thanks to rest, care, and his gardening—was better than it had been since it first collapsed in 1846. Psychologically, the war may well have helped to spur him into action again. Despite the necessity of not overstraining his newly recovered powers, it took him only two years to finish the *Pioneers*, which is one of the longest single works in the series. The nine chapters published in the *Atlantic* in 1863 and 1864 are from the earliest part of the book, and the preface is dated January 1, 1865. And not only had he completed the two distinct narratives, "Huguenots in Florida" and "Champlain and His Associates," which make up the work, but he had collected most of the material for the later volumes in the series and written a portion of the *Jesuits in North America* and perhaps of other works.

In the introduction to the *Pioneers* Parkman's belief that individuals rather than masses or forces make history is clearly set forth:

> The springs of American civilization, unlike those of the elder world, lie revealed in the clear light of History. In appearance they are feeble; in reality, copious and full of force. Acting at the sources of life, instruments otherwise weak become mighty for good and evil, and men, lost elsewhere in the crowd, stand forth as agents of Destiny. In their toils, their sufferings, their conflicts, momentous questions were at stake, and issues vital to the future world—the prevalence of races, the triumph of principles, health or disease, a blessing or a curse. On the obscure

strife where men died by tens or by scores hung questions of as
deep import for posterity as on the mighty contests of national
adolescence where carnage is reckoned by thousands.

And at the beginning of his great epic he sets forth his preconceived
view of the nature of the conflict which it chronicles, a struggle between liberty and absolutism:

> The subject to which the proposed series will be devoted is
> that of "France in the New World"—the attempt of Feudalism,
> Monarchy, and Rome to master a continent where, at this hour,
> half a million of bayonets are vindicating the ascendancy of
> regulated freedom—Feudalism still strong in life, though en-
> veloped and overborne by new-born Centralization; Monarchy
> in the flush of triumphant power; Rome, nerved by disaster,
> springing with renewed vitality from ashes and corruption, and
> ranging the earth to reconquer abroad what she had lost at
> home. These banded powers, pushing into the wilderness their
> indomitable soldiers and devoted priests, unveiled the secrets of
> the barbarous continent, pierced the forests, traced and mapped
> out the streams, planted their emblems, built their forts, and
> claimed all as their own. New France was all head. Under king,
> noble, and Jesuit, the lank, lean body would not thrive. Even
> commerce wore the sword, decked itself with badges of nobil-
> ity, aspired to forest seigniories and hordes of savage retainers.
>   Along the borders of the sea an adverse power was strengthen-
> ing and widening, with slow but steadfast growth, full of blood
> and muscle—a body without a head. Each had its strength, each
> its weakness, each its own modes of vigorous life: but the one
> was fruitful, the other barren; the one instinct with hope, the
> other darkening with shadows of despair.
>   By name, local position, and character, one of these commu-
> nities of freemen stands forth as the most conspicuous repre-
> sentative of this antagonism—Liberty and Absolutism, New
> England and New France. The one was the offspring of a tri-
> umphant government; the other of an oppressed and fugitive
> people: the one an unflinching champion of the Roman Catholic

reaction; the other a vanguard of the Reform. Each followed its natural laws of growth, and each came to its natural result.

*   *   *   *

The growth of New England was a result of the aggregate efforts of a busy multitude, each in his narrow circle toiling for himself to gather competence or wealth. The expansion of New France was the achievement of a gigantic ambition striving to grasp a continent. It was a vain attempt. Long and valiantly her chiefs upheld their cause, leading to battle a vassal population, warlike as themselves. Borne down by numbers from without, wasted by corruption from within, New France fell at last; and out of her fall grew revolutions whose influence to this hour is felt through every nation of the civilized world.

And then he paints one of his great word pictures, which reveals the hold this period had upon his imagination:

The French dominion is a memory of the past and when we evoke its departed shades, they rise upon us from their graves in strange, romantic guise. Again their ghostly campfires seem to burn, and the fitful light is cast around on lord and vassal, and black-robed priest, mingled with wild forms of savage warriors, knit in close fellowship on the same stern errand. A boundless vision grows upon us: an untamed continent; vast wastes of forest verdure; mountains silent in primeval sleep; river, lake, and glimmering pool; wilderness oceans mingling with the sky. Such was the domain that France conquered for civilization. Plumed helmets gleamed in the shade of its forests, priestly vestments in its dens and fastnesses of antique barbarism. Men steeped in antique learning, pale with the close breath of the cloister, here spent the noon and evening of their lives, ruled savage hordes with a mild parental sway, and stood serene before the direst shapes of death. Men of courtly nurture, heirs to the polish of a far-reaching ancestry, here, with their dauntless hardihood, put to shame the boldest sons of toil.

It is clear that Parkman, opposed as he might be by tradition, training, and bias to "Feudalism, Monarchy, and Rome," found more to admire in New France than in New England. As a matter of principle, he disliked the Society of Jesus, but some of his finest tributes are paid to the intrepid missionaries of that order; as a matter of principle, he approved of the Puritan, but he disliked his mentality and his manners, and made that dislike abundantly clear. Such was his position at the outset; as the series grew he tended more and more to sympathize with the French and to see the faults of the English colonial policy.

The *Pioneers* received a favorable, but not overly enthusiastic critical reception. The critics concerned themselves with the work at hand and showed little interest in the proposed series announced in the introduction. Parkman still had to make his audience, although the success of *The Oregon Trail* and *Pontiac* had given him a certain literary position. The *Spectator's* critic was troubled that the new work raised but did not answer the question "Why did the Huguenot and Jesuit succumb before powers which appear only to have strengthened the muscle of the Puritan?"—evidently he had not bothered to read Parkman's introduction. But more acutely he saw that "Mr. Parkman has thoroughly succeeded in imbuing himself with the spirit of the time, and written with the vivacity of an eyewitness." Again in this book, as in *Pontiac,* Parkman made frequent use of his own experiences of the wilderness and of his knowledge of the Indian to illustrate points in his narrative. The hold that his new pursuit of horticulture had on him is evidenced by his frequent references to the colonists' first attempts at planting, and his evident sympathy with Champlain's liking for a garden. There is a curious difference in style between the advance chapters in the *Atlantic* and the form they took in the book in the final version: there was a good deal of pruning of unnecessary epithets and a great gain in clarity and simplicity. Since Parkman acknowledges his debt to Charles Folsom's "skillful and friendly criticism," this former librarian of both the Athenaeum and Harvard College may be given credit for the marked improvement. Parkman's style was becoming less gaudy and rhetorical, although he still loved to create a set piece of description, such as that of the St. Lawrence as it appeared to the first French explorers. He could do such descriptive bits with a surer touch since he had carefully gone over the ground himself, taking notes on the appearance of the country. In the first section of the *Pioneers,* which deals with the Spanish and Huguenot attempts at colonization in Florida, he wrote for the first and only time of country that he had not personally inspected, and though the descriptions are vivid enough, he improved them when he revised the work years later, after making a visit to that region and carefully checking his local details. No point was too small to escape the attention of this historian who loathed the irksome task of research, but accomplished it with a terrifying thoroughness.

The book has a strong Protestant bias, and there are traces of the anti-clerical feeling which was to become an obsession with Parkman in his later years. It is clear that he thought that one of the reasons for the failure of French colonization in North America was the royal refusal to permit Huguenots to be among the colonists, except in the instances of the short-lived Florida settlements. To Parkman the Huguenots were the best stock of old France, and indeed their qualities were such as to fit them better for colonization than the Catholic nobles, gentry, clerics, clerks, and convicts who met with royal approval. But Parkman was not partisan enough to fail to be amused by the doctrinal dissensions which brought about the ruin of the Huguenot colony in Brazil. Some of the anti-clerical and particularly anti-Jesuit tone of this book may be due to Parkman's research difficulties, for despite the aid of the bishops of Boston and New York and the kind offices of George Bancroft and John Gilmary Shea, who enjoyed good standing with the Catholic authorities, he had found the Society of Jesus rather close-mouthed and secretive about its activities in the period with which he was concerned. Since the Jesuits have suffered considerably at the hands of literary men of other faiths, and sometimes at those of their own, this reluctance to reveal historical sources is not inexplicable. It would probably amuse Parkman to know that today there is a school of Jesuit historians, working in the field he did so much to clear, who have the greatest respect for his findings, if not for his interpretations.

It was typical of Parkman that as a vacation to celebrate the completion of the *Pioneers* he made a research trip to Washington and Richmond in the early summer of 1865 with his friend Dr. Algernon Coolidge. As a trustee of the Boston Athenaeum and a member of its library committee, he had concurred in its report:

> The sudden collapse of the Rebellion in the early part of the year seemed to the Committee to furnish an opportunity, which should be instantly used, of obtaining the newspapers and other publications issued by the South during the war; and of which very few had ever gone beyond the Confederate states. These fugitive publications had a peculiar historical interest and unless secured promptly, before they were destroyed or had fallen into the hands of collectors, they would be forever beyond our reach. . . .

So Parkman went to Richmond early in June with a fund of $500 assigned for his use in buying newspapers and documents of the war years. According to William F. Poole, the Athenaeum librarian to whom credit is usually assigned for its Confederate collection (which James Ford Rhodes called "second to none"), Parkman "made very valuable purchases, among which was a file of the Richmond *Examiner* from February 1861 to March 31, 1865, the last paper published before the city was evacuated. From this file not a paper is missing—not one torn or mutilated, in any manner. He also secured some important books and pamphlets." The Athenaeum recognized it was fortunate in its choice of an agent, for "more valuable than money were the training and experience applied to his task." Parkman not only displayed the resourcefulness of the trained historical researcher, but he evidently managed his task with considerable commercial ability, since incomplete files— the paper shortage in the South had made newspapers for 1861 and 1862 extremely scarce—of the *Examiner* alone were being offered for just the amount that he expended for all his purchases. Unfortunately there exists no account by Parkman of his visits to the battlefields of the war which had stirred him so much and of his conduct of his mission; there are only a few letters from Mr. Poole, full of advice, and a hasty note from the cigar-stand clerk of the Spotswood Hotel in Richmond, where Parkman put up, offering him a set of the Richmond *Enquirer*. Evidently all hands were speculating in Confederate relics amid the ruins of bombarded Richmond. Parkman was obliged by ill health to break off his excursion and return home in the middle of June, and when Dr. Coolidge, who had been visiting relatives in Albemarle County, returned to the Spotswood to meet his traveling companion, he found him gone and received a report from the hotel that Parkman was "a very fine gentleman" who did not seem well at departure. Evidently Parkman, despite his role of delver among the ruins of the Confederacy, did nothing to arouse the bitter feeling against Yankees which Dr. Coolidge found so strong in every Virginian.

Late in 1864, writing the autobiographical letter to George Ellis which is commonly dated 1868, Parkman could congratulate himself on having won—at least for the moment—the battle over "The Enemy," and on being well on the way at last to realize the great task he had set for himself more than twenty years before:

> At present the work, or rather the series of works separate, stands as follows. Most of the material is collected or within reach. Another volume, on the Jesuits in North America, is one-third written. Another on the French explorers of the Great West is half written, while a third, devoted to the checkered career of Louis de Buade, Comte de Frontenac, is partially arranged for composition. Each work is designed to be a unit in itself, independent of the rest, but the whole, taken as a series, will form a connected history of France in the New World.
>
> How far, by a process combining the slowness of the tortoise with the uncertainty of the hare, an undertaking of close and extended research can be advanced, is a question to solve for which there is no aid from precedent, since it does not appear that an attempt, under similar circumstances, has hitherto been made. Irksome as may be the conditions of requirements so anomalous, they are far less oppressive than the necessity they involve of being busied with the past when the present has claims so urgent, and holding the pen with the hand that should have grasped the sword.

While brief returns of "The Enemy" made work impossible for relatively short intervals in the years to come, Parkman was able to go ahead steadily with the production of his great history, and even to travel rather widely. He had emerged from the dungeon of the spirit, had passed through the dark shadow and the dark valley, and won his way back foot by foot to the realm of light where his spirit could flourish. He was not unmarked by the experience, which had taken nearly two decades of his prime, but his spirit was the stronger for having been tempered by the trial.

Part Four

A HISTORIAN IN THE STUDY
AND IN THE FIELD

1865–1893

14: "France and England in North America"

How far, by a process combining the slowness of the tortoise with the uncertainty of the hare, an undertaking of close and extended research can be advanced, is a question to solve which there is no aid from precedent, since it does not appear that an attempt, under similar circumstances, has hitherto been made. . . . The writer looks, however, for a fair degree of success.
F.P., LETTER TO ELLIS, 1864

HAVING laid the cornerstone of his great historical edifice with the publication of the *Pioneers* in 1865, Parkman proceeded to rear the rest of the structure as rapidly as his uncertain health permitted. Though he doubted his powers at the outset, after his long battle with "The Enemy," the next twelve years proved to be his most productive period. The histories appeared with almost mechanical regularity—though there was nothing mechanical within the lively volumes of *The Jesuits in North America* (1867), *The Discovery of the Great West* (1869), *The Old Regime* (1874), and *Count Frontenac and New France* (1877). In addition to the composition of the histories during these twelve years, Parkman made two trips to Europe, three to Canada, and an exhaustive tour of historic sites in the upper Mississippi Valley in search of materials and information. *The Book of Roses* appeared early in 1866, and during the next five years Parkman produced a multitude of horticultural papers, which brought him a professorship at Harvard's Bussey Institution in 1871. He also wrote many articles and reviews for the best magazines of the country. All this activity from a man in crippled health, who had received a death sentence from his doctors a few years before, is remarkable enough; but it was also mirrored in a correspondence of considerable proportions with fellow-workers in the field of Canadian history, both in Canada and in Europe as well as at home. These exchanges of letters are much more than professional in character; Parkman gradually made friends of his correspondents, as if he could not get enough of human companionship after his long period of isolation. Since his correspondents were distinguished men of very different backgrounds, Parkman thus escaped into a larger world than that of Boston, though he spent much of these years, as before, shut up in his studies at Chestnut Street and Jamaica Plain. His trips cemented the friendships which grew up through the exchange of letters, and his circle of friends was probably larger in Quebec than in Boston. And as the years went by, his great project attracted more attention from the public, and honors began to come to him from all directions in a swelling stream.

In 1866 Parkman made the first of a series of visits to Montreal and Quebec which had the twofold nature of research trips and pleasure excursions. The Reverend John Cordner, an Ulsterman who had been called in 1848 to preside over the first Unitarian Church in Montreal, had married Parkman's sister Caroline in 1852. With the Cordners and their three daughters Parkman was as much at home in Montreal as he was in Boston. He got along famously with his brother-in-law, who liked his company so much that he moved his family to Boston in 1882, when he retired from the pulpit, and spent the remainder of his years in a house close to Parkman's on Chestnut Street. The Reverend John Cordner was no milk-and-water cleric, but a hearty soul who delighted in Parkman's tales of frontier life as much as the latter did in his recitation of Irish ballads. In Quebec Parkman had firm personal friends in Judge Henry Black and Judge George O'Kill Stuart, to whose rock-ribbed Protestant company he retreated when the clerical atmosphere surrounding his friends at the Séminaire de Québec became too much for his layman's taste. Another close Canadian friend was Sir James Macpherson LeMoine, a notable antiquarian and man of letters and for many years president of the Quebec Literary and Historical Society, an organization which combined the private library function of Parkman's beloved Boston Athenaeum with the publication of historical documents. Parkman became an honorary member of this society, and his historical advice was gladly received by its heads. Another president of the "Lit." who was a

PARKMAN'S CHESTNUT STREET HOME
By courtesy of Miss Elizabeth Cordner.

good friend of Parkman was William James Anderson, an amateur of letters. In Quebec Parkman usually stayed with Judge Stuart at his beautiful old house in Ste. Ursule Street or at Russell's Hotel in St. Louis Street. His figure soon became familiar, striding vigorously with a slight limp up and down St. Louis Street, and there must have been many in the charming old city on the rock above the St. Lawrence who echoed LeMoine's sentiment in dedicating his *L'Album du Touriste* to Parkman in these terms: *"A qui, donc, devais-je, de préférence, dédier* L'Album du Touriste, *sinon au Touriste aimé, qui, chaque printemps, nous revient avec les hirondelles; au brillant et sympathique historien, qui a su entourer d'une auréole notre vieux Québec?* . . ." The Canadians welcomed with all their warm and generous hospitality the man who was revealing their past to the English-speaking world in all its life and color for the first time.

At the close of his preface to the *Jesuits,* dated May 1, 1867, Parkman announced his intention of devoting the next volume in the series to "the discovery and occupation by the French of the valley of the Mississippi." Following his custom of going over the ground himself, he devoted a good part of the following summer to a trip to Fort Snelling, Minnesota, visiting on the way Keokuk, Peoria and the Illinois River, Prairie du Chien, and St. Louis, where he saw Henry Chatillon, his guide on the Oregon Trail trip, with whom he had kept up a correspondence for twenty-one years. One purpose of the trip was to refresh his ideas on the Indians by seeing them once more in their own country. The changes in the region which he had first seen in its frontier stage were tremendous and appalling, and he echoed Chatillon's feeling that they were not for the better. But to console him he had a remarkable experience on this trip, which proved how well he had done his preliminary work. The site of the great village of the Illinois Indians was a matter of conjecture, and on this trip Parkman confirmed his theory as to its location in the most dramatic sort of way. He described the incident in a note to *La Salle:*

From a study of the contemporary documents and maps, I became satisfied, first, that the branch of the river Illinois, called the "Big Vermilion," was the *Aramoni* of the French explorers; and, secondly, that the cliff called "Starved Rock" was that known to the French as *Le Rocher,* or the Rock of St. Louis. If I was right in this conclusion, then the position of the Great Village was established; for there is abundant proof that it was on the north side of the river, above the Aramoni and below Le Rocher. I accordingly went to the village of Utica, which, as I judged by the map, was very near the point in question, and mounted to the top of one of the hills immediately behind it, whence I could see the valley of the Illinois for miles, bounded on the farther side by a range of hills, in some parts rocky and precipitous, and in others covered with forests. Far on the right was a gap in these hills, through which the Big Vermilion flowed to join the Illinois; and somewhat towards the left, at the distance of a mile and a half, was a huge cliff, rising perpendicularly from the opposite margin of the river. This I assumed to be Le Rocher of the French, though from where I stood I was unable to discern the distinctive features which I was prepared to find in it. In every other respect, the scene before me was precisely what I had expected to see. There was a meadow on the hither side of the river, on which stood a farmhouse; and this, as it seemed to me, by its relations with surrounding objects, might be supposed to stand in the midst of the space once occupied by the Illinois town.

On the way down from the hill I met Mr. James Clark, the principal inhabitant of Utica, and one of the earliest settlers of this region. I accosted him, told him my objects, and requested a half-hour's conversation with him, at his leisure. He seemed interested in the inquiry, and said he would visit me early in the evening at the inn, where, accordingly, he soon appeared. The conversation took place in the porch, where a number of farmers and others were gathered. I asked Mr. Clark if any Indian remains were found in the neighborhood. "Yes," he replied, "plenty of them." I then inquired if there was any one spot where they were more numerous than elsewhere. "Yes," he answered again, pointing towards the farmhouse on the meadow; "on my farm down yonder by the river, my tenant plows up teeth and bones by the peck every spring, besides arrowheads, beads, stone hatch-

ets, and other things of that sort." I replied that this was precisely what I had expected, as I had been led to believe that the
principal town of the Illinois Indians once covered that very
spot. "If," I added, "I am right in this belief, the great rock beyond the river is the one which the first explorers occupied as a
fort; and I can describe it to you from their account of it, though
I have never seen it, except from the top of the hill where the
trees on and around it prevented me from seeing any part but the
front." The men present now gathered around to listen. "The
rock," I continued, "is nearly a hundred and fifty feet high, and
rises directly from the water. The front and two sides are perpendicular and inaccessible; but there is one place where it is
possible for a man to climb up, though with difficulty. The top
is large and level enough for houses and fortifications." Here
several of the men exclaimed: "That's just it!" "You've hit it
exactly!" I then asked if there was any other rock on that side
of the river which could answer to the description. They all
agreed that there was no such rock on either side, along the whole
length of the river. I then said: "If the Indian town was in the
place where I suppose it to have been, I can tell you the nature
of the country which lies behind the hills on the farther side of
the river, though I know nothing about it except what I have
learned from writings nearly two centuries old. From the top of
the hills, you look out upon a great prairie reaching as far as
you can see, except that it is crossed by a belt of woods, following the course of a stream which enters the main river a few
miles below." "You are exactly right again," replied Mr. Clark;
"we call that belt of timber the 'Vermilion' Woods and the stream
is the Big Vermilion." "Then," I said, "the Big Vermilion is the
river which the French called the Aramoni; Starved Rock is the
same on which they built a fort called St. Louis, in the year 1682;
and your farm is on the site of the great town of the Illinois."

I spent the next day in examining these localities, and was
fully confirmed in my conclusions. . . .

Unfortunately there is no other record of this five weeks' journey
through a region so rich in historical interest for Parkman than this

account in a footnote to the text of *La Salle*. He no longer kept diaries, but on most of his later trips he used small notebooks to jot down topographical details and outlines of descriptive passages. If he kept such a record of this excursion, it has disappeared.

In the early spring of 1866 Parkman received a letter from the Abbé Henri-Raymond Casgrain of Laval University in Quebec, which was the forerunner of one of the most interesting historical correspondences on record. Parkman was acquainted with the abbé by reputation, for he had reviewed the latter's edition of the *Jesuit Relations* (done in collaboration with a colleague, the Abbé Charles-Henri Laverdière) at length in the July 1865 number of the *North American*. Parkman had used the book as a springboard for a long discussion of the manners and customs of the principal Indian tribes, finding that this great series of firsthand narratives constituted by far the "most full and trustworthy authority" and an excellent antidote to the erroneous views of H. R. Schoolcraft and L. H. Morgan. Since the *Relations* were one of the greatest sources for his history—he incorporated many passages from them directly into his text—and the series had long been out of print, except for a few modern reprints of individual narratives, Parkman was under a great debt to the two Canadians who had made the whole work readily available once more in three volumes. His new correspondent told Parkman that he had come across the latter's *Pontiac* by chance in the Parliamentary Library, and had been struck by the vivacity, brilliant imagination, and the breadth of view shown in it. He spoke flatteringly of the author's erudition, *"aussi rare que sûr,"* and offered his services if Parkman should find them of use. Parkman had sent in his subscription to a new magazine, *Le Foyer Canadien,* over which Casgrain presided, and the latter sent in return copies of all its publications. Parkman had been coached by John Gilmary Shea in the correct manner of approaching French men of letters, and he wrote a rather flowery reply in which he thanked the abbé for his compliments and for his gift, "both for their own sake, and as the gift of an eminent Canadian author." Casgrain replied with the present of a signed photograph, and the news that the second volume of the late Abbé Ferland's *Histoire du Canada* was being put through the press by his friends.

Parkman sent his photograph in return, as requested, though seemingly amused by this method of beginning a correspondence, and expressed his hope of meeting both Casgrain and Laverdière on his visit to Quebec that summer. But since he was in Quebec during August, when the professors at Laval were in the country on their summer vacations, he missed meeting his new friends.

The correspondence thus begun constitutes the largest single series of letters that Parkman wrote, for it continued until his death almost thirty years later. The Abbé Casgrain was eight years younger than Parkman, and a member of a distinguished Canadian family whose seigneury was at Rivière-Ouelle on the lower St. Lawrence, near Ile-aux-Coudres. A romantic, stirred by the history of his people as depicted by Garneau and Ferland, he early determined to dedicate himself to historical pursuits and the continuation of their task. He became the leading French Canadian historical writer of his period, and did much to make Canada and its early history better known abroad in a period when the world still tended to think of his country in the terms of Voltaire's "few acres of snow and ice." He was the center of a group, which included Antoine Gérin-Lajoie, Joseph-Charles Taché, Dr. Hubert La Rue, and P.-J.-O. Chauveau, who were responsible for a sudden flowering of the French Canadian genius. The movement, which was a deliberate attempt to create a French Canadian literature, began in 1860, deriving its inspiration chiefly from François-Xavier Garneau's historical work and the poetry of Octave Crémazie. The prominent place of the latter, whose promising career was cut off at the age of thirty-five when, in financial distress, he exiled himself from Canada, was soon taken by the Abbé Casgrain, who was a leading spirit in the launching in 1860 of a review dedicated to the program of the group, *Les Soirées Canadiennes*, which was succeeded in 1863 by *Le Foyer Canadien*. The movement was strongly patriotic in character: it was designed to keep alive the French tradition in Canada and to increase its influence and position. At first its members had to dwell on the glories of the past and local legends and traditions, but soon this deliberate attempt to create a French Canadian literature succeeded, and there were notable books of the day to discuss. The movement's progress can be fol-

lowed in Casgrain's own works: his first books were slight in substance and characterized by a gaudy and inept style. Gradually
he matured into a full-fledged historian whose style, while remaining lively and engaging, was purged of its early defects. His first
notable book was a *Histoire de la Mère Marie de l'Incarnation* (of
which Parkman made use in the *Jesuits*), and it was followed by his
Biographies Canadiennes (in which a sketch of Parkman's life and
works is to be found), a *Histoire de l'Hôtel-Dieu de Québec, Un
Pèlerinage au Pays d'Evangéline* (a book which brought him into
conflict with his American friend, though its conclusions have since
been ratified at the expense of Parkman's), and his great compilation, *Montcalm et Lévis.* The singular interest of his correspondence with Parkman derives from the difference in the natures and
backgrounds of the two men and their common concern with the
history of New France. Casgrain was regarded as a liberal in certain Canadian circles, but he never forgot that he was a priest of
the Catholic Church, and this brought him into conflict with his
rationalist American correspondent, though he championed Parkman in the Canadian press when the ultramontane party condemned *France and England in North America.* In many respects
his general views were more liberal than those of Parkman—which
is amusing in the light of the latter's opinion that Catholics had to
relinquish their freedom of thought under the harsh discipline of
their reactionary Church—and his share in the French tradition
and in the intellectual life of the Paris of his day made him more of
a broad-minded man of the world than his layman friend. Both
Parkman and Casgrain were romantics, motivated in their historical labors by a great love for the vivid past of New France; but
by nature and by environment they had violently opposed points
of view which frequently brought them into open conflict, despite
goodwill on both sides and Casgrain's rather remarkable tolerance
of his friend's opinions and crotchets. There is perhaps no other
instance of two historians, working in the same field simultaneously
from different points of view, who were close personal friends, and
recorded their agreements and differences so fully as Casgrain and
Parkman did in the two hundred-odd letters of their thirty years'
correspondence. Casgrain was so subjective a writer that he re-

vealed himself even in his formal works; a still clearer picture of the man may be found in his letters. And his confidences were met by those of the usually reticent Parkman, who let himself go uniquely in his letters to his fellow-worker and friend. The correspondence is sometimes in English, sometimes in French, and sometimes in both languages.

Some half-dozen letters, dealing largely with historical points, were exchanged before Casgrain went to Europe in the spring of 1867. Upon his return late that fall, the abbé reported upon the immense collection of documents relating to La Salle which Pierre Margry, an official in the Archives of the Marine and the Colonies in Paris, had assembled and was jealously guarding for his own use. Casgrain found him "*très avare de ces richesses, qui sont grandes.*" He also brought word that the Abbé Faillon would probably not complete his history, because of old age. But more important than these bits of shoptalk was Casgrain's reaction to Parkman's *Jesuits*, which he had sent to the abbé with a warning note: "Remembering that I am a heretic, you will expect a good deal with which you will be very far from agreeing. . . . I meant to give a candid view of my subject in the best light in which I could see it":

You speak of the impression that the reading of a book by one whom you call a heretic, and to whom I give the kinder name of *separated brother* (belonging to that chosen class who trample prejudices under foot to look the truth squarely in the face), must have made on me, a Catholic priest. Your book, in my opinion, is a *masterpiece*, and I dare not tell you so, for fear of passing for a flatterer, without adding that it is a *masterpiece* of contradictions. Pardon my frankness. It is useless for me to attempt to reconcile the conclusions with the premises; it would be a waste of time. We live at two opposite poles: you at the pole of naturalism; I at that of supernaturalism; but there is one point on which we meet: that is, the love of humanity.

Like me, you cannot withhold your admiration of these men who sacrificed themselves with so much constancy and heroism for the love of mankind. The only reproach you make them is that of an inoffensive credulity. What is this speck of dust, if it is one, before the grandeur of their deeds? What colossuses, you say, and justly. But are you indeed sure that they would have been such great men without their blind obedience, without their enthusiastic faith? Could you have written page 319 of your fine book if our missionaries had been, like the ministers of New England, good family men, not in the least credulous, passing their lives seated beside the hearth? Believe me, sacerdotal celibacy is more fruitful than many marriages.

However that may be, your book is the work of a thinker and of a great painter; and Canada owes you an eternal debt for having made its history so much admired.

In reply Parkman wrote:

. . . I am truly glad that, as a man of letters and as a Catholic priest, you can find so much to approve in my book, and I set an especial value on your commendation. We are, as you say, at opposite poles of faith—but my faith—such as it is—is strong and earnest, and I have the deepest respect for the heroic self-devotion, the true charity, of the early Jesuits of Canada.

Back and forth the letters went that spring, full of queries, answers, and hints on historical matter, and of bulletins on the condition of one another's sight, for Casgrain, too, was troubled by weakness of the eyes. His waning sight forced him to relinquish his plan of coming to Boston that spring and of having the pleasure of meeting his correspondent. Parkman consoled him by announcing a visit to Quebec that summer, but when he arrived there in August the abbé was again out of town. Soon after Parkman got back to Boston, a return of his illness made it necessary for him to go abroad for the winter; and since the abbé's eyesight remained in parlous state, the correspondence ceased for three years. But two men who had much in common had learned each other's quality, and these three years were a mere interlude in what was to be a great friendship.

Late in October 1868 Parkman began to feel the cerebral confusion which was a symptom of the return of "The Enemy." The attack was the worst in years, and since there was little improvement in the following month, he determined to go to Paris for the winter, choosing to be idle there rather than at home, since all work seemed out of question for the time being. He went prepared to offer M. Pierre Margry a large sum for the use of the great collection of documentary material on La Salle which the latter had formed. Margry was an old hand at the business of gathering historical materials. In 1839 General Lewis Cass had employed him to collect documents bearing on the old Northwest. This task had occupied him for three and a half years, and then he had performed a similar one for John Romeyn Brodhead, who was charged by the state of New York with the collection of materials dealing with its early history. Margry's vocation was thus fixed, and obtaining a position in the Archives de la Marine et des Colonies, he spent the rest of his active life there. Much of the next thirty years he devoted to searching not only the Archives in which he was employed and of which he eventually became the director, but also all the other public and private collections in France, for material throwing light on the French explorers in North America, with particular attention to La Salle. He planned to publish the results of his research, and carefully kept his collection inaccessible to other scholars until that object should be attained, though he indicated enough of its nature to convince both Casgrain and Parkman that the material was of the first importance. Parkman had been writing his *La Salle* on the basis of the Cass Papers, Margry's compilation of colonial papers for the Canadian government, various documents discovered by the Abbé Faillon (including the family papers of La Salle), and the collection formed by President Sparks of Harvard for a revised edition of his own work on La Salle, which never saw the light. Parkman was hardly established at 21 Boulevard St.-Michel in Paris before he began to lay siege to M. Margry. He won his friendship but not the use of the great collection. He did succeed, however, in getting some useful hints, and in engaging Margry to supervise the copying of a vast mass of papers in the Archives which would form the materials of Parkman's later books. The change of scene soon brought about a change of health, and Parkman led an active life in Paris. On February 24 he wrote to his sister Lizzie thus:

Have been troubled with want of sleep for five or six nights, but otherwise all right. If I accepted invitations, which I do not, I should have the run of the Faubourg St.-Germain. I have just declined an invitation from the Prince de Broglie to dine. Yesterday I saw the Marquis de Montcalm, great-grandson of Wolfe's antagonist, who was very civil. The post-stamps were very gratefully received. [Parkman had asked his sister to send some American and Canadian stamps for the collections of the concierge's little girl.] Don't let the doctor think that I am doing anything but amuse myself, for I am not. I meet a few people incidentally, but am very stiff in declining overtures. The Marquis placed his family papers at my disposal. I have not read one of them, but employed a man to copy them, who is now at work.

Despite this disclaimer of overdoing, Parkman was far from leading an invalid's life during his three months in Paris. Day after day he had long discussions with Margry, often lasting until midnight; he took notes in the various libraries on maps and on portraits, visited Versailles, and formed friendships with Count Adolphe de Circourt (a friend of the Ticknors and an amateur of history), M. Jules Marcou, another historian, and General Dix, the American Minister. He even visited the Paris sewers, perhaps as an antidote to too much high life in the Faubourg St.-Germain. It is not surprising that soon after his return to Boston late in March his sister noted in her diary that "Frank's head is almost as bad as before he went away." But despite sleepless nights and periods in which his head was too confused for work, Parkman kept at his task, and *The Discovery of the Great West* was published in the fall of 1869.

The anti-Jesuit feeling evident in this work, and Parkman's wholehearted support of La Salle's own opinion that his lieutenant Beaujeu was a tool of the Jesuits and as such wrecked his expedition to the mouth of the Mississippi, led John Gilmary Shea to protest that Parkman "had been led too far by Margry, who is of the modern French school continually yelping at the Jesuits." Parkman replied that Margry was "a most zealous Catholic" and that, as for himself, "should evidence turn up showing me to be anywhere in error, in fact or judgment, I shall recant at once, as I care for nothing but to get the truth of the story." A Canadian critic later put the case clearly when he observed that it was impossible for Parkman to tell the true story of New France, because his background and state of mind often made it impossible for him to see the truth which he so earnestly desired to present. But it is clear from the Margry-Parkman correspondence that the former did prejudice the historian against the Jesuits and that Shea was right in his judgment. Margry was a curious character about whom little enough is known. He spent most of his life shut up in a library, hoarding his documentary riches. The records that have been left of him were largely written by scholars who were deprived of the opportunity of using his resources for many years and hence were prejudiced against him. Though Parkman never questioned Margry's right to ownership of the materials he had gathered from the Archives while an employee of the state, others did so most vehemently, and accused him at best of a breach of duty and an abuse of office. But Parkman stood by his new friend, who had delayed his own work, and eventually made it possible for Margry to achieve the fruits of his labor by publication of his collection. And in return Margry favored him above the rest of the workers in the field, and in his letters to Parkman revealed a friendship of a strength and feeling of which many others would have believed the old watchdog of the Archives quite incapable.

Parkman's stay in Paris had another result. His friend Count Adolphe de Circourt introduced him by letter to Madame la Comtesse de Clermont-Tonnerre, a member of that Vaudreuil family which had played a great role in the history of New France. The countess later proposed, with Mr. Parkman's permission, to make available in France sections of his epic work on the history of France's greatest colony. He gave his consent freely, refusing any share of the profits that might result from a French edition of his works, though he was to regret his courtesy. The countess's version of the *Pioneers* was free enough to embarrass him, but he exploded when he discovered what the lady had done to the *Jesuits*:

You express a wish I may have been satisfied with the translation of the *Jesuits*. I am unable to regard it as in any proper sense a

translation at all. Large and essential parts of the book are
omitted. The arrangement of the rest is in some parts entirely
changed, sentences are in some places interpolated and sometimes suppressed, often in such a way as to make me appear to
express views contrary to those of the original. My name is put
on the title-page of a book which is not mine, either in form or
substance, and not an indication is anywhere given that any
alterations have been made.

The countess, a pious lady, had taken it upon herself to alter or
omit all passages that might give offense to the Church, and her
piety was very susceptible to the slightest reflection upon Catholicism or its priests. Parkman attempted to bring her version of the
Pioneers to the attention of the French Canadians, but he would
have nothing to do with her *Jesuits*. It is ironical that in the years
immediately after the Franco-Prussian War the only good translation of Parkman's work was the German version of Friedrich Kapp,
and that there never has been a full French translation, although
Ulric Barthe of Quebec began one just before the World War.
France had so far lost interest in her giant child that there was no
demand for one.

Late in December 1869 Parkman published in the *Nation*—for
which he wrote anonymous reviews for many years under E. L.
Godkin's editorship—his reflections on education, in an essay entitled "The Tale of the Ripe Scholar." He had been for two years an
overseer of Harvard, and took his duties in that post so seriously
that he produced a remarkably modern and thoroughgoing consideration of the American educational problem. He opened the
essay with a consideration of the past, when "New England colleges were . . . little more than schools for making ministers."
But as the clergyman, who "long held a monopoly of what passed
for learning," lost his influence, scholarship lost its repute, for reasons which seemed obvious to Parkman:

The really good scholars were exceptions and very rare ones.
In the matter of theology some notable results were produced,

but secular scholarship was simply an exotic and a sickly one. It never recovered from its transplantation and drew no vital juices from the soil. The climate was hostile to it. All the vigor of the country drifted into practical pursuits, and the New England man of letters, when he happened not to be a minister, was usually some person whom constitutional defects, bodily or mental, had unsuited for politics or business. He was apt to be a recluse, ignorant of the world, bleached by a close room and an iron stove, never breathing the outer air when he could help it, and resembling a medieval monk in his scorn of the body, or rather in his utter disregard of it. Sometimes he was reputed a scholar merely because he was nothing else. The products of his mind were as pallid as the hue of his face, and like their parent void of blood, bone, sinew, muscle, and marrow. That he should be provincial was for a long time inevitable, but that he was emasculate was chiefly his own fault. As his scholarship was not fruitful of any very valuable results, as it did not make itself felt in the living world that ranged around it, as in short it showed no vital force, it began at length to be regarded as a superfluous excrescence. Nevertheless, like the monkish learning of the Middle Ages, it served a good purpose in keeping alive the tradition of liberal culture against a future renaissance. . . . The most finished and altogether favorable example of this devitalized scholarship, with many graceful additions, was Edward Everett, and its echoes may still be heard in the halls of Congress, perplexing Western members with Latin quotations, profuse if not always correct.

Then, after thus blasting the intellectual tradition of his theocratic forebears, Parkman went on to point out the increasing demand for literary originality and force, as the nation grew in importance and in pride, "but neither originality nor force can be got to order. They must spring from a deeper root and grow by laws of their own." He found that culture came to be despised, because it was "weak, thin, and unsuitable" to a nation rejoicing in its untried strength. But to Parkman true culture was nevertheless a supreme necessity of the nation:

The presence of minds highly and vigorously developed is the most powerful aid to popular education, and the necessary condition of its best success. In a country where the ruling power is public opinion, it is above all things necessary that the best and maturest thought should have a fair share in forming it. Such thought cannot exist in any force in the community without propagating its own image, and a class of strong thinkers is a palladium of democracy. They are the natural enemies of ignorant, ostentatious, and aggressive wealth, and the natural friends of all that is best in the popular heart. They are sure of the hatred of charlatans, demagogues, and political sharpers. They are the only hope of our civilization; without them it is a failure, a mere platitude of mediocrity, stagnant or turbid as the case may be. The vastest aggregate of average intelligences can do nothing to supply their place, and even material growth is impeded by an ignorance of its conditions and laws. If we may be forgiven the metaphor, our civilization is at present a creature with a small and feeble head, a large, muscular, and active body, and a tail growing at such a rate that it threatens to become unmanageable and shake the balance of the vital powers.

He protested against the tendency of a partial education to produce an excess of self-confidence, which led incompetent persons to pretend to omniscience, with dangerous consequences to the nation. The remedy, as he saw it, was to substitute a broad knowledge and a vigorous reason for the effete and futile scholasticism of the past. This remedy was already being applied, but was threatened by the ascendancy of material interests in America— particularly since the Civil War:

> To the great mass of our population, the clearing of lands, the acquiring of new territory, the building of cities, the multiplication of railroads, steamboats, and telegraph lines, the growth of trade and manufactures, the opening of mines, with the resulting fine houses, fine clothes, and sumptuous fare, constitute the real sum and substance of progress and civilization. Art, literature, philosophy, and science—so far as science has no direct bearing on material interests—are regarded as decorations,

agreeable and creditable, but not essential. In other words, the material basis of civilization is accepted for the entire structure. A prodigious number of persons think that money-making is the only serious business of life, and there is no corresponding number who hold a different faith. There are not a few among us who would "improve" our colleges into schools of technology, where young men may be trained with a view mainly to the production of more steamboats, railroads, and telegraphs; more breadstuffs; more iron, copper, silver, and gold; more cottons and woolens; and consequently more fine houses and fine clothes.

This analysis applies neatly to America in the years that followed the World War, although with the growth of the nation different means had become necessary to achieve the same ends. Materialism was just as much in the saddle in the nineteen-twenties as it was in the seventies and eighties, and with the same effect upon intellectual pursuits as Parkman noticed in his own time:

> The drift towards material activity is so powerful among us that it is very difficult for a young man to resist it; and the difficulty increases in proportion as his nature is active and energetic. Patient and devoted study is rarely long continued in the vortex of American life. The dusty arena of competition and strife has fascinations almost irresistible to one conscious of his own vigor. Intellectual tastes may, however, make a compromise. Journalism and the lecture room offer them a field midway between the solitude of the study and the bustle of the world of business; but the journal and the lecture room have influences powerfully adverse to solid, mature, and independent thinking. There, too, is the pulpit for those who have an inclination that way; but in this also a mighty and increasing temptation besets the conscientious student. As for politics, they have fallen to such a pass that the men are rare who can mingle in them without deteriorating.

Again, taking a view that has been advanced frequently in our own time, Parkman found that mass education was working against the free development of the highest education and culture:

There has been a vast expenditure of brick and mortar for educational purposes, and, what is more to the purpose, many excellent and faithful teachers of both sexes have labored diligently
in their vocation; but the system of competitive cramming in our
public schools has not borne fruits on which we have much
cause to congratulate ourselves. It has produced an immense
number of readers; but what thinkers are to be found may be
said to exist in spite of it.

In this vast mass of the half-educated, the cheap newspapers,
magazines, and books had found an audience who pampered "their
mental stomachs with adulterated, not to say poisoned, sweet-
meats, till they have neither desire nor digestion for strong and
wholesome food." He found ever fewer serious and thoughtful
readers, and a public demand for elocution rather than reason from
orators. The public taste had been debased:

It rejoices in sweeping statements, confident assertions, bright
lights and black shadows alternating with something funny.
Neither does it care much for a terse, idiomatic, and pointed dic-
tion, but generally prefers the flatulent periods of the ready
writers. On matters of greatest interest it craves to be excited or
amused. Lectures professing to instruct are turned to a tissue of
jokes, and the pulpit itself is sometimes enlivened after a similar
fashion. The pill must be sugared and the food highly seasoned,
for the public mind is in a state of laxity and needs a tonic. But
the public taste is very exacting, and it offers great and tempting
rewards to those who please it.

✿   ✿   ✿   ✿

The amount of what we have been saying is, that the public
which demands a second-rate article is so enormously large in
comparison with the public which demands a first-rate article
that it impairs the quality of literary production, and exercises
an influence adverse to the growth of intellectual eminence.
Now what is the remedy? It seems to us to be twofold. First, to
direct popular education, not to stuffing the mind with crude

aggregations of imperfect knowledge, but rather to the development of its powers of observation, comparison, analysis, and reasoning; to strengthening and instructing its moral sense, and leading it to self-knowledge and consequent modesty. All this, no doubt, is vastly more difficult and far less showy in its results than the present system of competitive cramming, and requires in its teachers a high degree of good sense and sound instruction. The other remedy consists in a powerful re-enforcement of the higher education, and the consequent development of a class of persons, whether rich or poor, so well instructed and so numerous as to hold their ground against charlatanry, and propagate sound and healthy thought through the community. He who gives or bequeaths money to a well-established and wisely conducted university confers a blessing which radiates through all the ranks of society. He does a service eminently practical, and constitutes himself the patron of the highest and best utilitarianism.

Parkman's educational argument is so familiar to all who have concerned themselves with the subject in recent years that hardly any comment is necessary upon it, save that it was a remarkable one to make seventy years ago.

"The Tale of the Ripe Scholar" is the most notable of Parkman's contributions to periodicals. It reveals clearly his own ideas on the calling that he had adopted, and his hatred for emasculated scholarship. Though circumstance had confined him to "a close room and an iron stove" and made him a recluse, the products of his solitary toil were full of the life that he loved so passionately and far from being "void of blood, bone, sinew, muscle, and marrow." Though years were still to pass before the public demanded more than a few hundred copies of his histories upon their publication, Parkman never deigned to cater to its taste and went his own way:

That which pleases it pays so much better in money and notoriety, and is so much cheaper of production than the better article which does not please it, that the temptation to accept light work and high wages in place of hard work and low wages is difficult to resist. Nothing but a deep love of truth or of art can stand against it.

Yet in these years he was beginning to reap the rewards of his long toil. He was gradually recognized as the authority in his field of history and called on to weigh the merits of new work in that field. In July 1866 he wrote a long review * of Father Tailhan's edition of Nicolas Perrot's *Mémoire sur les Moeurs, Coutumes, et Religion des Sauvages de l'Amérique Septentrionale*. He took this occasion to flay Schoolcraft's huge work on the Indians, which had been published at government expense:

> It is a singularly crude and illiterate production stuffed with blunders and self-contradictions, giving evidence on every page of a striking unfitness either for history or philosophical inquiry, and taxing to the utmost the patience of those who would extract what is valuable in it from its oceans of pedantic verbiage.

He had formed high standards for the writing of history, as is revealed by his notice of John M. Read's *Historical Inquiry Concerning Henry Hudson:* †

> Americans are generally supposed to live in the present and the future, and to discard the past as a worn-out garment. But if the tide sets this way, there is nevertheless a strong undertow, which, from whatever cause it proceeds, is a phenomenon very marked and noteworthy. No people are more addicted than Americans to rummaging among genealogies and tracing out the sources of surnames, as a very copious literature to be found on the shelves of historical and genealogical societies can attest. Moreover, a very large proportion of what little the country has achieved in literature belongs to the department of history. We have a profusion of histories of all sorts, good, bad, and indifferent, and have histories and collections without number—many of them hasty, crude, and superficial, and some, too, evincing the most thorough accuracy.
>
> The work which furnishes the text of these remarks is a most

* For the *North American Review*.
† In the *Atlantic* for June 1867.

50 Chestnut St.

Boston.   Wed.

1868 Feb. 5

My Dear Gould,

How can I ascertain if a comet — a somewhat remarkable one — was visible from the site of Peoria, Illinois, in January, 1681?

Also, how can I ascertain on what day of the month Easter Monday, 1680, occurred?

I want the information to test the accuracy of certain journals in my possession.

Very truly yrs.

F. Parkman

Dr. B. A. Gould, Cambridge

AN APPEAL TO AN EXPERT

Parkman consults his former college roommate, become a famous astronomer, in order to verify the authenticity of the manuscript materials for his great history.

From a letter in the possession of the author.

scholarly and admirable example of a species of investigation which lies at the base of all accurate and trustworthy history.

In the following month he was able to pay a tribute to the father of Canadian history when he reviewed in the *Atlantic* John Gilmary Shea's labor of love, the first English translation of Père Charlevoix's *History of New France:*

> It is a well-written, scholar-like, and readable book, treating of a subject which the author perfectly understood and of which he may be said to be a part. Tried by the measure of his times, his research was thorough and tolerably exact.

And in 1868, at the request of the publishers, who lavished encomiums upon his standing in his profession, he wrote the introduction and revised the translation of a new edition of William Smith's *Account of Bouquet's Expedition against the Ohio Indians.* Thus brought back to his work on Pontiac's conspiracy, he had little changed his views: he still saw the peace of 1763 as the end of a "vast but frail French empire in the West" and a disaster to the Indians: "While the French had usually gained the goodwill, often the ardent attachment of the tribes with whom they came into contact, the English, for the most part, had inspired only jealousy and dislike. This dislike was soon changed to the most intense hatred." His judgment of the Indian had not changed, either: "One is almost constrained to admire the inflexible obstinacy with which he clings to his own personality, rejects the advances of civilization, and prefers to die as he has lived. Such indeed is the alternative; and it was after the peace of 1763 that this inexorable sentence of civilization or destruction was first proclaimed over the continent in tones no longer doubtful. . . . That the Indians understood the crisis it would be rash to affirm; but they felt it without fully understanding it. The result was the great Indian war under Pontiac."

The gift of the Bouquet and Haldimand Papers to the British Museum, and other material that had come to light in the nineteen years since the publication of *Pontiac,* led Parkman to revise the work thoroughly for the sixth edition. Thus he established a precedent which he followed with most of the other volumes in the series. It was his desire to have his books correct, even to the smallest detail, in the light of the most recent research, and so he kept all his books up-to-date. Despite the scale of his project, he never found himself in the position familiar to other ambitious historians, who saw their first volume outmoded before the last was finished. This constant revision took time and a good deal of money, not only for resetting of the text but for copying documents. Parkman spent considerable sums in obtaining copies of documents in the British Museum in 1870 for the revised edition of *Pontiac* which appeared in two volumes in that same year. Copies of the early editions of his books, corrected in his own hand, are among the works he left to the Harvard College Library, and these reveal the great pains he took in revision.

15: Friendships and Feuds

*Hostile, il pouvait l'être d'esprit, mais,
par une étrange contradiction, il ne
l'était pas de coeur.*
A. FAUTEUX, PARKMAN CENTENARY,
1923

THE new edition of *Pontiac* was about all that Parkman was
able to accomplish in 1870, for during most of that year he
was a prey to insomnia, which each night robbed him of all but
an hour or two of sleep, and sometimes permitted him none at all.
He was too old a soldier in the battle with "The Enemy" to give
way to despair, however; while the siege lasted he abandoned work
without complaint and amused himself and his children by inventing nonsense stories in which the leading roles were often
taken by the succession of cats that Parkman liked to have about
him. In the spring of the following year he was able to begin work
again. As if to mark the curious parallelism between the careers
of the two men, the Abbé Casgrain reopened his correspondence
with Parkman, reporting that his ailing eyes once more permitted
him to use them. Parkman replied with ready sympathy:

> . . . A matter in which I can wholly sympathize with you, my
> own having been useless for ten years or more, and even now
> permitting me to write or read only for a few minutes at one
> time.

That May the two men met for the first time, though they had cor-
responded for five years, when the abbé came to Boston with the
aim of obtaining material for a biographical sketch of Parkman.
Casgrain, an ardent French Canadian nationalist and the leader
in the movement to make his compatriots conscious of their great
heritage, felt that Parkman was shamefully neglected in Canada.
He was scarcely better known to English readers there than to the
French, who had only a mutilated translation to judge his work
by, if they did not read English. Casgrain discussed the matter

401

with his fellow-French historians, and they agreed that it would be a good idea to write the biography of this American who was bringing the history of New France to the attention of the world: *"C'était servir la cause nationale!"* So the abbé announced his impending arrival in the stronghold of Puritanism to his friend, who met him as he was mounting the steps of the Revere House, lost in admiration of the princely hotels of the Americans, *"Cette grande tribu nomade campée en Amérique."*

At last the two men met face to face and shook hands for the first time, after Parkman had twice gone in vain to Quebec to meet Casgrain, and Casgrain had twice come in vain to Boston to meet Parkman. The abbé found his friend of *"une simplicité toute américaine."* He saw the frailness hid beneath the sturdy figure, and a face which seemed to him one of the remarkable sort that Leonardo loved to paint: "a harmonious combination of intelligence, acuteness, and energy; a large forehead, a finely shaped nose, and a strong and prominent chin." He saw nothing to suggest the imaginative poet who had written the word pictures which had moved him so much; the face was that of a thinker rather than a poet, but something in the eyes half shut against the bright sunlight suggested the flame within. For his part, Parkman wasted no time in analyzing his new acquaintance, but immediately took him off in his carriage to make the grand tour of Boston, which the abbé soon found was justly called the Athens of America and the intellectual capital of the great republic. Casgrain seems to have been particularly impressed by his visit to Harvard and to the homes of two of its professors, Agassiz and Longfellow. He painted a charming portrait of Longfellow, the "American Lamartine":

> *L'auteur d'Evangéline est un beau vieillard, aux traits animés, au regard limpide et inspiré. Sa noble figure, sa longue et abondante barbe qui tombe en flots de neige sur sa poitrine, lui donnent un air de majesté qui rappelle les bardes ou les voyants des anciens jours. C'est ainsi qu'on représente Ossian, Baruch, ou le Camoëns.* *

---

* "The author of *Evangeline* is a handsome old man, with animated features and a calm and lofty look. His noble face, his long and abundant beard which falls in

Agassiz, the great scientist, also made a strong impression on Casgrain, but Mrs. Agassiz won his heart entirely by taking him aside and discussing with tears in her voice the heroism of the early Canadian missionaries and religious. He found that both his hosts had learned to admire Canada through reading Parkman; here in Cambridge, as elsewhere in the United States and in France and England, he heard his people praised in the words of his friend. Then Parkman took him out to his cottage on the banks of Jamaica Pond, among the wooded hills and the "opulent villas" of Jamaica Plain. Casgrain was struck by his friend's passion for roses, and learned with wonder how he had brought more than a hundred and fifty different varieties back from Europe. With Gallic grace, Casgrain pictured Parkman planning his histories amid this forest of roses and composing *"ces pages fleuries, tout embaumées de parfums exquis, qu'on croit respirer en ouvrant ses livres."*

All in all, the visit was a great success, and Parkman intended to return it by coming to Canada that summer. But one thing after another put him off: first an uncle died, leaving his family and affairs to be managed by Parkman; then his own mother died suddenly; then there were complications about the opening of the Bussey Institution, of which Parkman had been appointed professor of horticulture in the spring. Finally early in November he got to Quebec for a few days, of which his copyist, M. N.-E. Dionne—later head of the Quebec Parliamentary Library—gives a good picture in uncertain English:

Being poor, I was glad to gain some dollars, but I was chiefly proud to accompany this well-known Bostonian through his peregrinations from the Seminary to the Episcopal Palace, from the registrar Office to the Terrier's office, compulsing together every document which he intended to use. . . . So I must say, and everybody can say so, that if I am something today, I owe this to Mr. Parkman.

This trip to Quebec was not his only excursion of the year, for Parkman made a short tour of historic places in Nova Scotia and

snowy waves on his chest, give him a majestic air which recalls the bards or seers of ancient time: it is thus that Ossian, Baruch or Camoëns is painted."

New Brunswick during the last part of July and the first part of August. His mother's death occurred during his absence and cut short the expedition.

Early in the new year Casgrain informed Parkman that he planned to publish a criticism of his works in French in *L'Opinion Publique* of Montreal and in English in the *Canadian News: "Naturellement* it is the Catholic view: *mais large et généreuse. . . ."* Parkman saw the proofs, and found little to quarrel with. The essay appeared in four weekly installments during March and April in *L'Opinion Publique*—the proposed English version never saw the light—and then was reprinted as a small book. It is the only extended study of Parkman and his work by a French Canadian, and throws considerable light on the relationship between its author and its subject. Casgrain had made himself something of a name with a series of such critical and biographical studies; they were later collected under the title of *Biographies Canadiennes,* where Parkman found himself in the goodly company of F.-X. Garneau, Octave Crémazie, G. B. Faribault, Gérin-Lajoie, and Philippe de Gaspé. The essays were conceived as propaganda for the nationalist literary movement, and may be said to be the first French Canadian literary criticism of significance. Previously there had been so little literature that such criticism as there was had been confined to logrolling. Casgrain did not escape entirely from the tradition, for the interests of the movement were very close to his heart, but he had a talent for the form he adopted, he wrote with charm, and most of the essays remain of considerable interest today. He opened his essay on Parkman with an account of his meeting with the historian in Boston, and then gave a brief and none too reliable account of Parkman's life, in which he does not fail to point out the historian's great advantage in having completed *"ses études de cabinet par l'étude sur la Nature elle-même."* He saw that Parkman was both poet and historian, a romantic historian who was not content to dig up a skeleton from the tomb, but insisted on bringing it back to life clothed in flesh and blood. He found that the persons and places of Parkman's narrative were almost photographic likenesses of their originals. After sketching the contents of the published histories, and indicating—incorrectly—the contents of those yet to be written, the abbé proceeds to judge Parkman's work from the literary, national, and religious points of view. This was the more difficult since "the radiations of Mr. Parkman's style on the blue sky of our history have something of the nature of the splendors of the aurora borealis, producing on the spirit an equal fascination and making it impossible to view the matters it treats of in a critical spirit." But at the outset Casgrain made it clear that he had important reservations in his praise of Parkman's achievement. None of them is concerned with form, except a feeling that his author is too prodigal with footnotes, and he singles out for unreserved praise two of the great word pictures in the *Jesuits* and in *La Salle*. He rejects the criticism that some have made that Parkman indulges too much in set pieces, that his style and his narrative are too highly colored and too dramatic. The abbé joins his friend in the romantic school with the flat avowal that he prefers "a Correggio to an Overbeck, a page of Thierry to a whole narrative by Bancroft."

Reluctantly the abbé admits that he is far from agreeing with Parkman on more basic matters:

> . . . The work of Mr. Parkman is the negation of all religious belief. The author rejects the Protestant idea as well as Catholic dogma; he is purely rationalist. He admits no other principle than the vague theory that is called modern civilization. One glimpses a righteous soul, born for the truth, but lost without compass in an ocean without shores. Hence these aspirations toward the truth, these brilliant avowals, this homage to the truth, followed, alas, by strange declines, by outbursts of astonishing fanaticism.

The abbé takes up Parkman's assertion that New England stood for liberty and New France for absolutism, and using the historian's own words confutes the contention rather neatly, coming to the conclusion that Parkman's work is a bed of Procrustes on which he reduces everything to his own shape. He sees his friend, who rejects the supernatural, losing himself in trying to find merely human motives to explain the heroism of the early missionaries: "Too proud to alter his convictions, too enlightened to let himself be carried away by prejudice before the fact, but not enough to embrace the whole truth, he resembles belated travelers in our dangerous swamps. Everywhere he feels the ground give under his feet, and he advances, groping to right and left, searching in the shadow for a path that he does not find." Casgrain blames Parkman's lack of a philosophical education for his confusion of principle and application, and for his inability to understand that the divine Church might have all too human instruments. He neatly applies this truth about things human to Parkman's work:

> In short, the writings of Mr. Parkman, in which good and evil are mingled, are the image of human nature. The sky is not without clouds, the light not without shadows, but nevertheless it is day. One recognizes throughout the elevated mind, the honest heart, which, through all his gropings, admires the beautiful, searches for the truth, and loves the good.
>
> His history is a reparation and a work of justice which our enemies have too long refused us.
>
> A stranger to our country, ignorant of our party battles, he has not allowed himself to be prejudiced by calumnies invented before his coming. He has gone to the very sources of our history; he has studied them with a care, a love, worthy of all praise; he has then told the story, just as he has found it, and said: "Accept or reject my conclusions; but here are the facts."
>
> We can scarcely hope more of an impartial enemy.
>
> The eloquence of the facts, told truthfully and loyally, triumphs over erroneous interpretations; light breaks through the clouds, and the impression that is left is all to the advantage of our race.

Despite all the objections that a Catholic must make to Parkman's books, the abbé felt that Canadians owed Parkman a great debt, for no other writer had done so much to make their country's history known and admired abroad, and he pointed out that one could not admire the history without also respecting the religion which had played so great a role in it. In a remarkably farsighted conclusion the abbé expressed his belief that Providence had made use of

Parkman, quite without his knowledge, for the accomplishment of its designs: that his books helped to break down the barriers which divided the races of the New World, who were destined in time to unite in a civilization which would rule the globe. And then he paid a fine tribute to his friend:

> When you have come to the end of your career, you can lay down on your books your head whitened by toil, and give this testimony: I have used my life for the good of my fellows, with a right and pure purpose; I can lay myself down to sleep with the hope that this will be held to my credit.

Casgrain, not content merely to praise his friend's work, did a good deal to further it. Parkman was planning a trip to Europe in the summer of 1872, and during that June Casgrain arranged with the Abbé Villeneuve, the superior of the Montreal Sulpicians, that his friend should be well received when he made historical inquiries at St. Sulpice in Paris. To clinch the matter, Casgrain advised his friend to take copies of his books along, "to show the favorable appreciation you give of the Sulpicians." When Parkman got to Paris, he found the gentlemen of St. Sulpice well disposed toward him, but discovered "nothing of much account" in their archives. He had hoped to find something of interest in the Abbé Faillon's papers, which were in their keeping, but the four manuscript volumes that he was shown, "as all that Abbé Faillon had left," contained little to his purpose. But he met Gabriel Gravier of Rouen, the Norman authority on La Salle, and Henry Harrisse, who had perhaps a greater bibliographical knowledge of early Americana and Canadiana than any other living man. He ransacked the libraries and museums for maps and plans which would aid his work, and again he laid siege to Pierre Margry, who proved more helpful on this visit, putting down La Salle references in Parkman's little clasped notebook in his own cramped hand. The acquaintance had ripened into friendship, and Margry dined with Parkman and his sister Lizzie on September 16, producing a poem written in honor of the occasion, which was Parkman's forty-ninth birthday:

16 7bre. 1823–1872

A Francis Parkman, Auteur des "Français en Amérique"

Dans le monde où vous êtes né
Vos écrits disent notre gloire;
Nul n'a, comme vous, honoré
Les beaux actes de notre histoire.

Cependant presque inaperçu
Vous allez parcourant la France,
Et c'est par hasard que j'ai su
La date de votre naissance.

Aussi je veux pour mon pays
Fêter ce jour, selon l'usage,
Par la même pensée unis
Il m'est cher de vous rendre hommage.

Dans mes faibles remercîments
Ne comptez pas combien nous sommes.
Ecoutez à mes sentiments
L'écho que font nos grands hommes.

Ecoutez les voeux de Cartier,
Ceux de Champlain sur vos rivages,
Entendez ceux de Cavelier
Applaudissant à vos ouvrages.

. . . And so on, for five more stanzas. But despite his friendly feelings, Margry was still unwilling to allow Parkman to use his treasured La Salle collection. He did relent sufficiently to authorize him to offer the right of publication to his own publishers under certain rather impracticable conditions. But unfortunately Parkman found Boston in flames upon his return on November 17, and since the business section had been nearly wiped out by the great fire, no Boston firm felt like taking on an ambitious project which at best could only be considered as philanthropic from a commercial publisher's point of view. At first the firm considered publishing the work if a large number of subscribers could be obtained, but when these were not forthcoming, despite much effort on Parkman's part, they withdrew entirely. Far from being discouraged, Parkman set about creating a lobby for publication by the government, undaunted by the fact that Henry Harrisse and the American Minister to Paris had met failure in a similar attempt several years before. He wrote to all his friends in the historical societies to enlist their support, and besought the aid of literary men, members of Congress, and all who could help in any way to further the cause. Colonel Whittlesey of the Ohio Historical Society, Lyman Draper of the Wisconsin Historical Society, William Dean Howells of the *Atlantic*, and Senator Hoar and General Garfield were among those who helped along the appropriation of $10,000 by Congress for the purpose. The affair dragged on for months, as such matters do, but at last Parkman could tell Margry that the bill was passed and that he could begin printing the documents at Paris. But Parkman was not yet done with the matter: Margry was injured by the Librarian of Congress's failure to respond to communications, and for his part the Librarian clearly distrusted Margry's good faith, particularly when the first two volumes appeared without any indication of the sources of the documents they contained. Parkman by constant letter-writing kept peace between the two men through many such incidents, and at last Margry's great compilation, *Découvertes et Etablissements des Français dans l'Ouest et dans le Sud de l'Amérique Septentrionale (1614–1754), Mémoires et Documents Originaux,* was complete in book form. The work has been a treasure house for generations of historical investigators; all that Parkman got for his trouble was the opportunity to revise extensively his *La Salle*.

While he was still occupied with the Margry affair, Parkman heard from the Abbé Casgrain that the latter had been attacked by the ultramontane party in Quebec for favoring a heretic historian, and had written an article in reply in the *Revue Canadienne*, which he feared might alienate his friend. Parkman hastened to reassure him:

> Your article in the *Revue* has not affected in the slightest degree the cordial regard which I entertain for you. I know that you wrote it with pain and regret, in obedience to a sense of duty, and besides, I believe that when I feel confident in my position, I am not very sensitive to criticism.

If there was any friction between the two men at this time, it did not last long, for Parkman spent some weeks of that summer at Casgrain's family estate, Manoir Airevault, at Rivière-Ouelle on the St. Lawrence below Quebec. Here he obtained the firsthand acquaintance with seigneurial life that he required for his work on *The Old Regime,* then nearing completion. The Quebec country-side had changed little in the matter of manners, classes, and cus-toms since the days of New France, and Parkman got all that he required. It is clear that he also enjoyed himself thoroughly, for he fell a victim to the great charm of that beautiful countryside. And then, when he was not making excursions about the region with his host, he had long talks with the abbé's mother, Madame Casgrain, who spoke English well and proved so good a conversa-tionist that the meals lasted for hours. It was perhaps on this visit that he penciled into a notebook this description of one of the matchless sunsets of the St. Lawrence Valley:

St. Lawrence, near Saguenay, after a Shower

The setting sun, half sunk behind the hills of Tadoussac, bathes with soft golden fire the fleecy clouds that hang above the west, pours floods of level radiance athwart the falling drops, and paints a mighty rainbow against the gray eastern sky.

He marveled at the porpoises playing in the waters of the great river, and took so much interest in them that, after his return to Boston, Casgrain sent him a little pamphlet he had written about the porpoise fishery in the days of New France. With the abbé he visited some of the islands in the river, where isolation had kept the old order still more unchanged than on the mainland, and at last, with real regret, he returned home to another world than this bit of old France in the New World. Late in October he visited Lake George for a few days, and when he described his excursion by letter to the abbé, the latter replied that he wished he could have been at his side as he re-explored this old battleground of the colonists.

The abbé reported that his eyes were in such bad shape that he could neither read nor write, and that he was going to spend the winter in France and Italy in the hope that a change of climate would help them. Parkman commissioned him to find a copyist in Paris, and the abbé thought to oblige two of his friends at once by offering the job to Octave Crémazie, the great Canadian poet, then a bankrupt exile in Paris under the name of Jules Fontaine. The arrangement did not work out too well, however, for Parkman had given faulty directions and M. Jules Fontaine was prone to delays and long silences in correspondence, which, however appropriate to a poet, were maddening in a copyist. Several times Parkman had to invoke the abbé's assistance in prodding M. Fontaine into action or at least into correspondence. He did not know, of course, that his copyist was a broken man, often mentally ill and unable to work, for the abbé thought it best to preserve Crémazie's incognito.

During the spring of 1874 Parkman wrote regularly to the abbé, discussing points in *The Old Regime*, which he was then concluding. He gave warning that the book might not be so much to the abbé's taste as its predecessors:

> The papers which I brought from Paris—chiefly from the Marine & Colonies—have proved extremely rich in information as to the condition of the colony, on which they throw a great deal of light. Their revelations, unfortunately, are not always agreeable. In fact, the condition of Canada under the old regime was simply deplorable. My book is in the printer's hands.

In July Parkman came to Quebec with his two daughters, but the abbé was away. Parkman left a note saying that the next book in the series, *Frontenac*, would be "much more agreeable and much less difficult writing"—still in fear, evidently, that his conclusions in *The Old Regime* would grate on his friend's sensibilities. His fears were justified, for just before Christmas he heard from James LeMoine that *The Old Regime* had been well received by English Canadians, "but our friend the abbé does not relish it as much as your other works." The abbé preserved a discreet silence until he reviewed the book in the *Revue Canadienne* early in 1875. Parkman wrote him at once:

9 May '75, Jamaica Plain

Mon cher ami:

I am an *abonné* of the *Revue Canadienne* and have just read your article on *The Old Regime*. It is very much what I had expected, knowing your views and the ardor with which you embrace them, as well as the warmth and kindliness of your feelings. I could take issue squarely on the principal points you make, but it would make this letter too long, and I do not care to enter into a discussion with a personal friend on matters which he has so much at heart. Moreover, I wish to preserve an entirely judicial, and not controversial, frame of mind on all that relates to Canadian matters.

Let me set you right, however, on one or two points personal to myself. My acquaintance here would smile to hear me declared an advocate of democracy and a lover of the Puritans. I have always declared openly my detestation of the unchecked rule of the masses, that is to say of universal suffrage, and the corruption which is sure to follow in any large and heterogeneous community. I have also always declared a very cordial dislike of Puritanism. I recognize some most respectable and valuable qualities in the settlers of New England, but do not think them or their system to be praised without great qualifications; and I should not spare criticism if I had to write about them. Nor am I an enthusiast for the nineteenth century, many of the tendencies of which I deplore, while admiring much that it has accomplished. It is too democratic and too much given to the pursuit of material interest at the expense of intellectual and moral greatness, which I hold to be the true end and to which material progress should be but a means.

My political faith lies between two vicious extremes, democracy and absolute authority, each of which I detest the more because it tends to react into the other. I do not object to a good constitutional monarchy, but prefer a conservative republic, where intelligence and character, and not numbers, hold the reins of power.

If you have mistaken my views, I could also point out a good many other mistakes in your article. You say that I see Canadian defects through a microscope and merits through a diminishing glass. The truth is, I have suppressed a considerable number of statements and observations because I thought that while they would give pain, they were not absolutely necessary to the illustration of the subject; but I have invariably given every favorable testimony I could find in any authentic quarter; and after I had finished the volume, I made careful search in Ferland and Garneau to see if they had discovered anything which had escaped me. The materials of Canadian history, it is true, proceed almost entirely from the pens of persons born and bred in France —for the Canadians themselves wrote very little indeed—but only a very few of these persons wrote in an adverse spirit. Whenever it was possible, I have used their own language. As for d'Allet, I have indicated his proclivities by stating that his statements are printed in the *Morale Pratique*, a publication well known as hostile to the Jesuits. The end of the paper stops me. I have space only to tell you how much I value your testimony to my conscientiousness as a writer, and your remarks, too partial, I fear, on the literary qualities of the book.

Very cordially yours,

F. P.

[New Sheet]

P.S. I am well aware that the conduct of the British government towards the Canadians was for a long time unjust, and in some respects grossly so; but it is not the less true that it was the conquest to which Canada owes the introduction of the institutions by which she has so greatly prospered.

In exhibiting the different workings of the two political systems, it was necessary to make comparisons which seem invidious, but these comparisons are not, as you say, *continual;* for they are confined to three or four pages at the end of the book, and the points of military efficiency on which the system of authority had advantages are fully exhibited. You say I have more patriotism than impartiality. Let me beg you to turn to the foot of page 265 and the top of page 266 of the *Revue,* and judge as to which of us your remark best applies. As for the *cri de haine* which you impute to me, I assure you that my patriotism is not of the sort to be disturbed at this late day by any vision of Puritan scalps.

I am well on in the story of *Frontenac,* whose good and bad traits I shall endeavor, after my custom, to exhibit clearly. Perhaps when you read what I have written, you will not think me so partial after all.

I expect to receive from France about 6000 (or more) pages of entirely new material on the war of 1755–63. I have received about 3000 of them this winter, and have still several copyists at work in the Archives.

During 1875 Parkman pushed ahead with the writing of *Frontenac,* and by the end of November it was half written. As always, he kept more than one work on the stocks, and had already assembled and begun to digest more than 6000 pages of new papers on the Seven Years' War. In September 1876, with all but three or four chapters of *Frontenac* written, he spent a few days in Ottawa, but did not go down to Quebec to visit his friends there, being pressed for time. He gave warning to the abbé, in expressing his regret at not seeing him that summer, that *Frontenac,* after all, might not prove much to his taste:

> You will not like all parts of it. I have, as usual, given the facts good, bad, and indifferent, exactly as I found them; and, as in most things human, there is much in them both to blame and praise.

Despite the increasing differences of opinion in which the two men were becoming involved as each pursued his own line, there was no lessening of goodwill on either side. Parkman got his Boston engraver to do a portrait of Mère de St. Augustine for Casgrain's *Histoire de l'Hôtel-Dieu de Québec,* though he was occupied at the time in seeing his *Frontenac* through the press. A copy went to Casgrain upon its publication in September 1877, and in May 1878 Casgrain sent in return a copy of his book. Meanwhile the two friends had taken opposite positions in regard to a new work on the Acadian question, Rameau's *Une Colonie Féodale;* Casgrain approving of it and Parkman violently opposing its theories:

I am well acquainted with Rameau's *Une Colonie Féodale,* which I received about six weeks ago, and have studied with great attention. It is full of errors of fact, due partly to his having trusted such untrustworthy authorities as Haliburton, Williams, Charlevoix, Ferland, and Madame de Clermont-Tonnerre's extremely incorrect and garbled translation of my *Pioneers*—and partly to his own inexactness and want of critical discrimination . . .

M. Rameau is void of judgment, as well as of precision. . . .

He then takes his friend to task for urging him to be "diplomatic" and "not to compromise himself": "My business is to write true history, and I never consider whether, in doing so, I shall commit myself with your countrymen or my own." Unfortunately Parkman had already compromised himself in the view of some French Canadians, for he wrote a slashing review of Rameau's book in the *Nation,* and after it was in print was embarrassed to receive a complimentary copy from the author. He begged Casgrain to assure M. Rameau that he had written the review before he had received the gift.

In a postscript to the sharp letter about Rameau's book, he apologizes for his seeming curtness, and explains that he meant no moral aspersion on Ferland by calling his work "untrustworthy." But he put his foot in it again by showing his displeasure at Casgrain's announced intention of reviewing *Frontenac,* though the remarkable offer he makes at the same time takes something of the sting out of his attitude. Parkman proposed a historical duel:

As *Frontenac* is a relation of facts drawn from original authorities, it cannot be effectually criticized by anybody who is not familiar with these authorities. You will find a considerable part of them at Ottawa, but by no means all. I have a great deal on this period which is not to be found there, or anywhere in Canada. My MSS. are too bulky to send you, and I do not want to expose them to the risks of transportation; but if you will make me a visit here, they shall all be at your disposal, as well as my notes and memoranda, which form volumes in themselves. You shall have a quiet room to consult them in, and bring with you an amanuensis if unhappily you still require one. The only condition I wish to make is that your critique and my reply shall be printed together. This would put an end to all doubts as to the correctness of my positions, and show beyond question whether I or others have built on the firmest ground.

The Canadian critics were beginning to get under Parkman's skin and some months after writing this brisk challenge, he asked Casgrain to send him any adverse criticisms that appeared in Canada: "Some of these days I may perhaps answer my critics. At present I am too busy in writing strictures on my own countrymen of the present day. If they were written about Canada, and some of my Canadian friends saw them, they would say that they proceeded from prejudices of race and religion."

The "strictures" took the form of an essay on "The Failure of Universal Suffrage" which appeared in the *North American Review* for July–August 1878, and was widely noticed and commented upon both in America and in Europe. The essay was a vigorous protest against the modern tyranny of Demos—far more dangerous in Parkman's view than the former tyranny of kings and of feudalism—and a castigation of the political evils in which the country had become increasingly involved since the Civil War:

When a king makes himself oppressive to any considerable part of his subjects, it is not worthwhile to consider whether he wears one head or millions; whether he sits enthroned in the palace of his ancestors, or smokes his pipe in a filthy ward-room among blackguards like himself. Nevertheless, if we are to be oppressed, we would rather the oppressor were clean, and, if we are to be robbed, we would like to be robbed with civility. Demos is a protean monarch, and can put on many shapes. He can be benign, imposing, or terrible; but of late we have oftener seen him under his baser manifestations, keeping vile company, and doing his best to shake our loyalty by strange, unkingly pranks. The worst things about him are his courtiers, who in great part are a disreputable crew, abject flatterers, vicious counselors, and greedy plunderers; behind their master in morals, and in most things else but cunning. If the politicians would let him alone, Demos would be the exact embodiment of the average intelligence and worth of a great people; but, deluded and perverted as he is, he falls below this mark, and passes for worse than his real self. Yet, supposing that his evil counselors were all exterminated as they deserve, it would avail us little, for he would soon choose others like them, under the influence of notions which of late have got the better of his former good sense. He is the master, and can do what he will. He is answerable for all, and if he is ill-served, he has nobody to blame but himself. In fact, he is jealous of his nobles, and, like certain other kings before him, loves to raise his barber, his butcher, and his scullion to places of power. They yield him divine honor, proclaim him infallible as the pope, and call his voice the voice of God; yet they befool and cheat him not the less. He is the type of collective folly, as well as wisdom, collective ignorance as well as knowledge, and collective frailty as well as strength. In short, he is utterly mortal, and must rise or fall as he is faithful or false to the great laws that regulate the destinies of man.

Parkman saw our originally healthy democracy beset by two enemies under the new conditions of the age: an ignorant proletariat and a half-taught plutocracy. He believed that the hope of salvation for the country lay in its middle classes, "the natural enemies of the vulgar plutocrat and the natural friends of all that is best in the popular heart, but as they neither flatter, lie, nor bribe, they have little power over these barbarians of civilization that form the substratum of great industrial communities." The new political rallying cry was equality rather than liberty, and Parkman never accepted the doctrine of equalitarianism. He puts his political goal in sharp contrast to that of the popular party:

Shall we look for an ideal society in that which tends to a barren average and a weary uniformity, treats men like cattle, counts them by the head, and gives them a vote apiece without asking whether or not they have the sense to use it; or in that which recognizes the inherent differences between man and man, gives the preponderance of power to character and intelligence, yet removes artificial barriers, keeps circulation free through all its parts, and rewards merit wherever it appears with added influence? This of course is a mere idea, never to be fully realized; but it makes vast difference at what a republic aims, and whether it builds on numbers or on worth.

Parkman felt that the times had changed, and the original theory no longer worked well: a New England village was safely governed by the votes of every man in it, "but now that the village has grown into a populous city, with factories and workshops, its acres of tenement houses, and thousands and ten thousands of restless workmen, foreigners for the most part, to whom liberty means license and politics plunder, to whom the public good is nothing and their own most trivial interests everything, who love the country for what they can get out of it, and whose ears are open to the promptings of every rascally agitator, the case is completely changed, and universal suffrage becomes a dubious blessing." He believed that it worked well only where hereditary traditions of self-government existed, and among "those people, if such there are, who by character and training are prepared for it." Using much the same arguments as in "The Tale of the Ripe Scholar," he condemns the present system of popular education as an inadequate form of training for such responsibilities. What, then, was the remedy? A king would be ridiculous; an oligarchy, "made up of the 'boss,' the 'railroad king,' and bonanza Croesus" would be "a tyranny as detestable and degrading as that of the rankest democracy, with which it would be in league." Parkman saw clearly enough that "the low politician is the accomplice of the low plutocrat, and the low voter is the ready tool of both." The new gospel of imperialism offered no better prospect; an emperor would be "nothing but a demagogue on a throne, forced to conciliate the masses by giving efficacy to their worst desires." Parkman saw no hope for the nation save in a gradual purging and strengthening of the republic. He believed that "a debased and irresponsible suffrage" was at the root of the trouble; but he also blamed the spoils system, which barred the best men from public office in the interests of party. He placed his faith in the return of the better class to public affairs, and urged them to begin with the cities, where "the diseases of the body politic are gathered to a head." "The reform of the cities would be a

long and hopeful step toward the reform of the states and the nation." This essay, while arising from a state of mind that can only
be described as Federalist, and which shows all the Brahmin's
prejudice against immigrants and others who did not share the heritage of Beacon Hill, nevertheless anticipated the good-government
movements later formed in several of the chief American cities by
the very class that Parkman here tried to rally. He also displayed
considerable political insight by recognizing the importance of the
great city political machines at this stage of their development,
when others equally intelligent ignored them for twenty more years,
until their odor became too strong to ignore. But his sermon was
not to the taste of the day, as he indicated in replying to one of
Casgrain's periodic apologies for an unfavorable criticism of his
friend's work:

> I have always recognized in your writings *"la main amie der-*
> *rière le critique"*—so do not imagine for a moment that I am less
> heartily your friend.
>
> Did you get an attack on the sovereign Demos, which I sent
> you? It has drawn on me a good deal of barking and growling,
> and caused me to be branded as "audacious," "a foe of popular
> government," so you see I am shot at from both sides of the line.
> The article in question, however, has been very widely read, and
> has received a great deal of approval as well as denunciation.

But the shot was soon to come in the form of an overwhelming
bombardment from the French side, which Parkman had just dealt
with somewhat condescendingly in an anonymous *Nation* article,
"Mr. Parkman and His Canadian Critics."

After Parkman's visit to Quebec in November 1878, a bitter
newspaper controversy broke out in the French press of Canada
over the rumored intention of Laval University to award him the
honorary degree of *docteur-ès-lettres*. Parkman's friend LeMoine
started the row unwittingly by a letter to *Le Journal de Québec*,
announcing the historian's visit, comparing him with Garneau, Ferland, Bibaud, Faillon, and Laverdière as a great historian of the
Canadian past, and suggesting that he be honored by the Literary
and Historical Society and the Canadian Institute. Jules-Paul Tar-

divel, an ultramontane journalist of hot temper and great hatred for the United States—which had been his own birthplace and his mother's native land—promptly took up the cudgels and applied them to M. LeMoine, for whom he had no great love, and to Parkman. After amusing himself at the expense of LeMoine's tendency to blow his own horn, Tardivel developed a bitter attack upon Parkman:

> Mr. Parkman has permitted himself to insult our race and our religion; he has applied himself to the task of belittling us in the eyes of the world, of shattering our true national glories; he has falsified our history; he has calumnied our priests, above all the Jesuit missionaries, those martyrs of the faith who have watered the Canadian soil with their sweat and their blood.
>
> Mr. Parkman does us justice sometimes; but too often he tortures the facts, presenting them under an entirely false light . . . he falls willingly into exaggeration for the sole end, apparently, of throwing discredit on religion and its ministers. He constantly supports the State against the Church. . . . He represents the first settlers, our ancestors, under the most unfavorable colors. . . . He ridicules the miracles and the prodigies which marked the beginnings of the colony. . . . Priests, remarkable for their sanctity, are fanatics; pious laymen are enthusiasts.
>
> In a word, he, a Protestant and an American, has undertaken to write the history of a country Catholic and French. Not understanding the glorious destiny of the French Canadian people, he has been unable to raise himself above the materialist level. He has made some fine phrases, some well-rounded periods; he has not written a single page of history.

And then Tardivel set himself to picking out texts which would support his charges—no difficult matter since there are plenty of isolated statements in Parkman's books which met his need. So Parkman's slurs on the Jesuits, on Bishop Laval, and on the Church were copied out and interpreted in the worst possible light, with no mention of the statements which balanced them. Tardivel ended up in a fine fury by saying that Parkman was blinded "by prejudices, by a deplorable education, perhaps by hatred," and that there could be nothing in common between such a man and the French Canadians.

The *Journal de Québec* replied to the onslaught with the ingenious charge that Tardivel and another Quebec journalist who had taken up the cudgels in similar fashion had violated an ecclesiastical regulation which forbade criticism of the university, except privately to one of the bishops, in order to avoid public scandal. This was letting the cat out of the bag, for Tardivel was not aware of Laval University's intention, at the instigation of the Abbé Casgrain, the Grand Vicar Cazeau, Dr. La Rue, and others of Parkman's friends in Quebec, to grant an honorary degree to Parkman, and had not, of course, criticized the unexpressed intention of the university to do so. Tardivel made the most of his opening, and asked if the directors of the university really had the intention of honoring "this insulter of the Church." Then the Abbé Casgrain entered the fray in the interest of his friend with an article in the *Courrier du Canada*, which explained that the proposed honor was not intended to endorse all Parkman's ideas, but to give recognition to his work and its real merit. He made the excellent point that "Mr. Parkman is a Protestant, and consequently his works, from the Catholic point of view, are composed of both true and false, of good and bad. . . . To make an impartial judgment on them, it is necessary to consider them as a whole." And then he brought out Parkman's tributes to the Jesuit missionaries and to the Church, as Tardivel had brought out his criticisms. But Tardivel, who clearly was a master of controversy and might have confuted the Pope by quotations from the encyclicals, insisted that the truth lay either on the side of those who admired Parkman's books, or on that of those who condemned them. To him the middle way of the liberal abbé was anathema; for him, there was only a black-and-white choice between evil and good. And layman though he was, he did not refrain from accusing the abbé of theological error and confusion of the roles of priest and critic.

Naturally the anti-clerical papers and the Protestant press were delighted to find the Catholics fighting among themselves, and did their bit to fan the flames. The *Witness* of Montreal pointed out that Parkman's books had been a disagreeable surprise to those

French Canadians who were accustomed to see their early ecclesiastics painted in the pages of Ferland, Faillon, and Laverdière as saints and models of all the virtues; and then went on to praise Parkman for having written of men as they were and of events as they happened. Not content with that, the *Witness* congratulated Laval for having honored so frank a critic. Tardivel and the outraged ultramontane party were brought to the point of apoplexy by such insolence. For actually, of course, the degree had never been awarded, and its bestowal only rumored.

Parkman heard about the row from LeMoine and asked Casgrain to send him the details. In reply he wrote this admirable letter:

50 Chestnut St., Boston, 10 Dec. 1878

Mon cher ami:

I received your letter of the 7th yesterday, and at the same time the journals in which I am attacked by one Tardivel and defended by you. You need not fear that I shall find anything *qui puisse me blesser* in your kind article. I see in it, as in all you have written about me, the hand of a friend, who differs in opinion, but is united in feeling.

This outbreak is a very curious one. So far as I myself am concerned I find it rather amusing and am not annoyed by it in the least. But I regret it extremely on account of the trouble it has given you and Mr. LeMoine; and also on account of the embarrassing position in which I fear it places the University and the excellent ecclesiastics by whom it is directed. It was to me extremely gratifying that men like these, while differing profoundly from me and disapproving much that I have written, should recognize the sincerity of my work by expressing their intention to honor me with a degree of *docteur-ès-lettres*. It was this generous recognition which gave me particular pleasure; and greatly as I should feel honored by a degree from Laval University, I prize still more the proofs of esteem which its directors have already given me. I trust that they will not feel themselves committed to any course which circumstances may have rendered inexpedient, and that they will be guided simply by the interests of the University.

I shall be glad to receive any articles that may appear relating to this matter.

Please remember me to M. Hamel, Mgr. Cazeau, Mgr. Plaquet, and M. Letellier, as well as to Dr. La Rue, if you see him.

With cordial regard,

Faithfully yours,

F. Parkman

Unfortunately the "Tar-Devil," as LeMoine called him, had done his work so well that in the following March the rector of Laval, Monsignor Thomas Hamel, had to write Parkman that he had hoped fanaticism would yield to reason, but "if we persist, we will raise the tempest against us and you." The rector felt that it was better to defer the question of the degree until the excitement had died down. The degree was never awarded, for the fight had been too bitter to be forgotten. McGill University, the stronghold of the Protestant English, stepped in and awarded Parkman its honorary doctorate within a few months, while the Catholics were still fighting among themselves over the question, and by accepting it he convinced the ultramontane party of Quebec that he was on the side of the enemy. His later books did nothing to heal the breach, and as the opposition of historical views became more intense between himself and Casgrain, who had been the chief proponent of the award, leading to a long interruption of their familiar correspondence, the question of a Laval degree was never raised again. It seems more than possible, in the light of Parkman's correspondence with other Canadian friends of views akin to his own, that the incident, however well he took it at the time, strengthened his anticlerical and anti-Catholic feelings in the long run.

With the passage of the years, almost all French Canadian bitterness against Parkman has vanished. Casgrain's early estimate of him is now generally accepted, for it has been recognized that Parkman was a man of good will who stated the truth as he saw it, sincerely, without conscious bias, and without mockery. Parkman's reflections on the French Canadian's deeply cherished religion and civilization naturally cause reservations in praise of him from this quarter, but when Parkman's centenary was celebrated at Montreal in 1923, the historian received fully as much honor from the French Canadian representative as from the English. Parkman is now regarded by all Canadians as the greatest and most eloquent historian of their country's early days.

16: The Last Years

You have had the singular good fortune to complete successfully a great work which puts you at the head of our living historians. . . .

HENRY ADAMS TO F.P., 1892

AFTER the publication of *Frontenac,* Parkman turned his attention to *Montcalm and Wolfe,* the final volume of the series, temporarily putting off the preceding volume in chronological order, *A Half-Century of Conflict.* He had some fear that he might not be able to fulfill his self-appointed task and he wanted to finish the more important work, even if he should be unable to complete the series. Besides, the theme was close to his heart: it was that history of the Old French War which he had dreamed of writing since he was eighteen, and the rest of the series was merely preliminary to it. So in the summer of 1879 he returned to Quebec to examine the battlegrounds on the Plains of Abraham in the company of James LeMoine, and then, equipped with letters of introduction to priests of Cape Breton Island from one of his friends at the Séminaire de Québec, he examined Louisbourg, the great fortress which guarded the mouth of the St. Lawrence and changed hands so many times in the course of the struggle between the French and the English. Then he examined the fortifications of the Acadian peninsula and saw some Micmac Indians, finally returning home by way of St. John, New Brunswick. He had already visited the region of the Minas Basin and Annapolis Royal on an earlier excursion.

In both 1880 and 1881 he spent most of the summer with his sister in Paris and London, hunting out documents and maps. He was no longer an unnoticed figure, and these trips abroad now took on something of the nature of triumphal tours. James Russell Lowell was Minister to the Court of St. James's, and delighted in entertaining his old friend. Henry James, who had a great admiration for Parkman's work, opened the doors of the Reform Club to him;

and the Earl of Carnarvon, who became a good friend of Parkman, gave him a card to that most intellectual of English social institutions, the Athenaeum. At the British Museum the Bullens bade him welcome—Mrs. Bullen had done a good deal of copying for him—and everywhere he was given a warm reception. In Paris he found new friends as well as old, and his works were eulogized in the sacred precincts of the French Academy. His younger daughter, who had married John Templeton Coolidge, Jr., in the fall of 1879, was now a resident of Paris and made him feel at home there. Parkman was particularly fond of this artist son-in-law, who performed many services for him during his residence abroad, and upon his return to the United States insisted on having his company during the summer months at his home in Portsmouth, New Hampshire. Parkman, who was fond of youngsters, enjoyed the company of his four grandchildren thoroughly, even if their occupations sometimes interfered with the progress of his own work. His other daughter had also married in the same year as her sister, so his own household now consisted only of his sister, who devoted her life to furthering his work by acting as his secretary and amanuensis, as well as presiding over his home.

Perhaps this alteration in his family circle had something to do with the role he played in the founding of the St. Botolph Club in Boston, in whose evening gatherings he found the masculine companionship and good fellowship that was always welcome to him. Parkman was one of ten Boston men—including Phillips Brooks, William Dean Howells, and Henry Cabot Lodge—who thought that the city needed a club on the model of the Century Association in New York, which gathered together artists, writers, and professional men from many different fields in the interests of good society. The proposal met with great favor, and Parkman was chosen the first president of the new club. He was extremely faithful in attendance until increasing lameness confined him to his home in the closing years of his life. One of those originally invited to become a member, Edward Everett Hale, proposed at the first meeting that "the use of wines and liquors be interdicted in the clubhouse." The proposal was referred to a committee, and the club's historian remarked: "Incidentally, Edward Everett Hale resigned soon after the club was formed to find more congenial society." Since the patron of the institution was a legendary individual, a Lincolnshire saint who

> . . . loved a friend and a flagon of wine
> When the friend was true and the bottle was fine,

and its first president publicly viewed the temperance movement as the "corrupting force of a prohibition which does not prohibit, which in large communities does not prevent or even diminish drunkenness, but which is the fruitful parent of meanness, fraud, lying, and contempt of law," it would seem that Mr. Hale was well advised.

In the *North American* for October 1879 Parkman published an essay on "The Woman Question" in which he gave a masterly presentation of the arguments against woman suffrage—a movement which remained none too popular for many more years. To him female suffrage was clearly against the order of nature: man was made for war, business, and politics; woman for the home. He brought out the instances in history where women had enjoyed political power, and showed the evil results which sprang from that circumstance. He pointed out the unfitness of the vast majority of women for playing a part in politics, and insisted that the right of voting and the duty of fighting should not be disassociated. And then he brought out again some of his old arguments against universal suffrage. In the eyes of those who shared his views, his article left nothing more to be said by the suffragists, but nevertheless it was said by Julia Ward Howe, T. W. Higginson, Lucy Stone, Elizabeth Cady Stanton, and Wendell Phillips, and Parkman replied to his critics in another article the following January. And finally, nine years later, he published a pamphlet—"printed at the request of an association of women"—which summed up his two former essays, under the title of "Some of the Reasons against Woman Suffrage." Though Parkman's debt to the feminine sex was immeasurable, for it was largely through the aid of women relatives that he was able to work at all, he did not feel that he was neglecting an obligation to them by thus crusading against the suffragists. In view of his general ideas, it is hard to believe that he did not feel he was thus discharging his obligation to the sex.

Montcalm and Wolfe finally appeared in the fall of 1884, after advance chapters had been published in the *Atlantic*. It was the crown of his work, and a worthy one, for he reached the heights of historical writing in this great panorama of a vast struggle. It was recognized by Parkman's critics as his greatest work, even if the public demand called for a first printing of only fifteen hundred copies. Casgrain thought it "epic" and "gripping," even if it proved *"plus hostile à tout qui nous est cher."* Parkman probably valued more highly Henry Adams's tribute:

> 1607 H Street, Washington
> 21 December 1884

My dear Parkman:

Your two volumes on Montcalm and Wolfe, which you were so kind as to send me, deserve much more careful study than I am competent to give them; for my work lies in different times, and throws no light on the colonial period. To say nothing at all when I can say nothing which I think worth saying, has been the rule I have tried to follow in literature; and so far as I can see, you have so thoroughly exhausted your sources as to leave little or nothing new to be said. The book puts you in the front rank of living English historians, and I regret only that the field is self-limited so that you can cultivate it no further. The most curious fact connected with the French colonization seems to me to be its sterility. I do not know that the French Canadians have been more barren in influence than the Pennsylvania Germans; but the overpowering energy of the English stock has absorbed what was useful in both.

Your book is a model of thorough and impartial study and clear statement. Of its style and narrative the highest praise is that they are on a level with its thoroughness of study. Taken as a whole, your works are now dignified by proportions and completeness which can hardly be paralleled by the "literary baggage" of any other historical writer in the language known to me today. George Bancroft has the proportions but not the completeness; for, as I often tell him, he has written the History of the United States in a dozen volumes without reaching his subject. The English are just now poorly off. Except Gardiner and Lecky I know of no considerable English historians besides the old war-horses Freeman and Froude. My favorite John Green was the flower of my generation; and in losing him, I lost the only English writer of history whom I loved personally and historically.

Now that your niche is filled, I hope you will go over all the work. File and burnish. Fill in with all that you can profitably add, and cut out whatever is superfluous. Give us your ripe best, and then swing the whole at the head of the public as a single work. Nothing but mass tells.

My own labor is just half done. Two heavy volumes have been put into type, partly for safety, partly to secure the advantages of a first edition without the publicity. The more I write, the more confident I feel that before long a new school of history will rise which will leave us antiquated. Democracy is the only subject for history. I am satisfied that the purely mechanical development of the human mind in society must appear in a great democracy so clearly, for want of disturbing elements, that in another generation psychology, physiology, and history will join in proving man to have as fixed and necessary development as that of a tree; and almost as unconscious.

Ever truly yrs
Henry Adams

Francis Parkman, Esq.

From George Bancroft, the eighty-four-year-old dean of American historians, who had aided his first labors, Parkman had already received a moving letter:

Washington, D.C., 28 Nov., 1884

Dear Mr. Parkman:

I am delighted at receiving from you under your own hand these two new volumes with which you delight your friends & instruct readers in both worlds. You belong so thoroughly to the same course of life which I have chosen, that I follow your career as a fellow-soldier striving to promote the noblest ends, & I take delight in your honors as much or more than I should my own. You have just every thing, which goes to make an historian: persistency in collecting materials, indefatigable industry in using them, swift discernment of the truth, integrity & intrepidity in giving utterance to truth, a kindly humanity which is essential to the true historian and which gives the key to all hearts, & a clear & graceful & glowing manner of narration. I claim like yourself to have been employed earnestly.

I pray you to hold me to be in all sincerity & affectionate regard

Your fellow-laborer & friend
Geo Bancroft

Francis Parkman, Esq.

In order to revise his account of the French settlements in Florida, as given in the *Pioneers,* Parkman made a two-week trip through this region of the South in March 1885. He stopped first at Beaufort, South Carolina, to examine the site of Port Royal, and then went on to Fernandina and Jacksonville, Florida. The tropical vegetation caught his gardener's eye, and he filled several pages of his little notebook with remarks on its character. From Jacksonville he made excursions to Fort George, Palatka, and St. Augustine, noting always the character of the country, its flora and fauna, and sketching little maps of places of particular historical interest. Twenty years after publishing the book which dealt with this region, he took all these pains in order that he might correct the smallest details. Henry Adams's injunction to "file and burnish" had been taken to heart. Parkman hoped to revise all his books before death put an end to his career, but, with working hours limited by illness, he did not achieve his object completely. He brought out a new edition of *Pontiac* in 1870, of *The Discovery of the Great West* (under the new title of *La Salle*) in 1878, and of the *Pioneers* in 1885. In the very year of his death, 1893, he produced a revised edition of *The Old Regime,* but the *Jesuits, Frontenac, Montcalm and Wolfe,* and *A Half-Century of Conflict* remained in their original form at his death.

Parkman painted the best picture of the difficulties that beset him in his later years in a letter to Dr. S. Weir Mitchell, the great Philadelphia physician and literary man, who enjoyed more of his confidence than any other member of the medical profession:

Jamaica Plain, 5 Nov. 1883

My dear Dr. Mitchell:

I regret to bother you again with my troubles, but as you have done more for me than anybody else, I am tempted to do so.

For about two years I have observed an increasing tendency to insomnia. This autumn, within about two months, it has become extremely troublesome. Sometimes I do not sleep at all. Often I sleep only from one to three hours. The week before last, the average for seven days was about two hours. Last night I heard every clock but those of eleven and twelve. The preceding night, however, I slept—at intervals, and not continuously —to the amount of more than five hours, which was rather rare good luck.

Bromide, etc., produce no effect. . . . Bating sleeplessness and its effects, I have been better than before, with the exception of palpitation of the heart, which is sometimes very troublesome.

Throbbing in the ear at night is also annoying at times. The old distress in the head continues, but has been less distressing within the last few years than before I took your advice. Within the last year I have done a very moderate amount of work, and recently none at all. . . . Muscular strength is not exhausted, but nerves are set on edge, and the condition of the head entirely precludes brainwork. I have occasionally had attacks as severe, or more so —once four successive nights absolutely without sleep—but this is more persistent than any before, and is aggravated by the palpitation of the heart, which I have reason to believe is not from organic causes.

Yours very truly,

F. Parkman

There was little that Dr. Mitchell or any other physician could do to relieve this persistent insomnia. In one of his notebooks Parkman kept a cryptic chart over a period of months, which showed the number of hours of sleep he obtained each night under the influence of various sedatives, and it is clear that he regarded himself as fortunate if he got a full night's sleep once a month. It is not surprising that it took him eight years to fill in the missing link in his chain of histories with *A Half-Century of Conflict,* which did not appear until 1892, for often he had to suspend work for months at a time. And perhaps he did not drive himself quite so hard, for the goal was now in sight. After the publication of *Montcalm and Wolfe* he made fewer contributions to the periodical press, and most of these were brief book reviews which were hardly more than summaries of the works under consideration. His correspondence also dropped off considerably, although he always seemed to find time to reply to an old friend. This slackening of activity would be natural enough in a man of his age, even though not beset by invalidism as Parkman increasingly was.

That the same fire burned within him as in his youth is evident from the expedients he adopted to get relief from the insomnia which the doctors could not quell. In October 1883 he made a six-day horseback trip from Portsmouth to Crawford Notch and back, and with pride wrote Casgrain: "although I am a sixty-year-old grandfather I was not upset by the adventure." In June 1886 he spent a month camping in Canada on the Batiscan, which flows into the St. Lawrence near Trois Rivières. He heartily enjoyed returning to wilderness life after forty years' absence, and he found that he was still a fair shot, though his lame knee confined his shooting to target practice. He took up the art of fly-casting for the first time, and admitted its superiority to the lowly practice of bait-fishing. But canoeing gave him more pleasure than anything else, and he loved to go off on solitary expeditions on the lonely river, studying the forest and the beasts that dwelt there. James Le-Moine came to visit Parkman and his companion C. H. Farnham, at their camp, but for all LeMoine's love for the Canadian wilderness he could not be induced into a canoe excursion: "not being

FRANCIS PARKMAN AT FIFTY-NINE

From a photograph taken in 1882.

From C. H. Farnham's *Francis Parkman,* by permission of the publishers, Little,
Brown & Co.

an expert swimmer, I had to decline the honor of being paddled through the furious eddies of the Batiscan by the most eminent historian of Massachusetts in a canoe evidently intended for one man only." Parkman would have liked to stay at the camp all summer, but his duty as a fellow of Harvard called for his presence in Cambridge on Commencement Day. He had hoped to return to Canada afterward, but that proved impossible, so he contented himself with spending the latter half of the summer at the Bemis Camps on the Rangeley Lakes in Maine, not many miles from the scene of his youthful exploits on the Megalloway. Here he had a cabin built for himself and his sister, hoping that they could go there each summer, but his health never permitted him to return. The great lover of the wilderness had his last taste of it at the age of sixty-three.

His last major journey was to Europe in the summer of 1887 with his old friend Dr. Algernon Coolidge. He had determined to try the effect of the German spas upon his ailments, but shortly after landing at Santander and reaching Madrid, he underwent so severe an attack that he determined to return home at once by way of Paris. After this abortive excursion he never went farther from home than Portsmouth, New Hampshire, where he spent most of every summer with the J. T. Coolidges in the old Benning Wentworth Mansion at Little Harbor, whose historic walls were an appropriate shelter for the historian of pre-revolutionary America. Insomnia and lameness compelled him in 1888 to renounce one of his cherished honors, his office of fellow of the Corporation of Harvard. A letter to the Abbé Casgrain in the spring of the following year gives his own view of his case:

For the past 5 years I have done very little historical work, not so much from laziness as from the effects of insomnia. Two or three hours of sleep in the 24—which have been until lately my average allowance for long periods together—are not enough to wind up the human machine, especially when exercise is abridged by hereditary gout mixed with rheumatism, produced, according to the doctors, by numerous drenchings in the forests of Maine when I was a collegian (e.g., on one occasion, rain without shelter for 3 days and nights, just after being wrecked in a rapid of the River Megalloway).

Perhaps, however, the rheumatism is a stroke of retributive justice for writing *Montcalm and Wolfe*. Though I have slept better in the past year, it is still an open question whether I shall ever manage to supply the missing link between that objectionable work and its predecessor, *Count Frontenac.*

Despite his preoccupation with fulfilling his task, he could spare time to cheer on the abbé in his publication of a collection of manuscripts concerning the Chevalier de Lévis, Montcalm's aide in the death struggle of New France. The abbé had discovered the papers in Paris in the possession of a descendant of the chevalier, and arranged for their publication in eleven volumes in Quebec at the expense of the Provincial Government. Parkman gave what aid he could, and wrote an introduction for the volume containing Montcalm's letters to Bourlamaque, as well as those of the latter to Lévis. He also guided the abbé through the maze of archives in France and England which he knew so well.

Whatever the state of his health and however busy he might be with his own concerns, Parkman always found time to help fellow-workers. He wrote many letters of advice to William Kingsford of Ottawa, while the latter was preparing his monumental *History of Canada,* and aided Douglas Brymner in his great work as the first archivist of the Dominion. A list of Parkman's correspondents would include the name of almost every historical worker in Canada. He was even called upon to help determine the western boundary of Ontario by the provincial attorney-general, Oliver Mowat. He also found time to further the researches of those engaged in research in allied fields: he was in large measure responsible for the archaeological work of Adolph Bandelier in the Southwest and Mexico and of Captain John Bourke on the Indians. He gave money as well as time and influence to both these projects, although neither could be expected to benefit his own work. But though he was kindness itself to aspiring historians and scholars, he was still ruthless in dealing with historical fakers. In 1886 one such appeared in Boston with portraits of Washington and Alexander Hamilton and other revolutionary notables, supposedly the work of the painter Sharpless. This Major James Walter, who asserted that the paintings were heirlooms of his family, was not content with taking in a goodly sum at exhibitions in New York, Philadelphia, and Boston, but tried to top off his swindle by selling the portraits to the Massachusetts Historical Society. In support of their authenticity he produced letters from Washington, Colonel Trumbull, Albert Gallatin, Washington Irving, and R. W. Emerson. Parkman was commissioned by the Historical Society to prepare a report on the matter, which he did with considerable energy, branding the portraits as unauthentic, the letters as clumsy forgeries, and Major Walter as a swindler. The major seems to have been something of a psychopathic case, for he admitted his guilt partially, and then begged the head of the society to show mercy by paying his debts and enabling him to return home! And some years later, when safe in England, he tried to reopen the matter, demanding a second hearing in which new proofs of the portraits' authenticity would clear his good name, so grievously soiled by the society's report.

These years were also embittered by a feud with the Abbé Casgrain over the Acadian question, which came to a head with Parkman's review in the *Nation* for March 14, 1889, of Casgrain's *Un Pèlerinage au Pays d'Evangéline*. The book was the culmination of the abbé's efforts to refute Parkman's two Acadian chapters in *Montcalm and Wolfe*. The question of the removal of the Acadians by the English, as a result of their refusal to be good British citizens, is still a thorny one, confused by Longfellow's sentimentalization of the matter. In Parkman's time there were two schools of thought: the English, which he adopted and in which he was supported by Sir Adams Archibald, president of the Nova Scotian Historical Society and a former governor of the province, and the French, of which the leading supported was Casgrain, backed by Rameau de St. Pierre and M. Richard. Parkman based his view largely upon the collection of historical documents edited by Thomas Atkins of the Nova Scotian Archives. Casgrain, by industrious research, demonstrated that Atkins bowdlerized the evidence, and modern historians tend to accept more of his view of the matter than of Parkman's. But Parkman, upon the evidence at hand, decided that his view was the correct one, and at first was amused by Casgrain's efforts to disprove it. In reviewing Casgrain's argument for the *Nation,* he wrote with some condescension:

> He has chosen to make the question a national and religious one, and hence the remarkable heat with which he has pursued his task; a difficult one in view of the awkward circumstance that Mr. Parkman not only stated unwelcome truths, but proved them by unanswerable French and Catholic evidence.

Of course the question was nothing if not national and religious, for Parkman held that the Acadians, who were French, refused to accept English rule, and that they were led to revolt against it by their priests, whose role, as he paints it, was that of unscrupulous political agitators. In such circumstances, Casgrain's emotional temperament was apt to lead him astray, but Parkman's increasing bias against Catholicism and its clergy—shown in an 1890 pamphlet on "Our Common Schools," which defended the public school system and deplored the rise of parochial institutions—was also apt to influence his judgment of historical evidence, as is quite evident in his last work, *A Half-Century of Conflict.* Parkman rested on the sources already available to him; Casgrain found much new evidence by ransacking the Archives of the Marine and Colonies in Paris and the British Museum and the Public Record Office in London, and reported on it in a series of articles in a Canadian review, then in several papers read before the Royal Society of Canada, then in another series of articles, and finally compiled his whole case in *Un Pèlerinage.* The book was impressive enough to cause Parkman to abandon partially his view that the Acadians got their just deserts, and to remark: "The truth is that the treatment of the Acadians was a scandal on both sides." The coldness that had interrupted the friendship and correspondence of the two men for four years soon broke down after this admission, and Parkman wrote the most intimate letters of his last years to his old friend and enemy. Their tone is indicated by the following response to Casgrain's offer to bury the hatchet:

Old Wentworth Mansion
Portsmouth, N. H.
(Care of Mr. J. T. Coolidge)
14 Aug. 1890

My dear Abbé:

I was very glad indeed to get a letter from you. It reached me today, in this curious old colonial house, built in 1750 by Benning Wentworth, governor of New Hampshire. It now belongs to my son-in-law, J. T. Coolidge, and I usually spend most of the summer here. Being on the seashore, about 2 miles from the town, in a beautiful situation, and with some 30 acres of land attached to it, it makes a pleasant summer retreat. Though the house is large, my daughter and her four children—two of whom were born in France, and, till lately, spoke only French—make it lively enough. About a mile distant is the still older house of Sir William Pepperell, who commanded the expedition against Louisbourg in 1745.

I was much interested to see that your letter was written in part from Lake George, which has been a favorite resort of mine since I was a boy in college, when I spent two or three weeks there visiting the historical localities. I am glad to know that the ruins of Fort William Henry still exist. There was danger, when I saw them last, that vandals in the shape of directors of a railroad company would get possession of them and destroy them for their own stupid purposes.

❧   ❧   ❧   ❧

I am still engaged on the remaining volume of my series (1700–1748), which has given me more trouble than any of the others, from the want of unity in the subject, and the difficulty of weaving its complex parts into a continuous narrative. It draws, however, towards an end.

❧   ❧   ❧   ❧

My work has been extremely retarded by a poor state of health, arising chiefly from severe and persistent insomnia. Hoping to hear favorable accounts of your health and your sight,

> I remain,
> Yours very truly,
> F. Parkman.

Casgrain hastened to reply with an account of his visit to Lake St. John, at the head of the Saguenay, and the marvelous fishing there, which Parkman wished he could have shared with his friend, having been told that "the winonishe [ouananiche] are almost unequaled as a game fish." That fall the letters went back and forth almost weekly, and Parkman offered his help in the editing of the Lévis papers on which the abbé was then engaged. Early in 1891 the latter went abroad, equipped with a letter of introduction to the English owner of the Montcalm-Bourlamaque letters which Parkman had examined ten years before. After the abbé's return Parkman followed the progress of the work as closely as if it had been his own, and took great pleasure in the volumes which the abbé sent him as they came from the press. Their last exchange of letters, in the fall of 1892, was concerned with Lake George, which the abbé had just visited with his brother:

Jamaica Plain, 30 Sept.

My dear Abbé:

I was very glad to hear that you and your brother were so agreeably employed at a place to which I have always been especially attached, though I should be glad to have the big hotel and, above all, the railroad swept out of existence—from which, I suppose, you will conclude that I am a bad American—which is true inasmuch as I do not pin my faith on railroads and steam engines.

If I do not mistake, the Lake House is the old inn of Caldwell from which my friend White and I set out in June 1842 to circumnavigate and explore the lake in a rowboat. White did not sympathize with my ideas, and was sometimes rather disgusted at my persistency in searching after localities for which he did not care a pin.

I have not got *Le Voyage de Franquet* except in MS. extracts, and very gladly accept your kind and obliging offer. With warmest good wishes,

> Yours very truly,
> F. Parkman

To which letter mourning the old order Casgrain made an amusing reply:

> *Quebec, 3 Oct. 1892*

My dear historian,

Why was I not in your boat instead of your friend White? With what eagerness I would have shared your researches at Lake George; I would have searched the creeks, the promontories, and established each place marked by a memory. Lake House is probably the same inn as before, but become a grand hotel.

I am more American than you in regard to modern life. I swear to you that I was charmed by the new aspect of Lake George. The fashionable American set has respected the forest vegetation: Lake St. Sacrement retains its savage character. Rogers and Marin, Putnam and Langy could still fire shots from the thickets. Only, instead of the warwhoop, the air resounds with the whistles of locomotives and steamers. It is more prosaic, but less bloody.

The islands of the Narrows and the most picturesque places on the shores, always wooded, are ornamented with cottages and summer houses, designed and painted evidently by artists. It is a charming sight to see the elegant world pass in the avenues, half hidden by the handsome homes, or on the lake in small boats with sails of purple, blue, or white.

I do not think more of this exterior splendor than you, but it has its good side. It is like the cockle in the wheatfields: it produces nothing, but it pleases the eye.

Your letter suggests another reflection to me. In recalling the scenes of Fenimore Cooper and in reading Prescott's *Conquest of Mexico,* I said to myself, that these two writers paled beside you. . . .

I remain, as always, yours with all my heart,

H. R. Casgrain, Priest.

Parkman could not accept the abbé's view, and in his reply he railed at the *"nouveau riche,* who is one of the pests of this country"*: "*For my part, I would gladly destroy all his works and restore Lake George to its native savagery—which shows plainly that you are a better American than I am." And so closed a correspondence which had been carried on for nearly thirty years.

The abbé received one more token of friendship from Parkman, however: an inscribed copy of the new edition of *The Oregon Trail,* with illustrations by Frederic Remington. In correspondence with Parkman about the scenes to be illustrated, Remington, who knew the West as well as Parkman and fully valued his account of it, made an acute comment: "I believe that you have 'blazed a trail' which will produce a romantic literature and an art in America— the French period—the most romantic of all. You can see it coming." The comment was one worthy of a first-rate literary critic. G. A. Henty, Conan Doyle, Mary Hartwell Catherwood, and others made use of Parkman's work in their novels, and surely the recent flood of historical novels on colonial and revolutionary themes owes something to Parkman.

Beset by rheumatism and insomnia, often condemned to be *"plutôt pêcheur qu'écrivain,"* as he wrote Pierre Margry—he spent much time fishing at Little Harbor and Jamaica Pond—Parkman struggled on until *A Half-Century of Conflict* was finished in March 1892, and with it his great historical epic. The book is one of the weakest links in the chain: it not only lacks unity, as he saw himself, but the old dramatic command of narrative is missing, though the work is done as carefully as before. There is, too, an unfortunate tendency to editorialize, for Parkman gives his anti-democratic, anti-clerical, and anti-Jesuit feelings play when there is no occasion for their appearance. His Acadian chapters are marked by the bitterness of his struggle with Casgrain and others of the opposing party on that question. The great history was written, however, in the face of all the probabilities against its completion. Parkman permitted himself only a brief comment in the closing paragraph of the preface:

The manuscript material collected for the preparation of the series now complete forms about seventy volumes, most of them folios. These have been given by me from time to time to the Massachusetts Historical Society, in whose library they now are, open to the examination of those interested in the subjects of which they treat. The collection was begun forty-five years ago, and its formation has been exceedingly slow, having been retarded by difficulties which seemed insurmountable, and for years were so in fact. Hence the completion of the series has required twice the time that would have sufficed under less unfavorable conditions.

In submitting to the *Atlantic* an article on "The Feudal Chieftains of Acadia," which appeared in the revised edition of *The Old Regime,* Parkman was reminded of the length of his task, and how it had dragged on under "unfavorable conditions." Horace Scudder accepted the chapters with pleasure and the comment: "It gives me quite a sense of the stability of the *Atlantic* to find a contribution asked for by my first predecessor turning up thirty-five years afterward, and just as appropriate to the magazine now as when solicited!" But Parkman was still more pleased by the tribute paid him by Henry Adams:

1603 H Street
1 June 1892

My dear Cousin:

Your two volumes have lain on my table only long enough for me to read them before sending my acknowledgment. You have had the singular good fortune to complete successfully a great work which puts you at the head of our living historians; and I leave the dead ones out of account only because we cold-blooded Yanks detest the appearance of exaggeration so much more than we love what the French call *mesure.* Let the dead rest in peace, but pray accept my warm congratulations on your arrival.

Certainly it is an event in our literary history, and I wish you had been here to celebrate it with me, who am probably about the only man who has in this country grown sufficiently weary in the same service to join in the celebration in a thoroughly religious and penitent spirit. To be sure, I have none of your courage, for I have not even preserved enough self-respect to express so much as an opinion about our society or its tendencies. With abject selfishness, I recognize that our society has been much more civil to me than I deserve, and I feel grateful to it for leaving me alone. You hold up a higher ideal, and have worked in a more generous spirit. Peace be with you.

Ever yrs

Henry Adams

Francis Parkman, Esq.

Another writer did not hesitate to disturb the dead by making comparisons. Young Theodore Roosevelt, who had dedicated his *Winning of the West* to Parkman in the opinion that "your works stand alone, and that they must be models for all historical treatment of the founding of new communities and the growth of the frontier here in the wilderness," found it difficult to say anything about *A Half-Century of Conflict* "without seeming to use overstrained language. It must have been rather hard for anyone to whom Gibbon, for instance, sent his work to find perfectly fit words to use in acknowledging the gift." There was a great flood of such letters from fellow-historians, friends, and admirers, and surely in them Parkman found some compensation for his long struggle.

He had to put aside the project of revising the whole epic, and strengthening its connections so that the whole should be clearly one work, for the few months that were left to him were not blessed by good health. He spent his last summer lazily at the Wentworth Mansion, fishing or dreaming about the early days of Portsmouth as he drifted about Little Harbor in his boat. In the fall he returned to his beloved home on the shores of Jamaica Pond, where he celebrated his seventieth birthday among his flowers and his friends. His estate had been condemned to make way for the Jamaica Pond

Parkway, but the City of Boston ordained that Parkman was to be undisturbed as long as he lived. Even then he still enjoyed rowing about the pond, and it was upon returning from such an expedition that he felt ill and took to his bed. Peritonitis set in, and he died calmly, after three days' illness, on November 8, 1893. He eased his last suffering by reading *Childe Harold* once more, and with his last words he described a dream he had had about killing a bear. His last thought was of the American wilderness which he had loved so well and which he had immortalized for those who could know it only on the printed page.

Boston outdid itself to honor the passing of the last and one of the greatest of its Brahmins. His funeral took place at King's Chapel. Half his surviving classmates at Harvard were present, and the pall-bearers were old friends and associates: John Lowell, Martin Brimmer, Daniel Denison Slade, George Silsbee Hale, John Quincy Adams, Charles Sprague Sargent, and Edward Wheelwright. The Massachusetts Historical Society held a special meeting in honor of its most distinguished member on November 21, at which Dr. Ellis opened and read Parkman's autobiographical letter, written in 1864 and confided to him in 1868 under a cover marked "not to be used during my life." This account, written in the third person, was the first revelation of the odds that Parkman had faced and overcome, and its simple statement of facts is more eloquent than any of the panegyrics on that or later occasions. For days the newspapers were full of accounts of his life, and within a few months of his death every magazine of note in the country paid tribute to him. Harvard held a special commemorative service in his honor on December 6 in Sanders Theater, where Parkman had received the honorary degree of doctor of letters four years before, and where at so many Commencements he had sat on the platform as a fellow or an overseer of his university. President Eliot, Justin Winsor, and John Fiske paid tribute to Harvard's distinguished son. His fellow-historian, Professor Fiske, closed his address thus:

> The memory of a life so strong and beautiful is a precious possession for us all.

As for the book on which he labored with such marvelous

heroism, a word may be said in conclusion. Great in his natural powers and great in the use he made of them, Parkman was no less great in his occasion and his theme. Of all the American historians he is the most deeply and peculiarly American, yet he is at the same time the broadest and the most cosmopolitan. The book which depicts at once the social life of the Stone Age, and the victory of the English political ideal over the ideal which France inherited from imperial Rome, is a book for all mankind and for all time. Strong in its individuality, and like to nothing else, it clearly belongs among the world's few masterpieces of the highest rank, along with the works of Herodotus, Thucydides, and Gibbon.

Fiske justly referred to Parkman's series as a book, for a book it is, though one of many parts. Volume after volume carries on the story from the dawn of French colonization in America until its eclipse with the English conquest of Canada. The first, *Pioneers of France in the New World,* covers the abortive settlement of Florida by the French and the enduring labors of Champlain and his associates in Canada in the sixteenth century. The second, *The Jesuits in North America,* carries the story on into the seventeenth century with its account of the missionaries' great but short-lived effort to convert the Indians. The third, *La Salle and the Discovery of the Great West,* is the story of the exploration and first colonization of the Great Lakes and the Mississippi Valley. The fourth, *The Old Regime in Canada,* falls into three parts: the first dealing with the feudal era of Canada, the second with Canada as a mission field, and the third with the royal exploitation of New France in the interest of the mother country. The fifth, *Count Frontenac and New France under Louis XIV,* is an account of the colony in its heyday, with the conflict between state and church already straining its shaky structure. The sixth, *A Half-Century of Conflict,* covers the years between 1700 and 1748, which were filled with the border strife that marked the opening of the struggle to the death between New France and the English colonies which it almost encircled. The seventh and last, *Montcalm and Wolfe,* is the story of the conflict itself, which ended with the downfall of New

France on the Plains of Abraham in 1759. *The Conspiracy of Pontiac,* though not formally a part of the great history, fills out the story of the English conquest with its account of the subsequent great Indian uprising against the new rulers of North America. The whole constitutes the story of the conflict of two great European systems in the colonial field, and of the sources of a new civilization which was shortly to rival those of the Old World. To Parkman the struggle was one between liberty and absolutism, and so it was to a certain extent. But in less than two decades after its close France, his symbol of absolutism, was to aid the liberty-loving English colonies to wrest their freedom from that England which he viewed as the guardian of the rights of freemen. The struggle in America was intricately involved with the struggle for power in Europe, and one of Parkman's great historical contributions was the demonstration that obscure events in America had a vital effect on the course of history in Europe, as those in Europe did in America. Acquaintance with Parkman's great history is essential to every American and every Canadian who wants to understand his heritage, but it is also vital to all who wish to form a clear picture of world history, both in the past and today. The struggle between liberty and absolutism has not yet been concluded, and there are lessons to be learned from the past.

Epilogue

THE passing of nearly half a century since Parkman's death has both clarified and obscured his greatness. His books are more widely read than those of any other American historian of his period, and the historical value of his work has suffered little in the light of fifty years' research. Yet the triumph of the scientific school of historiography over the romantic and rhetorical has tended to place him in the shade, along with Motley and Prescott, in the minds of those who are not especially concerned with his field. He died at the summit of his career, and he was mourned almost fulsomely by his contemporaries, who saw in his passing the close of New England's great age. Those who came after have been suspicious of the critical verdicts of that age, and in the main justly so, for in instance after instance time has made radical changes in them. Despite the fact that Parkman's reputation has weathered the years with less loss of luster than has fallen to the lot of most of the great American names of the nineteenth century, it is by no means unnecessary today to point out once more his achievement and its nature.

As we look back over the period from the vantage point of today, it is difficult to avoid the foreshortening effect of our perspective; it is hard to grasp how original and how fresh Parkman's work was in its own day, and how nearly it approximated our modern notion of how history should be written. Parkman came close behind the pioneer writers of American history. He formed his great plan just three years after Jared Sparks filled the first chair of history ever established in any American college. The old classical discipline was then just beginning to relax sufficiently to permit the entrance of other subjects, considered basic today, into the academic curriculum. Prescott made his name by publishing *Ferdinand and Isabella* in 1838. The first volume of Bancroft's *History of the United States* had appeared four years before. Motley, almost exactly Parkman's contemporary, did not publish his first historical work until five years after the appearance of *Pontiac*. History was not an overcrowded or a popular literary field. Bancroft's measure of success was due in good part to his political prominence: there was virtually no interest in American history. Prescott and Motley for years attracted infinitely greater audiences with their works on Spanish and Dutch subjects than Parkman could hope to win with his accounts of the American past. The average American had no interest in his heritage, certainly none in the period before the Revolution, whose story had grown familiar to him through many retellings in the eagle-screaming orations which were long the core of Fourth of July celebrations. The American of the middle years of the nineteenth century still looked across the Atlantic, if he were of a literary or a scholarly turn of mind; in many respects his point of view was European. His taste in history was for works that made him more familiar with the European tradition. Parkman was the first to see the importance of the wilderness struggles which made America; the first to recognize that they were not mere backwoods skirmishes but conflicts of more than local importance and with considerable influence on the course of events in the European world. And to the task of chronicling this forgotten chapter of history he brought great gifts and a new historical method.

Parkman's contempt for "emasculate scholarship," for the moralizing, dogma-ridden writing of the ministerial New England past, was based upon his perception of the truth stated epigrammatically by a French statesman and historian: *"Ecrire l'histoire, c'est agir; et c'est pourquoi il convient que l'historien soit homme d'action."* With that principle in mind, he prepared himself for his chosen task perhaps more thoroughly than any other historian has ever done, not only studying every printed and manuscript record that he could lay his hands on, but familiarizing himself at first hand with every scene of action and actually living, as far as possible, the same life as the people of his drama had led. Despite his training under Jared Sparks, who was a product of the old New England order, he largely refrained from sentimental moralizing, and he was quite incapable of consciously shaping his narrative to a predetermined view. He exhausted himself and his personal resources in the service of historical integrity: he could not be content to write a page until he had mastered the most primary of sources, and he was highly scrupulous in his use of the materials which he amassed with great trouble and expense. He had the prejudices and biases of his environment and upbringing, but in great measure his honesty and thoroughness enabled him to overcome this disadvantage.

In addition to his thorough research and a distrust of secondary sources very rare in his period, he had the advantage of being a great writer—a talent only too rare among modern scientific historians. He could and did make his books better reading than the novels of the day without detracting a whit from their historical accuracy. There is no other explanation but sheer genius for his ability to reduce the conclusions of years of study of dusty documents and garbled accounts to a narrative of remarkable clarity and vigor. When it is considered that he was a pioneer in his chosen field, and had to make his own framework for his great narrative, establishing the outline of events, their connections and interrelations, and the relative importance of the roles played by the various figures of the drama, his achievement becomes still more remarkable. Parkman was at once the researcher, the monographist, the compiler, and the popularizer. Few historians today would care to attempt to combine all these roles.

It is no longer the fashion to write history in terms of great men, and to confine oneself to the chronicling of political and military events. But Parkman was writing the history of a colony whose destinies were absolutely controlled by a handful of men, and so his tendency to think of history in terms of individuals rather than masses and forces did not mislead him. To a very great extent New France was Champlain, La Salle, Frontenac, Laval, Bigot, or Montcalm in the several periods of those men's power. A decade before the effect of the new German school of history was felt in America, Parkman was devoting a whole book to the economic and social factors in the history of New France, and in his other works he did not neglect the effect of such economic factors as the fur trade on Canadian life. For a pioneer he did a remarkably thorough, detailed, and well-rounded piece of work, whose general outlines have not been changed and whose details have been corrected in only a few instances by later historians working in a different spirit and with a broader view of their subject. And his personal experiences enabled him to vitalize his accounts of such dry matters as tribal divisions and land tenure in a way that is seldom encountered today.

What Thackeray said of Macaulay might well be said of Parkman: "He reads twenty books to write a sentence; he travels a hundred miles to make a line of description." But all this painstaking labor was concealed in the final product; its results were fused into a lively narrative through Parkman's great literary gifts. Parkman's books offer a sharp contrast to most of the productions of the new scientific school of history, for the new historians are content to present the findings of their research without much concern for literary values. The tendency, in fact, has been to disparage style as a popularizer's trick used to conceal inadequate research. But the new historian here runs head-on into a literary problem: that of communication. All the research in the world, no matter how conscientious and scholarly, is of little value unless its results can be conveyed to the reader. The inability of the majority of modern historians to combine the roles of researcher and writer has brought about a vast decline in the reading of history. History, like the physical sciences, has largely become the private preserve of specialists: the layman is barred by his unfamiliarity with the professional jargon and by the specialist's inability or unwillingness to make his conclusions readily available to the general reader. Perhaps this condition has something to do with the increased popularity of biography, which humanizes the past in the way that the old history used to do. To a very great extent, biography has supplanted history, of which it used to be the raw material and the ally, in the favor of the general reader.

Parkman had one great literary advantage over the modern historian: in his day history was not regarded as the record of all man's activities. Economic, social, and cultural events were not given the same importance that they are today in connection with political and military occurrences. Parkman did not face the problem of composing a chronological narrative which would unite and relate the advances and declines in many different fields. And though his talent for construction was great, it is clear from the evidence of

The Old Regime that he would have shared the modern historian's inability to solve the problem satisfactorily. Even though he generally confined himself to political and military events, he needed a central figure around which to build his narrative. When such a protagonist was lacking, as in *A Half-Century of Conflict,* his work lost unity and clear and logical structure. His tendency to think of history in terms of eras dominated by one individual was one great literary asset; another asset was his physical handicap. Debarred from making much use of his eyes, he had to digest his materials thoroughly and arrange them in his mind before beginning to write. Without a preconceived outline, the tortoise-like method of composition forced upon him would soon have involved him in hopeless confusion. But driven as he was by a passion for his subject which ruled out almost all other considerations, and possessed of great mental energy, he used his enforced solitude and sleepless nights for mental composition, so that when he began to dictate a book, he was able to do so without halts for reference and in such finished form that few corrections were required. While his powers of memory were not those of Prescott, who could keep sixty pages in his head for several days, they were remarkable enough; for it was his practice to digest materials and take mental notes years before he wrote the books based upon them, and yet he used hardly any written notes or outlines. Generally his documents and reference works are annotated only with symbols calling attention to various important points, and again with a mark indicating that the material has been used. All the modern historian's cumbersome apparatus of filing cards and cabinets has produced no more accurate or detailed results.

Parkman also had the personal and literary qualifications for being a great writer of history. He believed so thoroughly in himself that he did not feel it necessary to parade all the factors that went into the making of his conclusions, though he was always ready to reveal them to fellow-students concerned about some point. After *Pontiac,* his first historical work, he did not load down his books with presentations of all his data and citations of all his authorities. He merely made it clear that he had been at great pains to ascertain all the facts, mentioned his chief sources of information, and then assumed the reader's confidence in his thoroughness and integrity, without continually producing his raw materials as so many modern pedants feel obliged to do. He had the literary taste to know when a quotation from a source would increase the flavor and color of his narrative, and when it was better presented in digested form. He was artist enough to be able to cloak his facts with the life that makes them stick in the reader's mind. A comparison of passages on the same topic from George Bancroft and from Parkman reveals the great difference between the historical pedant and the historical artist. In Bancroft most of the facts are to be found and the style is correct enough, but the narrative is lifeless; in Parkman the facts take on new meaning and become memorable through the warm life with which they are infused. Yet Parkman is a far more reliable historian, factually, than Bancroft.

In one respect Parkman fell short of the highest level of historical writing. *France and England in North America,* as a whole, lacks the sweep and majestic perspective of a whole period which such a masterwork as Gibbon's *Decline and Fall* possesses. The criticism may be unjustified, since Parkman was conscious of the necessity of tying the whole work together in the manner that his friend Henry Adams recommended, and was only prevented from doing so by ill health and death. But it remains dubious whether he could ever have accomplished his object, even if he had had the opportunity. History may be "a compound of innumerable biographies," as Parkman undoubtedly felt that it was, but he lacked both the philosophical equipment to concoct that compound on a large scale and the interpretive ability to draw general conclusions from it once it was made. Devoted to the great-man theory of history, he could hardly be expected to sense the laws of social evolution, to see, as Spencer put it, "that the forces which mold society work out their results apart from, and often in spite of, the aims of the leading men." He was an artist, not a sociologist, and he viewed his subjects pictorially, in much the same manner as the sculptors and painters of the period did theirs.

Parkman is notable for his detachment among his historical contemporaries, but he would hardly be considered the model of the impartial historian today. He was a New Englander of New

Englanders, and his heritage marked his opinions and ways of thought irrevocably. He was also a product of the romantic era, and though he shed some of his early Byronic romanticism as he grew older, he never lost it entirely. He began his work in the conscious belief that the story of New France demonstrated the innate superiority of the civilization of Protestant England over that of Catholic France, and such remained his view at the close of his career, though he had penned passages which indicate more than a little doubt about the principle in certain instances. *The Oregon Trail* shows how little capable this New Englander was of understanding the West of his own day, and there are evidences of such astigmatism in his treatment of western topics in the histories. Parkman cherished his ideal of the Indian and of the frontiersman and of the life they led, but his environment made him recoil before the reality. Conscious supporter that he was of the doctrine of Anglo-Saxonism, of the innate superiority of the plain man of English blood and Protestant faith to men of another race and creed, his own tastes made him sympathize with those of his characters who displayed the aristocratic virtues, who represented a mature European civilization rather than a raw and callow American one, despite their Latin blood and religion. Puritan that he was, he disliked the Puritans most cordially; republican that he was, he loathed democracy and fought its growing influence. For all the insight that his lifetime's labor gave him into the making of American democracy, he remained a Brahmin, shocked and grieved in his later years by the course that the country was following. Long buried in his work and isolated by his illness and his means, at his death he was already a monument to a vanished era and an anachronism. He was the last of the Brahmins; the last of that goodly company who did so much to make the name of Boston as the cultural capital of a young country and as the center of a civilization which was not to be that of the country as a whole. The enduring worth of the books he left behind him is such as to entitle him to recognition not only as the last but the greatest of that caste which has set its stamp upon our way of life.

Bibliographical Note

An exhaustive bibliography would be superfluous, since an adequate critical one may be found in Wilbur L. Schramm's *Francis Parkman*, a useful volume of representative selections (American Writers Series. New York: American Book Co., 1938). The following list is therefore confined to Parkman's published writings, of which a fuller account is now possible.

Most of Parkman's manuscripts—journals, letters, and historical papers—are in the Massachusetts Historical Society. Other manuscripts are widely scattered among private owners and the libraries mentioned in the preface. So far as he may, the author will gladly answer inquiries from students as to the location of manuscripts referred to in the text. Many letters have been printed in the biographies by Farnham and Sedgwick; more are available in Don C. Seitz's *Letters from Francis Parkman to E. G. Squier* (Cedar Rapids, Iowa: Torch Press, 1911) and in John Spencer Bassett's *Letters of Parkman to Pierre Margry* (*Smith College Studies in History*, VIII, Nos. 3 & 4, April–July 1923). Both collections are regrettably incomplete.

Of the great mass of biographical and critical literature on Parkman—much of it repetitious—the following titles have proved most useful as supplements to the manuscripts upon which this book is based:

Farnham, C. H. *A Life of Francis Parkman*. Boston: Little, Brown, 1900.
Sedgwick, H. D. *Francis Parkman*. American Men of Letters Series. Boston: Houghton Mifflin, 1904.
Wheelwright, Edward. "Memoir of Francis Parkman." *Publications of Colonial Society of Massachusetts*, I, 304–5. 1894.
Casgrain, H. R. "Francis Parkman." *Biographies Canadiennes*. Montreal, 1885.
Gould, G. M. *Biographic Clinics*. Philadelphia, 1904.
Fiske, John. *A Century of Science and Other Essays*. Boston: Houghton Mifflin, 1899.
Wrong, G. M., "Francis Parkman," *Canadian Historical Review*, December 1923.
Parkman Centenary Celebration at Montreal. Montreal: McGill Univ., 1923.

I. BOOKS

(Volumes of *France and England in North America* are numbered according to their place in the series, but listed in order of publication.)

The California and Oregon Trail. New York: Putnam, 1849. (For magazine version, see under the *Knickerbocker*). Later published as *Prairie and Rocky Mountain Life* and after 1872 as *The Oregon Trail*.
History of the Conspiracy of Pontiac. Boston: Little and Brown, 1851.
Vassall Morton: A Novel. Boston: Phillips, Sampson, 1856.
I. *Pioneers of France in the New World*. Boston: Little, Brown, 1865. Advance chapters in *Atlantic Monthly* for July, August, November 1863 and November 1865 (XII, 30–5, 225–40, 537–55; XIV, 530–7).
The Book of Roses. Boston: Tilton, 1866.
II. *The Jesuits in North America in the Seventeenth Century*. Boston: Little, Brown, 1867. Advance chapters in *Atlantic Monthly* for June 1867 (XIX, 723–31).
III. *The Discovery of the Great West*. Boston: Little, Brown, 1869. Published after 1879 as *La Salle and the Discovery of the Great West*.
IV. *The Old Regime in Canada*. Boston: Little, Brown, 1874. Advance chapters in *Atlantic Monthly* for December, 1872; July, December 1873 (XXX, 687–701; XXXII, 84–91, 691–8); and in *North American Review* for April 1874 (CXVIII, 225–55). Advance chapters of revised edition in *Atlantic Monthly* for January, February 1893 (LXXI, 25–31, 201–13).

V. *Count Frontenac and New France Under Louis XIV.* Boston: Little, Brown, 1877. Advance chapters in *Atlantic Monthly* for December 1876 (LIII, 719–32).

VI. *A Half Century of Conflict.* Boston: Little, Brown, 1892. Advance chapters in *Atlantic Monthly* for June 1888 and March, April, May 1891 (LXI, 783–93; LXVII, 314–25, 514–23, 621–30).

VII. *Montcalm and Wolfe.* Boston: Little, Brown, 1884. Advance chapters in *Atlantic Monthly* for September, October 1884 (LIV, 339–51, 444–56).

Parkman wrote the articles on Frontenac, La Salle, and Montcalm in *Appleton's Cyclopedia of American Biography* (1866–7).

He wrote the preface and revised the translation of a sketch of General Bouquet for *William Smith's Historical Account of Bouquet's Expedition against the Ohio Indians.* Cincinnati: Carter, 1868.

Many of Parkman's contributions to periodicals appeared as pamphlets in small editions. To be distinguished from these are the following:

Some of the Reasons against Woman Suffrage. Printed at the request of an association of women, n.d. (1887).
Our Common Schools. Boston: Citizens' Public School Union, 1890.
An Open Letter to a Temperance Friend. n.d.

II. PERIODICALS

The *Knickerbocker Magazine*

March 1845, "The Ranger's Adventure," XXV, 198–201.
April 1845, "The Scalp Hunter," XXV, 297–303.
June 1845, "A Fragment of Family History," XXV, 504–18.
August 1845, "The New Hampshire Ranger," XXVI, 146–8.
December 1845, "Satan and Dr. Carver," XXVI, 515–25.
February 1847, "The Oregon Trail: A Summer's Journey Out of Bounds," XXIX, 160–5.
April 1847, "The Oregon Trail: Breaking the Ice," XXIX, 310–16.
May 1847, "The Oregon Trail: Fort Leavenworth," XXIX, 389–98.
June 1847, "The Oregon Trail: The Big Blue," XXIX, 499–510.
August 1847, "The Oregon Trail: The Buffalo," XXX, 126–36.
September 1847, "The Oregon Trail: Taking French Leave," XXX, 227–37.
December 1847, "The Oregon Trail: Scenes at the Camp," XXX, 475–92.
January 1848, "The Oregon Trail: Hunting Indians," XXXI, 1–16.
February 1848, "The Oregon Trail: The Ogillallah Village," XXXI, 111–24.
March 1848, "The Oregon Trail: The Hunting Camp," XXXI, 189–203.
April 1848, "The Oregon Trail: The Trappers," XXXI, 326–32; "The Black Hills," 332–5.
May 1848, "The Oregon Trail: "A Mountain Hunt," XXXI, 398–406; "The War Parties," 438–46.
June 1848, "The Oregon Trail: Passage of the Mountains," XXXI, 482–93.
July 1848, "The Oregon Trail: The Lonely Journey," XXXII, 42–55.
August 1848, "The Oregon Trail: The Pueblo and Bent's Fort," XXXII, 95–102.
October 1848, "The Oregon Trail: Indian Alarms," XXXII, 310–21.
December 1848, "The Oregon Trail: The Buffalo Camp," XXXII, 504–15.
January 1849, "The Oregon Trail: Down the Arkansas," XXXIII, 1–12.
February 1849, "The Oregon Trail: The Settlements," XXXIII, 108–15.

The *Christian Examiner*

May 1851, Review, Squier's *Indian Antiquities of North America,* L, 417.
July 1851, Review, Squier's *Serpent Symbol,* LI, 140.
January 1853, Review, French's *Historical Collections of Louisiana,* LIV, 142.

The *North American Review*

January 1852, "The Works of James Fenimore Cooper," LXXIV, 147–61.
July 1865, "Manners and Customs of Primitive Indian Tribes," CI, 28–64.
July 1866, "Indian Superstitions," CIII, 1–18.
July 1868, Review, Morgan's *Bibliotheca Canadensis*, CVII, 370–1.
January 1875, Review, Bancroft's *Native Races of the Pacific States*, CXX, 34–47.
April 1875, Review, Higginson's *History of United States*, CXX, 469–71.
November 1877, "Cavalier de la Salle," CXXV, 427–38.
July–August 1878, "The Failure of Universal Suffrage," CXXVII, 1–20.
October 1879, "The Woman Question," CXXIX, 303–21.
January 1880, "The Woman Question Again," CXXX, 16–30.

Harper's Magazine

November 1864, "Exploring the Magalloway," XXIX, 735–41.
November 1884, "The Acadian Tragedy," LXIX, 877–86.
August 1890, "A Convent at Rome," LXXXI, 448–54.

The *Atlantic Monthly*

March 1867, Review, Stone's *Life and Times of Red Jacket*, XIX, 383.
June 1867, Review, Read's *Historical Inquiry concerning Henry Hudson*, XIX, 764.
July 1867, Review, Charlevoix's *History of New France*, XX, 125.
January 1868, Review, Madame Riedesel's *Letters and Journals*, XXI, 127–8.
April 1872, Review, Charlevoix's *History of New France*, XXIX, 499–500.
June 1885, Review, C. S. Sargent's *The Forest and the Census*, LV, 835–9.

The *Nation*

December 23, 1869, "The Tale of the Ripe Scholar," IX, 558–60.
September 14, 1876, Review, Margry's *Découvertes et Etablissements*, XXIII, 168–9.
May 3, 1877, Review, Bonnechose's *Montcalm et le Canada Français*, XXIV, 269.
December 27, 1877, Review, Rameau's *Une Colonie féodale*, XXV, 400.
April 4, 1878, "Note on Rameau," XXVI, 230
July 11, 1878, Review, LeMoine's *Chronicle of St. Lawrence*, XXVII, 30.
August 1, 1878, "Mr. Parkman and His Canadian Critics," XXVII, 66–7.
December 12, 1878, Review, Stewart's *Canada under Dufferin*, XXVII, 369.
June 10, 1880, "Note on Joliet's Map," XXX, 438.
April 27, 1882, Review, Ellwanger's *The Rose*, XXXIV, 366.
May 31, 1883, Review, Hole's *A Book about Roses*, XXXVI, 476.
November 6, 1884, "The Acadian Tragedy," XXXIX, 398.
January 22, 1885, "The Acadians Again," XL, 73.
April 15, 1886, Review, T. C. B.'s *Voyage au Canada*, XLII, 314–5.
April 12, 1888, Review, Hard's *Fall of New France*, XLVI, 308.
May 10, 1888, Review, Irving's *Indian Sketches*, XLVI, 385.
March 14, 1889, Review, Casgrain's *Un Pèlerinage*, XLVIII, 232–3.
August 23, 1891, Review, Lucas's *Appendiculae Historicae*, LII, 346.
September 14, 1893, Review, Girouard's *Lake St. Louis*, LVII, 200.

The *Critic*

October 31, 1885, "Revocation of the Edict of Nantes," VII, 205–6.
May 1886, Letter on Indian Rights Association, VIII, 248.

The *Youth's Companion*

April 4, 1889, "The Adventures of Pierre Radisson."
April 11, 1889, "The Adventures of Pierre Radisson."
April 18, 1889, "The Adventures of Pierre Radisson."

The Boston *Daily Advertiser*

August 28, 1861, "William H. Russell and Our Duty."
September 4, 1861, "The Nation's Ordeal."

January 8, 1862, "Where are Our Leaders?"
August 12, 1862, "To the Lingerers."
October 14, 1862, "Why Our Army Is Not the Best in the World."
October 17, 1862, "Conservatism."
June 30, 1863, "The Weak Side of Our Armies."
July 4, 1863, "The Chiefs of the Nation."
July 14, 1863, "Aristocrats and Democrats."
July 21, 1863, "Our Best Class and the National Politics."
September 30, 1864, "Southern Treatment of Federal Prisoners."

Bulletin of Bussey Institution

1877(?), "Hybridization of Lilies," II, 161–5.

Tilton's American Journal of Horticulture

January 1867, "Spring Flowers," I, 5.
February 1867, "Flowers of May," I, 74.
March 1867, "Cherokee Rose," I, 184.
May 1867, "Flowers of May," I, 264.
August 1867, "Aquilegia formosa," II, 111; "Aquilegia Durandii," 112.
February 1868, "Phlox," III, 76.
May 1868, "A Plant for the Millions," III, 295.
June 1868, "Manure and the Flower Garden," III, 351.
September 1868, "Fire Lily," IV, 133.
October 1868, "New Dwarf Perpetual-Flowering Carnations," IV, 206; "Florist Pyrethrums," 223.
July 1869, "Lilium longifolium," VI, 13.
October 1869, "Hybrids of Lilium auratum," VI, 206; "Tree Weigelias," 220.
November 1869, "Variations of Flowers from Seed," VI, 276; "A Distinction with a Difference," VI, 341.
March 1870, "How to Propagate Shrubs," VII, 146.
May 1870, "The Japanese Lilies," VII, 265.
June 1870, "Rose Victor Verdier," VII, 333.
July 1870, "Propagation of Shrubs," VIII, 1.
August 1870, "The New Pyrethrums," VIII, 65.
September 1870, "Clematis Jackmani," VIII, 139.
November 1870, "Lilium pomponium," VIII, 272.
December 1870, "Spanish Iris," VIII, 338.
April 1871, "Lilium tenufolium," IX, 104.
May 1871, "Hardy Spring Flowers," IX, 129.
December 1871, "Rose Mrs. Charles Wood," X, 354.
January 1872, "Stuartia Pentagyria," XI, 40.
March 1872, "What Shall I Plant?" XI, 111.

Garden and Forest

February 29, 1888, Appeal for Preservation of White Mountain Forests, I, 1.

Index

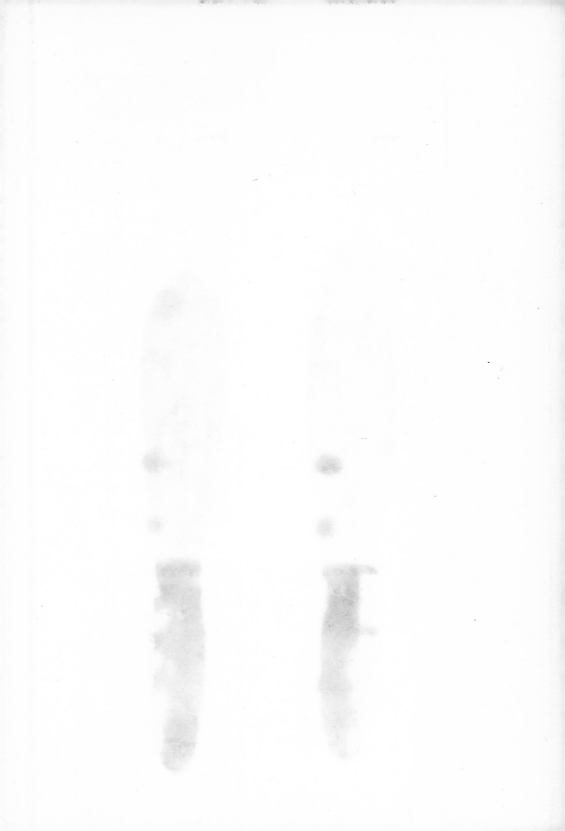

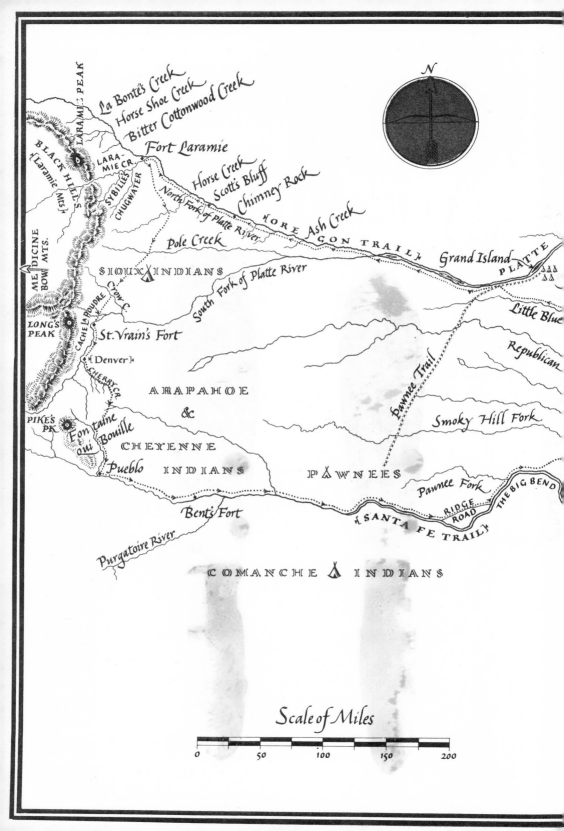

La Bonté's Creek
Horse Shoe Creek
Bitter Cottonwood Creek

LARAMIE PEAK

BLACK HILLS
{Laramie Mts.}

LARAMIE CR.

Fort Laramie

SYBILLE'S

CHUGWATER

North Fork of Platte River

Horse Creek
Scott's Bluff
Chimney Rock

HORE Ash Creek

GON TRAIL

Pole Creek

MEDICINE BOW MTS.

SIOUX INDIANS

Crow C.

CACHE LA POUDRE

South Fork of Platte River

LONG'S PEAK

St. Vrain's Fort

{Denver}

CHERRY CR.

ARAPAHOE

&

CHEYENNE

Pawnee Trail

PIKE'S PK.

Fontaine qui Bouille

Pueblo

INDIANS

PAWNEES

Grand Island

PLATTE

Little Blue

Republican

Smoky Hill Fork

Pawnee Fork

RIDGE ROAD

THE BIG BEND

Bent's Fort

SANTA FE TRAIL

Purgatoire River

COMANCHE INDIANS

N

Scale of Miles

0   50   100   150   200